MACROECONOMICS AND THE REAL WORLD

Volume 2

MACROECONOMICS
and the REAL WORLD

Volume 2
Keynesian Economics, Unemployment, and Policy

Edited by
ROGER E. BACKHOUSE
ANDREA SALANTI

OXFORD
UNIVERSITY PRESS

OXFORD

UNIVERSITY PRESS

Great Clarendon Street, Oxford OX2 6DP
Oxford University Press is a department of the University of Oxford.
It furthers the University's objective of excellence in research, scholarship,
and education by publishing worldwide in

Oxford New York

Athens Auckland Bangkok Bogotá Buenos Aires Calcutta
Cape Town Chennai Dar es Salaam Delhi Florence Hong Kong Istanbul
Karachi Kuala Lumpur Madrid Melbourne Mexico City Mumbai
Nairobi Paris São Paulo Shanghai Singapore Taipei Tokyo Toronto Warsaw

and associated companies in Berlin Ibadan

Oxford is a registered trade mark of Oxford University Press
in the UK and certain other countries

Published in the United States
by Oxford University Press Inc., New York

British Library Cataloguing in Publication Data

Data available

Library of Congress Cataloging in Publication Data

Macroeconomics and the real world/edited by Roger E. Backhouse, Andrea Salanti.
p. cm.
Includes bibliographical references.
Contents: v.1. Econometric techniques and macroeconomics.—
v. 2. Keynesian economics, unemployment, and policy.
1. Macroeconomics. 2. Econometrics. 3. Keynesian economics. I. Backhouse, Roger.
II. Salanti, Andrea, 1950–

HB172.5. M3355 2000   339—dc21   00-057111

ISBN 0-19-829795-5 (Vol. 1, Hbk.)
ISBN 0-19-924204-6 (Vol. 1, Pbk.)
ISBN 0-19-829796-3 (Vol. 2, Hbk.)
ISBN 0-19-924205-4 (Vol. 2, Pbk.)

10 9 8 7 6 5 4 3 2 1

Typeset by Newgen Imaging Systems (P) Ltd., Chennai, India
Printed in Great Britain
on acid-free paper by T.J. International Ltd., Padstow, Cornwall

ACKNOWLEDGEMENTS

The essays and comments collected in these two volumes were originally presented at, or arose out of, a conference on 'Theory and Evidence in Macroeconomics', held at the University of Bergamo on 15–17 October 1998. The editors would like to thank all the participants for their valuable contributions and, last but not least, Ms Laura Capelli and Ms Paola Bortolotti of the secretarial staff of the Department of Economics of the University of Bergamo for their invaluable assistance. Very grateful acknowledgements are also due to the same Department for the financial support which made possible the organization of the conference. Editing these volumes took place whilst Roger Backhouse was holding a British Academy Research Readership and he wishes to thank the British Academy for its support. Five papers from the conference (by McCallum, Vercelli, Smith, Juselius, and Dixon) were included as a symposium in the *Journal of Economic Methodology* (6(2), July 1999). Two of these have been substantially revised and the remaining three are published here with the permission of Routledge.

CONTENTS

1 Introduction to volume 2

ROGER E. BACKHOUSE AND ANDREA SALANTI

1. Introduction

Macroeconomics poses important and difficult methodological questions, some of which do not arise in microeconomics. These are important for practising macro-economists because there is widespread disagreement in macroeconomics, both over policy and over how data should be analysed. It may be the case that there is more of a consensus over macroeconomic theory than in the days when the 'monetarist–Keynesian' controversy was at its height, with widespread agreement that theories should be based on individual optimization and rational expectations, but differences remain. On top of this are differences over the type of evidence that should be used and how it should be used. What, for example, should be the relationship between the assumption of individual rationality, microeconomic evidence, historical studies, and statistics? Even if we confine our attention to statistical evidence, there remain acute divisions over how such evidence should be used.

Furthermore, macroeconomics has always represented a sort of methodological paradox within economics. On the one hand, if only because of the problem of aggregation, macrotheories and models look less rigorous and theoretically justified than their counterparts in microeconomics. On the other hand, due to its having to deal with 'analysis applied to facts' (Hicks 1979: p. ix) in the shape of either 'commonsense perception' and 'everyday experience' (Solow 1998: 1–3) or 'empirical modelling' (Granger 1999), it should be more easily approachable by means of the conceptual tools of the philosophy of (hard) science, at least those traditionally connected with the empiricist tradition. Somewhat surprisingly, however, the traditional methodological literature (see, for example, Blaug 1992; Caldwell 1993) offers little guidance. Induction versus deduction, confirmation versus falsification, the Duhem–Quine problem, piecemeal theorizing, adhocness, and the tenacity of theories are all issues that have to be faced but in order to say something about them it is necessary to discuss the subject in far more detail than has often been done.[1]

It was to address such problems that we organized a conference on the theme, 'Theory and Evidence in Macroeconomics', held in the University of Bergamo on 15–17 October 1998. We took the view that, in order to make progress, it was

---

[1] This is not to say that methodological discussions of macroeconomics and/or (macro)econometrics have been completely absent. Examples include Backhouse (1995, 1997); Darnell and Evans (1990); Dow (1996); Epstein (1987); Granger (1999); Hands (1993); Hoover (1988, 1995); Klein (1994); Mayer (1993); Morgan (1988, 1990); Pagan (1987); Vercelli and Dimitri (1992). Macroeconomics has, however, been comparatively neglected in the recent literature on economic methodology.

necessary to bring together practising macroeconomists and econometricians as well as specialists in economic methodology. We decided on eight topics, and for each of these we commissioned two papers, one from someone more committed to econometric research, the other from someone nearer the theoretical end of the spectrum. Specialists in methodology were selected as discussants. We then allowed considerable time for discussion from the floor, correctly anticipating that this would be one of the most valuable aspects of the conference.

The result of that process (involving, as usual, a few unavoidable deviations from the envisaged ideal) is the papers contained in this and the companion volume. Though the division is to a certain extent arbitrary, the papers fall broadly into two categories. Volume 1 is focused on alternative econometric techniques and the impact these have had, or should have, on macroeconomics, whilst Volume 2 is centred on the closely related questions of Keynesian economics, employment, and policy. However, there is enormous overlap between the two volumes, which should be considered as a whole.

2. Methodological questions in macroeconomics

Macroeconomics would seem a particularly important subject for methodological analysis, for a variety of reasons:

- When critics point to the failure of economics, it is frequently macroeconomics (in particular macroeconomic forecasting) to which they point.
- There is believed to be much greater disagreement amongst economists on macroeconomic questions than on microeconomic ones.
- Though the increased availability of micro data sets and suitable computing technology has changed the situation substantially in recent years, econometrics has generally been more prominent in macroeconomics than in microeconomics.
- Macroeconomics raises specific questions about the use of econometrics due to the nature of the data, in particular the time-series properties of much macroeconomic data.
- The agenda for macroeconomics is, to a greater extent than that for microeconomics, determined by factors outside the discipline. Macroeconomics has to provide diagnoses and remedies for problems such as unemployment, inflation, productivity slowdowns, and financial crises, whether or not these are the topics that, from a scientific point of view, are the ones the discipline is best equipped to tackle.

Thus Blanchard and Fisher (1989: p. xii) write:

Working macroeconomists, like doctors treating cancer, cannot wait for all the answers to analyse events and help policy. They have to take guesses and rely on a battery of models that cannot be derived from first principles but have repeatedly proved useful.

In this respect macroeconomics is more like social science as seen by Kuhn (1970: 164).

The latter [social scientists] often tend, as the former [natural scientists] almost never do, to defend their choice of a research problem—e.g. the effects of racial discrimination or the causes of the business cycle—chiefly in terms of the social importance of achieving a solution.[2]

Even if there are doubts about how far Kuhn's characterization is appropriate for all natural sciences and even if the difference between micro and macro is not a sharp one, there is nonetheless an important difference in emphasis.

The main reason why macroeconomics poses distinctive methodological questions is that it has to look in two directions: towards macroeconomic evidence about the real world and towards microeconomics. These raise different sets of problems and in addition to these, questions arise about how these two types of evidence should be combined and what should be done when they conflict.

2.1. Macroeconomics and macroeconomic evidence

The most familiar form of macroeconomic evidence is statistical: aggregative data such as national income accounts, employment statistics, interest rate and price data, and so on. These are usually taken to refer directly to variables that appear in macroeconomic models, though even this is sometimes problematic. For example, it can be unclear which measure of national income to use and switching from one to another may give different results. More difficult, once it is established what data set to use, there arises the question of how to analyse it and how to confront it with the model. Should testing comprise confirmation or falsification: is it better to find a model that fits the data or to use the data to reject models that are unsatisfactory? Whichever choice is made, the biggest question turns out to be what statistical techniques to employ in order to estimate parameters and decide whether the fit between the model and the data is satisfactory.

Though such issues arise in any discipline where statistical evidence is used, macroeconomics faces particular problems because of distinctive characteristics of macroeconomic data. The data are typically aggregative. There is aggregation over commodities, with data on real variables often being obtained, in practice, by deflating income data with more or less appropriate price indices. Data on stocks, notably capital, are often calculated by perpetual inventory methods—as cumulative sums of net investment. There is also aggregation over time. The macroeconomist typically works with a model specified in continuous time (or based around a time-period of arbitrary length) and has to fit this using monthly, quarterly, or annual data.

These features of macroeconomic data raise methodological problems at two levels. They clearly pose practical questions that must be answered whenever statistical work is undertaken. However, they are also relevant to deeper methodological issues that relate to those discussed in the methodology literature. The most obvious set of

---

[2] Kuhn goes on to ask, 'Which group would one then expect to solve problems at a more rapid rate?'

problems arises in studies based on time-series data sets. Time-series data pose specific statistical problems, with a range of competing methods having been developed to solve them. It is hard to comment on strategies for testing theories, and even on the possibility of confirming or refuting theories, without taking these into account for they raise the question of how far it is in practice possible to test a theory and what would constitute such a conclusive test. Cross-section studies, such as those often used in the growth literature, raise a different set of issues. Neither case, for example, conforms to the type of experimental situation for which classical statistical methods were developed. The difference between the processes by which macroeconomic data are generated and laboratory experiments also creates conceptual problems about what constitutes replication.[3]

In addition to statistical data, macroeconomics also uses institutional and historical evidence about the real world. Economists have direct information about central bank operating procedures, about the way in which fiscal decisions are made, legislative changes, and many other things that are believed to be relevant to macroeconomic phenomena.[4] There is also a wealth of historical evidence. This may include statistical information but this is combined with other evidence and, more importantly, relates to specific events. Thus where an econometric study might represent the unique features of the Great Depression or World War II as random shocks, elements of a stochastic process with particular properties, the historian may see more significance in them and reach a conclusion very different from that reached by the econometrician. This raises the question of how these different types of evidence should be reconciled.

2.2. Macroeconomics and microeconomics

The relationship between micro- and macroeconomics raises a different set of methodological questions. The contemporary consensus is that macroeconomic theories should be derived from microeconomic foundations and that these should be based on the assumption of individual rationality. A major problem, however, is that the conditions under which it is possible to aggregate from microeconomics to macroeconomics are almost never satisfied. How should economists respond to this? One is to disregard aggregation problems, using devices such as the representative agent, trusting that if this is illegitimate, this will show up when the resulting macromodels are confronted with macro-evidence. Another response is that aggregation problems undermine the search for microfoundations and economics should instead be searching for regularities at the macrolevel.

Both these strategies, however, raise further problems of their own. The strategy of seeking regularities can be criticized by arguing that they can never be established by induction, however many data are available and because the processes whereby they are collected and aggregated mean they can never be free of theory. The theoretical

---

[3] See Cartwright (1991); Backhouse (1997: ch. 11).

[4] It is this kind of evidence about the institutional environment which offers, for instance, some insights on how to shape the behaviour of economic policy authorities in a way suitable for game-theoretic analysis.

strategy is always open to the criticism of simply begging the relevant questions in more than one respect. Indeed, even apart from doubts about aggregation conditions, the representative agent fiction ends up by preventing macroeconomics from exploiting all the richness of modern microeconomic theory.

For its part, microeconomic evidence is often contradictory and ambiguous. During the last three decades microeconomists have abandoned the constricting neo-Walrasian idea of general equilibrium analysis as the overarching theoretical framework in order to exploit the wider descriptive flexibility allowed by a range of partial equilibrium approaches. In doing this, however, they have had to incur a cost. Many such models reach interesting results only *because* they are deliberately biased caricatures (in the sense of Gibbard and Varian 1978) that are thought to provide interesting insights into some microeconomic situations. This means that they are inadequate as general microfoundations.[5]

All of these questions relate to issues that methodologists and philosophers of science have discussed. To provide effective answers, however, requires attention to detail—to attend to the practicalities of what can actually be done. This can make things more complicated but equally it may point to solutions. Difficulties that seem significant in the abstract may in practice turn out to be much less important.

3. Microfoundations

It is nowadays widely accepted that macroeconomic models need microfoundations and that these should be based on assumptions of rational expectations and intertemporal utility maximization. This view is best represented in the paper by Burnside, Eichenbaum, and Fisher (1-3). [Note: references of this form denote volume number and chapter.] They model behaviour in terms of a representative household maximizing a discounted sum of expected utility and a perfectly competitive firm maximizing profit. Even though the model is calibrated to fit certain macroeconomic evidence, its properties reflect the values chosen for the parameters that describe microeconomic behaviour. It is, therefore, an attempt to base macroeconomic theory on rigorous microfoundations. This view that macrotheories need microfoundations is shared by Delli Gatti and Tamborini (2-8) and Dixon (2-9). The difference is that they seek to establish different microfoundations involving rationing and imperfect competition.

This view contrasts with the approach taken by Hendry (1-5) and Juselius (1-8) for whom theory does no more than suggest a behavioural relationship and a list of variables that might affect the macroeconomic problem they are tackling. Microfoundations are implicit, in that there are well-known microeconomic theories that will produce money-demand functions of the form that they use but the detail is left in the background. There are several microtheories that could be used. This contrasts with the view that microfoundations should be explicit.

---

[5] For a different opinion on the possibility of exploiting an eclectic mixture of different microfoundations for different aggregate markets, see Stiglitz (1992).

The problem with seeking to base macromodels on explicit, formal, microfoundations is that the conditions required for aggregation are either unknown or are not met. Sims (2–4B) made the point that, given that we know that many markets are oligopolistic, the ideal would be to work with oligopolistic microfoundations. The problem is that we do not know how to aggregate such models, which is why much of the imperfect-competition literature assumes monopolistic competition. However, this is an interesting line of defence, for it seems clear that, even if markets exhibit perfect or monopolistic competition, the conditions required for aggregation are unlikely to be met. Rigorous aggregation in these models is possible only through assuming away aggregation problems, such as by postulating a single representative agent or markets populated by identical firms. Rigour has been purchased at the cost of making assumptions that are contradicted by the evidence or, at least, that introduce some *ad hoc* specifications just in order to obtain the solvability of the model.[6]

This raises the question of how one can justify such an approach. The obvious answer is that the assumptions are justified by the success of the model—which in Burnside, Eichenbaum, and Fisher's case is its ability to mimic the response of the economy to a fiscal shock. If this criterion is met, the implied conclusion is that aggregation problems and departures from competitive, optimizing behaviour are in practice not sufficiently important to matter. Thus Pagan (2–10B) responds to New Keynesian models by saying that he does not see what implications they have for the data, and that some of them output dynamics that are more complicated than anything one does see in the data.

What is probably the most widely held defence of formal microfoundations based on optimizing behaviour was articulated by Eichenbaum (2–4B). It has two strands. The first is that understanding a phenomenon means knowing what it means in terms of agents' motivations. For him, merely fitting equations, or finding regularities, does not constitute understanding. The second is that optimization is a way of being precise so that it is not necessary for people to guess what you mean. His objection to Keynes is not that he was wrong but that it is impossible, even decades later, to work out what he meant. In another session (2–7B) he added a third—that one of the merits of 'optimization-based' models is that they break down the separateness of macro and micro. If the goal is not so much to generate the best theory as to develop conditions under which progress is likely to occur, this may be important if it leads to the exploration of avenues that would otherwise remain closed. The sociological effect of a theory may be significant. This opens up the questions of whether the sociology of the profession (also referred to by Morgan (2–4B)) may merit more attention.

Arguments against this were offered by Hendry. He (1–7B) introduces the idea that behaviour may mimic rationality even though it is not rational. Expectations, he argued, could not possibly be rational because the sort of information that would be needed is obviously not available. Some behaviour is clearly irrational. However,

---

[6] Think for instance of the widely employed Dixit–Stiglitz assumption that goods are symmetrical imperfect substitutes in models of monopolistic competition. Many would agree that this assumption is far from satisfactory in a number of respects but, as noted by Lipsey (2–4A) and Sims (2–4B), it is nonetheless widely employed because of its analytical tractability.

under some circumstances agents may mimic rationality. During the sample covered by his model, for example, agents could have formed unbiased expectations simply by assuming $\Delta^2 \log P = 0$ and assuming that inflation would be the same as in the previous period. Such a forecasting rule would not be efficient, but one might defend it as boundedly rational in the same way that Dixon (2-10B) points out that cost-plus pricing rules may be boundedly rational. Such rules can imply behaviour that is different from what one would derive from full optimization models—cost-plus pricing, for example, implies price stickiness.

Perhaps the most radical response to the project of seeking formal microfoundations, also offered by Hendry (1-7B), is that macroeconomic models should be about discovering system properties—properties of macroeconomic systems that are not to be found at the level of individual agents. He likens his models, not based on formal microfoundations, to the models used in hydrology.[7]

Hendry, therefore, is arguing that macroeconomics (though it clearly has to be consistent with what we know of microeconomic behaviour) is partly autonomous in that it may uncover relationships that emerge only at the macroeconomic level and that these relationships can provide the basis for explanations. This is in marked contrast with the RBC programme, exemplified by Eichenbaum, who seeks to explain macroeconomic phenomena in terms of behaviour at the microeconomic level. Similar issues are raised by Ferri (2-5) who argues that the Phillips curve should be seen as a system relationship, depending on the operation of the entire economic system. He also raises the possibility that it may be derived from microfoundations other than optimization in perfectly competitive markets.

This choice between theories with rigorous microfoundations and theories that represent purely macroeconomic properties is linked to other methodological issues, notably the virtues of simplicity and the relative weights to attach to theory versus stable statistical relationships. Eichenbaum (1-7B) points out that McCallum's paper (1-6) 'points to some of the tensions in the desire for simplicity when we model and the desire for richness of detail when we actually go to the data'. One reason why Hendry differs from Eichenbaum and McCallum, being much more sceptical about the value of simple models, is that he attaches great weight to the data and he attaches great significance to the enormous number of factors that have to be taken into account in order to explain the historical record.

However, the significance of these issues depends on specific contexts. This is illustrated by the discussion of the labour market. Oswald and Trostel (2-6) share with Burnside, Eichenbaum, and Fisher the view that the microeconomic foundations of macroeconomics are important, but they use statistical, microeconomic evidence to challenge some of the simplifying assumptions that macrotheorists frequently make. Hendry (2-4B), though sharing their desire to place a high weight on observable statistical regularities, is sceptical about the value of their results. The reason, he

---

[7] 'I think it is simply unimaginable where hydrology would be today if hydrologists had insisted on working out the theory of turbulence from quantum dynamics. They wouldn't have made one iota of a contribution to understanding it because it is a system property and it is enormously complicated how turbulence behaves, how waves behave, how they propagate, etc.' (1-7B, p. 156)

argues, why there is so much more consensus amongst labour economists using large-sample cross-section data sets is that they are failing to apply statistical tests that are as rigorous as those used in the analysis of macro time-series data. Hausman made the point that it is hazardous to use any observed relationship in a theory if we do not know why it obtains. However, even if they represent correlations that correspond to no causal relationship, they may nonetheless be phenomena that theorists ought to be trying to explain.

4. Can macroeconomic theories be tested?

A basic tenet of the modern conception of science is that the ultimate criterion for appraising theories is, or should be, that they should fit with what happens (or seems to happen) in the real world or in the laboratory. Given the obvious difficulties with conceiving of experiments in macroeconomics, econometrics might therefore appear as the best set of tools at our disposal for testing theories. This requires, of course, that theories are properly designed for testing and that appropriate data and quantitative techniques for their treatment are available. Because these conditions are hard to meet, the problem of testing is never as trivial as one might expect from this commonsense account of scientific research activity.

Macroeconomics (and microeconomics too, for that matter) is no exception. Indeed, economic methodologists have, following philosophers, made much of the Duhem–Quine problem and the impossibility of conclusively testing any scientific theory. Methodology textbooks all point to the auxiliary assumptions and *ceteris paribus* conditions that make it possible to save any theory from refutation. In macroeconomics and econometrics this problem arises in four guises: (i) identification; (ii) model specification; (iii) observational equivalence; and (iv) evaluation of (possibly alternative) models. The papers and discussions brought together in these volumes touch on all four of these, discussing both their implications in practice and how they might be reduced.

Sometimes, in the methodological literature, a distinction is made between 'testing theories' and 'building empirical models' (or similar expressions), as if the respective outcomes would require two quite different *methodological* appraisals.[8] In what follows very little emphasis is placed on this distinction because, in our opinion, it is at most a matter of degree and not one of real substance. 'Measurement without theory' may surely be a neat and impressive label for an academic manifesto but if taken literally, it is simply false: what actually happens when people say that they are not trying to test any particular theory it is that they are testing (possibly particular versions of) a theory or a model of their own instead of one provided ready-made by 'theorists'. Admittedly, such models may well have been designed according to criteria and priorities very different from those usually endorsed by theorists, but this just means that we are dealing with a different kind of theory (which, is *per se* perfectly legitimate).

---

[8] Cf., e.g. Granger (1999) and Morgan (1988, 1990).

4.1. Identification and specification

The traditional view about identification and specification problems is based upon a distinction which sees identification as primarily a statistical matter and specification as something to be approached with reference to some *a priori* knowledge provided by economic theory. Such a view was repeatedly challenged during the conference—there was close to a consensus that the two issues are strictly intertwined.

On the one hand, for instance, Smith (1-9) argues that identification is an economic problem, not the statistical one that econometrics textbooks sometimes lead readers to assume it to be. It is fundamentally a matter of data interpretation. Textbook discussions of the properties of relevant matrices may be important in helping economists to sort out the statistical properties of their models and hence whether their assumptions are consistent with what the econometrician claims to have identified. In the last resort, however, identification involves making a judgement about the data that takes into account more than simply the structure of the model and the numbers fed into the computer. On the other hand Hendry, in his own contribution (1-5) as well as in a number of scattered observations in general discussions, advocates a more 'data-driven' approach to model specification. Taken together, both these positions undermine the traditional view that identification is a purely statistical problem and model specification is a theoretical issue.

Another source of tension between theoretical representations and properties of data emerges from Harding and Pagan's (1-2) proposal to (re)focus applied research on business cycles onto the time-honoured task of identifying the 'turning points' in economic activity (a perspective that recent theories of business cycles tend to neglect). The subsequent comment by Hartley (1-4A) and general discussion (1-4B) remind us that our perception of facts is theory-laden to the point that even the definition of what constitutes a business cycle is controversial.

For these reasons, among others, identification and model specification can never be completely conclusive and therefore, as McCallum (1-6) points out, single econometric studies are generally not decisive. What happens is rather that evidence has a cumulative effect to the point where the weight of evidence becomes convincing. Evidence from different studies is brought together in an informal, but nonetheless persuasive, way.

Juselius (1-8) approaches the problem of whether economic theories can be tested by posing a challenge to macroeconomic theorists from another perspective. As an econometrician, she argues that the possibilities for confronting models with evidence depend crucially on how they are formulated. The traditional approach involves formulating a deterministic theoretical model to which error terms are added so that inferences can be made concerning parameter values. This, she argues, means that it will never be possible to test models against all the stochastic properties of the data. To do this, models need to be formulated as stochastic models from the start. In other words, Juselius suggests that economic theories could be constructed so as to be more testable than they are at the moment.[9]

---

[9] The points made in the previous two paragraphs are related to points made in Backhouse (1997) in the context of replication. There it is suggested that replication is informal, involving a series of studies rather than ones that are individually persuasive, and is a question of how economic theories are formulated.

A related point is that in practice the testability of a theory may depend on how one approaches the relationship between theory and data. A common approach is to start from a theoretical model, add stochastic components, and then test the model. An alternative approach is to start with a general stochastic model, testing theoretical relationships as restrictions on this. These two approaches can produce very different results. The contrast between these two methods is one way in which the conflict between deduction and induction emerges in practice. It would be going too far to classify either method as deductive or inductive but there is a clear difference of emphasis. Juselius's method, of starting with a general stochastic model, obviously involves theory at the start (for no model can be completely general) but it allows maximum scope for data to influence the final model. This is very much in the spirit of induction. In contrast, the standard approach tests a model the detailed specification of which comes from economic theory.

4.2. *Observational equivalence and evaluation*

Identification and specification, however, do not exhaust the problem of testability of macroeconomic theories. When theories and their applications are subjected to overall evaluations of their predictive or explanatory power a number of other problems come into the foreground. Two issues, in particular, deserve to be mentioned.

The first arises from theorists' attitudes towards theoretical models which are not suited to empirical testing but which they nonetheless consider useful in other respects.[10] In Vercelli's paper (2-2), for example, the question is raised of whether a successful theory *should* be testable. It is argued that the longevity of the IS–LM model arises not from its success in meeting empirical tests but in its flexibility. This model which, at its minimum, comprises equilibrium loci for the product and money markets, is compatible with numerous assumptions about what lies behind these loci.[11] The IS–LM model is thus not testable, but provides a framework within which testable models can be constructed. Such an argument immediately suggests scope for a Kuhnian or a Lakatosian analysis. For example, we might reconstruct the IS–LM model itself as a Lakatosian hard core with the microfoundations of the two loci lying in the protective belt. The problem with such an interpretation, however, is that they have no commitment to the IS–LM independently of the assumptions on which the curves are based. They are derived relationships, not something about which

---

[10] Such an attitude is by no means confined to macroeconomics. In the introductory chapter of one of the most acclaimed advanced textbook in microeconomics the author is very explicit:

What constitutes better understanding? ... The standard acid test is that the theory should be (a) testable and (b) tested empirically, either in the real world or in the lab. But many of the models and theories ... have not been subjected to a rigorous empirical test, and some of them may never be. Yet, I maintain, models untested rigorously may still lead to better understanding, through a process that combines casual empiricism and intuition. (Kreps 1990: 7)

[11] It could be formulated even more generally if, following Tobin (1969), the LM curve is seen as the equilibrium locus for the entire financial sector, which may not even involve a single asset that is designated 'money'.

economists have commitments. It would therefore be paradoxical if something that is a derived feature of the model, and which is not in itself testable, were something to which economists were committed.[12] Vercelli explores some of the reasons, other than the model's predictive success and mainly related to the adaptability of IS–LM models to changing macroeconomic environments, why the model might have persisted for so long.

Economists' theoretical commitments seem to play an important role in evaluating theories in another respect—in accepting or rejecting particular causal explanations that empirical evidence seems to suggest as the most likely among those contemplated as possibilities within a given class of models. Indeed, one way to characterize the explanatory role of theoretical models is to say, following Rappaport (1998: ch. 8, in his turn referring to Miller 1987), that formal modelling helps to delimit the set of possible (causal) explanations appropriate to specific situations. According to this interpretation, causal explanations emerge from the comparison of rival hypotheses, among which the most plausible should be selected on the basis of the available empirical evidence in any specific circumstance.

What happens, however, is that some hypotheses are regarded as more (or less) plausible than others on a priori grounds, quite independently of the robustness of the available empirical research. A number of general discussions in the two volumes (see, for instance, 1-4B on business cycles; 1-7B on monetary policy; and 2-7B on the labour market; 2-10B on new Keynesian economics) provide clear examples of how people of different theoretical persuasions react differently to the same kind of 'evidence'.

5. Do macroeconomic theories change in response to evidence?

McCallum (1-6) argues that though the evolution of macroeconomic theory has in part been driven by theoretical considerations (pre-eminent amongst which is the assumption of rational expectations), theorists have undoubtedly taken account of evidence. Behind this general claim, lies his judgement that the balance between the roles of theory and evidence is about right. Two things are worth noting about this. The first is that he sees the problem as one of a balance between two influences. This is consistent with a view whereby theory and evidence both impact on macroeconomists' views about the world. It is not consistent with the 'conventional view' of the role of evidence as being to test theories—in such a context it does not make sense to speak of the relative impacts of theory and evidence. The second is that McCallum's is a pragmatic, empirical judgement. Consider, for instance, his views concerning price stickiness as a phenomenon that arises in many macroeconomic models but for which there is no theoretical reason whatsoever. Models can be built to explain price

---

[12] This is not to say that it is not possible to offer a Lakatosian interpretation of the evolution of IS–LM models. For example, one might suggest that such research in the 1950s and 1960s could be explained as a programme based on: (i) the analysis of a small number of aggregate relations; (ii) the analysis of market equilibrium conditions; and (iii) the possibility of an equilibrium with less than full employment. But the IS–LM model itself does not form part of such a hard core.

stickiness, but that is a different matter. The main reason why price stickiness is assumed is, McCallum claims, that it is necessary in order to explain the evidence. In a similar vein he argues that contemporary models take the interest rate, not the money supply, as the authorities' monetary policy instrument because this is how monetary authorities are known to operate. One of the significant features of these two examples is that evidence is convincing, if not overwhelming, even though there is no formal econometric test that has been decisive.[13] McCallum even expresses doubts about the limited work that has been done (in particular by Blinder) to test price stickiness directly.

However, although decisive tests are rarely possible, some papers cite one example where such a test occurred: the rejection of the hypothesis that monetary shocks were the cause of the business cycle. This led directly to the emergence of real business-cycle theory. McCallum claims simply that 'the upsurge of the RBC movement can be viewed as principally empirical' (McCallum 1-6). Smith goes even further, writing of Nelson and Plosser's work that:

[t]heir results killed the previously fashionable model which explained GDP variations by money-supply surprises; there was no way this could be true since money-supply surprises were white noise by construction and GDP variations were highly persistent. The Lucas supply curve, found in most theoretical models at that time, just could not provide an interpretation of summary statistics of the time series properties. (Smith 1-9, p. 206)

This is as close to a decisive result as one could reasonably hope for. It is, of course, important to bear in mind, however, that though empirical work did have this effect, it was within the context of a very specific set of theoretical assumptions such as rational expectations and competitive market clearing. In the context of Juselius's claims cited in the previous section it is worth noting that it was only because the stochastic properties of the theoretical model were precisely specified (money-supply shocks are white noise) that the model was testable.

Looking at IS–LM analysis, Vercelli (2-2) argues that macroeconomic theory made major changes directly in response to evidence. These changes took two forms. The major structural change in the economic environment that took place in the 1970s led to a new generation of IS–LM models. These were based on forward-looking expectations and the assumption that the classical dichotomy must hold in the long run. These are theoretical requirements but the motivation of making such modifications was that the models could not otherwise explain the new economic regime. In addition minor changes in the environment produced minor amendments to the model. The simplest IS–LM model, Vercelli claims, was successful in the 1950s because the world fitted the model, with few significant supply shocks. When such shocks occurred in the 1960s, the model had to be augmented with a Phillips curve. In other words, though the IS–LM model itself survived, evidence was crucial in causing changes in the way the model was used and in the way it was understood. It remains to be established, however, whether or not these changes can be regarded as examples of progressive

---

[13] This is consistent with the claims made by Summers (1991).

improvements in macroeconomic theory. More detailed analysis would be necessary to exclude the possibility that in some cases the modifications to which supporters of IS–LM resorted were *ad hoc* (one doubtful case being the addition of the Phillips curve).[14]

Dixon's paper (2-9) also supports the idea that theories may persist despite anomalous evidence. Faced with evidence that Walrasian models could not explain, such as the persistence of unemployment and shocks to output, resort was made to the *ad hoc* assumption of sticky prices. This was *ad hoc* in the sense that it was inconsistent with the assumption of competitive equilibrium. Economists were also prepared to ignore the fact—obvious to most people—that when people become unemployed their welfare falls.

This example raises two further methodological points. The first is that the role of theory and evidence may depend critically on the time-period that is investigated and the stage of development of a theory. The pattern Dixon points out, which is compatible with Kuhn's account of scientific revolutions, is that evidence produces anomalies and *ad hoc* modifications of the theory. There then follows a stage in which the resulting theoretical inconsistencies are removed. In some cases this can be regarded as saving the paradigm. In others it results in the creation of a new paradigm.[15] If we look only at this second stage, theoretical considerations appear decisive. The second point concerns whether or not it is undesirable to rely on *ad hoc* modifications to a theory. McCallum (1986), for example, has argued that when the world is more complicated than any model we could analyse, it cannot be assumed that theories containing *ad hoc* assumptions are necessarily inferior to ones that do not.[16]

There is a further aspect of the relationship between theory and evidence that may encourage the practice of having recourse to *ad hoc* assumptions in macroeconomics. As a number of papers point out, empirical evidence is often far from being decisive. Sometimes it may offer clear suggestions about things that were *less* important than expected together with much less clear insights about the relevant determinants.[17] In other cases, as Durlauf (1-11) maintains, apropos of the econometric evidence provided by the empirical work connected with new growth theory, applied research turns out to be inconclusive because it offers too many different explanatory variables. Finally, it may happen that empirical evidence cannot properly be exploited, simply because theorists are unable (given the theoretical strategies to which they are committed) to build up a theory consistent with it. Oswald and Trostel (2-6, p. 139) are quite explicit on this point. After having presented six alleged regularities in labour-market data (they are modest enough to avoid to call them 'stylized facts'), they conclude that:

[t]hese disparate types of evidence suggest that labour markets do not operate in a simple competitive spot-market fashion. The emerging findings will face opposition—because the competitive

---

[14] For a useful discussion of the various ways in which the term '*ad hoc*' has been used, see Hands (1988).

[15] We leave open the question of whether the new Keynesian imperfect competition approach to macroeconomics amounts to a new paradigm in Kuhn's sense.

[16] The Dixit–Stiglitz assumption of goods that are symmetrical imperfect substitutes in models of monopolistic competition (see n. 6 above) could be regarded as a case in point.

[17] Cf. e.g. Hendry's (1-5) conclusions about what determined UK inflation during the 1960s and 1970s.

spot-market paradigm is the dominant way the profession thinks (both formally and informally). ... The profession's modelling strategies will not change quickly. There are significant obstacles. First, and probably most importantly, the appropriate alternative strategy is not clear.

All in all, it seems possible to conclude that empirical evidence drives theoretical changes in macroeconomics when two conditions are satisfied: evidence must be unambiguous (as far as it can be reasonably expected) *and* suited to theoretical rationalization (notably with reference to the problem of aggregation). Otherwise the door remains open for theories grounded on more doubtful and somewhat compromising assumptions.

6. Macroeconomics and policy

The relationship between macroeconomics and government policy raises methodological questions that have implications for the choices economists make between theories. It is usually taken as given that one of the main reasons for doing macroeconomics is to improve the quality of the advice that can be offered to policy-makers. This argument, however, can be taken in several directions. If the main requirement of policy-makers is accurate forecasts, economic theory is relevant only in so far as it leads to this end. If they offer better forecasts, for example, VARs or other time-series models may be all that is required, even if they cannot be interpreted and even if there is no theoretical rationale for the variables that appear in them. The problem with this strategy is that, should the system change, models may cease to forecast well. Macroeconomic theory becomes relevant as a means for finding models that will be more robust. In other words, our belief about the likely robustness of a model may depend not only on its past performance (what statistical analysis can measure) but also on our beliefs about whether or not it corresponds to features of the economy that are likely to remain unchanged in the presence of shocks to the system. This is a theoretical as much as a statistical question.

Policy-makers, however, require more than forecasts. They want to understand why things are happening and how the economy will respond to actions they might take. This is a statement not just about the relationship of macroeconomic models to the real world (whether the models seek to explain rather than just to forecast), but it is also a statement about the relationship of macroeconomic models to the questions policy-makers are asking and what they are able to understand. This issue arises sharply in the discussion of the business cycle. Harding and Pagan (1-2) claim that what concerns policy-makers is fluctuations in output, especially turning points. This leads them to argue that any model that purports to be a model of the business cycle should explain the key features of the classical cycle and they present algorithms that can be used to extract the required information. Pagan (1-4B) therefore argues that before he will take a business-cycle model seriously he wants to know what sort of business cycle it generates. They are critical of Burnside, Eichenbaum, and Fisher (1-3) for not providing this information. Burnside, Eichenbaum, and Fisher (1-4B) respond by arguing that the cycle generated by their model will depend on how the exogenous technology shocks are modelled and so they do not answer this question. They argue that what matters to policy-makers is how a model responds to policy interventions and so they prefer to evaluate their model by seeing how it responds to different shocks.

Whether or not one judges a business-cycle model on the basis of its ability to explain turning points in a variable such as real GDP or in terms of its ability to explain co-movements of various series depends on what one is trying to explain. Harding and Pagan argue that if one is claiming to explain the business cycle, then one should explain turning points in a variable such as real GDP since that is the way in which the business cycle is understood by most policy-makers. Burnside, Eichenbaum, and Fisher, they contend, claim to be offering a business-cycle model, but fail to show whether their model does generate a business cycle as the term is generally understood. This raises the question of whether the question of how one defines the business cycle is a purely semantic issue, of no real importance. Thus Eichenbaum points out that the business cycle is merely a construction we place upon the data: all there really is out there is 'a bunch of decision-makers and a bunch of data' (1-4B). Sims makes a similar point in a different way when he argues that to require every business-cycle model to explain turning points in output is to impose a lexicographic ordering on the criteria by which models are tested and that there is no justification for doing so. One might wish to trade off performance in one dimension in order to obtain better performance in another dimension. Morgan responds by questioning whether it is necessary to have congruence between models, definitions, and concepts in the same piece of applied work. Different answers to the question of what policy-makers are interested in may lead to the use of different models. Given economists' different starting points, it is going to take different things to make different economists have confidence in a model. As Eichenbaum puts it, 'it is not going to be one size fits all' (1-4B).

In the course of this discussion, Eichenbaum questions the extent to which research should be driven by the concerns of policy-makers. First, he suggests that policy-makers are unduly driven by day-to-day considerations and that research ought not to be driven by these. Second, he is concerned not just with operating within existing institutions but with designing different institutions. Macromodels provide laboratories that can be used to test these. Eichenbaum's view on the concerns of policy-makers is reinforced by Mayer's (2-11) reading of the US Federal Open Market Committee's use of academic research, at least in the 1970s. The FOMC's discussions focused on the current state of the economy and on the very immediate effect of minor changes in the federal funds rate, two issues on which the academic literature had little to say. Though it can be argued that academic economists should take more interest in these questions, it is possible that this represents an appropriate division of labour.

Thus although the argument that macroeconomics should be judged by the extent to which it provides useful advice to policy-makers, this must be qualified. The advice that policy-makers find useful at any particular time may not relate to fundamental issues but it may depend on prior beliefs about optimal policies. It may also, as was revealed in Maes's paper (2-12) and the ensuing discussion (2-13B), depend on the nature of the training received by government officials and hence on the types of arguments they are equipped to understand.

7. Keynesian economics, unemployment, and policy

The first group of papers in this volume is devoted to the IS–LM model and its evolution over time. Since its inception in 1937, IS–LM has played the role of macroeconomic model *par excellence*. For more than three decades it represented the main theoretical framework for macroeconomic research and it provided the way in which generations of students were introduced to Keynesian ideas. Even now, after three decades of (sometimes devastating) criticism, it survives in macro-textbooks and behind some of the large macroeconometric models used for policy evaluation and forecasting. The IS–LM model has well-known shortcomings when employed either for heuristic purposes or for descriptive and policy uses (when used for heuristic purposes, it fails to highlight the specificity of the Keynesian approach and when used for descriptive and policy purposes, the strict requirement of structural stability poses a problem) but has survived for more than six decades. Vercelli (2-2) argues that its longevity is due to its flexibility and adaptability in response to changes in (i) the relevant 'stylized facts', (ii) the outstanding policy issues, and (iii) the prevailing theoretical and methodological approaches. According to Vercelli, this endurance of the model is due to its capacity to be 'interpreted as the semi-reduced form of different structural models which may have different theoretical foundations' (Vercelli 2-2)—in other words, it is due to its ultimate ambiguity. To show this he distinguishes, among other things, a 'first generation' of IS–LM models (originating with Hicks 1937) and a 'second generation' (exemplified by McCallum 1989 and McCallum and Nelson 1997). The second generation has explicit microfoundations and a somewhat different scope.

If we take dynamic analysis versus short-run comparative statics as the dividing criterion between the two generations of IS–LM model,[18] the model proposed by Sims (2-3) may be regarded as belonging squarely to the second one. In order to overcome two shortcomings of traditional IS–LM models, namely the lack of expectations and the missing link between monetary and fiscal policy (due to the government budget constraint), he develops a dynamic IS–LM framework assuming a representative consumer and a representative firm both optimizing over an infinite time-horizon, together with a Phillips curve and a mark-up equation for wage and price adjustment respectively. Under the government budget constraint, the model shows how different combinations of active and passive monetary and fiscal policies affect the properties of equilibrium.

Lipsey (2-4A) chooses to comment of these two papers by offering his own alternative account of the IS–LM story, leaving to the reader the task of assessing possible

---

[18] During the general discussion (2-4B) McCallum points out a further distinction, arguing that McCallum and Nelson (1997) should be better considered as an example of a third generation of IS–LM models because of a more appropriate treatment of expectations.

differences of interpretation. Despite his direct and significant participation in part of this story, it is not centred around his personal reminiscences. Rather, he offers a quasi-Lakatosian reconstruction in which IS–LM: (i) belongs to the protective belt of the research programme; (ii) suffers from its inability to deal with expectations along truly Keynesian lines; and (iii) leaves open the problem of 'closure', necessary in order to identify what determines the price level. Nevertheless, his reconstruction of the evolution of IS–LM (as marked by different types of closure), together with the monetarist challenge and the new classical critique, lead him to maintain that Keynesians were less naïve than subsequent critics would have us believe. Warning against excessively simplistic textbook accounts of why the programme was finally superseded, he concludes that not all its insights should be swept under the carpet.[19] The ensuing discussion (2-4B) touches on a number of issues, most of which can be traced back either to the reduced-form nature of IS–LM models or to the question of how far microfoundations can be imported into such models without losing sight of their specific goals.

The first paper in the section on labour market takes up again, with reference to Phillips curve, the issue of what type of microfoundations are compatible with a Keynesian perspective. Ferri (2-5) maintains that the Phillips curve cannot be completely reduced to any sort of microbehaviour. In his view the relationship between *nominal* wages and unemployment is a macrorelation that depends on the institutional environment and policy regime, which jointly govern the distribution of the productivity gains. Moreover, the Phillips curve is shown to be compatible with different kinds of wage dynamics (not necessarily implying money illusion). Because of this, appending a Phillips curve to the IS–LM model is only one way in which it can be used. Other ways emerge from considering different macroeconomic regimes.

The second paper, by Oswald and Trostel (2-6), focuses on empirical findings in labour economics. Some evidence of six alleged regularities is presented. One of them, the relation between wages and lagged profits-per-worker (suggesting a mechanism of rent-sharing), challenges macroeconomists' habit of modelling the labour market as a competitive spot-market. Two others (the failure of minimum wage laws to have a significant effect on low-wage employment, and the positive correlation across counties between unemployment rates and home-ownership rates) stimulated much debate during the discussion (2-7B). This focused in particular on the correct interpretation of results obtained from cross-country or panel data.

Commenting upon these two papers, Backhouse (2-7A) hints at a number of methodological questions that arise when theory seems to conflict with facts that cannot be easily accommodated within a consistent theory. In addition to this, macroeconomic models always raise the problem of aggregation: the variables suggested by microeconomic theory do not always relate directly to macroeconomic evidence. He notes that while some consensus has emerged around a standard microeconomic framework in which individual optimization is central, this framework, coupled with

---

[19] He goes as far as to note, with agreement, that 'to many Keynesians the new classical programme replaced messy truth by precise error' (Lipsey, 2-4).

devices such as representative agents, can result in neglect of possible emerging systemic properties at a purely macroeconomic level. This generates a tension within the subject, due to the different research strategies needed to deal with the two different kinds of phenomena. In the ensuing discussion (2-7B) Lipsey suggests that one should avoid a dogmatic attitude on this issue. After all, however fruitful a research strategy based upon explicit optimizing microfoundations may have been, we cannot exclude the existence of phenomena not suited to such a theoretical reduction.

The issue of the possible malfunctioning of markets reappears in the two papers on new Keynesian economics. Unlike in other sections, both papers deal with theoretical models. Delli Gatti and Tamborini (2-8) offer us a quite detailed survey of the 'new Keynesian' literature on capital market failures and their consequences for economic activity, employment, and prices. Theories of the business cycle based upon the hypothesis of financial fragility are also reviewed. Their conclusions are, with some qualifications, generally in favour of the new Keynesian approach, in spite of their recognition that the proliferation of models makes it difficult to find a shared view on policy prescriptions. Finally, in a somewhat post-Keynesian mood, they maintain that 'liquidity preference as a cause of capital market failure remains a key issue in macroeconomic theory which is not addressed in new Keynesian models'. Dixon (2-9) reviews the other side of new Keynesian economics, i.e. the menu-costs and imperfect-competition explanations of nominal rigidities together with possible justifications for the notion of involuntary unemployment. His view of the role of theory and evidence comes from the conviction that empirical testing is never decisive because of the theory-laden nature of our interpretations of empirical evidence. In his view, therefore, the choice among different approaches in macroeconomics is heavily influenced by one's particular worldview. In his comment, Blaug (2-10A) accepts the conclusions of Delli Gatti, Tamborini, and Dixon about rationing and imperfect competition. The surprise, he argues, is that it is necessary to argue for them when all economists prior to Arrow and Deloren knew that the world was not, and could not be, perfectly competitive. Interestingly enough, the ensuing discussion (2-10B) is devoted not so much to the main theoretical tenets of new Keynesian macroeconomics as to the possibility of justifying theories by appealing to a set of 'stylized facts'. The whole discussion shows that when economic theorists and econometricians debate the pros and cons of taking stylized facts as the main source of inspiration in theory-building, it turns out to be quite controversial. While the former are ready to attach some value to such evidence, the latter are highly suspicious of it (going as far as to deny the possibility of placing any confidence on such illusory knowledge).

The last group of papers explores how academic macroeconomics actually influences policy decisions. Hints for a possible answers to this question were sought in (a small sample of) official documents. Mayer's paper (2-11) concentrates on documents relative to monetary policy in the USA but one section is nonetheless devoted to Europe and Japan. He points to some difficulties that make it difficult to provide a precise answer. First, it does not seem possible to quantify the influence of academic research in a meaningful way (for example, in the form of a citation count). Second, terms like 'academic ideas' and 'government documents' are somewhat ambiguous.

Third, some episodes of successful cooperation between academics and policy-makers seem to be due more to personal attitudes than to any general trends. Mayer (2-11, Section 6) discusses at some length the content of the *Report of the Council of Economic Advisers* and the *Transcripts of the Federal Open Market Committee* and comes to the conclusion that the nearer documents are to policy-making, the less likely they are to make use of academic research. Implicit influence seems more pervasive, especially when the results of academic research may be employed to support policy-makers' preferred viewpoints.

Maes (2-12) focuses on macroeconomic thought at the European Commission in the early 1980s. His reconstruction confirms that, even in this case, personal inclinations and links seem to have played a significant role. Moreover, his detailed account of the institutional framework within which economic policy proposals take shape shows that, at least in the European case, differences between macroeconomic approaches are intertwined with national idiosyncrasies. The result, as Maes stresses in his conclusions, is that the influence of academic ideas is clearly detectable but almost always filtered by the needs of consensus building and, therefore, by the consequent inclination to put out official documents that are eclectic and reconciliatory. Hausman (2-13A) does not respond to these papers in detail, but uses his philosopher's perspective to argue that economists typically take for granted two propositions. These are (i) that 'to decide rationally among competing policies requires information concerning their outcomes; [and that] (ii) science (and even economics) can sometimes provide this information'. He describes these as platitudes, but argues that because they are sometimes questioned, it is worthwhile to make explicit the arguments that can be adduced in support of them. The following discussion (2-13B) confirms that economists do accept these two platitudes. Another theme to emerge, perhaps not surprisingly in view of the background of those present, related to the ability of policy-makers and their staffs to understand what economic research is about.[20] This is linked to recruitment policies and the extent to which government organizations employ staff trained in advanced theoretical and econometric techniques. This suggests that the link between macroeconomics and policy may raise issues of sociology as well as methodology.

REFERENCES

Backhouse, R. E. (1995) *Interpreting Macroeconomics: Explorations in the History of Macro-economic Thought* (London and New York: Routledge).
——(1997) *Truth and Progress in Economic Knowledge* (Cheltenham and Lyme, NH: Edward Elgar).

[20] For a somewhat dissenting voice, see Mayer's rejoinder. He is concerned with the lack of intuition (without which good policies can hardly be designed) often displayed by technically competent economists. Further, he notes that the issue of how fast new economic ideas should be adopted faces the problem of the time needed to establish their soundness.

Blanchard, O. J. and S. Fisher (1989) *Lectures on Macroeconomics* (Cambridge, Mass. and London: MIT Press).

Blaug, M. (1992) *The Methodology of Economics. Or How Economists Explain*, 2nd edn. (Cambridge and New York: Cambridge University Press).

Caldwell, B. J. (1993) *Beyond Positivism. Economic Methodology in the Twentieth Century*, revd. edn. (London and New York: Routledge).

Cartwright, N. (1991) 'Replicability, reproducibility, and robustness: Comment on Harry Collins', *History of Political Economy* 23: 145–55.

Darnell A. C. and J. L. Evans (1990) *The Limits of Econometrics* (Aldershot and Brookfield, Vt.: Edward Elgar).

Dow, S. C. (1996) *The Methodology of Macroeconomic Thought. A Conceptual Analysis of Schools of Thought in Economics* (Cheltenham and Brookfield, Vt.: Edward Elgar).

Epstein, R. (1987) *A History of Econometrics* (Amsterdam: North-Holland).

Gibbard, A. and H. Varian (1978) 'Economic models', *Journal of Philosophy* 75: 664–77.

Granger, W. J. (1999) *Empirical Modelling in Economics. Specification and Evaluation* (Cambridge and New York: Cambridge University Press).

Hands, D. W. (1988) 'Ad hocness in economics and the Popperian tradition', in N. de Marchi (ed.), *The Popperian Legacy in Economics* (Cambridge and New York: Cambridge University Press): 121–37.

——(1993) *Testing, Rationality and Progress. Essays on the Popperian Tradition in Economic Methodology* (Lanham, Md: Rowman & Littlefield).

Hicks, J. R. (1937) 'Mr Keynes and the "classics": A suggested interpretation', *Econometrica* 5: 147–59.

——(1979) *Causality in Economics* (Oxford: Blackwell).

Hoover, K. D. (1988) *The New Classical Macroeconomics. A Sceptical Inquiry* (Oxford and Cambridge, Mass.: Blackwell).

——(ed.) (1995) *Macroeconometrics. Developments, Tensions, and Prospects* (Boston and Dortrecht: Kluwer).

Klein, P. A. (ed.) (1994) *The Role of Economic Theory* (Boston and Dortrecht: Kluwer).

Kreps, D. M. (1990) *A Course in Microeconomic Theory* (London: Harvester Wheatsheaf).

Kuhn, T. S. (1970) *The Structure of Scientific Revolutions*, 2nd edn. (Chicago and London: University of Chicago Press).

Mayer, T. (1993) *Truth Versus Precision in Economics* (Aldershot and Brookfield, Vt.: Edward Elgar).

McCallum, B. T. (1986) 'On "real" and "sticky-price" theories of the business cycle', *Journal of Money, Credit and Banking* 18: 397–414.

——(1989) (*Monetary Economics: Theory and Policy* (London and New York: Macmillan).

—— and E. Nelson (1997) 'An optimizing IS–LM specification for monetary policy and business cycle analysis', MS., Carnegie Mellon University.

Miller, R. (1987) *Fact and Method* (Princeton: Princeton University Press).

Morgan, M. S. (1988) 'Finding a satisfactory empirical model', in N. de Marchi (ed.), *The Popperian Legacy in Economics* (Cambridge and New York: Cambridge University Press): 199–211.

——(1990) *The History of Econometric Ideas* (Cambridge and New York: Cambridge University Press).

Pagan, A. (1987) 'Three econometric methodologies: A critical appraisal', *Journal of Economic Surveys* 1: 3–24.

Rappaport, S. (1998) *Models and Reality in Economics* (Cheltenham and Northampton, Mass.: Edward Elgar).

Solow, R. M. (1998) *Monopolistic Competition and Macroeconomic Theory* (Cambridge and New York: Cambridge University Press).

Stiglitz, J. E. (1992) 'Methodological issues and the new Keynesian economics', in A. Vercelli and N. Dimitri (eds.), *Macroeconomics. A Survey of Research Strategies* (Oxford and New York: Oxford University Press): 38–86.

Summers, L. H. (1991) 'The scientific illusion in empirical macroeconomics', *Scandinavian Journal of Economics* 93: 129–48.

Tobin, J. (1969) 'A general equilibrium approach to monetary theory', *Journal of Money, Credit and Banking* 1: 15–29.

Vercelli, A. and N. Dimitri (eds.) (1992), *Macroeconomics. A Survey of Research Strategies* (Oxford and New York: Oxford University Press).

Part I

THE IS–LM MODEL

2 The evolution of IS–LM models: empirical evidence and theoretical presuppositions

ALESSANDRO VERCELLI

1. Introduction

IS–LM models have played a crucial role in the evolution of macroeconomics in the last sixty years. Despite growing criticism in the profession, particularly after the mid-1970s, they still play a crucial role in macroeconomics. They remain the core of many introductory and intermediate-level textbooks (e.g. Dornbusch and Fischer 1978; Gordon 1987; Hall and Taylor 1988; Blanchard and Fischer 1989; Mankiw 1992; Blanchard 1996). In addition they are still the backbone of disaggregated macro-econometric models utilized by public authorities and firms for policy evaluation and economic forecasting (e.g. in the USA the MPS and the DRI models). The survival of IS–LM models in a prominent position in macroeconomics is quite surprising since in the last sixty years both the real world and economic theories and methods have apparently changed considerably. The longevity of IS–LM models has been made possible by the great adaptability they have shown in the face of changing perceptions of the economic environment within which they have been applied (which I will call, for short, 'the environment' throughout the paper) that depend on the evolution of the relevant stylized facts and of the salient policy problems as well as on the evolution of the prevailing theoretical assumptions and methodological approaches. How can we explain the adaptability of IS–LM models to a changing environment and their resilience after many, apparently crippling, criticisms?

In order to answer these questions we have to distinguish from the very outset different roles performed by IS–LM models during their career:

- *Propaedeutic role* for didactic or heuristic purposes. No doubt the success of IS–LM models has relied very much on a comparatively high benefit–cost ratio attributable to their use since they have often shown a significant heuristic and analytic power obtained through very simple means. In fact IS–LM models are able to represent the demand side of a whole economy by using just two equations and two endogenous variables (income and the rate of interest). Since one equation (IS) represents the real sector and the other (LM) the monetary sector, the IS–LM model is likely to be the simplest conceivable model which allows an analysis of the interaction between the real and the monetary sectors of the economy (at least as far as the demand side is concerned). Finally, the extreme simplicity of the model and the possibility of representing it by a two-dimensional graph allow an intuitive understanding of its implications for economic analysis and policy, thus permitting easy communication between macroeconomists and a broader public (journalists, politicians, and any audience sufficiently conversant with basic macroeconomics).

- *Hermeneutic role* in order to clarify the interpretation of one macroeconomic theory in comparison with other theories. Since their appearance (Hicks 1937), IS–LM models have played a crucial role as a common ground for theoretical and policy debates involving macroeconomists and policy-makers with different theoretical and policy perspectives: Keynes versus the classics until the late 1960s Keynesians versus the monetarists in the late 1960s and early 1970s, new Keynesians versus new classical economists more recently.

- *Descriptive role* for representing, explaining, or forecasting the performance of particular economies. IS–LM models have formed the backbone of most macro-econometric models. This explains in part their early success, for their pregnant simplicity made them easy to apply in the early days of econometrics (the early work by Klein is a prominent example). Subsequently IS–LM models have inspired the construction of more sophisticated multi-equation disaggregated econometric models.

- *Prescriptive role* for choosing the best policy measures or rules. Generic theoretical versions have been used for discussing which are the best policy rules under different hypotheses. Econometric versions of IS–LM models have been used for choosing the best policy measures for particular economies in particular periods. The policy implications of IS–LM models have proved to be very sensitive to competing assumptions on the slope of the two curves.

Of these four roles only the first one is relatively uncontroversial. Even a radical critic of IS–LM models wittily remarked a few years ago that 'IS–LM is the best mousetrap built so far in macroeconomics' (Leijonhufvud 1983: 64). The clever simplicity of IS–LM models is sufficient to justify their use as didactic or propaedeutic devices, provided that it is kept in mind, and made clear to the audience, that conclusions drawn from them may be wrong or misleading and require further analysis with more sophisticated arguments and instruments.

In the light of the severe limitations of the IS–LM models we might wonder how we can explain their resilience, for their range of application has gone well beyond what might be considered justified for over sixty years. Clues about how we might answer this question can be found by reflecting upon the surprising adaptability shown by IS–LM models to a changing environment. In this paper we intend to document this adaptability and to clarify the reasons for it and its implications. In order to do this we examine first, in Section 2, the prototype IS–LM model suggested by Hicks just after the publication of the *General Theory*. We then examine in Section 3 the evolution through time of IS–LM models based on Hicksian foundations and, in Section 4, the different foundations and implications of an emerging new generation of IS–LM models which aim to be consistent with new classical tenets. We are then in a position to hazard, in Section 5, a few remarks on the evolution of IS–LM models, trying to sort out the influence of empirical evidence and theoretical and methodological presuppositions. In the concluding section, the resilience of IS–LM models is related to their intrinsic ambiguity rather than to their good performance in macroeconomic analysis.

2. The prototype of the first-generation IS–LM models: Hicks (1937)

As is well known, the prototype IS–LM model was introduced by Hicks (1937) as a hermeneutic device for clarifying the relationship between Keynes's *General Theory* (from now on GT) and *General Equilibrium* (from now on GE) classical theory in a language that could be understood also by the emerging group of econometricians and mathematical economists (Hicks, 1982: 100).[1] At that time Hicks was writing *Value and Capital* (1939), meant to clarify the foundations of Walrasian GE theory in order to build on them more manageable models for economic analysis and policy. It therefore came naturally to him to represent the essence of GT in a small-scale semi-aggregate GE model and compare it with an analogous GE model of Walrasian inspiration in order to isolate and discuss the differences between them.

The GT model in Hicks's suggested interpretation considers explicitly only three aggregate markets (money, capital, and goods) and postulates that in the short period neither the market for labour nor price changes play a significant 'active' role in the determination of macroeconomic equilibrium. The result is the following simple model:

$$L = G(i), \quad I = F(i), \quad I = S(Y), \tag{1}$$

where the symbols (which do not always correspond to those, now obsolete, utilized by Hicks)[2] have their usual meaning: L is the aggregate demand for money (which is in equilibrium equal to the aggregate supply of money M), i is the nominal rate of interest, I is aggregate investment (in plant and machinery), and Y aggregate income. The variables are measured in nominal terms but, owing to the assumption of fixed prices, their changes also represent changes in real terms.

The classical (Walrasian) GE model assumed as a benchmark by Hicks is formally very similar although its foundations are quite different:

$$L = kY, \quad I = F(i), \quad I = S(i, Y), \tag{2}$$

where the first equation represents the simplest version of the 'Cambridge quantity equation', while the other two represent as before the investment and the saving equations.

---

[1] Not by chance 'Mr Keynes and the "Classics"' was written to be given at a meeting of the Econometric Society, held in Oxford in September 1936, and was published in *Econometrica*. The author himself underlines the role played by these circumstances (Hicks 1982: 100).

[2] By the way, the name given by Hicks to what is now called IS–LM was originally IS–LL and became SI–LL in his subsequent writings probably to emphasize, with a touch of typical Hicksian self-irony, the idea that this apparatus has to be taken just as a preliminary step towards more serious analysis (see Hicks 1983).

The only formal differences between (1) and (2) are in the first equation which in the classical case relates the aggregate demand for money to aggregate income (according to the 'Cambridge quantity equation'), not to the interest rate (as maintained by the Keynesian theory of liquidity preference) and in the third equation where in the classical case saving depends also on the interest rate. This second amendment is considered by Hicks a mere simplification (1937: 107). It is the first difference that leads to the 'startling conclusion, that an increase in the inducement to invest, or in the propensity to consume, will not tend to raise the rate of interest, but only to increase employment' (ibid.) Hicks calls the system of equations (1) 'Mr Keynes's *special theory*'. However, 'in spite of the fact that quite a large part of the argument runs in terms of this system' (ibid.), Keynes's *General Theory* recognizes that the aggregate demand for money depends also on aggregate income which plays a crucial influence in the transaction and precautionary motives of demand for money. Therefore the final model suggested by Hicks as a representation of the GT is the following:

$$L = G(i, Y), \quad I = F(i), \quad I = S(Y). \tag{3}$$

This model reintroduces the interdependence between the market for money (transaction, precautionary, and speculative motives) and the market for goods (investment and consumption goods) which is crucial in Walrasian GE models and was absent in the special theory of Keynes. The two models become substantially equivalent because the reduced and implicit form of the equations obscures the implications of their different foundations.

It is at this stage of the argument that Hicks has a real stroke of genius. He sees that it is possible to push further the discussion of the differences between Keynes and the classics without losing touch with economic intuition through a graphic method based on a further simplification of the model. By analogy with the first equation of the system (3), which expresses a relationship between income and the rate of interest under the assumption of equilibrium in the market for money, a relationship between the same variables may be derived by equating equilibrium investment and savings. He can then describe macroeconomic equilibrium in terms of the intersection of two curves in a two-dimensional Cartesian diagram: the LM that takes account of the equilibrium constraints arising in the market for money and the IS that takes account of the equilibrium constraints arising in the market for goods. The differences between Keynes and the classics are now reflected in different assumptions about the slopes of the two curves. The peculiar Keynesian results depend, according to Hicks, on the so-called *liquidity trap*—which implies a horizontal section of the LM curve when the economy is far from full-employment equilibrium. Keynes's *special theory* which neglects the feedback of income on the rate of interest may now be better understood not as based on the denial in principle of the interdependence between the monetary and real sectors but as the result of offsetting forces which may work adversely under given circumstances. Hicks seems inclined to believe that these circumstances are reasonable only in a depression (1937: 111). Analogously, if the axes measure the nominal rate of interest and real aggregate income, as in many IS–LM models, the classical dichotomy should imply a vertical LM and a horizontal IS curve (Hicks 1937,

1967*b*); however, many classical economists recognized some degree of interdependence between the monetary sector and the real sector in the short period (Hume, Thornton, Marshall, Lavington, etc.).

The final verdict by Hicks on the difference between GT and GE is completely clear: the only fundamental difference concerns the assumption of flexible prices. In the classical models this ensures the stability of full-employment equilibrium and the long-run dichotomy between the real sector and the monetary sector. However, in his opinion, in the short period the passive role of the supply side of the economy (and possibly even the stickiness of prices) may be justified as an approximation and could be accepted as such also by classical economists. In any case, the extent to which these assumptions are justified depends on contingent circumstances (phase of the cycle, industrial sector, country, and historical period) rather than on theoretical or methodological fundamentals. Therefore, according to Hicks, the residual differences between Keynes and the classics should be discussed mainly in empirical or econometric terms.

This interpretation based on the IS–LM apparatus has been found appealing because it provides a common ground for the discussion and comparison of different theoretical approaches to the determination of short-term macroeconomic equilibrium. It plays down fundamental or irreducible contrasts between them and sets common rules of the game for debating the issues and adjudicating arguments case by case. Therefore, the IS–LM apparatus offered both of the competing camps (Keynesians and classics) a very honourable compromise. This took the form of an alleged synthesis between two basically correct, but partial, points of view. It set, at the same time, a framework for future research that was perfectly attuned with the emerging tendencies in econometrics and mathematical economics. Therefore the tremendous, and relatively rapid, success of IS–LM models is perfectly understandable in historical terms. However, it involved costs that were by no means negligible. Profound theoretical and methodological questions raised by Keynes in the GT were completely ignored or trivialized in IS–LM-style macroeconomics. In order to understand this we have to go deeper into the relationship between the IS–LM apparatus and Keynes's theory.

As is well known, the main argument of the GT is developed in two stages. In the first stage (occupying the first part of the book and summarized in ch. 18), a fix-price heuristic model is developed which is meant to demonstrate and justify Keynes's own peculiar approach to short-period economic problems. In chs. 19–21, Keynes applies this approach to the explanation of unemployment equilibrium and to sorting out the most efficient policy remedies to it. In the second stage Keynes drops the assumption of fixed prices and grounds his conclusions on the structural instability[3] of the

---

[3] *Structural* instability indicates the propensity of a certain (macroeconomic) system to change the qualitative features of its dynamic behaviour (number and type of equilibria, their stability or instability, out-of-equilibrium behaviour, etc.) in consequence of a small shock. This property should not be confused with the usual concept of instability, which may be called *dynamic* instability, routinely utilized in economic analysis, which indicates progressive divergence of a system from equilibrium whenever a shock pushes it out of equilibrium. (For a more detailed discussion of instability concepts along these lines see Vercelli 1991.)

relationship connecting the endogenous variables (which implies a marked structural instability for both the IS and LM curves). This structural instability depends mainly on, possibly abrupt, changes in the long-term expectations of investors and speculators in the financial and productive capital markets, triggered by shocks which may be produced by policy interventions (for further details on this reconstruction of the GT argument see Vercelli 1991). In this view the IS–LM apparatus is a fairly faithful reconstruction of the Keynes's first-stage fix-price heuristic model, although restricted to the demand side of the economy. However, in the second stage, Keynes explicitly rejects the applicability of the first-stage fix-price heuristic model to situations characterized by structural instability, such as those which had led to the persistence of 'unemployment equilibrium' in the 1930s. He explains in the GT and elsewhere that this is not the exception but the rule in a sophisticated monetary economy (see in particular his review of Tinbergen, Keynes (1939)). Therefore, the crucial and more general second stage of the Keynesian argument contains implicitly a clear refutation of the descriptive and prescriptive roles of the IS–LM apparatus. Of course this does not exclude its propaedeutic use which is implicitly fully exploited by Keynes himself in the first stage of the argument, but its applicability as a reliable apparatus for drawing conclusions for the real world is explicitly denied. In order to cope with the structural instability exhibited by a sophisticated monetary economy, Keynes suggests a very innovative methodological approach based on strong uncertainty, probabilistic causality, attention for the time-sequence of changes, and a crucial role for long-term expectations (see Vercelli 1991). These innovative ideas, hardly consistent with Walrasian methodology, completely disappear from IS–LM models. Their hermeneutic, descriptive, and prescriptive implications are therefore in general completely different from Keynes's own. In particular, Keynes's specific results on the severe limitations of monetary policy for recovering from unemployment equilibrium and on the weakness of the feedback of income on the rate of interest depend neither on special assumptions concerning the slope of the relevant functions nor on the assumption of fixed prices. On the contrary, the stickiness of prices and their inability to bring the relevant variables to their optimal values as well as the so-called 'liquidity trap' were both explained as a consequence of the structural instability of a sophisticated monetary economy.[4] This leads to the conclusion that IS–LM models ignore and cloud the most interesting methodological and theoretical insights put forward by Keynes in the GT.

3. The evolution of IS–LM models

The prototype IS–LM model suggested by Hicks was mainly motivated by the need to clarify theoretical and methodological issues raised by the GT. The first reason for its

---

[4] Keynes also stresses institutional reasons for the stickiness of wages and prices, but this should not obscure the fact that in the second stage of his analysis he aims at a general theory which should apply also under the assumption of flexible prices, since 'a theory cannot claim to be a *general* theory, unless it is applicable to the case where (or the range within which) money-wages are fixed, just as much as to any other case' (Keynes 1936: 276).

success was its (alleged) ability to reconcile the Keynesian representation of the economy as a whole with that of classical GE theory under the assumptions of short-period fixed prices. This gradually produced a substantial consensus on the basic framework of macroeconomics (the so-called 'neoclassical synthesis'). It is also possible to claim that the appearance of the IS–LM apparatus contributed to the emergence of a broad consensus on macroeconomic policy—the need for policy intervention to get out of the Great Depression, to finance the war, and to convert war industries and reconstruct economies damaged by the war (the Marshall Plan). But these were exceptional circumstances under which it was relatively easy to agree. IS–LM models were worked out and discussed in the late 1930s and in the 1940s mainly in order to clarify the relationship between Keynes and the classics. It was only in the 1950s that they became the cornerstone of econometric models aiming to describe the perform-ance of the economy and to *fine-tune* it in ordinary times. However, in a sense, even the 1950s were not ordinary times. The success of IS–LM models in that period in the above role is strictly related to the (with hindsight) peculiar economic environment of the 1950s. This was characterized by:

- substantial monetary stability and relatively peaceful industrial relations which justified the assumption of fixed prices and wages (in the short period),
- slow and steady shifts of the supply curve which could be fairly well approximated, in the short period, by a given supply curve,
- substantial structural stability of the two curves which was sufficient to allow a safe use of IS–LM models for descriptive and policy purposes.

The descriptive use of IS–LM models which caught on in the 1950s and was consolidated in the 1960s could not emerge in the troubled times of the late 1930s and 1940s for reasons already clearly expressed by Keynes and which were discussed in Section 2 (structural instability of the two curves fed by strong systemic uncertainty).

In the 1960s the environment began to change as the industrialized countries experienced the first relevant supply shocks of the post-war period (mainly wage pushes). In the late 1960s these deepened and became more general. In this period it became progressively clearer that the IS–LM models could not represent the whole economy, not even as a first approximation, because the supply side and the process of formation of prices and wages could not be ignored any longer, even in the short run.[5] In that period it became obvious that traditional IS–LM models could at best be only a simplified representation of the demand side of the economy. However, IS–LM models were promptly rescued by appending a third equation—the Phillips curve just introduced into the literature by Phillips (1958) and Lipsey (1960)—which could somehow represent the supply side and the process of price and wage change.

The new augmented IS–LM models, however, had still to assume the structural stability of their equations, while since the late 1960s a series of connected shocks

---

[5] This was clearly anticipated by Hicks himself in his review of Patinkin (1956) published in 1957 (reprint with editorial changes in Hicks 1967*a*), and accurately examined in a few pioneering works (such as Bailey 1962).

(generalized wage-push in the late 1960s and early 1970s, the breakdown of the Bretton Woods system, and the two oil shocks) introduced a climate characterized by strong uncertainty and pronounced structural instability of the three curves. Attempts at rescue focused on more complex formulations of the Phillips curve or alternative formulations of the supply side as well as more sophisticated versions of the IS and LM curves. However, notwithstanding all these efforts, in the late 1970s a period of decline started for IS–LM models. This was due not only to the structural instability of the late 1960s and 1970s (which could not be accommodated within IS–LM models) but also to the growing success of the new classical economics and its basic challenges to the fundamental theoretical and methodological tenets of IS–LM economics.

The growing success of IS–LM models in the post-war period had not gone unchallenged, but until the mid-1970s the main opposition was from currents of thought that had not managed to exert a particularly deep influence on mainstream macroeconomics (for example, orthodox Keynesians such as Kaldor, Joan Robinson, and Pasinetti, or monetarists such as Friedman[6] and Brunner and Meltzer).[7] After the mid-1970s a more radical opposition came from the main leaders of the emerging school of 'new classical economics' (Lucas, Sargent, Barro, etc.). IS–LM models were severely criticized for their lack of sound microfoundations (consistent with new classical standards), the complete neglect of endogenous and forward-looking expectations, an obsolete concept of equilibrium, a static approach (which restricts their use to comparative statics), and systematic violation of the classical dichotomy between the monetary and the real sectors of the economy. The most crippling and influential criticism was the so-called Lucas critique (Lucas 1976) which argued that functions such as the IS and LM curves are in principle not invariant to changes in economic policy rules and therefore cannot be used for policy evaluation. More generally the so-called Lucas critique in its *pars destruens* correctly underlines that the main trouble with IS–LM models lies in their irremediable structural instability triggered by policy shocks.[8]

In consequence of the new classical revolution (or, better, counter-revolution) of the 1970s the use of IS–LM models for hermeneutic, descriptive, and prescriptive purposes declined sharply. This did not affect their prominent role in textbooks of

---

[6] Friedman who in the 1950s and 1960s raised the most influential criticisms to mainstream 'neoclassical synthesis' never liked the IS–LM apparatus but did not reject it altogether, at least as a possible vehicle of communication with Keynesian economists (see e.g. Friedman 1976: 310–17).

[7] Brunner and Meltzer who must be reckoned among the early critics of the Keynesian use of IS–LM models did not exclude the use of a more sophisticated version of IS–LM models extending the range of substitution between assets (for a recent restatement of their approach see Brunner and Meltzer 1993).

[8] It is ironic that the most crippling and influential critique of Keynesian, IS–LM style, models has been (independently) based on concepts already clearly expressed by Keynes, in particular in his critique of Tinbergen (Keynes 1939). However, the argument is inserted by Lucas in a different theoretical and methodological perspective. The structural instability is according to Keynes an ontological property of socio-economic systems and is particularly pronounced in a sophisticated monetary economy so that economic models cannot escape from it while their correct use must adapt to it. On the contrary, structural instability is according to Lucas either an illusory appearance of economic phenomena or, in any case, a property outside the reach of sound scientific methodology, so that models must be built and utilized in such a way as to avoid it.

Keynesian inspiration (for example, Dornbusch and Fischer 1978; Gordon 1987; Hall and Taylor 1988; Mankiw 1992; Blanchard 1996). In textbooks of new classical inspiration they were mentioned, and to some extent discussed, exclusively as expression of an approach considered out-of-date[9] (see, for example, Sargent 1979; Barro 1993). The harsh confrontation between new classical economists and new Keynesian economists implies in particular a divergent view on the legitimate roles of IS–LM models. The new classical economists are prepared to recognize some residual value for IS–LM models as a propaedeutic device, but strongly refute their descriptive and prescriptive roles,[10] while these are still vindicated by many new Keynesian economists (see, for example, Gali 1992; Taylor 1993; Ball and Mankiw 1994).

The influence of facts on the genesis and evolution of IS–LM models is recognized by both camps in a symmetric way. New classical economists consider the Keynesian revolution (which led to the birth of IS–LM models) to be an overreaction to the Great Depression of the 1930s, while new Keynesians consider the new classical counter-revolution (which led to the alleged demise of IS–LM models) to be an overreaction to the supply-side turbulence of the 1970s. It is clear that both episodes, as well as more ordinary factual developments, are seen in a completely different perspective because of different theoretical and methodological frameworks. The evolution of IS–LM models depends, no doubt, on the environment within which they are formulated, but the environment depends not only on the stock of accumulated empirical evidence and the flow of new additions to it, but also on their interpretation, which is grounded on the theoretical assumptions and methodological approaches adopted.

4. A second generation of IS–LM models?

In the new environment of the 1970s, a period of decline started for IS–LM models, at least as far as their descriptive and prescriptive roles are concerned. However, a more stable economic environment in the 1980s and 1990s has contributed, since the mid-1980s, to a revival of IS–LM models also in their descriptive and prescriptive roles.

The revival of IS–LM models since the late 1980s is characterized on the one hand by more refined foundations provided by new Keynesian economists, relating particularly to the assumption that prices are sticky in the real world (see Mankiw and Romer 1991), and on the other hand by the emergence of a family of IS–LM models which try to cope with the theoretical and methodological tenets of the new classical

---

[9] A partial exception is the textbook of McCallum (1989). On that see the next section.

[10] This point of view has been recently reasserted by Lucas (1994: 153):

Sometimes, as in the US Great Depression, reductions in money growth seem to have large effects on production and employment. Other times, as in the ends of the post-World War I European hyperinflations, large reductions in money growth seem to have been neutral, or nearly so. Observations like these seem to imply that a theoretical framework such as the Keynes–Hicks–Modigliani IS–LM model, in which a single multiplier is applied to all money movements regardless of their source or their predictability is inadequate for practical purposes.

For other recent critical assessments of IS–LM models on similar lines see e.g. Sims (1992); King (1993); and Leeper and Sims (1994).

economics. The authors of this family of models derive IS–LM models from explicit maximizing analysis of rational economic agents, being convinced that the lack of proper microfoundations is the main shortcoming of traditional IS–LM models. As a matter of fact, the individual equations on which traditional IS–LM models are based have received through time rigorous microfoundations: examples are the theory of consumption by Modigliani, and liquidity preference by Baumol and Tobin. However, these microfoundations are not fully consistent with those deemed sound by new classical economists, in particular because they ignore expectations or consider them exogenous or because they do not grant the classical dichotomy at least in the long term. Therefore the representatives of this new family of IS–LM models aim first of all to provide explicit microfoundations consistent with the theoretical and metho-dological tenets of new classical economics. Among the most interesting examples of IS–LM models of this kind we may reckon Fane (1985), McCallum (1989), Koenig (1989, 1993), Auerbach and Kotlikoff (1995), and McCallum and Nelson (1997, 1998). Although this family of models is not yet very numerous or very homogeneous, it could start a new generation of IS–LM models which might rehabilitate them with new classical economists and give a new impulse to their use. In any case these models confirm the great adaptability of IS–LM models to a wide range of theoretical and methodological environments by beginning to conquer even the school of thought which has been so far more sceptical on their virtues. The models belonging to this new family can be labelled as a 'new generation' of IS–LM models in order to emphasize that, notwithstanding unquestionable formal analogies between their equations and those of first-generation IS–LM models, the different foundations imply a quite different range of applicability for the models, as well as different results.

In order to clarify these assertions we are going to examine in some detail one emblematic representative of this new generation of IS–LM models which is parti-cularly interesting and coherent: the model recently suggested by McCallum and Nelson (1997) which restates the model first worked out in McCallum (1989). While Fane (1985) and Koenig (1989, 1993) confine their analysis to comparative statics and Auerbach and Kotlikoff (1995) derive the IS–LM apparatus from an overlapping generation framework only under the restrictive assumption of rigid prices, McCallum and Nelson (1997) provide a fully-fledged dynamic analysis, in the new classical sense, applicable also under the assumptions of sticky prices.

McCallum (1989: 102–7) and McCallum and Nelson (1997: 3) maintain that useful insights into monetary policy and business-cycle behaviour may be provided by the following semi-reduced macroeconomic structure:

(IS) $\log y_t = b_0 + b_1[i_t - E_t(\log P_{t+1} - \log P_t)] + E_t \log y_{t+1} + v_t,$

(LM) $\log L_t - \log P_t = c_0 + c_1 \log y_t + c_2 i_t + \eta_t,$ (4)

(AS) $\log y_t = a_0 + a_1(\log P_t - E_{t-1} \log P_t) + a_2 \log y_{t-1} + u_t,$

plus a policy rule for M_t (or i_t), where y_t is real income at time t, P_t the price level at time t, L_t the nominal money balances equal to nominal money supply M_t, i_t the nominal interest rate, $E_t(\cdot) = E(\cdot|\Omega_t)$ designates the rational expectations of $(\cdot)$ with Ω_t representing the set of information available in period t.

The first thing to notice is that the IS–LM equations are correctly considered as a semi-reduced form representation exclusively of the aggregate demand side of the economy so that they must be used in conjunction with a representation of aggregate supply (AS curve). This role is played not by a version of the Phillips curve as in traditional models but by a simple version of the new classical supply curve. This reveals a deep conceptual shift because it reinstates the long-run classical dichotomy between the monetary and the real sectors of the economy while short-run deviations are due to stochastic shocks on prices. The same new classical approach also consistently underlies the foundations provided for the IS and LM curves. These seem at first inspection to be the usual IS and LM curves but this appearance is highly misleading as they are based on alternative foundations aimed at making them fully consistent with the basic tenets of new classical economics. To this end McCallum and Nelson show that they can be derived from the optimizing behaviour of fully rational agents under standard simplifying assumptions. Consistency with optimizing behaviour just requires one simple but crucial modification to the usual specification of the IS curve: the expected value of next period's output has to be added as a crucial determinant of the output demanded in the current period. McCallum and Nelson (1997: 19) stress that this extra term gives a forward-looking aspect to the IS–LM curve that is not present in typical IS–LM models, and which is likely to have a major effect on the dynamic properties of the representation of a macroeconomic system.

Despite the strong formal analogy between McCallum and Nelson's IS–LM curves and the usual ones, the conceptual and methodological differences are quite deep and must be fully understood in order to avoid potential confusions. In particular:

- The underlying model assumes flexible prices although the derived relations are meant to 'be used sensibly in a setting with slow price adjustment' (McCallum and Nelson 1997: 15).
- The derivation of IS and LM curves from maximizing behaviour is developed first in a deterministic setting and is then carried on in a stochastic setting by employing commonly made approximations. Uncertainty is introduced in the usual way of the new classical macroeconomics by assuming a stationary distribution of stochastic shocks impinging upon one or more endogenous variables and by assuming that economic agents entertain rational expectations over the future. The stochastic microfoundations are particularly interesting because they promise to amend a crucial weakness of IS–LM analysis by introducing uncertainty explicitly and because they assure a deeper consistency with new classical tenets.
- Differently from the first-generation IS–LM models, McCallum and Nelson's model does not restrict IS–LM analysis to short-period (versus long-period) issues but to business-cycle (versus growth) issues. This is a crucial conceptual difference between first-generation IS–LM models and the McCallum and Nelson model since the dichotomy short/long period does not overlap at all with the business-cycle/growth one. In the Marshallian tradition underlying both Keynes's and

Hicks's models, as well as first-generation IS–LM models, the assumption of short period implies a given and invariant quantity and quality of capital stock and, in the absence of stochastic shocks, also a given and invariant supply curve. This simplifying assumption permits comparative-statics exercises to choose the best policy interventions in a given situation but is not appropriate for a satisfactory analysis of either business cycle or growth issues. The McCallum and Nelson model is fully dynamic (in the new classical sense) even in its supply curve which therefore plays a crucial role in the determination of income and, indirectly, of the other endogenous variables. The model supports comparative dynamics exercises which, however, are restricted to business-cycle issues because it is assumed that the time path of capital is exogenous. McCallum and Nelson assume in their theoretical analysis that the stock of capital grows at a given steady rate while in empirical applications they approximate the behaviour of the stock of capital as a random walk with drift so that investment is assumed to have a constant expected growth rate (1997: 7). This simple treatment of the dynamics of the capital stock does not prevent a satisfactory analysis of business-cycle issues because 'there is very little connection at cyclical frequencies between capital stock movements and aggregate output' (1997: 8). However, this assumption of course prevents any meaningful analysis of growth issues. This difference is crucial for defining the range of applicability of the model. The assumption of the short period, typical of first-generation IS–LM models, implies that the model cannot be applied to too long a series of data (exceeding, say, one year) while the assumption of a steadily growing capital stock is 'designed for quarterly time-series data over sample periods of many years' duration (e.g. ten to fifty years)' (1997: 7). Unfortunately this longer time-horizon is obtained only at the cost of a stringent assumption of stationarity for the relevant time-series which is not necessarily assumed in the traditional IS–LM analysis and was definitely not assumed in the second-stage heuristic model of Keynes.

- Strictly related to the last point is another important feature of McCallum and Nelson's model. While traditional IS–LM models may be used for choosing the optimal policy interventions in a given short-period situation but could not safely be used to choose the best policy rule under given assumptions, McCallum and Nelson's model is fitted for this second goal rather than for the first one. Notice that the model assumes a given policy rule for the nominal supply of money M_t (or for the nominal interest rate i_t) and not a given value as in traditional IS–LM models. The results that can be derived from the model are therefore conditional to the assumptions made on the monetary policy rules.

We may now attempt a preliminary assessment of the second generation IS–LM models in the light of the analysis of McCallum and Nelson's model. The main targets of these models seem to be the following:

- to provide common ground for macroeconomists and policy-makers with different perspectives, in particular new Keynesians and new classical economists (Koenig 1993);

- to choose optimal policy rules (McCallum and Nelson 1997, 1998) in given circumstances.

These targets are both problematic. First-generation and second-generation models really address different issues. The first-generation user (at least according to the original point of view of Keynes himself) may be likened to the captain of the *Titanic* who sees the iceberg and wants to know how to avoid the impact, while the user of a second-generation model aims to choose the best route for the *Titanic* taking account of all the possible shocks (including floating icebergs) but the solution to the second problem does not help solving the first one and vice versa.

We are not going to discuss here whether the second-generation models may really help to choose the optimal policy rules. Of course the validity of the results obtained from them are subject to all the limitations typical of the new classical models that have often been discussed in the literature (see for example, Vercelli 1991; Vercelli and Dimitri 1992). In any case we do not intend to deny that there may be a role for second-generation IS–LM models which is similar and complementary to that of the first-generation models—a simple propaedeutic presentation and discussion of the behaviour of a macroeconomic system and of its reaction to different kinds of external shocks or changes in policy interventions or rules. In particular its didactic value is quite evident: after having presented the characteristics of a typical first-generation IS–LM model, a teacher may substitute the new classical supply curve for the Phillips curve, may introduce uncertainty and rational expectations and show why the model has different implications for theory and policy applications.

5. The role of empirical evidence versus theoretical and methodological presuppositions

We are now in a position to advance a few tentative remarks on the evolution of IS–LM models. According to the cursory reconstruction of the evolution of IS–LM models outlined here we have to distinguish two generations of IS–LM models which have completely different foundations. While it is not yet clear whether the second generation, which temporally overlaps with the most recent examples of the first one, will catch on in the future, it has to be sharply distinguished from the first generation since it has completely different foundations, as well as different implications for macroeconomic analysis and policy. The first generation is based on the deterministic version of GE suggested by Hicks and Samuelson (see, in particular, Hicks 1939; Samuelson 1947), while the second generation is based on the Arrow–Debreu stochastic version of GE in agreement with the microfoundations suggested by Lucas and Sargent (see, in particular, the introduction to Lucas and Sargent 1981; comments may be found in Vercelli 1991). According to the foundations of GE models suggested by Hicks and Samuelson, disequilibrium is a meaningful concept and expectations do not need to be rational, while in the second case disequilibrium is meaningless and expectations must be rational. These different foundations imply a different conceptualization and a different range of applicability of the two generations (short period in the first case and business cycles in the second case, despite strong formal analogies between the two models). Generally speaking, it is possible to say that a new generation of IS–LM models appears after a major structural change in the environment: the first generation as a response to the Great Depression of the 1930s and the second generation as a response to the supply-side crisis of the 1970s and early 1980s.

Each generation of IS–LM models is characterized by many specific models which may differ considerably (for example, because they add further parameters and even, sometimes, further endogenous variables) and may be classified according to the standard 'routine' of application to empirical evidence (for example, with or without an aggregate supply curve). A change in the operational routine, i.e. in the way the models are implemented, is sensitive to structural changes less radical than those which led to new generations of models: the positive and normative use of IS–LM models as a complete representation of the economy establibed itself in the 1950s and 1960s in a period of price stability and steady shifts of the supply curve, while the addition of a third relationship in order to represent the supply side of the economy established itself in the late 1960s in consequence of the growing importance of supply-side shocks.

All the evolutionary changes which we have discussed typically lag behind the originating structural changes in the environment with a delay of about five to ten years. The Hicksian prototype of IS–LM models emerged as a means of modelling the Keynesian fix-price heuristic model that was designed to represent the causes of, and to design remedies for, the Great Depression triggered a few years before by the collapse of Wall Street. Its systematic use for fine-tuning starts at the end of the 1950s after almost one decade of steady growth in industrialized countries. The integration of a third equation to represent aggregate supply constraints is almost contemporaneous with the growing influence of supply shocks in the 1960s, while the eclipse of IS–LM models starts only in the late 1970s, almost ten years after the breakdown of the stability of the Phillips curve. The revival of IS–LM models since the late 1980s reflects almost a decade of recovered structural stability in the growth process and in prices after the troubled 1970s.

As for the specific role of cumulated empirical evidence on this process of evolution, it may be observed that successive models in each generation characterized by the same operational routine may be very sensitive to new empirical evidence made available by official sources and econometric models, while a new routine typically emerges only when different pieces of evidence systematically violate the tenets of the preceding routines (for example, the irrelevance of the supply side in the short period); a new generation of models requires in addition a radical reconceptualization of empirical evidence which is based on completely new theoretical and methodological assumptions.

6. Concluding remarks

The cursory overview of the evolution of IS–LM models reported in this paper has documented the remarkable resilience of IS–LM models which have been able to adapt to frequent and radical changes in the environment. A first possible explanation could be the good performance of IS–LM models for the purposes for which they have been designed and utilized. This may be part of the truth: the clever simplicity of these models could be sufficient to explain their continuing success in textbooks, with the media and in research reports for propaedeutic, didactic, or heuristic purposes. What about the other roles of IS–LM models? Let's consider them separately following the classification suggested in the first section of this paper:

1. Since their first introduction by Hicks, IS–LM models have been often praised for setting a common ground for competing theories and for helping their inter-pretation and assessment. Unfortunately the conclusions drawn by this hermen-eutic use of IS–LM models have often been misleading, as shown by the following three crucial episodes. (a) In the 'Keynes versus the classics' controversy, the suggested synthesis relied on the false conclusion that the main difference between Keynes's GT and Walrasian GE classical theory was rooted in the Keynesian assumptions of sticky prices and the special slope of (part of) the LM curve (because of the so-called 'liquidity trap'). The ensuing compromise (i.e. 'neoclassical synthesis') was sufficient to justify 'Keynesian' policy measures (deficit spending) and practices (fine-tuning) but trivialized the message of Keynes and ignored the deep methodological differences between GT and Walrasian GE theory which had led Keynes to reach his policy conclusions under fairly general assumptions (as argued in Section 2). (b) In the 'Keynesians versus monetarists' controversy, the crucial difference between the two camps was reduced again to a question of slope of the LM curve (assumed to be horizontal by Keynesians and vertical by monetarists). This dichotomy characterizes only one aspect of the conflict between fix-price Keynesianism and that variety of extreme monetarism that assumes the irrelevance of the rate of interest in the quantity theory of money. However, it completely clouds the deep methodological differences involved in the debate: Friedman's Marshallian method, the Walrasian GE method of the 'neoclassical synthesis', and Keynes's own method. (c) In the recent 'new Keynesians versus new classicals' controversy the use of IS–LM models again risks muddling the main issues by obscuring the deep methodological and conceptual differences underlying the different foundations of IS–LM models. The main differences between the two approaches, apart from those underlying different supply functions, seems still to reside in the Keynesian assumption of stickiness of prices. This gives the wrong impression that a compromise between the two schools of thought is possible provided that price stickiness is explained in rational terms as the systemic consequence of the optimizing behaviour of economic agents. However, as we have suggested (Section 4) the two approaches address different problems and what is common is seen in a different light.
2. The use of IS–LM models for descriptive purposes is restricted to cases in which the structural instability of the economy is fairly irrelevant. In industrialized countries this may have been approximately true for long spells of time in the 1950s and 1960s and part of the 1980s but it is certainly not true in general. This problem is

particularly severe for predictive uses because it is almost impossible to hazard forecasts on the future developments of processes characterized by structural instability. This crucial limitation in the application of IS–LM models was lucidly anticipated by Keynes and rediscovered by Lucas in a different perspective.

3. The use of IS–LM models for policy purposes is barred again by the necessary requirement of structural stability. The choice of the optimal policy interventions in a given situation, or of the best policy rule under standard assumptions, both involve forecasts as they involve a comparative assessment of the consequences of alternative policy measures or rules. In addition, as has been lucidly perceived by both Keynes and Lucas, the introduction of a new policy rule, or of a new policy measure, may produce discontinuous changes in the behavioural rules of the agents and therefore discontinuous shifts in the IS and LM curves, increasing the degree of structural instability of the economic system.

We have to conclude that the performance of IS–LM models applied to hermeneutic, descriptive, and prescriptive issues has been very poor and often misleading. The reason of the resilience of IS–LM models has to be related more to their adaptability to different theoretical and economic milieux than to their good performance, with the only exception of their propaedeutic function for each of their possible uses. Therefore we are led to conclude that the main reason of their enduring popularity is to be found in their flexibility which is ultimately rooted in their ambiguity. What is common to all the IS–LM models is after all not very demanding:

• The useful but quite obvious idea that the equilibrium aggregate demand of a certain economy implies equilibrium in both the market of goods and the market for money. In other words the IS–LM models perform a sort of minimal dis-aggregation of the determinants of equilibrium aggregate demand which is, no doubt, particularly convenient for a first study of the interrelations between the monetary and the real sectors of the economy. This very basic idea underlying IS–LM models is consistent with any theory prepared to accept the relevance for macroeconomic analysis of the equilibrium concept and of the distinction between a monetary and a real sector. For the same reason IS–LM models, short of precise a priori restrictions on the slope and position of the two curves, are consistent with almost any sort of empirical evidence and are therefore virtually non-falsifiable.

• Each curve represents the locus of all the possible couples of equilibrium values for the same endogenous variables by taking account separately of the constraints originating in the real and monetary sectors. The choice of the aggregate income and the rate of interest as the endogenous variables of the model, i.e. as the crucial bridges between the two sectors, is hardly controversial.

Summing up, we may conclude that IS–LM models are consistent with most eco-nomic theories because a certain IS–LM model can be interpreted as the semi-reduced form of different structural models which may have different theoretical foundations, and it may have different theoretical or policy implications according to the operational routine chosen. This suggests that the adaptability of IS–LM models to different environments is basically due to their ambiguity. Unexpected empirical evidence has always been accommodated in one way or another, by changing the specification of the curves, or the operational routines, or the theoretical foundations. This ambiguity of IS–LM models may well explain why they have been often utilized for suggesting compromises between different theories (e.g. the so-called 'neoclassical synthesis'). Unfortunately, the dialogue between different theories based on IS–LM models has always proved rather sterile, neither succeeding in providing a genuine and sound synthesis between competing theories, nor clarifying very much the issues at stake.

The former criticisms are not meant to deny that IS–LM models may have a useful propaedeutic role, for didactic or heuristic purposes, as a first stage of inquiry preceding a deeper analysis of macro problems and theories. Therefore there is no reason to anathematize IS–LM models for the restricted uses for which they are fit, provided that the usual warning is taken very seriously: 'handle with care'.

REFERENCES

Auerbach, A. J. and Kotlikoff, L. J. (1995) *Macroeconomics: An integrated Approach* (Cincinnati: South-Western).
Bailey, M. J. (1962) *National Income and the Price Level* (New York: McGraw-Hill; 2nd edn. 1971).
Ball, L. and Mankiw, N. G. (1994) 'Sticky price manifesto', *Carnegie-Rochester Series on Public Policy* 41: 127–51.
Barro, R. J. (1993) *Macroeconomics*, 4th edn. (New York: John Wiley).
Blanchard, O. J. (1996) *Macroeconomics* (Saddle River, NJ: Prentice-Hall).
——and Fischer, S. (1989) *Lectures on Macroeconomics* (Cambridge, Mass.: MIT Press).
Brunner, K. and Meltzer, A. H. (1993) *Money and the Economy: Issues in Monetary Analysis* (New York: Cambridge University Press).
Dornbusch, R. and Fischer, S. (1978) *Macroeconomics* (New York: McGraw-Hill).
Fane, G. (1985) 'A derivation of the IS–LM model from explicit optimizing behaviour', *Journal of Macroeconomics* 7: 493–508.
Fitoussi, J.-P. (1983) *Modern Macroeconomic Theory* (Oxford: Blackwell).
Friedman, M. (1976) 'Comments on Tobin and Buiter', in J. L. Stein (ed.), *Monetarism* (Amsterdam: North-Holland): 310–17.
Gali, J. (1992) 'How well does the IS–LM model fit postwar data?', *Quarterly Journal of Economics* 106: 709–38.
Gordon, R. J. (1987) *Macroeconomics*, 4th edn. (Boston: Little, Brown & Co.).
Hall, R. E. and Taylor, J. B. (1988) *Macroeconomics: Theory, Performance, and Policy*, 2nd edn. (New York: Norton).
Hicks, J. R. (1937). 'Mr Keynes and the "Classics": a suggested interpretation', *Econometrica* 5: 147–59, repr. in Hicks, 1967a, 126–42, and Hicks, 1982: 100–15. (Quotations are from the last reprint).
——(1939) *Value and Capital* (New York: Oxford University Press).
——(1967a) *Critical Essays in Monetary Theory* (Oxford: Clarendon Press).

Hicks, J. R. (1967*b*) 'The classics again', in Hicks 1967*a*, 143–54.

—— (1974) *The Crisis in Keynesian Economics* (Oxford: Blackwell).

—— (1982) *Money Interest and Wages, Collected Essays on Economic Theory*, ii (Oxford: Blackwell).

—— (1983) 'IS–LM: an explanation', in Fitoussi (1983: 49–63).

Keynes, J. M. (1936) *The General Theory of Employment, Interest and Money* (London: Macmillan).

—— (1939) 'Professor Tinbergen's method', *Economic Journal*, 49: 34–51.

King, R. G. (1993) 'Will the new Keynesian macroeconomics resurrect the IS–LM model?', *Journal of Economic Perspectives* 7: 67–82.

Koenig, E. F. (1989) 'A simple optimizing alternative to traditional IS–LM analysis', MS, Federal Reserve Bank of Dallas.

—— (1993) 'Rethinking the IS in IS–LM: adapting Keynesian tools to non-Keynesian economics, Part 1', *Federal Reserve Bank of Dallas Economic Review*, Third Quarter, 33–49.

Leeper, E. M. and Sims, C. A. (1994) 'Toward a modern macroeconomic model usable for policy analysis', in S. Fischer and J. Rotemberg (eds.), *NBER Macroeconomics Annual 1994*, MIT Press: 81–118.

Leijohnufvud, A. (1983) 'What was the matter with IS–LM?', in Fitoussi (1983: 64–90).

Lipsey, R. G. (1960) 'The relation between unemployment and the rate of change of money wage rates in the United Kingdom, 1862–1967: a further analysis', *Economica* 27.

Lucas, R. E. (1976) 'Econometric policy evaluation: a critique', in K. Brunner and A. H. Meltzer (eds.), 'The Phillips curve and labour markets', *Carnegie–Rochester Conference Series* 1: 19–46, repr. in Lucas (1981: 104–30).

—— (ed.) (1981) *Studies in Business-Cycle Theory* (Cambridge, Mass.: MIT Press).

—— (1994) 'Comments on Ball and Mankiw', *Carnegie–Rochester Conference Series on Public Policy* 41: 153–5.

—— and Sargent, T. J. (eds.) (1981) *Rational Expectations and Econometric Practice* (London: George Allen & Unwin).

Mankiw, N. G. (1992) *Macroeconomics* (New York: Worth).

—— and Romer, D. (1991) *New Keynesian Economics* (Cambridge, Mass.: MIT Press).

McCallum, B. T. (1989) *Monetary Economics: Theory and Policy* (New York: Macmillan).

—— and Nelson, E. (1997) 'An optimizing IS–LM specification for monetary policy and business cycle analysis', MS, Carnegie Mellon University.

—— and —— (1998) 'Nominal income targeting in an open-economy optimizing model', MS, Carnegie Mellon University.

Patinkin, D. (1956) *Money, Interest, and Prices* (New York: Harper & Row).

Phillips, A. W. (1958) 'The relation between unemployment and the rate of change of money wage rates in the United Kingdom', *Economica* 25: 283–99.

Samuelson, P. A. (1947) *Foundations of Economic Analysis* (Cambridge, Mass.: Harvard University Press).

Sargent, T. J. (1979) *Macroeconomic Theory*, 2nd edn., 1987 (San Diego: Academic Press).

Sims, C. A. (1992) 'Interpreting the macroeconomic time series facts: the effects of monetary policy', *European Economic Review* 36: 975–1000.

Taylor, J. B. (1993) *Macroeconomic Policy in a World Economy* (New York: Norton).

Vercelli, A. (1991) *Methodological Foundations of Macroeconomics: Keynes and Lucas* (Cambridge: Cambridge University Press).

—— and Dimitri, N. (eds.) (1992) *Macroeconomics: A Survey of Research Strategies* (Oxford: Oxford University Press).

3 Whither IS–LM

CHRISTOPHER A. SIMS

1. Introduction

Keynes considered expectations a central factor in macroeconomic dynamics. Much of his discussion of them treats them as volatile but exogenous ('animal spirits'), but in places he elaborates on the importance of particular types of endogenous expectations. Since the equations he wrote down did not include an explicit role for expectations, the IS–LM codification of Keynesian orthodoxy could plausibly ignore them, and did so. This not only distorted Keynes's thinking, it ironically weakened Keynesian orthodoxy in the face of the rational expectations critique. The standard Keynesian position came to be that expectations, or at least endogenous expectations, were not as important as the RE critics made them out to be. This was a substantively weak position in itself, and it had the further weakening effect of keeping Keynesian attention away from developing a strong response to Keynes's new classical critics.

The fact is that it is possible to develop general equilibrium models with endogenous expectations and price and wage stickiness that are completely in line with the way Keynes thought about the economy. Such models deliver the Keynesian conclusion that monetary and (under some conditions) fiscal policy have powerful real effects and that there is no automatic tendency of the economy towards optimal behaviour in the absence of good monetary and fiscal policy. The models are not subject to some of the standard criticisms of Keynesian models as incomplete or internally inconsistent. But we do not arrive at these models by modifying or modernizing IS–LM. They represent a different approach to modelling entirely.

IS–LM continues to be used, especially in undergraduate teaching, because sophomores and juniors—and their professors—can understand it and because it claims to give answers to interesting and important questions. But an appealing, teachable, falsehood is still a falsehood. Finding equally teachable simplifications that are not so distorted is not easy, but we need to proceed in that direction.

2. Critique of IS–LM and AS–AD

The most common intermediate textbook approach to Keynesian modelling has an investment function that depends on an interest rate and output, but not explicitly on expected future values of anything. It is part of an IS sector derived entirely in real terms. This means the IS curve relates the *real* rate of interest to output, while of course in the standard derivation the LM curve relates the *nominal* rate to output. The combined IS and LM curves imply a single number—output or labour—as a solution, reflecting what is known as aggregate demand. Aggregate demand then feeds into the Phillips curve, which generates wage and/or price dynamics, without any explicit feedback into the IS–LM part of the model. The rational expectations critique of Keynesian modelling is often taken to be focused on the Phillips curve, and sophisticated textbook modelling often explicitly allows for rational expectations, or at least long-run rational expectations, in the Phillips curve. It is much less common for textbook modelling to allow for an explicit real–nominal interest rate distinction,[1] and still less so for there to be explicit treatment of the role of expectations in forming the real rate.

The set of modelling choices that lead to this standard set-up seems hard to justify. If money illusion, lack of foresight, and decision-making inertia are important in macroeconomic dynamics, it seems more likely that they are important in labour markets than in the majority (value-weighted) of investment and savings decisions. One would think therefore that the first place to examine the implications of forward-looking behaviour would be in savings and investment decisions, and that 'irrational' inertial elements in labour-market behaviour might be well worth retaining.

These modelling choices are nonetheless understandable. It is essential to Keynesian reasoning about the business cycle that adjustment of the capital stock is costly, so that a rise in the marginal product of capital can lead to a sustained rise in investment. This implies that the expected growth rate of the relative price of capital goods is an essential determinant of investment. There will be no way to write down the real rate of interest as a function of K, L, and I based on production technology and firm optimization alone. When this fact is augmented by the need to distinguish real from nominal rates, we are confronted with an essentially multivariate rational expectations system. Even today graduate students in economics are often not taught how to handle such systems as part of their core training in macroeconomic theory. The prospect of explaining such systems to undergraduates with only a shaky grasp of calculus is daunting.

Besides the fact that the IS–LM framework mishandles expectations, there is reason to regret the mental habit of breaking models into IS, LM, and AS sectors. Both for econometric and analytic purposes, the reason for breaking a model into 'structural' blocks is that it is useful to consider perturbations in one block while the other blocks hold constant.[2] This may be because we think historical stochastic disturbances in the separate blocks are more or less unrelated, because we contemplate taking policy measures that affect one block but not others, or some mixture of these reasons. In academic exercises we do move around the IS, LM, and AS curves independently. But what is the basis for thinking such exercises useful?

These blocks do not correspond to the behaviour of distinct groups of economic agents. In discussing IS, Keynesian modellers do distinguish the behaviour of firms, who control production technology, from that of workers, who control labour supply and consumption, and this distinction is clearly justifiable. But the arbitrage condition

---

[1] Dornbusch and Fischer (1978) include an appendix discussing a version of IS–LM that distinguishes real and nominal rates, but the resulting model, as it does not include other forward-looking aspects of investment and consumption, is ill-behaved.

[2] This is an old point, made precisely by Hurwicz (1962), for example.

relating bond interest rates to money holdings that goes into the LM curve is generated by the behaviour of some mixture of firms and workers. What reason is there to think that the disturbances to this block will be distinguishable from those to the IS block? The same goes for AS. Despite their names, the Keynesian AS–AD distinction carries nothing like the microeconomic SS–DD distinction between technological and taste influences on equilibrium. Keynesian 'AS' describes price and wage-setting behaviour, and this behaviour involves the same workers and firms that are making investment and consumption decisions and monitoring their real balances.

It is standard to assume that the block distinctions do correspond to components of the economy that can be separately disturbed by monetary and fiscal policy actions. Only the IS block contains G and T variables that are thought of as controlled by a fiscal authority, while only the LM block contains M, controlled by a monetary authority. Monetary policy intervention is modelled as a shift in LM, fiscal policy intervention as a shift in IS. A Keynesian model that takes endogenous expectation formation seriously will still contain a block that, in terms of raw variable counts and which variables appear where, will look in these respects like IS–LM. Indeed some writers take modern models with forward-looking components and label the components with IS–LM terminology. But in models with careful dynamics, these equations are differential or difference equations with forward-looking terms. They cannot be used to produce relationships among current levels of variables that correspond to IS and LM. Furthermore, the absence of M from the IS block depends on ignoring the existence of the government budget constraint as a separate relationship connecting monetary and fiscal variables.

Ideally at this point the paper would go into a discussion of how to get the ideas of Keynesian economics across to a non-technical audience. There are existing approaches to this, and I have some ideas of my own, but it is far from a solved problem.

Instead we proceed directly to laying out a complete Keynesian model with endogenous expectations, observing in what respects it emerges as familiar and unfamiliar.

3. A coherent Keynesian model

The actors in this model are a representative consumer–worker–investor, a representative firm, and a government that sets fiscal and monetary policy. The worker saves in the form of bonds and money and receives dividends as equity-holder in the firm. The firm hires workers and invests to maintain or increase its capital stock. It borrows and lends in the same bond market that workers participate in. Investment and consumption goods are not perfect substitutes, so the capital stock does not adjust instantly in response to shifts in the marginal product of capital.

Both firms and workers are dynamic optimizers. The distinction between the Keynesian model as presented here and a classical version of the same model is that both workers and firms consider employment L not to be under their direct control, so that firm and worker first-order conditions (FOCs) with respect to L do not take their places among the model's behavioural equations. Instead there is a Phillips curve and a mark-up equation. The former makes nominal wages rise when workers feel over-worked—measured by when the marginal utility of leisure exceeds the real wage. The latter makes prices rise when firms feel that revenues are not covering costs—measured by when the marginal product of labour falls below the real wage.

A model like this does not have an elaborate story, based on forward-looking optimizing behaviour, for its price and wage dynamics. New Keynesian-style models do provide such stories. The stories are arguably in disagreement with microeconomic evidence, however. Actual industries have highly skewed distributions of firm sizes, and regular turnover of firms, with entry and exit decisions a key component of competition. None of these elements is present in the microeconomics underlying New Keynesian macroeconomics. Our objective here is to show that the somewhat old-fashioned and somewhat more transparent 'disequilibrium' style of modelling can incorporate dynamically optimizing agents and in the end give results for macro-economic behaviour similar to those from New Keynesian models. Both types of model imply strong, quick responses of real variables to nominal disturbances—in particular to monetary policy. In fact, the empirical weakness of these models is that they imply stronger real effects of monetary policy than clearly emerge in the data.

The model of this section includes money illusion in the Phillips curve. There is no a priori argument that this must be irrational, however, so long as fluctuations in prices are stationary, as is assumed here. The assumption of a real cost to nominal changes in prices, as in New Keynesian models, is a similarly arbitrary introduction of non-neutrality, with no greater a priori justification. Both kinds of assumption would need to be reconsidered if the models containing them were being used to project the effects of large and permanent changes in the inflation rate. It is useful to recognize where we are introducing non-neutrality into a model and to bear in mind the limitations of non-neutrality assumptions. But it was one of Keynes's central insights that in this respect a little ad hockery is not too high a price to pay for maintaining a model's grip on reality.

3.1. Consumer

Optimization problem:

$$\max_{C,L,V,M,B_C} \int_0^\infty e^{-\beta t} \frac{C_t^{\mu_0}(1-L_t)^{\mu_1}}{\mu_0 + \mu_1} \, dt \tag{1}$$

subject to

$$\lambda: \quad PC^* + \dot{B}_C + \dot{M} + \tau \leq WL + \pi + rB_C, \tag{2}$$

$$\psi_C: \quad C^* \geq C \cdot (1 + \gamma V), \tag{3}$$

$$\psi_V: \quad V \geq \frac{PC^*}{M}. \tag{4}$$

Note that the demand for money arises out of the γV term in (2). This term implies that the budgetary cost of the consumption C that enters utility is blown up by a transactions cost factor $(1 + \gamma V)$ before it enters the budget constraint (as C^*). Larger real balances therefore make possible increased consumption.

FOCs:

$$\partial C: \quad \frac{\mu_0 U}{C} = (1 + \gamma V)\,\psi_C, \tag{5}$$

where U is instantaneous utility, the undiscounted integrand in (1).

$$\partial L: \quad \frac{\mu_1 U}{1 - L} = W\lambda. \tag{6}$$

(Equation above not used directly.)

$$\partial C^*: \quad P\lambda + \frac{P\psi_V}{M} = \psi_C, \tag{7}$$

$$\partial B_C: \quad -\dot{\lambda} + \beta\lambda = r\lambda, \tag{8}$$

$$\partial M: \quad -\dot{\lambda} + \beta\lambda = \psi_V \frac{PC^*}{M^2}, \tag{9}$$

$$\partial V: \quad \gamma C\psi_C = \psi_V. \tag{10}$$

3.2. Firm

Optimization problem:

$$\max_{\pi, I, K, L, C^*, B_F} \int_0^\infty e^{-\beta t} \phi(\pi_t)\, dt \tag{11}$$

subject to

$$\zeta: \qquad\qquad \pi \le PC^* - WL + \dot{B}_F - rB_F, \tag{12}$$

$$\omega: \quad C^* + \left(1 + \xi\frac{I}{K}\right)I \le AK^\alpha L^{1-\alpha}, \tag{13}$$

$$\sigma_K: \qquad\qquad \dot{K} \le I - \delta K; \tag{14}$$

FOCs:

$$\partial I: \qquad\qquad \sigma_K = \left(1 + 2\xi\frac{I}{K}\right)\omega, \tag{15}$$

$$\partial K: \quad -\dot{\sigma}_K + (\beta+)\sigma_K = \omega \cdot \left(\alpha \cdot A \cdot \left(\frac{K}{L}\right)^{\alpha-1} + \xi\frac{I^2}{K^2}\right), \tag{16}$$

$$\partial L: \qquad\qquad \zeta W = \omega \cdot (1 - \alpha) \cdot A \cdot \left(\frac{K}{L}\right)^\alpha. \tag{17}$$

(Equation above not used directly.)

$$\partial B_F: \quad -\frac{\dot\zeta}{\zeta} = r - \beta,$$

(18)

$$\partial C^*: \quad P\zeta = \omega.$$

(19)

3.3. Price and wage adjustment

Phillips curve: $$\frac{\dot W}{W} = \eta_L \frac{\mu_1 U}{(1-L)W\lambda},$$

(20)

Mark-up equation: $$\frac{\dot P}{P} = -\eta_C \log\left(\frac{A(K/L)^\alpha \omega}{W\zeta}\right).$$

(21)

These equations can only be interpreted as temporary local approximations. Certainly the expected 'normal' rate of inflation will change over time if the economy's actual inflation level drifts. This normal level of inflation will tend to become the reference point for price adjustment, shutting off, or at least greatly attenuating, long-run effects of changes in the inflation rate on real equilibrium. However, as we have already noted, this caveat applies equally to other, 'microfounded' models of wage and price adjustment. Theories that postulate a cost of adjustment for prices, or that postulate an exogenously determined contract length or mean time between opportunities to adjust price, will not be quantitatively stable if the inflation rate drifts. It is a fact that contract lengths change when the inflation environment changes. Whatever the costs of price adjustment are, institutions will adapt to change those costs if the inflation rate drifts. The question of which type of potentially unstable description of price adjustment is best is empirical, and as yet has no clear answer.

3.4. Government

Constraint:

$$\frac{\dot B_C - \dot B_F + \dot M}{P} + \tau = r\frac{B_C - B_F}{P}.$$

(22)

Behaviour: Monetary and fiscal policy equations must be specified jointly in a model like this, as was explained in Leeper (1991). Monetary policy can be given the form

$$\dot r = -\theta_1 r + \theta_2 \log M + \varepsilon_M$$

(23)

and fiscal policy the form

$$\tau = -\phi_0 + \phi_1 \frac{B}{P} + \varepsilon_F.$$

(24)

This model behaves as Leeper would suggest: existence and uniqueness of equilibrium requires a combination of active fiscal with passive monetary policy, or vice versa. Active monetary policy combined with active fiscal policy leads to non-existence, while passive monetary policy combined with passive fiscal policy leads to non-uniqueness. In Leeper's definition, 'active' monetary policy increases interest rates with the price level, or else increases them more than one-for-one with the inflation rate. Active fiscal policy commits to a level or path of τ, the real primary surplus, that does not respond strongly to B/P—in particular with a coefficient less than the steady-state real rate (β in this model). Passive monetary policy pegs r or otherwise makes it respond to inflation by too little to make inflation increases raise the real rate of interest. Passive fiscal policy[3] commits to increasing τ with B/P by enough so that the increased interest expense in the budget is more than offset.

3.5. Can this model be IS–LM'd?

Because it has firms that make an investment decision, consumers who make savings and money-holding decisions, and a government that controls interest rates and deficits, this model has at least the sectoral structure of an IS–LM model. And indeed we can derive analogues of the elements of the IS–LM model.

There is a standard liquidity preference, or money-demand, relation in this model, which emerges if we equate the right-hand sides of (8) and (9), then use (7) and (10) to eliminate the Lagrange multipliers. The result is

$$r = \gamma V^2. \tag{25}$$

From (5), (7), and (10) we can get an expression for λP as

$$\lambda P = \frac{D_C U}{(1 + \gamma V)^2}. \tag{26}$$

In a model where for simplicity the dependence of transactions demand on C (or on any other measure of aggregate activity) were suppressed, the right-hand side of (26) would be just the marginal utility of consumption.

Substituting (26) into (8) gives us the usual forward-looking consumption Euler equation:

$$\frac{-(d/dt)D_C U}{D_C U} = r - \beta - \frac{\dot{P}}{P} - \frac{2\gamma \dot{V}}{1 + \gamma V}. \tag{27}$$

---

[3] Woodford calls such fiscal policies 'Ricardian', though the Ricardian equivalence proposition does not rest on policy taking this form.

The only non-standard (for rational expectations models) element of this equation is the term in V on the right-hand side. This term is important, though, as it implies (after substituting for V using the money-demand equation) that there is strong dependence of the rate of growth of $D_C U$ on $\dot{r}$ as well as on r itself.

To derive an investment function, we introduce

$$P_K = 1 + 2\xi \frac{I}{K}, \tag{28}$$

the price of capital goods in terms of consumption goods (if they were traded). Then from (15), (16), (18), and (19) we can derive

$$\frac{\alpha A (K/L)^{\alpha-1} + \xi(I^2/K^2)}{P_K} = r - \beta - \frac{\dot{P}}{P} - \frac{\dot{P}_K}{P_K}. \tag{29}$$

This equation matches the real interest rate in terms of capital goods prices to the marginal product of savings (i.e. of capital measured in consumption goods units).

We have arrived at a pair of equations that characterizes household savings behaviour ((27) and (2)), an investment equation, and a money-demand equation. Is it useful to think of this as a version of IS–LM? There is no harm in observing that there are parallels between this system and IS–LM, but the difference between this system and the usual aggregate supply vs. aggregate demand (AS–AD) reasoning that emerges from traditional IS–LM is great—so great, I would argue, that to label this system 'modern IS–LM', or the like, is a barrier to understanding. Perhaps equally important, calling a system like this IS–LM legitimizes the version of IS–LM taught in undergraduate textbooks, as if it were a simplified distillation of this kind of model, which it is not.

There are two crucial characteristics of this system that make an AS–AD interpretation of it untenable. The inflation rate as well as the interest rate (or equivalently, real and nominal rates separately) enter the 'aggregate demand' portion of the model; and investment depends on the expected rate of growth of real capital goods prices. The wage and price dynamics equations do provide growth rates for W and P as functions of real variables and the price and wage levels, but even holding P and W levels fixed, there is no possibility of solving the 'IS–LM' sectors of the model for C and L, treating these as determined by 'demand', and then reading off $\dot{W}$ and $\dot{P}$ recursively from 'aggregate supply' in the form of the Phillips curve and mark-up equations, (20) and (21). The system is fundamentally simultaneous, and fundamentally forward-looking. The price level is predetermined, but the inflation rate is not and appears in both 'aggregate demand' and 'aggregate supply' portions of the model. As current levels of C and L change, expectations about their future paths necessarily change also, which will affect $\dot{P}_K/P_K$. Thus we cannot even derive aggregate demand as a schedule connecting C and L to the inflation rate. The effects of given changes in the current values of the interest rate or the government's primary surplus can be drastically different according to how persistent they are expected to be.

3.6. Responses to policy

With a 'standard' active-money, passive-fiscal policy combination, the response of the economy to a monetary policy expansion takes the form shown in Figures 3.1 and 3.2.[4] The policy parameters underlying these responses are $\theta_1 = 0.2$, $\theta_2 = 0.01$, $\phi_0 = 0.4$, $\phi_1 = 0.06$. An interest rate reduction, initially of about 1 percentage point, produces an instant 18 per cent rise in M, humpshaped responses of wages and prices peaking at about 6 and 2 per cent, respectively, and immediate expansion in employment, consumption, and investment. The initial expansion in L is 16 per cent, roughly the same as that in M. With this policy configuration, the model is Ricardian, so that disturbances to the fiscal policy equation affect nothing except the time paths of τ and B/P.

The model also has a well-behaved equilibrium when monetary policy is passive and fiscal policy is active. For this case we set $\theta_2 = 0$, $\phi_0 = -0.4$, and $\phi_1 = 0$, with all

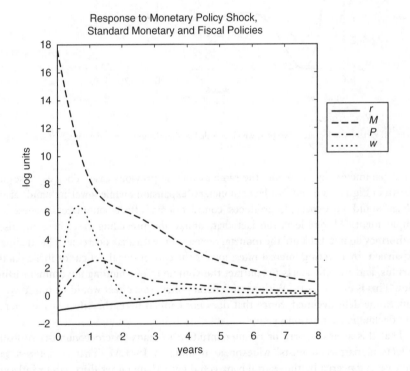

FIG. 3.1. *Nominal variables*

Note: All variables in log units except r, which is in natural units (not per cent)

---

[4] All the responses shown are based on linearization of the model about its steady-state. The calculations were carried out with the matlab program gensysct.m, available through the author's web page at www.princeton.edu/~csims. The complete set of parameter values used to generate the responses are shown in the appendix.

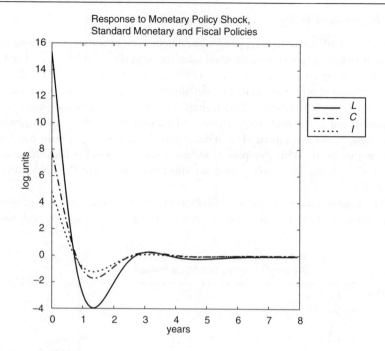

FIG. 3.2. *Real variables*

Note: All variables in log units except *I*, which is scaled so that the units are a percentage of steady-state *C*

other parameters in the model the same as for the previous case. The responses are shown in Figures 3.3 and 3.4. Here monetary 'expansion', while lowering *r* and raising *M* as would be expected, produces contractionary effects on prices, wages, and employment. This reflects the fact that, unlike the preceding case, here the fiscal authorities do not 'back up' the monetary expansion with a tax decrease. The monetary expansion, by lowering interest rates, lowers the conventional deficit, or increases the surplus, and thereby starts to contract the volume of outstanding government liabilities. This is deflationary. With passive fiscal policy, this effect would be offset by tax cuts as the debt declined. Since that does not happen here, the effect of the interest rate decline is contractionary.

That this seems bizarre or counter-intuitive to many macroeconomists probably reflects in part economists' widespread training in IS–LM. That an interest rate increase engineered by the central bank could exacerbate rather than reduce inflation, is commonly recognized in current policy discussions, even though it is not mentioned in most (any?) intermediate macroeconomics textbooks. It is particularly likely to occur in economies where the political ability to adjust taxes to public obligations is weak, as in many poorer countries.

With this combination of policy reaction functions, a positive disturbance to the fiscal policy equation has a contractionary effect. The responses are displayed in

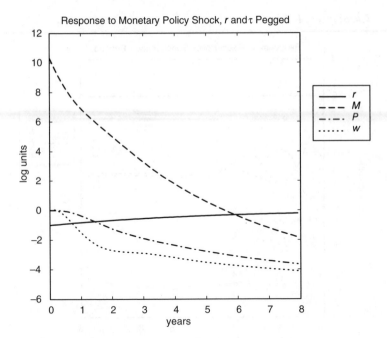

FIG. 3.3. *Nominal variables*

Note: All variables in log units except r, which is in natural units (not per cent)

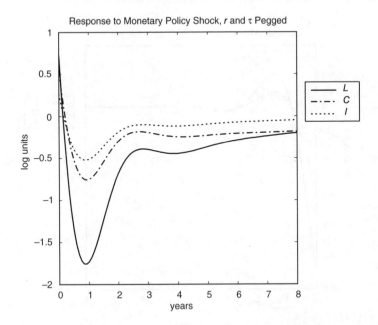

FIG. 3.4. *Nominal variables*

Note: All variables in log units except I, which is scaled so that the units are a percentage of steady-state C

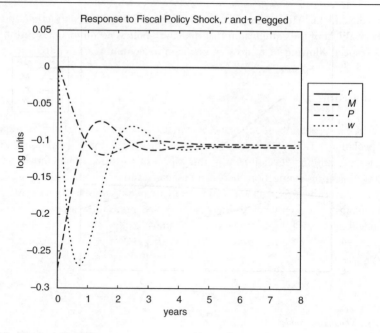

FIG. 3.5. *Nominal variables*

Note: All variables in log units except *r*, which is in natural units (not per cent)

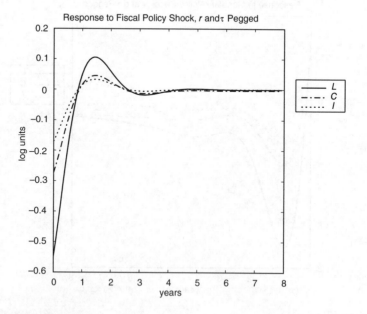

FIG. 3.6. *Nominal variables*

Note: All variables in log units except *I*, which is scaled so that the units are a percentage of steady-state *C*

Figures 3.5 and 3.6. Money does decline in reaction to the fiscal contraction, and it is a necessary aspect of the equilibrium that monetary policy 'accommodates' fiscal policy in this respect, allowing M to drop to maintain its commitment to a fixed r.

4. Conclusion

- Keynesian reasoning ought to be essentially forward-looking and to emphasize expectational factors in savings and investment decisions. Traditional IS–LM hides and inhibits development of this aspect of Keynesian modelling.
- IS–LM ignores connections between monetary and fiscal policy that are enforced by the government budget constraint. In many policy contexts, this is a major gap.
- It remains to be seen whether there is a way to capture these aspects of Keynesian modelling in a package as neat and non-technical as IS–LM, but that should not be an excuse for continuing to make IS–LM the core of our teaching and informal policy discussion.

APPENDIX: PARAMETER SETTINGS

α:	0.3
β:	0.05
γ:	0.01
δ:	0.07
A:	12.211
ξ:	1.0
μ_0:	-0.9
μ_1:	-0.3
θ_1:	0.2
θ_2:	0.01/0.0
η_C:	0.5
η_L:	0.5
ϕ_0:	0.4/-0.4
ϕ_1:	0.06/0.0

REFERENCES

Dornbusch, R. and S. Fischer (1978) *Macroeconomics* (New York: McGraw-Hill).
Hurwicz, L. (1962) 'On the structural form of interdependent systems', in *Logic, Methodology and Philosophy of Science* (Stanford, Calif.: Stanford University Press): 232–9.
Leeper, E. M. (1991) 'Equilibria under active and passive monetary and fiscal policies', *Journal of Monetary Economics* 27: 129–47.

4A   IS–LM, Keynesianism, and the new classicism

RICHARD G. LIPSEY

Rather than give detailed critiques of the other papers in this session, I will give my own account of 'what happened to IS–LM?' My criticisms of the other accounts presented at this conference are implicit in some contrasts between my paper and the others. Because the conference has a methodological focus, and because the current session is billed as retrospective, I will try to keep to both of these themes, while giving my interpretation of the historical events as seen by someone who lived through them and who, in some small way, contributed to them.

1. Methodological preliminaries

Theory focuses the mind on certain issues. Prevailing research programmes (in the Lakatosian sense) present a whole programme for research built around a set of maintained assumptions.[1] They tell us what to look for, and those who suggest looking for something else are usually ignored. Basic research programmes are thus simultaneously both powerful and constraining.

Maximization over infinite time-horizons by agents operating in perfectly competitive markets and guided by rational expectations is a major part of the core of the current 'new classical' research programme. In some ways it has been a fruitful programme but, like all programmes, it can become a dogma in the hands of its more extreme practitioners, cutting off potentially fruitful lines of investigation. Later in my remarks, I will say more about these dangers.

My concern is with changes in research programmes. To deal with them, I need to establish a number of points. First, Lakatos (1978) distinguished the untestable 'core' of any programme from its protective belt. The core is a set of maintained assumptions that are typically too general to be directly testable. An example is the maximization hypothesis of neoclassical theory. Less general assumptions allow the core to yield more specific predictions that are part of the programme's 'protective belt' and that are

I am indebted for comments and suggestions to Roger Backhouse, Ken Carlaw, Peter Howitt, Robert Leeson, and Mark Blaug.

[1] I use the Lakatosian concepts of a research 'programme' with a non-testable core and a 'protective belt' of lower-level models with testable predictions. But nothing that I say really depends on this. The whole argument could be recast in the terms used by Thomas Kuhn (1970) without altering its substance. I hasten to add that I agree with Freeman Dyson (1999) that the kind of paradigm shift that Kuhn talks about in general, and I discuss here with respect to Keynesian and new classicists, is only one type of scientific revolution—a concept-driven one. Other revolutions are driven by more seemingly mundane developments, such as new and better ways of observing and measuring things.

testable. An example is that maximizing consumers will buy more of a product when its price falls.

Second, all progressive programmes must live with unexplained anomalies and some refutations of theories that are part of their protective belts. The anomalies present research opportunities. Explaining them in ways that make new predictions that pass test enriches an evolving research programme. In contrast, a degenerate programme explains each new anomaly in an *ad hoc* fashion that merely saves the programme without yielding any new testable predictions. Continued pursuit of this latter strategy makes the programme consistent with any imaginable facts and hence empty of empirical content.

Third, if unresolved anomalies accumulate over the years, a time eventually comes when practitioners begin to consider abandoning the prevailing programme. Supporters and attackers then do battle. Not every attack is successful. The prevailing programme usually repulses attacks from several competing theories before it finally succumbs to a successful assault.

Fourth, when it finally does come, the replacement of the old programme by a new competing programme is not the result of a single crucial test. Instead, in response to the accumulation of anomalies, a broad consensus slowly develops that some competing programme deals with these anomalies better than does the established one. Since judgement is involved, the timing of the replacement is partly a matter of psychology.

Fifth, the outcome looks inevitable after the event. Those who supported the old, now-displaced programme seem, in retrospect, to have been fighting a rearguard action against the advancement of knowledge. But this is not so, since unsuccessful attacks on any prevailing programme are much more common than are successful ones. Only after each particular battle has been fought, does it become clear whether the prevailing programme will continue or will be replaced.

Sixth, when a new research programme arises, its originators do not consciously construct its core and then move on to more specific assumptions that provide the protective belt. These are *ex-post* constructs. They are useful because they provide a method of analysing the implications of the fact that some assumptions are more fundamental than others; some can be shed without affecting the basic thrust of some general theory, while the abandonment of others threatens the very basis of that theory. Thus, it is not surprising to find that different observers sometimes disagree as to the specific nature of some programme's core and its protective belt.

2. The Keynesian research programme

2.1. The Keynesian core

In the Keynesian case, I would venture that the core of the new research programme that came into the world in the late 1930s and early 1940s, as propounded by Keynes's followers, although not necessarily by Keynes himself, was the hypothesis of non-market clearing with disequilibrium adjustments taking place in real time.[2] Wages did not adjust quickly to clear labour markets, particularly in the face of excess supply, and the velocity of circulation of money was a function of the interest rate. As a result, quantities rather than prices did much of the adjusting to short term shocks in the labour market—even if the money supply were held constant. The fiction of the Walrasian auctioneer, who prevented transactions from occurring out of equilibrium, was dropped and adjustments were assumed to take place in real time as quantities moved towards equilibrium, often over long periods. Although Keynes himself tried to embed his theory in a world of perfectly competitive goods markets, followers quickly extended the hypothesis of price stickiness to oligopolistic goods markets. Swedish and Robertsonian process analyses were typical protective belt constructs in this core tradition.[3]

Keynesians were never quite sure if their core included maximizing behaviour or rejected it in favour of the hypothesis of conventional behaviour. Price stickiness of firms was formalized in the full-cost-pricing hypothesis (Hall and Hitch 1939)[4] which could be regarded either as conventional, non-maximizing behaviour, or as maximization in the face of costly price adjustments. Similarly, resistance to downward adjustment of wages could be rationalized as irrational money illusion or as a rational response to the uncertainties of dynamic adjustments.[5] As time passed, the emphasis slowly shifted from irrational to rational price stickiness.

2.2. The place of IS–LM

Where does IS–LM fit in to this scheme? Is it an expression of the core assumptions or is it part of the protective belt? With regard to the LM curve, a basic Keynesian innovation was to place the interest rate in the demand for money function—as a result of the liquidity preference motive—giving rise to a downward-sloping LM curve. This allowed the velocity of circulation to vary and hence broke the quantity theory of money's tight relation between the money supply and nominal national income. In its extreme form of the liquidity trap (never part of the Keynesian core), the LM curve produced another sticky price, this time the interest rate. What lay behind the IS curve was a model of the goods market in which prices were sticky and output adjusted to equate desired expenditure to actual output. With suitable lags, the IS and

---

[2] This is more or less the Patinkin–Leijonhufvud interpretation. Many post-Keynesians argue that it does not apply to Keynes himself. Perhaps they should paraphrase Bernard Shaw's comment that there was only one true Christian—and he died on the cross.

[3] In the *Journal of Political Economy*'s symposium on Friedman's theoretical framework, Paul Davidson defined the Keynesian core (although he did not, of course, use this term) as including: '(1) the concept of uncertainty in the Knight–Keynes sense, (2) the inapplicability of a Walrasian system to a real world production economy where false trades occur, and (3) the essential properties of money which follow from the existence of uncertainty,' (1972: 864).

[4] The early debate over full-cost-pricing is well summarized in Gordon (1948).

[5] Okun (1981) gives a clear statement of what had been in the oral tradition much earlier. Also in Lipsey (1981) I expressed rational versions of wage and price stickiness that I had used in my lectures at least since the early 1970s.

LM curves could trace out a dynamic multiplier process in which income and the interest rate moved towards their equilibrium values over real time.

To construct these curves, one has to add to the core assumptions a number of subsidiary ones concerning the determinants of such variables as consumption, investment, the interest rate, and the money supply, any one of which could be modified without abandoning the hard core of the programme. Furthermore, the existence of these curves and their assumed shapes of an inelastic IS curve and an elastic LM curve were in principle testable. Indeed, over time, empirical evidence forced both monetarist and Keynesians to alter their assumptions about the shapes of these curves. This strongly suggests that the IS–LM model is best seen as part of the protective belt.

2.3. The nature of the IS–LM model

The IS–LM model is the generic form of all income flow models, many of which are still used in macroeconomic modelling. Its basic characteristics are the following.

First, expenditure categories are divided between those that are endogenous, consumption, investment, and imports, and those that are exogenous, government expenditure and exports. Second, the equilibrium condition is that desired expenditure on national output should equal actual output.[6] Third, there is no explicit price adjustment mechanism that operates when equilibrium occurs at less than 'full employment'. Fourth, the demand for money depends on both national income and the interest rate while the money supply is exogenous.

The IS–LM model omitted many of the more subtle parts of Keynes's own vision; in particular it lacked explicit expectations. When I was a student in the early 1950s, we heard very little about expectations, except to learn that animal spirits caused the investment function to be quite unstable. Occasional instability might be thought of as a cause of occasional exogenous disturbances to an otherwise stable equilibrium. But the more or less continuous major instabilities envisaged by some Cambridge followers of Keynes could make the IS–LM equilibrium analysis misleading—and indeed, many of them rejected the model as not adequately capturing the Keynes of the *General Theory*. To most Keynesians, this was regarded as a remote possibility and hence a tolerated anomaly. We went on using that model, while carrying the verbal qualification that animal spirits might make the whole system unstable, or at least subject to large and unpredictable shocks. When we came to study inflation, we understood that expectations did matter. The usual assumptions were extrapolative or adaptive expectations, both of which were 'backward-looking' in the sense that expectations of inflation were some function of past experience, rather than the expected future consequences of current events.

---

[6] This equilibrium condition was the source of endless confusion through the whole period 1935–80. Many assumed it to be an identity even though nothing empirical can be deduced from a definitional identity. The correct statement that the equilibrium condition was $E = Y$ not $E \equiv Y$ is not usually found in macro textbooks until sometime around the late 1970s. For a full discussion see Lipsey (1972) especially the appendix entitled 'A short history of the muddle' reprinted in Lipsey (1997, vol. 2).

2.4. The evolution of closure

The IS–LM model determined real income for any given price level. The problem of simultaneously determining income and the price level was referred to as the problem of 'closure'. Over the years, several versions of closure succeeded one another.

The first closure, the one that I was taught at the LSE in 1953–5, used the kinked, ratcheting AS curve. Below full-employment income, the price level was fixed so that fluctuations in desired expenditure caused fluctuations in income and employment. If desired expenditure exceeded full-employment income, prices would rise. The operation of the monetary adjustment mechanism would then shift the LM curve to the left, raising the interest rate and lowering desired real expenditure until it equalled full-employment output. Since the price level was rigid downwards, a further reduction in desired expenditure would lower income and employment at the new higher price level. This was the upward ratcheting, kinked, aggregate supply curve where the kink occurred at full-employment income and the perfectly elastic part was always at the current price level.

Beginning in the late 1950s, a simple form of the Phillips curve slowly became the preferred method of closure, replacing the kinked aggregate supply curve, at least in the UK. To close the model, one needed to transform the Phillips curve from 'wage-adjustment–unemployment' space in which it became famous to the 'income–price-adjustment' space, which is where Phillips located it in his early papers.[7] The transformation is trivial under the following circumstances: unemployment is assumed to be a function of national income; the rate of productivity growth is assumed to be exogenous; and money wages change at a rate equal to productivity growth plus a demand component that is a function of the difference between actual and full employment income. This may be why the transformation was so seldom laid out formally. The $\dot{P}$–Y Phillips curve then determined how fast the price level changed and hence how fast the LM curve shifted when the current positions of the IS and LM curves created either an inflationary or deflationary gap.[8] (Dots over variables stand for percentage rates of change.) Thus Sims is incorrect when he says that this curve *did not* feed back to the IS–LM part of the model (see ch. 3).

At the time, many economists misunderstood the place of the Phillips curve in the IS–LM model. Most of these probably only knew the curve from its $\dot{W}$–U version in Phillips's famous 1958 article rather than its $\dot{P}$–Y version which is needed to close the IS–LM model.[9] Phillips used the $\dot{P}$–Y version in his earlier, but less well-known, publications to relate excess demand to price level changes.

---

[7] Phillips used a $\dot{P}$–Y form of his curve in his stabilization models (1954 and 1957). He then used the $\dot{W}$–U form (Phillips 1958) to give empirical verification of a relation he had been assuming as obvious in these earlier models. Once the $\dot{W}$–U form of the curve became famous, it became common for other writers to use Phillip's original $\dot{P}$–Y curve to close Keynesian models rather than the kinked AS curve. See e.g. Dow and Dicks-Mireaux (1959).

[8] This form of the Phillips curve closure of the IS–LM model is laid out, among other places, in Lipsey (1977).

[9] See e.g Meiselman (1968: 745) who argued that the curve was based on a 'labor theory of the value of money—one which contains neither a demand nor a supply of money.' I have dealt with such misunderstandings in Lipsey (1977) and the essence of this argument is reproduced in the text that follows.

At this point I have two small caveats to add to Vercelli otherwise excellent account (in Chapter 2). First, British economists and policy-makers were worried about wage push as early as the 1950s. Indeed early Keynesians such as William Beveridge worried that if Keynesian economics solved the unemployment problem, there would be no labour-market discipline to stop unions imposing substantial wage inflation on the country. Second, the Phillips curve was used to close the IS–LM model well before that model got into empirical difficulties. Phillips used it in 1954 and Dow and Dicks-Mireaux among many others used it in a two-equation empirical model in 1959. Empirical difficulties did not arise until the late 1960s and only became acute in the 1970s after the first OPEC oil shock.

The Phillips curve was immediately embraced, at least at the LSE, as a method of closure superior to the kinked AS curve for several reasons.

- It dispensed with the kinked Aggregate Supply curve's dichotomy between P fixed and Y variable below full employment income and Y fixed and P variable at full employment income. Since the Phillips curve was usually drawn as becoming increasingly steep as unemployment fell towards zero and increasingly flat as it rose above 10 per cent, the kinked AS curve could be thought of as a special case of the curved relation (although one uses P and the other $\dot{P}$ as the dependent variable).
- It linked the model back to the labour market and allowed the *ad hoc* assumption of rigid wages to be dispensed with.
- Of course, evidence mattered and the articles by Phillips (1958) and Lipsey (1960) provided it. But the Phillips curve replaced the kinked AS curve (at least in the UK) because it was on all counts a superior method of closure.

Because it was used in empirical work everywhere and in much UK theorizing, Friedman surprised us at the LSE by stating in 1970 that Keynesians closed the IS–LM model (provided the 'missing equation' as he put it) by assuming that 'the price level is determined outside the system ... [by] an institutional structure that is assumed either to keep prices rigid or to determine changes in prices on the basis of "bargaining power"' (1970: 219–20). This caused many of us in the UK to wonder about the apparent absence of a transatlantic diffusion of knowledge.[10] Throughout the 1970s, I used the Phillips curve closure in my graduate lectures at Queen's University in Canada in the form that it appears in Lipsey (1977). It appeared in an intermediate macroeconomics text book by Wilton and Prescott in 1982 who

---

[10] It should be pointed out, however, that this form of closure spread only slowly, even in UK teaching. I am indebted to Roger Backhouse for pointing out that he was taught the kinked aggregate supply curve along side the Phillips $\dot{W}/U$ curve as late as 1970–1 at the University of Bristol. In his lecture notes (which he has kindly shown me), inflationary gaps appear to cause the price level to rise but cause no transitory increase in income and employment as the economy is temporarily pushed into the inflationary range of the Phillips curve. Indeed it was this slow spread of understanding of the Philips curve closure that led me to feel as late as 1977 that an article was still necessary on this form of closure.

observed: 'It is Lipsey's integration of the Phillips curve into the IS–LM framework that forms the basis of the model developed and used in this textbook' (preface p. xv).[11]

What did not get a lot of notice was the comparative static properties of the IS–LM model closed by the $\dot{P}-Y$ Phillips curve. These restored the orthodox classical properties.[12] To see them, call the level of income where the Phillips curve cuts a horizontal line indicating the exogenous rate of productivity growth, macro-equilibrium.[13] Consider a monetary expansion starting from this macroequilibrium. The LM curve shifts to the right and, according to the Phillips curve, leads to a higher level of national income and a rising price level. As prices rise, the real money supply falls and the LM curve shifts to the left. This continues until the curve has returned to its original position with macroequilibrium re-established at the original level of income. If we start at an IS–LM equilibrium below macroequilibrium, wages rise more slowly than productivity, thus reducing unit costs and the price level. This shifts the LM curve slowly to the right until full employment is obtained. Thus when the Phillips curve is added to the IS–LM model, both the neoclassical unique macro-equilibrium and the neutrality of money are restored. The equilibrium level of income is determined by the real IS–LM relations and the Phillips curve dynamics which ensure that there is only one level of income at which the price level (and hence the LM curve) will be stable.

Referring to this point of macroequilibrium as 'full employment' requires the added assumption that, when full employment occurs, money wages will rise at a rate equal to productivity growth, leaving the price level constant. This was not accepted by many Keynesians, some of whom rejected the whole Phillips curve method of closure.

2.5. Money and monetary policy in the IS–LM model

As observed by Bennett McCallum in this conference, it is odd that the LM part of the model used money as a control variable. Right through the controversies with the monetarists in the 1960s, key English Keynesians and banking specialists were quite clear on how the Bank of England operated its monetary policy. It set the interest rate and let the money supply be endogenously determined. (See e.g. Cramp (1970) and Kaldor (1970).)

Yet in most textbook treatments on both sides of the Atlantic, the money supply was taken as an exogenous constant fixed by the central bank. How did this come about?

---

[11] It is important to note that I am speaking of one strand of Keynesian economists who were modellers and empirical testers. The Cambridge economists who were closest to Keynes, such as Joan Robinson, Richard Kahn, and Nicholas Kaldor all rejected the Phillips curve and kept to a theory that they held was closer to what Keynes himself had intended. But, unlike Friedman, they never specified their complete model. In correspondence with Kaldor, I was never able to get him to commit himself to writing down his model in equations.

[12] Perhaps this explains the enormous hostility that Cambridge Keynesians had towards this curve.

[13] In Phillips's and most other formulations, productivity increases are assumed to be positive and exogenous. Macroeconomic equilibrium then occurs where the rate of increase of money wages equals the rate of increase of productivity, i.e. where the Phillips curve cuts not the wage axis but a horizontal line whose height above the wage axis indicates the exogenous rate of productivity increase.

Keynes (1936) and Hicks (1937) were written shortly after the gold standard had been abandoned but before it was clear whether this was just another in a series of temporary suspensions or a permanent change of regime. At the time, it was probably reasonable to take the money supply as exogenous. However, by the end of World War II and the beginnings of the Bretton Woods system, it was clear that monetary policy had to be directed at maintaining a fixed exchange rate with consequences soon to be formalized in the Mundell–Flemming model of a small open economy. Nonetheless, the closed economy model with an exogenous money supply continued to be taught and used for many analytical purposes.

Later when Friedman embarked on his enormous task of persuading Keynesians that monetary policy mattered, he put his policy advice in its sexiest way: 'control the money supply'. We do not know if Friedman himself saw this as a heuristic device or if he really thought that central banks could and did use the money supply as an instrument. Certainly many in the generation of economists that were raised on IS–LM and the textbook treatments of the money multiplier, assumed that banks directly controlled the money supply. (I know that I did until I really thought out monetarism sometime in the early 1970s.) Of course, central bankers understood their own behaviour and, when they adopted monetarism, they made the money supply a target, never assuming it was an instrument. They continued to set short-term interest rates but now with the object of holding the money supply within some predetermined band.

Friedman gradually persuaded Keynesians that monetary policy mattered. But the unfortunate legacy of this battle was to strengthen the persistent belief among many economists that central banks use M as a control variable—a belief that can be traced at least as far back as the early teaching of the IS–LM model.

When we accept how central banks really behave, the IS–LM model must be altered to a form not found in standard textbooks until recently. The money supply is endogenous as was insisted by Kaldor, and many other critics of monetarism. But the central bank can control the interest rate. This makes the LM curve perfectly elastic at the going rate of interest. The analysis now proceeds as follows.

If the IS curve cuts the horizontal LM curve at full-employment income, macro-economic equilibrium ensues. If it cuts it at an income in excess of full employment, the price level will start to rise (as shown by the expectations-augmented Phillips curve). If the Bank insists on holding to the constant rate of interest, the inflation will accelerate and the endogenously determined money supply will also increase at an accelerating rate. The Bank's correct policy is to raise the interest rate until the horizontal LM curve cuts the IS curve at full-employment income. Finally, if the LM curve cuts the IS curve below the full-employment level of income, the appropriate monetary policy is for the Bank to lower the interest rate until the IS curve cuts the horizontal LM curve at full employment.

The whole of this analysis can be done without the IS–LM apparatus. All we need is the 45° line, 'diagonal cross' diagram with the aggregate expenditure curve drawn for the rate of interest fixed by the Bank. Expenditure equilibrium is where the AE curve cuts the 45° line and the appropriate monetary policy is to lower or raise the interest rate according as equilibrium is below or above full-employment income.

Some have suggested that the sheer simplicity of the model with an exogenous Bank-determined interest rate explains the persistence of the exogenous money supply version.[14] Exogenous money is needed to get the interdependence and simultaneity that is essential to making the model more technically demanding than the simple aggregate expenditure model that students learn (or at least used to learn) in their introductory macrocourse. The presumption seemed to be that being more technically demanding implies being somehow better! No one can be sure that this was the real motivation. It is, however, a possible explanation to be set against mine that Friedman's version of monetarism persuaded a generation of economists that central banks really did directly determine the money supply—at least outside of the relatively small number who understood Bank operating procedures.

In the 1980s, one central bank after another decided to get serious about controlling inflation. In spite of all the controversies about whether or not they could control the money supply, banks found that, if they were determined enough, they could force interest rates high enough to bring any inflation under control (at the cost of a temporary recession). Throughout the world, they did just that. Note that the success of their policy required them to be able to use open market operations to control the rate at which the high-powered money supply was expanding.

Interestingly, although the current directives to many central banks allow the required policy reaction to an inflationary gap, the required reaction to a deflationary gap is not allowed. Told to worry about the price level only, the banks must sit by and wait for some other mechanism to alter the national income when it is below full employment. Given the current reluctance to the use of fiscal policy as an anti-cyclical device, policy is back where it was in pre-Keynesian era with respect to recessions and unemployment. The authorities must wait for the price mechanism to produce a cure independently of any actions taken by policy-makers.

In a sense we now have the *policy equivalent* of the kinked AS curve. Because excess demand produces rising prices, central banks are supposed to deal with it. Because excess supply produces low income and high unemployment, central banks (and the fiscal authorities) are not supposed to deal with it. This may, however, be too stark a contrast for actual policy. By setting a positive floor to the target inflation rate, central banks may be led to adopt an expansive monetary policy, at least in periods of severe recession.

2.6. Accelerating inflation: anomalies arise

We have observed that the static equilibrium properties of the IS–LM model closed by the Phillips curve were quite orthodox. What was not orthodox was the model's non-equilibrium behaviour. Let the central bank expand the money supply sufficiently to shift the IS–LM equilibrium above the full-employment level. The price level begins to rise. But now let the bank further expand the money supply at the same rate as prices are rising. According to the model, the LM curve will not be shifted to the left by the

---

[14] I am indebted to Roger Backhouse for making this suggestion.

inflation; the disequilibrium will persist with lower unemployment bought at the cost of a steady inflation. Thus, although in the IS–LM model closed by a simple Phillips curve makes money neutral in its level, money is not neutral in its rate of change.

The absence of any theory of forward-looking expectations led to the conclusion that the bank could maintain a steady-state of excess demand with employment held above its full-employment level accompanied by a steady rise in prices accommodated by a steady increase in the nominal money supply.

In the 1960s and early 1970s, many governments tried this policy. Eventually—but as usual over a longer time than the critics had expected—the Phillips curve began to shift upwards. Ever-increasing inflation rates required ever faster monetary expansions in order to maintain a particular disequilibrium position on the Phillips curve.

By the beginning of the 1970s, the rate of inflation associated with any given level of unemployment, or output gap, was accelerating. This was a nagging but tolerated anomaly until the first OPEC oil shock in 1973. The ensuing full bout of stagflation baffled most observers. Nothing in conventional wisdom seemed able to explain the combination of rising rates of unemployment and rising rates of inflation. Stagflation was a mystery.

2.7. The expectations-augmented version of closure

Nonetheless, the resilience of the IS–LM model showed itself in that within a very few years stagflation had been incorporated into its framework. Analysis of the OPEC shock persuaded many economists that what was missing from the prevailing model was the supply side. As a result, the demand side was compressed into the aggregate demand curve which showed how the equilibrium national income determined by the IS–LM curve varies with the price level—changes in the price level shift the LM curve but move the economy along a given AD curve. The short-run aggregate supply curve was added, showing how desired output would vary with the price level on the assumption that input prices remained constant. To deal with accelerating inflation, an expectations term was added to the Phillips curve. The simple Phillips curve was seen to apply, as Phillips probably intended, to periods in which a stable price level was expected. It showed the effects of excess demand on wages and prices. To this was added the expectations of price level increases so that what happened to prices and wages was the sum of expected increases and a demand component read off the curve for zero-expected price inflation. This removed the two big anomalies in the existing model.[15]

First, stagflation was explained. OPEC price shocks, as well as effective union pressure, shifted the SRAS curve upwards, pushing the economy to the left along its AD curve. Prices rose while output fell—stagflation. Second, money became neutral not only in its level but in its rates of change (superneutrality). If the central bank tries to hold income above its full-employment level by validating any price rise, the

---

[15] The simplest version of the expectations-augmented Phillips curve is $\dot{W} = F(U) + e(\dot{P})$ where the second independent variable is the expected rate of price inflation.

expectations term in the expectations-augmented Phillips curve kicks in, causing inflation to accelerate. Expectations were still assumed to adjust with a lag so that the policy could be sustained for some time, but only at the cost of an accelerating inflation (accommodated by an accelerating rate of monetary expansion). This reconciliation could be found in a growing number of writings over the late 1970s. It is fully worked out in Otto Eckstein's book *Core Inflation* (1981). It entered elementary first-year textbooks around 1980, some of the earliest being Lipsey and Steiner (1981) and Baumol and Blinder (1979).[16]

3. The monetarist challenge

For three decades, from 1945 to 1975, the Keynesian programme was challenged by a group of monetarists led by Milton Friedman.

3.1. Early Keynesianism

Some early Keynesian models had no place for monetary influences—these models were, however, definitely in the protective belt, not the core. They used extreme forms of the LM and IS curves. The LM curve was perfectly elastic because the demand for money was assumed to be highly sensitive (in the limit, infinitely sensitive) to changes in the interest rate—the liquidity trap. The IS curve was perfectly inelastic because investment was assumed to be insensitive to variations in the interest rate. Not all Keynesians ascribed to this extreme version (see, for example, Tobin 1972). But it was widespread in textbooks and courses. (I was taught it at the LSE in the mid-1950s, but as an extreme case, applicable mainly in severe recessions.)

This early Keynesian model had two key characteristics. First, changes in aggregate desired expenditure caused large changes in income and employment, changes that were not damped by variations in either the interest rate or the price level. Second, changes in monetary aggregates did not affect income because the perfectly elastic LM curve was unaffected by changes in the quantity of money.

The main policy implication of the model was that government fiscal policy is needed to restore full employment whenever the economy shows signs of settling down to a period of substantial unemployment. Weaker versions used assumptions of an interest-elastic demand for money and an interest-inelastic investment function to produce the predictions that fiscal policy was relatively strong while monetary policy was relatively weak.

3.2. Early monetarism

Early monetarists disputed these conclusions. For some time it was thought that Milton Friedman based his dissent on a radically different model. However, when

---

[16] The lags between writing and publishing confirm what I would in any case report, that these two versions were written independently of each other.

challenged to produce his theoretical framework, he used an IS–LM model (Friedman 1970). He asserted that monetarists closed the model with a perfectly inelastic AS curve, reflecting the adjustment powers of flexible wages and prices to eliminate any transitory divergences from full-employment income. He contrasted this with the Keynesian closure which, he asserted, used a perfectly elastic AS curve on the assumption that the price level was set exogenously. As mentioned earlier, this splitting of the kinked AS curve and assigning the vertical half to the monetarists and the horizontal half to the Keynesians surprised those of us in the UK who had long ago abandoned the kinked AS curve in favour of the Phillips curve closure.

The early versions of the extreme monetarist model contained a vertical LM curve because the demand for money depended only on income and not on the interest rate. The consequence of this was 100 per cent crowding-out of any fiscal stimulus. Monetary policy, however, had powerful effects on the economy because shifts in the LM curve interacted with a highly elastic IS curve. Early monetarists also assumed that prices and wages were flexible downwards. This implied that any deviation from full employment would be corrected relatively quickly by adjustments in wages and prices that would shift the LM curve to the right.

3.3. The great debate

A great debate, accompanied by much empirical work, raged between the two camps in the 1950s and 1960s.[17] One by one, however, Keynesians and monetarists abandoned their extreme positions and moved towards common ground until, finally, little but rhetoric divided the two groups. Eventually, both sides agreed on a negatively sloped IS and a positively sloped LM curve, which allowed the economy to respond to both monetary and real expenditure shocks. Keynesians agreed that there was some downward flexibility in wages and prices. They argued, however, that wage reductions were too slow to be an effective mechanism for restoring full employment quickly after a downward shift in aggregate desired expenditure. Monetarists agreed that there was sufficient downward inflexibility of wages and prices to cause serious deviations from full employment when the economy was hit by a severe contractionary shock, either from the monetary or the real expenditure side. Nonetheless, these monetarists opposed fine-tuning, saying that the lags in the economy's responses to monetary shocks were too long and too variable to allow fine-tuning to do more good than harm. (It is worth noting that Phillips (1957) had given a very effective critique of fine-tuning in his second article on stabilization policy.)

---

[17] Patinkin (1956: 237) mounted a theoretical criticism which he argued 'forces upon Keynesian economics the abandonment of the once-revolutionary "diagonal-cross" diagram with which it swept its way into the textbooks.' His work was mainly seen, however, as providing micro-underpinning for such famous quantity theory predictions as the direct proportional relation between changes in the quantity of money and changes in the price level. As Archibald and Lipsey (1958) pointed out, however, the underpinnings of his first edition were deficient because Patinkin only considered one-period equilibria, rather than steady-state equilibria. This deficiency was corrected in his second edition.

Keynesians came to accept this view but continued to hold that the economy occasionally settled into slumps that were prolonged enough for there to be time to diagnose the situation. According to this view, corrective monetary and fiscal policies could then be applied at leisure, without having to worry about the pitfalls of fine-tuning in the face of sharp, transitory fluctuations.

In 1980 the Keynesian, James Tobin, joined the monetarist, David Laidler, in a debate that was subsequently published in the *Economic Journal* (Tobin 1981; Laidler 1981). Neutral observers could find little difference between them. Tobin and Laidler disagreed, as one might expect, on matters of judgement about speeds of reaction and the precise slopes of some curves. They revealed, however, no discernible differences of underlying models or of fundamental assessment of what were the key relations that governed the economy's behaviour.

The long monetarist–Keynesian debate was over. It could be regarded as a case study in positive economics. Although a great deal of heat had been generated over the decades, the end result was much light. Empirical evidence about such things as the income and the interest elasticities of the demand for money, and wage and price flexibility, were amassed. The extreme position of each of the two schools was moderated in the light of the accumulating evidence, until their differences were slight compared with their agreements.

Just as that apparently satisfactory situation was being reached, a new challenge arose in the form of the more basic critique of the Keynesian–monetarist synthesis, made by the new classical economists led by Robert Lucas. The original call to arms had come from Friedman's AEA presidential address (1968) where he argued that the Phillips curve implied money illusion and that the correct form would have real not money wages as the dependent variable. Edmond Phelps (1968) developed the first formal criticism. He criticized the Phillips curve for violating rationality assumptions and argued that only misinformation could lead to deviations from full-employment income. These critiques continued as non-fatal comments until Robert Lucas defined the new programme in full and elegant terms in a way that seemed to build on the assumed Keynesian failure to explain accelerating inflation and stagflation in the 1970s.

4. The new classical critique

The new research programme is often called rational expectations although that was only one of its parts. In contrast to Keynesian theories, the new programme was based on a general equilibrium model of the sort developed in the 1950s by Arrow and Debreu. Markets were perfectly competitive and always in equilibrium so everyone was able to buy or sell what he or she wished at the going set of prices—there were no unsatisfied sellers of either goods or labour services, no involuntary unemployment. Expectations were rational which meant that people held unbiased expectations over all relevant future variables. Given rational expectations, people maximized expected utility over either their expected lifetimes or over an infinite time-horizon (depending on which variant of the new classical model was used). Markets always cleared.

Given correct information, the random errors made by individuals would cancel out in aggregation, so that aggregate errors that could cause a macro-departure from equilibrium could only result from misinformation. In short, deviations from full-employment equilibrium could only be caused by policy-induced surprises.

During the ensuing conflict with the new research programme, the 'IS–LM plus expectations-augmented Phillips curve model' was accused of a number of failures that I consider below. Each alleged failure is stated in the heading and considered in the text that follows.

4.1. No government budget restraint

Carl Christ (1968) had pointed out in the 1960s that the addition of a government budget constraint altered the Keynesian model's long-run behaviour. Blinder and Solow (1974) then worked this out in some detail. Thus the Keynesian model had incorporated this important complication well before the new classical attack. In Chapter 3 of this volume, Sims gets his mileage from a combination of the budget constraint and rational expectations. How far these assumptions can take us in understanding reality is considered below.

4.2. Confusion of real and nominal interest rates

It was certainly well known to Keynesians—and I taught this in the 1970s when I returned to teaching macroeconomics after a sojourn as administrator at the new university of Essex from 1964–70—that the LM curve contained the nominal interest rate while the IS curve contained the real interest rate. Although some careless writers acted as if the rates were the same in both curves, the difference could be accommodated within the model, if not within the usual IS–LM diagram. As long as one was doing comparative statics, there was no problem because the two rates were equal in constant-price equilibrium. Furthermore, when doing steady-state inflation analysis in which the rate of inflation was constant, the divergence could be accommodated by a fixed gap between the real interest rate and the nominal rate.

4.3. The Phillips curve incorrectly used $\dot{W}$ rather than $\dot{W}-P$ as the dependent variable

Shortly after I published my first Phillips curve article (Lipsey 1960), Milton Friedman visited me at the London School of Economics. He argued that I was perpetrating money illusion by putting a nominal wage variable on the vertical axis of my figures rather than using some variant of the rate of change of real wages. My response to him then was the same as my response now. The variable that workers bargain over is the nominal not the real wage (with rare exceptions). If workers care about the real wage, then their expectation of how the nominal and the real wage may differ should enter the wage formation equation as an independent variable. But the dependent variable should be the true behavioural variable, the nominal wage change, $\dot{W}$.

When preparing my 1960 paper, I tried to take account of inflationary expectations, but lacking a good theory of expectations, I used Phillips's own catch-up hypothesis that the current wage bargain would be influenced by the previous increase in the price level.[18] I found no evidence of a statistically significant effect of this sort, and hence abandoned the price level as an explanatory variable, not because Phillips and I thought it intrinsically uninteresting, but because we could not find evidence of its affecting the wage bargain. If we had had it to do again with a more satisfactory expectations hypothesis, we might have found the evidence we looked for and did not find—although in that era of low inflation rates, it is not clear that British unions were as sophisticated as they later became in their ability to distinguish actual nominal from expected real wage rates.

4.4. No endogenous expectations

Of more force was the criticism that the model paid too little attention to expectations in general. The IS curve contained no formal modelling of expectations—all was certainty. Of course the LM curve did contain uncertainty in the explanation of the precautionary and the speculative demands for money.

Early Keynesian-style models of inflation and cycles did have expectations, usually in an extrapolative or adaptive backward-looking form. Later, when the two research programmes were in conflict, the new expectations-augmented Phillips curve did incorporate expectations, and in such a way that there was no long-run trade-off between income and employment on the one hand and inflation on the other. But even when presented with the new theory, Keynesian theorists refused to use full rational expectations. They thought that the implications were empirically wrong.

Keynesians accepted that there were deficiencies in their backward-looking theories of expectations formation which did not allow agents to anticipate the effects of policies that were obvious to most observers. Nonetheless, they argued that the substitution of fully rational expectations was even more unrealistic in assuming a knowledge of the economy that even professional economists did not have (since up to that time they had debated the causes of inflation each time inflation had become a serious problem).

4.5. Disequilibrium behaviour

One of the distinctive parts of Keynesian economics was its assumption that markets could be in disequilibrium in the sense that groups of unsatisfied buyers or unsatisfied sellers could exist over real time. New classical economists are not always clear as to

---

[18] In Lipsey (1960: 8–11) I gave detailed consideration to the possibility that the price level may influence the wage bargain. I considered a number of hypotheses, including Phillips's catch-up hypothesis and the possibility that the wage bargain would be influenced by the current rate of inflation. What I did not do was to estimate and use the *expected* inflation rate. In rereading these pages in order to write this footnote, I was surprised to find how many possibilities I had carefully investigated. Even I have been influenced by the folklore of how naïve we were and had forgotten just how careful we actually were—at least when seen in the light of what was then known!

whether they are stating an empirical prediction or a definitional identity when they assert that markets are always in equilibrium. If it is an empirical statement, it must predict something about the world such as that groups of unsatisfied buyers or unsatisfied sellers will not be found or that, if they are found, their failure to buy or sell will be due to mistaken expectations. In this usage, we can meaningfully define unsatisfied buyers and sellers and disequilibrium and then state as an empirical prediction that they will not be observed. Alternatively, it may be a definitional identity such that disequilibrium cannot exist and hence cannot be observed. This seems to be Vercelli's interpretation when he states that in new classical models 'disequilibrium is *meaningless* and expectations *must be* rational' (Chapter 2, p. 37). The statement that disequilibrium is meaningless seems to mean that it could not be observed. In this case, all situations, no matter how bizarre, are equilibrium situations and the statement is a definitional tautology consistent with all states of the universe. But this renders it uninformative and hence uninteresting.[19] If we are to make empirically interesting statements about disequilibrium and equilibrium, statements that have potential empirical content, we must define these two terms so that both are meaningful and both can be observed—in order to say that in fact we do not observe one of them.

4.6. Inadequate micro-underpinnings

Inadequate micro-underpinning was the most interesting charge and, to deal with it, two questions must be considered. First, what were the Keynesian underpinnings? Second, how do they compare with the new classical underpinnings that replaced them?

The consumption function, both time-series and cross-section, had been studied from the late 1930s in great detail. After the failure to predict the immediate post-World War II boom, the difference between the behaviour studied in, and the predictive power of, cross-section and time-series functions were fully worked out. Then Modigliani in a series of papers starting in 1954 (Modigliani and Brumberg 1954), and Friedman in an influential book (1957), gave life-cycle/permanent income underpinnings to this important function. Investment demand had a micro-underpinning stretching back to Irving Fisher, and earlier. In Keynesian times, it was also researched in great detail by many scholars. Dale Jorgensen's work provided microfoundations for investment behaviour, although not ones that were accepted by all Keynesians because of their underpinnings of perfect competition and continual market equilibrium.

The Keynesian money-demand functions were developed by Baumol (1952), with respect to the dependence of money demand on income, and by Tobin (1956 and 1958), with respect to the dependence of money demand on interest rates. Tobin's elegant derivation of the speculative demand for money (Tobin 1958) gave rise to a whole new discipline—portfolio analysis.

Long before the new classicism challenged the Keynesian programme, a whole generation of general equilibrium theorists lead by Frank Hahn tried to develop a

---

[19] This is strongly reminiscent of the saving–investment controversy where many economists argued that definitional identities could be used to make empirical predictions.

theory of the demand for money within the framework of the Arrow–Debreu GE model. To Keynesians, this seemed to reveal a typical GE theorists' misunderstanding of how their model related to more empirically oriented models. All the elements that Keynes, Tobin, and Baumol pointed to as the basis of the demand to hold money balances were abstracted from in typical GE models.[20]

The goods-market underpinnings were intensively researched by Keynesian economists.[21] Here the most prevalent micro-underpinnings were based on the theory of oligopoly—although some Keynesians still talked in terms of perfectly competitive models. Countless studies by Keynesian (and neoclassical) economists confirmed two main facts. First, short-run cost curves were flat up to capacity output.[22] Second, oligopolistic firms were price-setters responding to short-term fluctuations in demand by varying output, holding their prices constant. So the first signal that firms get of a change in the market demand for their products is a change in their sales at their administered prices. For just one of many examples see Neild (1963). These two propositions were initially put forward on the basis of strong empirical evidence. Subsequently, Okun (1981) and others provided theoretical underpinnings in which menu costs of price changes played an important part.

Labour-market underpinnings were also part of an evolving Keynesian research programme. Early Keynesian economists had argued that it was rational for labourers to resist a reduction in real wages through a fall in money wages while accepting it through a rise in the price level because the latter preserves relative wages during what can be a long transition while the former does not.[23] For this reason, equilibrating mechanisms that relied on reducing money wages might operate very slowly. Early followers sometimes turned this position into the more dubious proposition that the money wages were completely rigid downwards.

The non-linear nature of the Phillips curve provided more acceptable empirical evidence to the effect that, although money wages can rise rapidly under inflationary pressure, they tend to fall only slowly under deflationary pressure. According to the Phillips curve evidence, the price level could be pushed downwards as long as money wages rose less fast than productivity. But because the process was a slow one, the operation of the monetary adjustment mechanism would be long-drawn-out whenever a significant fall in the price level was required to restore equilibrium.

Beginning in the 1970s with implicit contract theory, Keynesian economists, and others, went much deeper into labour-market behaviour. In a research programme that has carried on through the modern new Keynesians, many reasons why wages do

---

[20] Excessive abstraction is a persistent criticism made of neoclassical general equilibrium theory. In the cases of economies of scale and of the demand for money, there is no doubt in my mind that the theory abstracts from all the interesting sources of these phenomena, leading to futile attempts to generate them in a context that denies the real reasons for their existence.

[21] I have reviewed this literature in the context of the debate between Keynesians and new classicists in Lipsey (1981).

[22] For a contemporary review of the evidence on cost curves see Johnston (1960) and for a discussion of its significance in Keynesian models see Lipsey (1981: 274–6).

[23] This argument, which was clearly stated by Keynes in ch. 2 of the *General Theory*, is discussed in Lipsey (1981: 278–81).

not fluctuate to clear markets were studied both theoretically and empirically. A survey of this work contemporary with the height of the battle between the Keynesians and the new classicists can be found in Hall (1980).

The charge that Keynesian economics had no clear microeconomic underpinnings is clearly wide of the mark, although my casual survey of newly trained graduate students suggests that this is the prevailing belief.[24] How then do these underpinnings compare with the new classical ones that succeeded them?

On expenditure, the consumption function has been extended for better or for worse from the horizon of one lifetime, as in Modigliani and Friedman's versions, to infinite time-horizons in some versions and overlapping generations of households, each with finite time-horizons, in other versions. However, the basics of the investment function have not been significantly altered.

On money, there is no rational reason for demanding money in a continuous-time, new classical, GE model. A positive demand for money is created in one of two ways. First, money can be inserted into the utility function (which provides no explanation of *why* it is valued.) One of the first economists to attempt this was Patinkin (1956). He used a random receipts and payments process to generate a utility for money balances. Second, a time lag can be created between receipt of income in one period and expenditure of that income in the next period. This requires a discreet time-period model of the sort used by Patinkin (and many others before him). It cannot be used in a continuous time model.

Money is neutral in both the infinite time and the overlapping generations models and it is superneutral (neutral in its time derivatives as well as its level) in many of the infinite time-horizon models. It is not, however, neutral in its time derivatives in the overlapping generations model because inflation redistributes consumption through time.

In the goods market, Keynesian underpinnings were oligopolistic while the new classical underpinnings are perfectly competitive. New classical firms get signals about market conditions only through prices. But this clearly is not what we see in real markets for manufactured goods and most services where producers of differentiated products must set prices and let sales provide signals about the state of the market. So Keynesian underpinnings were clearly closer to goods-market reality than are new classical ones.

---

[24] Any defeated programme in economics is typically taught (outside of the history of economic thought) as an unflattering caricature. Students of the new theoretical programme are typically trained to regard those who espoused the replaced programme as foolish or misguided—as I was trained to regard the so-called classical economists during the early days of the Keynesians revolution. It seems a shame to me that students are not trained to understand the progress of science rather than being given a travesty of all that went before whatever new programme they are studying. Among other things, the travesty takes no notice of the probability that when the current programme is replaced by another, as it certainly will be sooner or later, those who espouse the present orthodoxy will be dismissed in their turn in the same way that they now dismiss all who went before them. When I put this point to young economist colleagues, they often in effect reply that 'this will not happen because we have discovered the truth while everyone who went before was in error.' I remember Joan Robinson saying much the same thing to me about her Keynesian colleagues and the classicists who went before them.

Similar remarks apply to the labour market. New Keynesians argue that the evidence overwhelmingly conflicts with the theory that the labour markets in which most workers operate are in any sense competitive markets in which wage fluctuations act as the equilibrating mechanism. As Hall said in his 1980 review 'There is no point any longer in pretending that the labour market is an auction market cleared by the observed average hourly wage. In an extreme case, wages are just instalment payments on a long-term debt and reveal essentially nothing about the current state of the market.'[25]

Another important issue involving micro-underpinnings concerns the place played by relative prices in the behaviour of agents. Although this is critical to new classical theory, it has received almost no comment. In the standard theory of the firm that has been taught since Alfred Marshall's day, all the information that firms need is the money prices of their inputs and their output. Since the input and output prices are all divided by the price level to make them real variables, the determination of the firm's profit-maximizing output is the same whether it is carried out in real or in nominal terms. Although the firm is concerned with its output price relative to its input prices, it need not be concerned with the price of its product relative to the prices of other products.

Shifting the goods-market focus from oligopoly to perfect competition in a GE setting seemed to put the relative prices of products into the firm's behaviour functions. This led to the errors-only aggregate supply curve that is associated with the name of Robert Lucas, but which originated with Edmond Phelps (1968). In this approach, firms are only led to depart from their long-run equilibrium outputs when they mistake a change in the money price of their product for a change in its relative price. Indeed, the relative prices of products do appear in GE market-demand functions for goods. But these functions are not meant to describe the behaviour of individual firms. As we have already observed, to determine its profit-maximizing output, all a firm needs to know is the money prices of its inputs and its output. How the price of its output compares with other product prices is simply irrelevant.

By making the correct behaviour of the firm depend on a mass of knowledge external to its direct experience, namely the prices of all other products, the new classical approach denies one of the fundamental advantages of the price system that has been emphasized since Adam Smith—that a welfare-maximizing equilibrium can be obtained when each agent acts in response to only a small amount of easily accessible information, all of which is within the agent's own experience. It seems to me that one of the great anomalies in the new classical programme that few have pointed out and that no one has tried to resolve, is between the errors-only explanation of variations in aggregate output and the received theory of the perfect (and monopolistic) competition. In the former, each firm's action is in response to a mis-perception of relative product prices; in the latter, each firm only needs to know its own demand and cost curves, all defined in nominal prices, neither knowing nor caring about the prices of other products.[26]

---

[25] Since that time, masses of additional evidence has been collected about the non-market-clearing behaviour of labour markets. For a survey see Chrystal and Lipsey (1997: 322–42).

[26] Of course, when making long-run investment decisions, the firms' investors need to know how profits compare across industries.

In conclusion, it seems clear, in retrospect, that the charge of inadequate micro-underpinnings did not refer to the extent to which Keynesian underpinnings were absent or unrealistic. It referred instead to the fact that the Keynesian underpinnings were developed piecemeal and could not be formally aggregated to yield precise macroeconomic behaviour. The new classical model accomplishes this aggregation by employing a series of strong assumptions, some of the most important of which are market clearing under perfect competition and representative agents which can be blown up to become the aggregate of all producers and consumers.[27]

Keynesians argue that the world is irretrievably one of price-setting not price-taking in virtually all manufacturing and service industries, and often one of small group oligopoly rather than of large group monopolistic competition. They agree that no one knows how to aggregate from such microeconomic behaviour to macro-relations. But, they say, if that is the way the world is, there is no point in pretending that it fulfils the competitive conditions needed for aggregation.[28]

Thus to many Keynesians the new classical programme replaced messy truth by precise error.

5. Anomalies

Three of the anomalies which the new classicism currently tolerates are mentioned below.

5.1. Predicting the effects of policy shocks

Keynesians argue that the new classical model invests agents with a superhuman ability to solve the general equilibrium equations of the economy, not just in static form but in the unspecified dynamic form required to predict the paths of dynamic adjustments. Keynesian models clearly erred in allowing for only backward-looking expectations. No theory should imply that agents go on holding unrevised expectations that are repeatedly and systematically falsified. Keynesians (and others) argue, however, that to replace Keynesians' backward-looking expectations with fully rational expectations is to assume an ability to predict the future that no professional would claim. For example, getting things right on average at all times implies efficient markets devoid of the kind of speculative boom that we have just witnessed in Eastern Asia. It also implies that the outcome of any fully perceived shock, such as a policy-induced change in the interest rate, can be predicted on average by all agents.

---

[27] As Lancaster (1979) and Eaton and Lipsey have argued, the behaviour of agents who operate in a characteristic space that captures what we know about differentiated goods cannot be aggregated into a single aggregate function that describes their collective behaviour as if they were a representative consumer. Eaton and Lipsey's arguments are summarized in the introduction to Eaton and Lipsey (1997).

[28] In a series of articles (reprinted in Eaton and Lipsey (1997)) Curt Eaton and I have argued that the version of monopolistic competition that is now used by GE theorists bears as little relation to economic reality as does perfect competition. But this Dixit–Stiglitz version continues to carry the day, not because it relates to anything we see in the world, but because it introduces product differentiation in a way that can be inserted into GE models and can be aggregated to the macrolevel.

Say, for example, that in the midst of a recession, the central bank decides to drive up the short-term interest rate by 1 per cent in response to a flight of capital. Agents are assumed to be able to predict on average the effect on the money supply, the term structure of interest rates, the rate of inflation, and the level of economic activity, as well as the changes in relative prices and wages. In a simple model, the neutrality of money implies no real effects once long-run equilibrium is re-established, assuming an initial state of long-run equilibrium. But in the circumstances of a recession and a capital flight, there is no guarantee that the correct answers would be given by the average of the predictions of all economists, let alone by the average of the predictions of all agents. How large the effects will be, and how long they will persist, is beyond the ability of most economists to predict.

5.2. The formation of expectations

The hypothesis of rational maximization of the value of expected outcomes is a powerful one that predicts well in many circumstances. But it goes against two well-established sets of observations of how people form explanations of what they observe and of how much can be known about a future in which technology (and probably tastes) are changing endogenously.

Economists are used to deducing consequences from explicit models. But evidence from psychology is that once humans go beyond very simple and fully understood situations, crossing what Brian Arthur (1992) calls the 'complexity barrier', people behave inductively. They search for patterns in what they see, even when such patterns are not there; they then predict the future by extrapolating these assumed patterns. This is a part of the rational explanation of why so many people believe weird things, superstitions, and such pseudo-sciences as astrology (see, for example, Shermer (1997) and Vyse (1997)).

5.3. Knightian uncertainty

It is a basic assumption of neoclassical theory in general and GE theory in particular that tastes and technology are exogenous. But this is clearly wrong, at least with respect to technology.[29] Because R&D is an expensive activity which is often undertaken by firms in search of profit, innovation is to a great extent endogenous to the economic system, altering in response to changes in perceived profit opportunities. Indeed, much interfirm competition in non-perfect markets takes place in innovation.

---

[29] Endogenous technical change has a long history in microeconomic analysis. The nineteenth-century economist, John Rae, studied endogenous technical change and pointed out that it undermined the case for complete *laissez faire* in general and for free trade in particular. Joseph Schumpeter made the innovating entrepreneur the centrepiece of his theory of growth. In the early 1960s, Nicholas Kaldor developed models of endogenous growth (Kaldor and Mirrlees 1962) that inspired a generation of European scholars. Also in the 1960s, the historian Schmookler (1966) developed detailed evidence that innovation was endogenous. A decade later, in his classic work, *Inside the Black Box*, Nathan Rosenberg (1982) established beyond the shadow of a doubt that technological change was endogenous at the microeconomic level, in the sense that it responded to economic signals. Rosenberg (1982: ch. 7) also made a persuasive case that pure scientific research programmes also respond endogenously to economic signals.

One of the most important implications of endogenous technical change is that many decisions involve uncertainty rather than risk. Risky events have well-defined probability distributions and, hence, well-defined expected values. Uncertain events have neither.

When major technological advances are attempted, it is typically impossible even to enumerate in advance the possible outcomes of a particular line of research let alone assign objective probabilities to each. This uncertainty does not arise from a lack of information that one might feasibly obtain given enough time and money. It arises from the nature of knowledge. Until one obtains new knowledge about some researched phenomenon, no one can know what the nature of that knowledge will be. (To know this is to have the knowledge already.)

A key characteristic of *risk* is that two agents possessed of the same information set, and presented with the same set of alternative actions, will make the same choice—the one that maximizes the expected value of the outcome. A key characteristic of *uncertainty*, however, is that two equally well-informed agents presented with the same set of alternative actions may make different choices. If the choice concerns R&D, one may back one line of research while the other backs a second line, even though both know the same things and both are searching for the same technological advance.

Because firms are continually making R&D choices under uncertainty, there is no unique line of behaviour that maximizes their expected profits—if there were, all equally well-informed firms would be seeking the same breakthrough made in the same way. Profit-seeking in the presence of uncertainty, rather than profit-maximizing in the presence of risk, implies that technological trajectories are non-unique and path-dependent. If we could return to the same initial conditions and play the innovation game again, there is no guarantee that we would retrace our steps exactly. Of course, agents must form subjective assessments of uncertain situations but equally rational agents will make different assessments. It follows that under uncertainty there can be no such thing as rational expectations or a unique optimal allocation of resources.[30]

Although we can get a long way with short-term models in which technology is given, it is clear that in the real world technology is continually changing in response to economic signals. Yet, given technology and given tastes are the two fundamental exogenous variables in neoclassical theory. If these are endogenized, the whole structure of the new classical research programme is undermined.

So what is known about (i) how much people can reasonably know about the future effects of current policy shocks, (ii) how people form explanations of complex events, and (iii) the uncertainty that pervades many economic decisions when technology is changing endogenously, provide anomalies with which the current programme must live. There is no scandal here, except where the anomalies go unrecognized or are knowingly suppressed. But the anomalies should suggest an element of humility for those who feel that the present programme is obviously true and obviously better in all respects than all the previous programmes.

---

[30] Kenneth Carlaw and I have developed these arguments, along with their profound policy implications, in a series of papers. See e.g. Lipsey and Carlaw (1997) and (1998). Paul Romer has reached similar conclusions starting from the perspective of macro-endogenous growth models. For a comparison of his approach and ours see Lipsey (2000).

6. Victory for the new classical programme

I return now to where I began, with the replacement of one programme by another. Although new Keynesian economics is alive and well, particularly in labour economics, the ground occupied by macroeconomics textbooks belongs almost exclusively to the new classicists. What now is taught in standard macro courses is almost wholly post-Lucas and, except for short caricatures, it is devoid of what Keynesians or monetarists would have regarded as conventional wisdom in say 1980.

Popular accounts often ascribe the success of the new programme to the complete failure of the old one. This is not a correct version of history. When closed by the expectations-augmented Phillips curve, the IS–LM model did succeed in explaining what were anomalies for the earlier versions, particularly accelerating inflation and stagflation. Furthermore, when closed by that curve, the complete long-run neutrality and superneutrality of money was restored and the charge that the model implied irrational behaviour was dispelled.

The Keynesian programme appealed to those who saw theory as formalizing real world observations that did not all fit into a simple maximizing model. The new programme appealed to a generation raised on Arrow–Debreu general equilibrium theory and a rigorous application of the maximizing hypothesis. To them, the older more *ad hoc* theorizing that incorporated many diffuse observations seemed fatally unscientific.

It is impossible to be sure just what persuaded observers that the Keynesian anomalies were sufficient to justify a complete change in programme. But the Phelps critique, plus Friedman's presidential address broadside, coupled with Lucas's new classical model and rational expectations were there to give the basis of a competing programme making the anomalies facing the Keynesian programme seem critical. Also, Lucas's devastating and correct point that empirical regularities were often conditioned by particular policy regimes, and could not be used to predict the results of regime changes, went a long way to establishing the new theory's credentials.

We cannot today know how the new classical economics will be regarded when its research programme is close to fulfilment and when it is challenged by what becomes its successor. Nor can we know how much of the ideas of the Keynesian programme will survive to be incorporated (probably anonymously) by new programmes. But several points about programme transitions are worth restating in this context. First, the reasons given in the textbooks for the replacement of one programme by another are usually gross caricatures. Second, the replacement of one programme by another is a matter of judgement based on an impressionistic assessment of the overall weight of accumulated evidence, the persuasive power of the protagonists, and the way in which those making the judgement have been trained. (It is impossible, for example, to imagine the new classical programme replacing the Keynesian one were the new generation of economists not well versed in Arrow–Debreu GE theory.) Third, many of the insights of any replaced programme are still valid and one of the challenges facing any new programme should be (but usually is not) to salvage what was valuable in the old, rather than sweeping all previous knowledge under the carpet.

Lest it be thought that these comments are just directed at the transition from the Keynesian to the new classical programme, let me say that I believe that most of what I have just said also applies to the replacement of the so-called old classical programme of the 1920s (insofar as there was one) by the new Keynesian programme of the 1940s. Also I would be very surprised if the same points would not also be relevant when some future observers discuss the replacement of the new classical programme by whatever programme succeeds it sometime in the twenty-first century. Just for fun, I will conclude with the speculation that the new programme will include better ways of incorporating three things: (i) Knightian uncertainty, (ii) what psychologists now know about how people form explanations of what they see, and (iii) (what will be very difficult) the endogeneity of technological change and tastes.

REFERENCES

Archibald, G. C. and R. G. Lipsey (1958) 'Monetary and value theory: a critique of Lange and Patinkin', *Review of Economic Studies* 26: 129–45.

Arthur, Brian (1992) 'On learning and adaptation in the economy', MS, Stanford University.

Baumol, W. J. (1952) 'The transitions demand for cash: an inventory theoretic approach', *Quarterly Journal of Economics* 66: 545–56.

—— and A. S. Blinder (1979) *Economics: Principles and Policy*, 1st edn. (New York: Harcourt Brace Jovanovic).

Blinder, A. S. and R. M. Solow (1974) 'Analytical foundations of fiscal policy', in *The Economics of Public Finance* (Washington: Brookings Institution).

Christ, C. F. (1968) 'A simple macroeconomic model with a government budget restraint', *Journal of Political Economy* 76: 53–67.

Chrystal, K. A. and R. G. Lipsey (1997) *Economics for Business and Management* (Oxford: Oxford University Press).

Cramp, A. B. (1970) 'Does Money Matter?', *Lloyds Bank Review*, 98: 23–37.

Davidson, Paul (1972) 'A Keynesian view of Friedman's theoretical framework for monetary analysis', *Journal of Political Economy* 80: 864–82.

Dow, J. C. R. and Leslie Dicks-Mireaux (1959) 'The determinants of wage inflation: United Kingdom, 1946–56', *Journal of the Royal Statistical Society* 122: 145–74.

Dyson, Freeman J. (1999) *The Sun, the Genome, and the Internet: Tools of Scientific Revolutions* (Oxford: Oxford University Press).

Eaton, B. C. and R. G. Lipsey (1997) *On the Foundations of Monopolistic Competition and Economic Geography: The Selected Essays of B. Curtis Eaton and Richard G. Lipsey* (Cheltenham: Edward Elgar).

Eckstein, Otto (1981) *Core Inflation* (Englewood, NJ: Prentice-Hall).

Friedman, Milton (1957) *A Theory of the Consumption Function* (Princeton: Princeton University Press).

—— (1968) 'The role of monetary policy', *American Economic Review* 58: 1–17.

—— (1970) 'A theoretical framework for monetary analysis', *Journal of Political Economy* 78: 193–238.

Gordon, R. A. (1948) 'Short-period price determination in theory and practice', *American Economic Review* 38: 265–88.

Hall, R. L. and C. J. Hitch (1939) 'Price theory and business behaviour', *Oxford Economic Papers* 2: 12–45.

Hall, Robert E. (1980) 'Employment fluctuations and wage rigidity', *Brookings Economic Papers*, Tenth Anniversary Issue: 91–123.

Hicks, J. A. (1937) 'Mr Keynes and the classics', *Econometrica* 5: 147–59.

Johnston, J. (1960) *Statistical Cost Curves* (New York: McGraw-Hill).

Kaldor, Nicholas (1970) 'The new monetarism', *Lloyds Bank Review* 98: 1–18.

—— and J. Mirrlees (1962) 'A new model of economic growth', *Review of Economic Studies* 29: 174–92.

Keynes, J. M. (1936) *The General Theory of Employment Interest and Money* (London: Macmillan).

Kuhn, Thomas S. (1970) *The Structure of Scientific Revolutions*, 2nd edn. (Chicago: University of Chicago Press).

Laidler, D. (1981) 'Monetarism: an interpretation and an assessment', *Economic Journal* 91: 1–28.

Lakatos, Imre (1978) *The Methodology of Scientific Research Programmes* (Cambridge: Cambridge University Press).

Lancaster, K. (1979) *Variety, Equality and Efficiency* (New York: Columbia University Press).

Lipsey, R. G. (1960) 'The relation between unemployment and the rate of change of money wage rates in the United Kingdom, 1862–1957: a further analysis', *Economica* 27: 1–31.

—— (1972) 'The foundations of the theory of national income: an analysis of some fundamental errors', in B. A. Corry and M. H. Preston (eds.), *Essays in Honour of Lionel Robbins* (London: Weidenfeld & Nicolson).

—— (1977) 'The place of the Phillips curve in macro economic models', in A. R. Bergstrom *et al.* (eds.), *Stability and Inflation* (Chichester: Wiley & Sons).

—— (1981) 'The understanding and control of inflation and unemployment: is there a crisis in macro economics?', *Canadian Journal of Economics* 14: 545–76.

—— (1997) *The Collected Essays of Richard Lipsey; i, Microeconomics Growth and Political Economy; ii, Macroeconomic Theory and Policy* (Cheltenham, UK: Edward Elgar).

—— (2000) 'New growth theories and economic policy for the knowledge society' in K. Rubenson and H. G. Schuetze (eds.), *Transition to the Knowledge Society: Public Policies and Private Strategies* (Vancouver, BC: University of British Columbia Press).

—— and P. O. Steiner (1981) *Economics*, 6th edn. (New York: Harper & Row).

Meiselman, D. (1968) 'Comment: is there a meaningful tradeoff between inflation and unemployment?', *Journal of Political Economy* 76: 743–9.

Modigliani, F. and R. E. Brumberg (1954) 'Utility analysis and the consumption function', in K. Kurihara (ed.), *Post-Keynesian Economics* (New Brunswick, NJ.: Rutgers University Press).

Neild, Robert (1963) *Pricing and Employment in the Trade Cycle* (Cambridge: Cambridge University Press).

Okun, A. M. (1981) *Prices and Quantities* (Washington: Brookings Institution).

Patinkin, Don (1956) *Money Interest and Prices*, 1st edn. (White Plains, NY.: Row, Peterson).

Phelps, E. S. (1968) 'Money wage dynamics and labor-market equilibrium', *Journal of Political Economy* 76: 678–711.

Phillips, A. W. (1954) 'Stabilisation policy in a closed economy', *Economic Journal* 64: 290–323.

—— (1957) 'Stabilisation policy and the time-forms of lagged responses', *Economic Journal* 67: 265–77.

Phillips, A. W. and K. Carlaw (1998) 'Technology Policies in Neoclassical and Structuralist-Evolutionary Models', *OECD Science, Technology and Industry Review*, No. 22, Special Issue, 31–73.

—— —— (1996) 'A Structuralist View of Innovation Policy', in Peter Howitt (ed.), *The Implications of Knowledge Based Growth* (Calgary: University of Calgary Press), 255–333.

Phillips, A. W. (1958) 'The relation between unemployment and the rate of change of money wage rates in the United Kingdom, 1861–1957', *Economica* 25: 283–99.

Rosenberg, N. (1982) *Inside the Black Box* (Cambridge: Cambridge University Press).

Schmookler, J. (1966) *Invention and Economic Growth* (Cambridge: Harvard University Press).

Shermer, Michael (1997) *Why People Believe Weird Things: Pseudoscience, Superstition and Other Confusions of Our Time* (New York: Freeman).

Tobin, James (1956) 'The interest-elasticity of the transactions demand for cash', *Review of Economic Statistics* 38: 241–47.

—— (1958) 'Liquidity preference as behaviour towards risk', *Review of Economic Studies* 25: 65–86.

—— (1972) 'Friedman's theoretical framework', *Journal of Political Economy* 80: 852–63.

—— (1981) 'The monetarist counterrevolution today—an appraisal', *Economic Journal* 91: 29–42.

Vyse, S. A. (1997) *Believing in Magic: The Psychology of Superstition* (Oxford: Oxford University Press).

Wilton, D. A. and D. M. Prescott (1982) *Macroeconomics: Theory and Practice in Canada* (Reading, Mass.: Addison-Wesley).

Piero Ferri: I had the impression, when Vercelli was discussing IS–LM models, that we are probably using the term to cover too many things. When you consider a general equilibrium model which is made up of four markets, you only consider three of them because of Walras's Law and then you call it the IS–LM model. In other words, whenever you consider a simplified general equilibrium model you end up with an IS–LM model. So I would like you to be more precise about what you mean by IS–LM models. In my background I thought you excluded the models that are explicitly micro founded.

I like Sims's model very much and am working on a similar model, but with two differences. One is that, with my American colleagues, we are working on bounded rationality. We know very well that there is an expectation problem but we think rational expectations is probably too simple and so we are putting in some learning. At the same time we also have imperfect competition and we get into trouble because, as Lipsey said earlier, it is very difficult to have a general equilibrium with imperfect competition. You are then reduced to having some symmetry hypothesis. So the question is, 'Can we build a macromodel with symmetry hypothesis, or with a representative agent?'

David Hendry: A couple of comments to Lipsey. When you consider long runs of data, the now is the long run of the past and you don't need rational expectations for that at all. I also think it is quite extraordinary that Keynes was building these models with so-called sticky prices when, if you look at the data sets that I just showed, they had just fallen by 25 per cent in the previous couple of years. It really is rather an amazing idea that he has of the world.

My other comments are addressed to Sims. I have difficulties at three levels with what he is doing: his basic assumptions; his model and its properties; and the relation of the model to modelling and learning anything about the world from data. On the first, we really seem to suffer from a Humean-type problem in that we look at the world and we see very different things. Sims made the comment that he didn't see much jumping in the data. I see enormous jumping in the data, all the time. I see the consumption–income ratio jumping by 15 per cent from one quarter to the next against a growth of $2\frac{1}{2}$ per cent per annum in GNP. I see house prices changing by 25 per cent in a quarter nationally, and much more in London. I see explanations for this, as forecast failure out needs forecast failure in and all the big models have suffered forecast failure, repeatedly through history. They abandoned Keynesian-type models in the 1970s because of it. They failed again in the mid-1980s, the late 1980s, the early 1990s, and so on. So it seems to me that it is a world of enormous jumps in data and the historical series seem to bear that out.

How do I explain this sort of thing? I see something like competition and credit control getting introduced by the British government. It changes from eligible reserves to eligible liabilities. I see a gigantic increase in the money stock because they don't need the same high-powered money to finance broad money. That leads to a large increase in mortgages. That leads to a large increase in house prices because there is credit rationing, and instantly we have got non-neutrality. We have real things changing in response to monetary shocks. What is this big deal about non-neutrality? That leads to a huge increase in the construction sector, to a boom in Britain and causes enormous problems for the government. So I don't see why we have to build models with properties that are counterfactual from the outset.

Let's take the sort of model you are putting up here. It doesn't seem to have the property that it could generate this sort of forecast failure. It is a very static model, there is no growth in it, and all the parameters are fixed. I can't make any sense of equations (20) and (21), because by equation (17) the right-hand side of equation (21) is a constant and by equation (6) the right-hand side of (20) is a constant. Suddenly constants have become variables in your model. I don't see where they come from. On the other hand, the kind of equation I find historically for $\dot{P}/P$ is an equation which needs a lot of shifts. In addition, if you were to take equation (17) and substitute $\log(1 - \alpha)$ and let the wage share change greatly over time, then you would have it as being the input into this.

Christopher Sims: Under equation (17) is the sentence, 'Equation above not used directly'.

Hendry: But it is derived from your model. And the same with equation (6).

Sims: This is the first-order condition, but the model assumes that agents do not take α under their control. So it is not part of the model. It is only used indirectly to generate (20) and (21).

Hendry: That is the sort of thing I am baffled by. Why did they take this rather than something else? How do we suddenly decide which equations of a model agents use and don't use? The model and its properties do leave me baffled, particularly equation (23). Historically, over the long run, the log of money in Britain is the log of a variable that has changed six hundred-fold, and interest rates haven't changed anything like that. I can't see how there is a conceivable monetary rule to stick into a model to start analysing things and likewise with fiscal policy.

Now how is this going to be implemented when we come to do things? There are about fifteen or sixteen variables here and if one is going to set this up in a VAR then all existing VARs are dramatically marginalized representations of this sort of reality. There is no test of the adequacy of the marginalizations that have been undertaken. The constancy assumptions that are built into the model also seem to hang out there against the background, that I see, of all these rapid jumps in variables, the large differences that follow from legislation. It seems to me that the model also doesn't discriminate between the sort of factors that underlie these shifts (which are often those in conditional means of agents' plans) and the sort of shifts that follow from the random shocks to the economy (perhaps from outside, perhaps from other factors). When you try to study these impulse-responses they are just a conflation of all the residuals from the model that are renamed shocks to try to use language as a sort of game to give them more credibility than they could conceivably have. Residuals represent ignorance and shocks, in a sense, represent knowledge but these two things are suddenly becoming one. You try to use the analysis of these to say what will happen when policy is undertaken. Until your remarks in the session on official documents, I was getting totally baffled by this paper but if it really is just a language game, I begin to understand it much more. However, if it is a language game we are doing very different things indeed. I am trying to find out how reality works, not trying to play language games.

Bennett McCallum: Vercelli said that my second-generation model, which has a distinction between real and nominal interest rates, and includes rational expectations, is quite different, conceptually, from the first-generation IS–LM models. Well, I agree enthusiastically with that proposition. Mine is dynamic, whereas the other is short-run, comparative static. Thus mine applies to calendar time, whereas the other one applies to hypothetical thought experiments that do not correspond to anything operational. Having said that, two things need to be added. I call this my model, but I did not create it. It was written down well before by Tom Sargent in quite a few writings and he was drawing on the old textbook by Martin Bailey (1962) that distinguishes clearly between real and nominal interest rates in an IS–LM set-up. His model is static, however, and doesn't have in the kind of expectations that I have.

My model with Nelson, which is the one I was referring to in the first equation of that tiny system (Volume 1, Chapter 6, equation (1)), is really a third-generation one. It is quite different from the second generation due to the effect of the expected value of future income or future consumption or whatever that is in it. The fact that the other term needs to be in there shows that my previous belief that the old-fashioned IS function could actually be used to represent optimizing behaviour was wrong. So there is a significant difference between the second- and third-generation models. A lot of people are using this third-generation formulation right now. Michael Woodford has used it in quite a few papers and there is also King and Kerr (1996).

Let me move on to Sims. My kind of set-up does not try to explain investment. It is all about consumption and saving at the household level, so the question is whether Sims's consumer problem is like the one in my model. It is very similar but they are not just alike. To get the set-up that Nelson and I (1999) worked with, we had transactions costs for money represented in an indirect utility function instead of in the budget constraint. There are two different ways to enter the same sort of transactions services. I don't think either can be shown to be superior to the other. If I could make that change and make utility separable, within a period, over consumption and the other things, then I could take Sims's equations (5), (7), (8), and (10) and write out exactly my IS function at the consumer level. So I think that what is, admittedly misleadingly, called the demand side is essentially the same in Sims's set-up as in the one that I am talking about.

Interestingly, however, putting the transactions cost for money balances in the way in which he does, seems to me, preliminarily to imply that what I would call the

IS function does have a real-money-balance term appearing in it. This is a possibility that monetarists would be more inclined to be interested in than would other people. I also have a comment on the importance Sims gives to fiscal policy coming from the joint appearance of rational expectations and the government budget constraint. His paper, of course, says that with 'standard active money–passive fiscal policy combination' then the economy works in a Ricardian equivalence way and everything looks normal. When he goes to other policy-rule formulations he gets very different results. Because Sims and I have different rational-expectations solution concepts, I would always get the first solution and he wouldn't. This is a highly technical and debatable problem that I don't think we really need to go into. It has little to do with IS–LM.

One more comment, pertaining to everybody, including Lipsey. I agree with all of them that IS–LM is not like what was in Keynes's *General Theory*, but I come down on the other side. I think that Hicks, Patinkin, and Modigliani improved upon Keynes, who was a very brilliant man but just not very interested in economic theory and not inclined to write a book that was theoretically coherent.

Mary Morgan: I would like to comment on these two papers from the point of view of the sociology of science. We have two papers, one from an Italian and one from an American, which start off by agreeing that the IS–LM model was a mean, rather meagre attempt to translate the Keynesian system but thereafter diverge very radically in their discourse and their style. Vercelli's contribution has a rather historical survey which is what one might expect from the Italian tradition, but with the use of a nice functional analysis, so that we get a lot of insight into how this model has been used and why it is still around. I found this nice and unusual. In comparison, the American paper is somehow very un-American, if I may make that comment. It seems very unusual to have an American paper which is motivated by the failure of the model to be a useful teaching tool and by what has been left out from Keynes. What has been left out from Keynes would be a perfectly good way to motivate a paper, I think, in the Italian tradition, but it is somewhat unusual in the American tradition. I wonder whether Sims might comment on how far he would agree with the kind of analysis in Vercelli's paper about why IS–LM is still around, not just in textbooks but at a more professional level.

James Hartley: Sims's model is the second representative agent model we have seen, and this is the second time the representative agent model has had an aggregate restriction that was not derived from the individual optimization problem. This is rather striking and it is fairly new in this sort of representative agent modelling. Lipsey remarked that in any research agenda, anomalies build up and people begin to change their paradigm. I wonder whether that is what we are seeing here. Is this a sign that people are beginning to acknowledge that it was wrong for others to insist, for twenty years, that every model must be built up from individual optimization?

Huw Dixon: I would like to take up a point that was made earlier about oligopoly and prices. I had a hard time with my paper, being told I should look at the evidence.

There is quite a lot of evidence in the micro literature, I-O evidence as well as labour economic evidence, for cost-plus pricing. It is not universal and it is controversial but there is quite a lot of evidence that that is how things work. What relevance does this have for the macro literature? There are a few papers by Howard Naish (1990, 1993*a*,*b*) where he looks at rule-of-thumb, cost-plus pricing rules in a business-cycle model to see how well they do. It obviously depends on how big the mark-up is but they can do quite well. So there might be some sort of bounded-rationality justification for cost-plus sorts of rule. What has this to do with macro? From the new Keynesian perspective, getting that will give you some quite strong elements of price rigidity. With a cost-plus pricing rule, prices tend to respond to changes in costs, not demand, giving you a degree of nominal inertia quite nicely. In the longer run, of course, you have to go back and start worrying about wage equations. In the short run, one of the insights of the menu-cost literature was that a sufficient condition for nominal conditions to affect real output is just the rigidity of nominal prices. I think that might be an interesting way of proceeding.

Adrian Pagan: Listening to Hendry and Sims, I wondered whether the model Sims is giving us is really intended to be an operational model or a pedagogic model. I don't think IS–LM has been used in an operational sense almost anywhere for at least the last fifteen years. There is an enormous expansion in the types of models involved, using forward-looking expectations and so on, and it seems to me that IS–LM always has been a pedagogic model. Once you make anything pedagogic, you have got to choose what to leave out in order to make it simple enough for people to grasp the basic ideas. Then, if you look at the history of people developing extensions of IS–LM, most people have chosen to think of simple rules-of-thumb for the real side, and they have tried to introduce rational expectations on the financial side. We have a lot of simple models that people use for teaching that actually do that and I can't see that the empirical evidence is really against it. Whenever I think about real decisions and the Phillips curve, I am impressed by the enormous amount of evidence that people are much more backward-looking than they are forward-looking. It seems to me that it captures much more closely what actually goes on in the economy than the type of model that you are presenting here.

Finally, it seemed to me that the reason why you are doing this is because of the intertemporal budget constraint but I am left wondering how important the intertemporal budget constraint is. Why don't I just ignore it? You effectively told us that the Brazilians ignored it. Well, no one took any notice of the Brazilians because they didn't believe that they would actually raise taxes in order to compensate for the change in interest rates. I am sure that all the countries in the world who have tried to defend their exchange rate by raising interest rates would be very happy to know that there is a huge expansionary fiscal policy going on, which is going to expand their economies. So far they don't seem to have seen it.

Katarina Juselius: I had also great difficulties seeing how your (Sims's) relations could ever fit any data in a way that could be sensible and could give, say, likelihood-based estimates. I agree with Hendry's criticism. I also feel that we have been discussing empirical econometrics versus theoretically based models for three days and my expectation is that at the next conference we go to we will say exactly the same thing. Nothing will have happened. That is why I have a constructive suggestion. *You have formulated a model with many interesting features.* I think we could easily find a sample you think is interesting and then we should both analyse the same data and criticize each other's approach using the assessment criteria you gave for the IS–LM model. I think *this would produce results* that are important in many different dimensions. I am suggesting this in a friendly and constructive way, not in order to have a personal fight. This would be a way of bringing understanding a little bit closer.

I have another comment related to using rational expectations. I have great difficulty in understanding how the long run could be today. I will cite a survey, which was very wide-ranging, performed by a Danish economist, Martin Paldam (Nannestad and Paldam, 2000). He asked a lot of agents in the economy, informed and non-informed, educated and non-educated, and so on, about what they knew about the inflation rate and what they expected about it, about unemployment, about the balance of payments deficit—important macroeconomic variables. It turned out that they did not even know what the inflation rate was. It was actually around 2 or 3 per cent, and the average reply was something like 10 per cent. *Altogether, the level of knowledge was remarkably imprecise, and that was only knowing what the key variables are today, not to mention what they would be tomorrow or next year, knowing say monetary policy decisions.* There was a journalist reading about this, who thought that it was a very interesting study and he asked the same questions of the government, with equally bad results. That I think proves that one should use rational expectations with some care.

Martin Eichenbaum: I remember many years ago going into my adviser's office and saying, 'Gee, this IS–LM stuff is so nice because you get all this intuition and these other models seem so complicated.' Sargent said, 'Go back into the library and solve some more of these other models and you will develop intuition too.' So this siren-like appeal of IS–LM—it is very easy to shift these curves around—but I think it is for people who find the alternatives difficult. You just have to solve lots of the other models and then you get just as good intuition. Intuition does not just come—you are not born with it.

The question is why one does not see IS–LM style models or I think what was referred to as systems analysis (I hadn't heard that word in the journals or in the job market, certainly in North America—I make no statement about Europe). The point, from an American perspective, is that these optimization models are simply a language, a way of being precise, so that I don't have to guess what you mean. Frankly, when I read Keynes, I have no idea what he means and if we haven't figured it out after forty years, time's up.

The final point I want to make is 'What does it mean to understand?' I think a little bit of this ongoing debate with Hendry and Sims, is to do with this. For me, fitting the curves does not constitute understanding. For a lot of researchers it means being able to couch what the end of a complicated econometric procedure means in terms of agents' motivations. What do they think they are responding to? Using optimization models is just a way of being precise, so that I do not have to guess what you mean. No one has ever had to guess what Bob Lucas means because you can read the equations and you can debate them. When Lipsey says this is a really stupid assumption, or maybe it is a mistake, you don't have to guess—it is equation (16). That is hard to do with Keynes and I don't see why we have to pay this price of wading through masses of prose to figure out just what the guy meant.

Sims: I second Lipsey's point about the observation that industries are oligopolistic, not symmetrically monopolistically competitive and that it is bothersome that, to the extent that we do provide microfoundations for sticky prices, the model seems to rely on this counterfactual microeconomics. That is one reason why I am willing to experiment with ordinary Phillips curves, because I really don't trust whatever restrictions I get out of this symmetric equilibrium. I agree it would be better if we could figure out how to aggregate oligopoly and I am not sure it won't start to become more feasible in the next few years. There are a lot of microeconomists and macro-economists who are beginning to work with each other in this direction. What Keynes said (and this is the point of the chs. 18–19 versus the rest distinction) was, 'Here is what happens if prices are sticky. Actually we know they are not—they go down.' He then gave an argument that it is not just that there is herd behaviour, as Vercelli said, but that when wages are going down it raises the real rate, cuts back investment, reduces employment, and adds to deflation. So, even though we know wages decline in conditions of low demand, this actually makes things even worse than in the static analysis. It is just that he never completed the analysis.

In this model, consumption–investment ratios do jump. There are no house prices, but in a related model that I have worked with there are commodity prices that do jump. In a model like this there has to be something that reacts right away. If you put in enough prices, some of them will jump. The important thing is to distinguish between things that jump and things that don't. When I referred to the data and the evidence, there is a lot of evidence for jumps on the diagonal of the impulse-responses of VARs. Lots of variables jump, but what you don't see is much co-jumping as Hendry describes it. When you look at these VARs, a shock that occurs clearly in some other sector—a price signal that is trying to influence lots of individual agents—you do not see the individual agents jumping. In fact, that is what is wrong with this model. It implies that price signals can make individuals jump, which I think is unrealistic. He is right to criticize equation (23). I have worked out this model with versions where instead of M, r responds to inflation with a coefficient bigger than 1. That will produce drifting inflation and will give us more realistic long-run behaviour. After that, the rest of what Hendry said reminded me once again that an effective player of language games never admits that he is doing so.

As for McCallum, I agree his paper is third-generation IS–LM and the expected output is very important in differentiating it from IS–LM. I question whether it is worthwhile calling it IS–LM any more because I think that once we start seeing the world this way the question arises whether we have done anything any good by teaching them the old static IS–LM. I don't think it is true that the government budget constraint questions on which McCallum and I differ are not related to the IS–LM formulation. The counter-intuitive or strange results I showed for passive money–active fiscal equilibria are not a different solution—it is a unique solution to a different policy pair. From previous discussions with McCallum I think he might argue that the policy pair is infeasible—that the monetary or the fiscal authorities can't actually commit to the kind of policy that I am solving for and that is a difference we can't work out here. McCallum's view of what rational expectations equilibrium is may be conditioned by thinking that starts from IS–LM.

On Hartley's question about whether it was wrong for people to insist for twenty years that every model must start from individual optimization. I didn't. When I was at Minnesota I was a leftist, closet Keynesian. It was only when I moved to Yale that I became a rightist, closet classical economist, and I never thought I had changed at all. Leeper and Sims (1994) estimate a more complicated version of this model and it had price and wage stickiness in it, so at worst it is sixteen years not the last twenty.

I agree with Adrian that this paper is meant mainly to be pedagogical but to some extent it is meant to be pedagogical to economists as well as students. I agree with him that a lot of real decisions are rule-of-thumb, and this model doesn't get that in. I don't think investment decisions are. I think a lot of models, even now, are not as sophisticated as they ought to be in modelling expectational effects of inflation on investment. The Brazilians did not ignore the budget constraint. This model and the equilibrium I displayed with fixed r and passive fiscal is particularly relevant to explaining what happened when people tried to defend exchange rates by raising interest rates. What this model says is that if you don't have the fiscal guns to back up an interest rate rise, the interest rate rise is not deflationary and it will not succeed in maintaining the value of the currency. You need to convince the markets that you are not going to inflate. A high interest rate is what we think, from IS–LM, will convince them of that, but if it is not backed up by fiscal policy it won't. My view is that that is what happened.

Finally, in response to Katarina's suggestion that we should go out and fit these models, we already have. The models that we presented did not fit all that well—we had difficulty with the numerical properties. Our excuse for going ahead with presenting it is that it fitted a whole lot better than RBC models and we think we can do better. I don't think it is very hard to do better. The data are all publicly available.

Alessandro Vercelli: On the relationship between IS–LM and general equilibrium models. Let me start with a metaphor. Why do I think IS–LM models are ambiguous? Because they project on a screen a general image of the economy which may be projected by completely different objects. Unless you clarify from which object this shadow is projected, you do not know exactly the meaning of the image you see. The implications are quite different according to the choice you make about the object projecting the image. This is true in general in my opinion, but in particular it is true in trying to characterize the relationship between IS–LM and general equilibrium. I see two completely different relationships between IS–LM and general equilibrium.

According to whether you believe in one or the other one, it changes completely the conceptualization of what you say, the range of application, and the implications for policy. Let me be more precise. It is well known that in this century we have had two completely different foundations for general equilibrium theory. The first one was given by Hicks and Samuelson and was dynamic. Equilibrium was seen as the resting point of a process. It is all right to start with that if you view unemployment as a disequilibrium phenomenon, and from there come implications for policy. The Arrow–Debreu foundation, at least in the prevailing version, which is formalist in the sense of the formalist school of mathematics, is different. If you follow this road as, in my opinion, Lucas and Sargent follow it in their foundation of new classical macro-economics on general equilibrium, you have a completely different conceptualization. Disequilibrium doesn't have any sense. Equilibrium is essentially a logical phenom-enon. It is the only set of values that avoids a logical contradiction. You cannot adopt any assumption about expectations apart from rational expectations if you start from there. This is not true if you start from the other general equilibrium. To give another example, what new classical economists call the business cycle is a completely different object from what Keynesian economists call the business cycle. This was underlined in the session on business cycles. If you were in the old school of business cycles, what you were after was an explanation of regularities in the oscillation of the main variables, believing that there was such regularity. However, if you start from the point of view of Lucas and Sargent, they deny that there is a regularity of this kind. What they are after is the co-movements, the correlations, between variables and this is a completely different thing. Someone said, in that session, that this implies regularity in the first sense. I am not convinced about that. So we should be very careful when we discuss different ideas on business cycles held by different schools because we are speaking of different objects. This is true for IS–LM as well in that there is a different con-ceptualization in the first- and second-generation models. In relation to this, I agree with Lipsey when he said that it is not true that Keynesian economics had no microfoundations. He mentions the attempts to give microfoundations in terms of oligopoly. This is an important research line, but it was not the only one. The attempt to give microfoundations to IS–LM was done immediately. It was an attempt to explain behaviour in terms of maximization but it was done in a different style. First of all it was piecemeal—the consumption function by Modigliani and Friedman; then liquidity preference by Baumol and Tobin; and more recently the microfoundations of investment functions. So each of the parts of IS–LM received a Keynesian micro-foundation related to that conception of general equilibrium. It was a different kind of microfoundations. This reveals the difficulty of communication between different points of view.

Hendry said that in the 1930s, according to his graphs, prices and wages fell a lot. He mentioned this fact to say that the relation between facts and theories is not so strict. However, I have a few counter-arguments. (i) In the part of the GT where he applies his IS–LM model (which was expounded in the first part of the book) to explain persistent unemployment in the 1930s and provide remedies, he does not assume fixed prices. He made the argument assuming a fall of wages and has an argument notwithstanding that this is not sufficient to restore equilibrium. (ii) Hendry's data suggest a very interesting thing about the relationship between facts and theory. The 1930s were the only period in which there was a strong lack of aggregate demand, so it was natural for economists of the period to concentrate their attentions on the lack of aggregate demand.

Morgan is right to suggest that we could learn a lot from comparing different mechanisms of the sociology of knowledge in different countries but such an approach has limitations. I would not accept that the approach used in this paper is representative of the approach used in Italy, or even my own. It depends very much on the way I interpreted the question posed by the organizers, so the style is very much relative to that. Though Sims and I have very different backgrounds, I was surprised to see how similar was our interpretation of the main points of Keynes's arguments.

Sims tries to develop Keynes's argument about endogenous expectations. It may be possible today to give that argument interesting, rigorous foundations by utilizing new ideas in the theory of decision under strong uncertainty. These may be able to explain in a rigorous way many of the intuitions Keynes had in that part of the book.

Richard Lipsey: I must reply to Eichenbaum's outrageous suggestion that you have to be a new classical economist in order to be precise. We all prefer precision to vagueness. Most modern economics is more precise than the economics of thirty years ago. But I can show you some very precise economics that is in a different tradition to the Lucas tradition. Second, I agree with Sims that people are thinking about how to aggregate oligopoly. If I had an urgent research agenda it would be that, because the world is in many areas oligopolistic and it has certain characteristics that are very different from perfect and monopolistic competition, we ought to be thinking about how to do it. The big problem, as Curt Eaton and I have shown in a string of papers (see Eaton and Lipsey 1997), is that when you build oligopolistic models that meet the five or six obvious empirical observations concerning the characteristics of differentiated products, you get non-uniqueness, and then you are in trouble when you come to aggregate. The world of oligopoly is generally not a unique world. Third, I did not mean fully to embrace rational expectations. In some situations rational expectations are impossible to form. I am doing all my current research on technological change over the last 10,000 years. Whenever you go for a big technological breakthrough there is no way you can even enumerate the possible outcomes, let alone attach a probability distribution to each. You are dealing with what Frank Knight called uncertainty, not risk. I noticed that in all the papers people talked about uncertainty but then did risk analysis. The characteristic of risk is that you can get unique equilibria where people maximize the expected value of the outcome, but with uncertainty you can't. You don't know, so with uncertainty, which is a characteristic of technological change, you lose all optimality and you lose uniqueness and you gain path dependency and are in a really different world. If we look at the longer term, we are in a world of technical change in which over ten to twenty years what happens is to a great extent dominated by technical change. If you want an intractable problem, think about modelling technical change in a world that is uncertain as opposed to risky.

REFERENCES

Bailey, Martin J. (1962) *National Income and the Price Level*, 1st edn.; 2nd edn. 1971 (New York: McGraw-Hill).

Eaton, B. C. and Lipsey, R. G. (1997) *The Foundations of Monopolistic Competition and Economic Geography: The Selected Essays of B. Curtis Eaton and Richard G. Lipsey* (Chelthenham: Edward Elgar).

Kerr, W. and King, R. G. (1996) 'Limits on interest rates in the IS–LM model', *Federal Reserve Bank of Richmond Economic Quarterly* 82 (Spring): 47–75.

Leeper, E. M. and Sims, C. A. (1994) 'Toward a modern macroeconomic model usable for policy analysis', in S. Fischer and J. J. Rotemberg (eds.), *NBER Macroeconomics Annual 1994* (Cambridge, Mass. and London: MIT Press): 81–118.

McCallum, B. T. and Nelson, E. (1999) 'An optimizing IS–LM specification for monetary policy and business cycle analysis', *Journal of Monetary Economics* 10: 139–62.

Naish, Howard (1990) 'The near optimality of mark-up pricing', *Economic Inquiry* 28(3): 555–85.

—— (1993a) 'The near optimality of adaptive expectations', *Journal of Economic Behaviour and Organization* 20(1): 3–22.

—— (1993b) 'Real business cycles in a Keynesian macro model', *Oxford Economic Papers* 45(4): 618–38.

Nannestad, P. and Paldam, M. (2000) 'What do voters know about the economy? A study of Danish data, 1990–93', *Electoral Studies* (forthcoming).

Part II

THE LABOUR MARKET

5 Wage dynamics and the Phillips curve

PIERO FERRI

1. Introduction

When dealing with the theory of wage dynamics, one must state at the beginning whether nominal or real magnitudes are at the centre of the analysis. Even though in the current literature the emphasis is almost exclusively put on real variables, nominal wages are the object of the present analysis. Of course, one cannot neglect the interrelationships between the two concepts but we think that in a monetary economy an inquiry on nominal wages is worth pursuing.

In the case of nominal wage dynamics a paradox seems to have occurred: an empirical object, the 'Phillips curve', seems to have been a dominant theoretical issue for a long period of time. This is why wage dynamics and the Phillips curve are so closely linked.[1]

This association, however, entered a period of turbulence for both theoretical and empirical reasons, leaving the theory of nominal wage dynamics in a state of discomfort. On the one hand, the famous Friedman's article that appeared in 1968, suggested a new theoretical justification to the curve, where only real wages matter.[2] This line of research contributed to the emergence of the new classical economics or supply-side theories, where the role of microfoundations and hence the importance of rational expectations were the basic elements. On the other hand, during the early 1970s, the so-called stagflation period, the traditional Phillips curve seemed to have disappeared so pronounced having been its shifts.

It is worth stressing that also in the new approach there remains an isomorphism between micro-behaviour and macro-results, but it seems to work in the opposite direction. In fact, while the macro-results originally were supposed to indicate how the micro-units were operating, the new theories stress the opposite. It is the micro-behaviour that governs the wage dynamics, and this, by the assumption of the representative agent, should shape the macro-pattern.[3]

The author wishes to thank S. Fazzari and E. Greenberg (Washington University) for stimulating suggestions. Financial support from the Italian Ministry for University and Scientific Research and the University of Bergamo is acknowledged.

[1] In the present paper, we maintain the distinction between a Phillips curve, where the dependent variable is represented by changes in nominal wages and a trade-off curve where the dependent variable is represented by inflation rates (see Samuelson and Solow 1960).

[2] As stressed by McCallum (1989), even though the most frequently cited article is Friedman (1968), 'The ideas were presented earlier, by Phelps (1967) and Friedman (1966). The latter is a beautifully insightful yet informal discussion of only a few pages' (1966: 181).

[3] According to Ramsey (1996: 293), these two processes are called respectively, interpretability (the ability to provide a micro-interpretation of parameters that are estimated within a macro-equation) and recoverability (the identification of parameters in the macro-equation with the corresponding equations in the micro-formulation).

The thesis put forward in this paper is based upon an important methodological aspect that contrasts both these kinds of isomorphism. The Phillips curve is a system result that is not easily reducible to micro-behaviour. It is a macro-curve that reflects the systemic results of the interplay between micro-conditions and a macro-institutional setting. This methodological point of view implies four kinds of consequences, both analytical and practical. First, the existence of the Phillips curve does not necessarily imply the presence of money illusion as a long IS–LM tradition has sustained. Second, it is compatible with different kinds of wage dynamics. Third, the instability of the curve occurs because different economic and institutional regimes imply different results. Finally, it is this dynamic instability that prevents its use as a mechanical economic policy tool.

The structure of the paper reflects these points. In particular, in Section 2 the problem of wages in the General Theory is briefly presented. In Section 3 the theoretical role of an empirical object such as the Phillips curve is considered within the IS–LM tradition, while Section 4 considers the emergence of the Phillips curve in the so-called Keynesian era. Section 5 deals with the reasons for the crisis of this regime, the breakdown of the Phillips curve, and the emergence of models based upon a conflict theory of inflation and unemployment. Section 6 presents a regime-switching model, whereas Section 7 discusses recent events characterizing the labour market. Section 8 examines the common features as well as the differences among the various models examined, while Section 9 contains concluding remarks.

2. Keynes's four lessons

Even if one limits consideration to the labour market, there are many places in the General Theory where some of the methodological aspects just mentioned can be identified. In particular, there are four lessons that are worth considering.

Lesson 1 refers to micro–macro relationships. Keynes writes: 'The classical conclusions are intended, it must be remembered, to apply to the whole body of labour and do not mean merely that a single individual can get employment by accepting a cut in money-wages which his fellow refuse' (1936: 11).[4]

In this macro-perspective (i.e. a reference to the whole body of labour), one wonders how it is possible that, according to the classical school, 'the wage bargains between the entrepreneurs and the workers determine the real wage' (ibid. 11). The answer is macro: they are convinced of the idea that prices depend on the quantity of money' (ibid. 12). If one drops this assumption, as Keynes did, real wages are not determined by the labour market but they rather become a system result. This is lesson 2.

---

[4] It must be stressed that Pigou's analysis was one of the most important classical studies considered. See J. Robinson (1971).

In this perspective, lesson 3 follows: 'labour stipulates (within limits) for a money-wage rather than a real wage' (ibid. 9). 'Within limits' implies that the validity of the assumption of given money wages is analytically and historically determined.

In this framework, the main macro-variables are expressed in 'wage units': income, investment, and money supply are all defined in terms of this unit. The fact that the wage is given does not imply that it is rigid. This distinction is best illustrated by referring to what Hicks (1974) called the 'wage theorem'. According to this theorem, a general and proportional increase in money wages is bound to generate an identical increase in prices on the condition that money supply is augmented by the same amount. Under these circumstances, income and investment are independent of the level of money wages.[5]

Keynes exploited the wage theorem in a negative way, mainly to prove how deflation could not be a serious therapy for unemployment (ibid.: ch. 19). In fact, the dynamics of money wages did not seem to be an interesting question in the mid-1930s. However, a dynamic principle was clearly stated and this is lesson 4. According to Keynes 'In actual experience the wage-unit does not change continuously in terms of money in response to every small change in effective demand, but discontinuously. These points of discontinuity are determined by the psychology of the workers and by the policies of employers and trade unions' (ibid. 301).

These lessons are still valid and we shall try to verify what happened to them in the various approaches that followed. It must be stressed, however, that the determination of the wage dynamics in an economy that is neither in a Great Depression nor in a state of full employment remains a challenge from both a theoretical and empirical point of view. In order to partially overcome this indeterminacy, one has to refer to the set of institutions prevailing, the accepted laws and customs, and the macro-environment. In other words, one has to refer to the particular historical regime in which wage dynamics is studied. Three of them will be considered: the Keynesian era (approximately from the end of the World War II to the late 1960s), the stagflation period (the time of the two oil shocks), and the new paradigm that seems to be prevailing in the labour market in the most recent times. Within these historical periods, different models of wage dynamics will be taken into consideration.

3. The Phillips curve and the IS–LM models

The Phillips curve, i.e. the relationship between the rate of change of money wages and unemployment, has been considered as a relationship that completed the Keynesian paradigm, by introducing continuous change in place of discontinuities. In fact, it was supposed to provide the missing link between the General Theory and the actual working of the economy after World War II.

---

[5] According to Hahn and Solow (1995: 114) this result is called homogeneity property: 'an equal proportional change in M and W causes the equilibrium P to change in the same proportion and leaves the real variables unchanged'.

Phillips (1958) identified the empirical relationship between the rate of growth of money wages and unemployment, which he interpreted as the dynamic law governing the process of adjustment in the labour market.

When the demand for labor is high and there are few unemployed we should expect employers to bid wage rates up quite rapidly, each firm and each industry being continually tempted to offer a little above the prevailing rates to attract the most suitable labour from other firms and industries. (1958: 283)

This analytical interpretation of the Phillips curve was used as a motivation to append such an equation to the traditional IS–LM model (see Tobin 1975).[6] In this context, wage is represented by a dynamic variable and the rigidity 'querelle' becomes obsolete.[7] Since the original wage equation has been supplemented with a price variable, however, different analytical results can be produced according to the value of the coefficient measuring the impact of this variable. To obtain Keynesian results the coefficient must be less than one, but this implies that money illusion has taken the place of wage rigidity as a characterization of the working of a Keynesian labour market.

According to the criticisms started from Phelps (1967) and Friedman (1968) and deepened by the rational expectation supporters (Lucas 1981), this compromise is untenable. For instance, Phelps *et al.* (1973: 337) claimed that: 'A landing on the non-Walrasian continent has been made. Whatever further exploration may reveal, it has been a mind-expanding trip: we need never go back to $dp/dt = a(D - S)$ and $q = \min(S, D)$.'

Since the traditional justifications given for the Phillips curve were of this type, they had to be abandoned. Furthermore, the Phillips curve, if it exists, is merely considered in the new framework as a negative correlation between wage inflation and unemployment (Sargent 1987: 438) that seems to work in the opposite direction of the causal link identified by Phillips (1958).[8]

4. The Phillips curve and the economy of the 'big three'

There seems to be a parallelism between the Keynesian paradigm and the destiny of the Phillips curve. However, we claim that this parallelism must be looked for at a deeper level. To this purpose, let us start by considering the institutional arrangements characterizing wage dynamics in the quarter century after World War II, which is considered the Keynesian golden age period. The interplay between macroeconomic conditions and institutional arrangements is responsible for the canonical shape of the Phillips curve during this period.

[6] For a critique of these models and their contrast with Keynes, see Minsky (1975) and Davidson (1994). For the role of the Phillips curve in the IS–LM see also Ferri (1978).

[7] To be precise, Sargent (1987: 483) states that the derivative of wages is endogenous at each moment, 'even while the level of W is fixed'. For a criticism of this model, see Flaschel, Franke, and Semmler (1997).

[8] According to Friedman (1975), a Phillips curve, if it exists, works with a reverse causality from prices to unemployment, as Fisher taught a long time ago. It worked because of the Fisher effect and through wage and price surprise as shown by Lucas (1981).

This period was characterized by the presence of an institutional regime dominated by big firms, big unions, and big government that interacted in a way that can be stylized along the following lines (see Ferri and Minsky 1992). Firms generated an increase in productivity. Unions pursued an increase in the standard of living by asking for wages in line with productivity increases. Government ensured full employment (or welfare benefits in case of unemployment) and an increase in money supply adequate to the growth of income. In this situation, prices remained substantially stable and were thought to remain so.

In this context the Phillips curve can be generated as a system result, and therefore it is not necessary to impose an isomorphism between micro and macro, as Phillips (1958) himself claimed (see Ferri 1997). In order to prove this statement, one has to consider four other 'macro-laws' that were characterizing the economy at that time. (i) 'Ford's law', according to which the dynamics of productivity $(\hat{pr})$ constrains the dynamics of nominal wages $(\hat{w})$. (ii) 'Kaldor's law', also called 'Verdoorn's law', according to which the rate of growth of productivity is a function of the rate of growth of output (g) and this relationship is supposed to capture the role of the economies of scale. (iii) 'Okun's law' according to which there is a negative association between the rate of growth of output and the rate of unemployment (u).[9] (iv), in order to close the model, there is the 'Phelps-Brown's law' about the constancy of the income distribution shares (where $\hat{p}$ in equation (2) represents the dynamics of prices). From these macro laws, one obtains the following system:

$$\hat{w} = \hat{pr} \qquad \text{Ford's law,} \qquad (1)$$

$$\hat{p} = \hat{w} - \hat{pr} \qquad \text{Phelps-Brown's law,} \qquad (2)$$

$$\hat{pr} = f(g) \quad f' > 0 \qquad \text{Kaldor's law,} \qquad (3)$$

$$u = h(g) \quad h' < 0 \qquad \text{Okun's law.} \qquad (4)$$

This four-equation system contains four unknowns (i.e. the variables in the left-hand-side) and is driven by the exogenous growth rate g. In graphical terms, one obtains Figure 5.1 where in quadrant II a Phillips curve is generated.

According to this interpretation, the Phillips curve is a macro-relationship reflecting the working of the whole system, not only that of the labour market in particular.[10] In the second place, the existence of the Phillips curve does not imply any kind of money illusion. On the contrary, it is compatible with rational expectations (or preferably, consistent expectations). The 'big three' actors have in mind the same model. Price stability is assumed and at the same time is realized (see also Leijonhufvud 1981). It is therefore rational to reason only in terms of money wages because these also imply real

---

[9] This is a generalization of Okun's law that originally linked the unemployment gap to the output gap. This version of the Okun's law reflects the impact of productivity, labour-force participation and production function considerations (see Blinder 1997).

[10] Paradoxically, this is the same conclusion reached by Rogerson (1997) even though his approach is radically different, being totally microfounded.

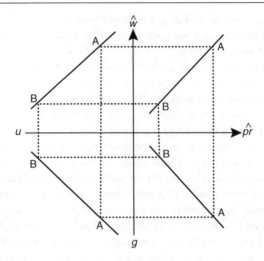

FIG. 5.1. *The Phillips curve and the other macro laws*

wages. In terms of game theory (see also Maital and Lipnowski 1985), one can assume that firms are the 'Stackelberg' leaders that operate through the increase in productivity and that unions and the government follow by setting, respectively, wages in line with productivity growth and money supply in line with the increase in monetary income.

Of course, one can complicate these stylized facts. For instance, some form of indexation can be added to the wage equation, but this was heritage of the war period and does not alter the core of the model. Furthermore, there are at least two labour-market sectors, the primary and the secondary one; the latter is disciplined by a mechanism similar to the 'reserve army' of the classical writers. For this reason, the rate of unemployment can appear directly in the wage equation. Finally, the presence of different sectors in the economy explains why there can be some structural inflation rather than absolute price stability, due to the presence of differences in productivity greater than wage differentials.

5. Conflict, inflation, and unemployment

During the two oil crises period, the previous illustrated 'stylized' working of the economy was no longer operative. Price-stability anchor had disappeared, and 'the big three' had to take that into account. In particular, agents had to protect themselves from price changes to defend their standard of living. In this new environment, not only a wage equation that somehow referred to real targets had to be introduced, but also a price equation spiralling with the wage equation had to be considered. As far as the wage dynamics is concerned, an equation (in logs) based upon an error-correction mechanism was reconsidered (see Nickell 1988):[11]

$$w(t) = w(t-1) + \{[cp(t)^e + (1-c)p(t)] - p(t-1)\}$$
$$- [w(t-1) - p(t-1) - pr(t-1)] - bu(t) + z. \tag{5}$$

According to this formulation, when wages are set, a proportion c of agents do not know the aggregate price level and so the term in brackets reflects the relevant expected (p^e) inflation rate. pr is the log of productivity and the value of term inside the square bracket implies a negative correlation with wage increase, while z reflects exogenous forces.

This wage equation was contrasted with a price-setting equation within the framework of a conflict theory of inflation (see Rowthorn 1977) where firms set prices given some expectations of wages and unions set wages given some expectations of prices becomes relevant. In this imperfect competition setting, Layard *et al.* (1991) identify the equilibrium rate of unemployment as NAIRU, i.e. the non-accelerating inflation rate of unemployment. The restraint placed by price and wage formation constrains the achievement of a full-employment target, which is outside the reach of a demand policy. In fact, the NAIRU is a long-run natural rate of unemployment governing the labour market and wage-determination problem.

But the NAIRU concept is debatable for at least two reasons. First of all, it is the result of a labour demand and a wage curve (not to be confused with the labour supply) both expressed in real terms. In the second place, it implies the existence of a unique long-run equilibrium in which the agents are supposed to operate in the same regime forever. In fact, the long run is a period where regimes, i.e. the set of rules, behaviours, and institutions that characterize for instance the labour market, can change.

One has to investigate what happens when the regimes can change. In fact, it is not necessarily true that, even in the presence of an inflationary environment, wage dynamics must be determined in real terms.

6. A regime-switching model

In a sense, the regime-switching model is compatible with the hypothesis envisaged by Keynes of an economy that behaves discontinuously in different economic situations. In this spirit, Ferri and Greenberg (1992) have studied a macro-regime-switching model grounded upon a wage–price subsystem. It is supposed that the wage–price subsystem undergoes discontinuously a change when a strategic variable passes some threshold level.[12]

---

[11] This specification was introduced much earlier from Sargan (1964) in relation to the UK economy that did not share the characteristics of the virtuous growth model described in the previous Section.

[12] The regime-switching model considered in this paper is a piecewise linear model. In order to avoid abrupt changes in the parameters, smooth autoregressive transition models (STAR) have been suggested, see Granger and Terasvirta (1993). For a comparison with other ways of producing non-linearities, see Acemoglu and Scott (1994) who also consider state space formulations. For a general discussion on the non-linearity property of the Phillips curve, see Clark and Laxton (1997).

In order to simplify the exposition, let us consider the following system based upon three equations:

$$w(t) = a + p(t-1) - bu(t), \tag{6}$$

$$p(t) = m + w(t), \tag{7}$$

$$u(t) = d + hp(t). \tag{8}$$

Although stated in a very simple way, all three equations have clear interpretations. (All the variables are in logs, except the rate of unemployment). First, nominal wages are set in advance based on the previous price level but responds contemporaneously to the unemployment rate. (This is a simplified version of equation (5)). Second, the price level is determined by a constant mark-up (m) over wages. Third, a higher price level reduces the real stock of money and aggregate demand, and thereby induces higher unemployment.

It follows that the equilibrium unemployment rate is given by

$$u^* = \alpha/b, \tag{9}$$

where $\alpha = m + a$, while the wage dynamics and the dynamic adjustment of unemployment are respectively represented by the following equations:

$$w(t) - w(t-1) = \alpha - bu(t), \tag{10}$$

$$u(t) = \phi u(t-1) + (1 - \phi)u^*, \tag{11}$$

where $0 < \phi = 1/(1 + hb) < 1$.

The Phillips curve is generated in equation (10). Two observations are worth making at this stage of the analysis. First of all, the Phillips curve is a system result that differs from the specific labour-market equation (6). This latter takes price into consideration, while in the specification (10) prices are not present in an explicit way. In the second place, this curve can shift for different reasons. For instance, it may shift as the result of the various shocks (see Nickell 1988). By the way, this is just what happened in the stagflation period, when these conflict models of wage determination based upon some form of imperfect competition were considered. However, the curve can shift for endogenous reasons. For instance, in the case of equation (6), the parameters a and b can change when unemployment exceeds the threshold level of unemployment u^T:

$$u > u^T, \tag{12}$$

where a new regime becomes operative.

To this purpose, let us start from the easiest case and suppose that the wage-equation parameter a changes when a threshold level of unemployment (u^T) has been reached. In particular, let us suppose that a^{II}, which rules in regime II where unemployment is bigger than the threshold level, is smaller than a, i.e. $a^{II} < a$.

This assumption is reasonable. When the unemployment rate is above a certain threshold, the exogenous forces that impinge on the dynamics of wages weaken. One

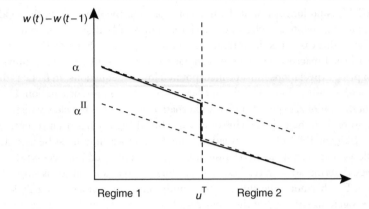

FIG. 5.2. *Two Phillips curves*

can think of the strength of the union, the role of unemployment benefits, the probability of finding a job elsewhere in the economy.[13]

In the case of the switching in this parameter, we can obtain a Phillips curve of the type illustrated in Figure 5.2.

Some observations are worth making. The change in the parameter a modifies in the same direction α and therefore shifts down the Phillips curve. In this case, one has two Phillips curves, one for recessions (or stagnation) and one for expansions. Secondly, changes in a modify the unemployment rate in such a way that

$$u^{*\mathrm{II}} < u^{\mathrm{T}} < u^{*}.$$

In other words, the rate of unemployment in regime II $(u^{*\mathrm{II}})$ is smaller than the one prevailing in regime I. In such a case, an endogenous cycle can be generated (see Ferri and Greenberg 1992).[14]

The advantages of this approach are various. First of all, one has to stress that the parameters of the equations need not necessarily be constrained to produce stability, because a change in regime can bring about stability by other means. In the second place, a regime-switching model implies the presence of multiple equilibria. It follows that in this context, the equilibrium rate of unemployment (or *mutatis mutandis*,

---

[13] Two points are worth making at this stage of the analysis. The first is that the justification of the change depends on the micromodel one has in the background (i.e. turnover model, insider–outsider, efficiency models). The second is that it depends on the time-horizon, in other words whether one wants to refer to high-frequency fluctuations or to lower-frequency ones. In the first case (see Acemoglu and Scott 1994), the two regimes refers to boom and recession, in the latter case to expansion and depression. Phelps (1994) studies unemployment in the latter perspective.

[14] Given $u^{*\mathrm{II}} < u^{\mathrm{T}} < u^{*}$ and $\phi < 1$ and $\phi^{\mathrm{II}} < 1$, there exists a unique, asymptotically stable cycle of period ≥ 2. It is also important to stress that the cycle is not due to the presence of nominal rigidities in the labour market, but to the presence of the threshold mechanism. What the nominal rigidities can do is to modify the profile of the cycle. This is brought about by changes in the parameter ϕ that regulates the permanence in one regime or in the other.

the NAIRU) is no longer a well-defined concept.[15] In the third place, the model can endogenously generate a cycle, where different kinds of Phillips curves can be generated. Also in this case, it is the interaction between specific labour-market institutions and then broad macro-conditions in generating them. Finally, in this context, some forms of price expectations must be incorporated into the equations. In fact it is difficult to assume that indexation is satisfactory because of its backward orientation. However, we doubt that rational expectation is the alternative because it is not clear which 'regime' is going to replace the old one. (In some sense this difficulty has been recently recognized by Sargent 1993.) In this situation some form of learning must be introduced.

It follows that even in an environment of conflict, one need not necessarily have to state wage determination in real terms, even though a real wage target is surely behind the scene. Furthermore, the shifts in the Phillips curve may not necessarily be attributed to exogenous shocks, but they may simply reflect endogenous changes in the laws governing wage dynamics.

7. Towards a new paradigm

The laws governing wage dynamics are historically determined. In fact, two changes have happened that are worth considering in order to understand the new environment within which wage dynamics takes place. The first is the modification of monetary policy. With the advent of monetarism in the economic policy of the early 1980s, government (or better, central banks) became the 'Stackelberg' leader. Central banks set the monetary targets: inflation control becomes the main target, while employment follows. The second refers to changes in the real aspects of the model based upon the three 'big actors' illustrated above.

One can discuss whether these changes are reducible to a regime-switching model or rather the expression of more structural and therefore irreversible changes. The answer is mixed. In fact, it is in the logic of a regime-switching model to have new rules and hence new parameters governing the equations and this can create a dynamic transition that mimics the present experience of contained nominal wage dynamics. However, some changes are deeper and modify the equations in a more structural way.

Owing to the globalization of markets, the diffusion of information technology, and the pre-eminence of the service sector one is tempted to conclude in favour of irreversible structural changes. In this context, the power of unions has strongly diminished above all in the US economy.[16] Furthermore, a competitive pressure has implied

---

[15] One must qualify this statement. In fact, one has to observe that there is no stationary state in this model: a point which begins in one phase zone is 'drawn towards' the equilibrium value it would have if it were the only regime but, when the switching threshold is crossed, the other phase equation takes over so that the process moves cyclically from one regime to the other. As long as the above conditions hold, neither equilibrium can be reached—even in the long run. It must be stressed that it is the presence of this assumption that explains the difference with the conditions set by Tong (1990: 67) for the stability of piecewise linear systems.

[16] In the case of the USA, one must also mention the relevant increase in labour supply, due to demography, family policy, and immigration. It is also important to stress that the different regimes had a different impact in Europe compared to the USA.

a different way of distributing the benefits of technical progress: lowering relative prices more than increasing nominal wages. Finally, full employment is no longer the main target of economic policy.

In this new environment, not only the parameters of the equations can change (as predicted by a model based upon regime-switching) but the nature of the relationship can undergo deeper changes, as predicted by the presence of more structural changes. In the new economic situation, money wages can even decrease. The insiders can accept a reduction only if they experience a fall in employment (see Fazzari *et al.* 1998) and this is what happened.[17]

Actually, wage reduction raises another question because it can break that sense of 'fairness' that was one of the reasons underlined by Keynes against wage reductions. However, as Hicks (1973) has pointed out, this aspect is important mainly for a labour market that is based upon 'long-term' relationships, but it is not necessarily valid for relationships that become short term or even precarious. And this is what seems to be happening in the US economy, where a new regime with global firms, small government, and flexible labour markets has replaced the 'big three' model that prevailed until the end of the 1960s. In this new regime, the working of the labour market seems to be reverting to the pre-Keynesian or Pigouvian world.

Those who oppose this view, insisting on the cost of downward wage rigidity (see Akerlof *et al.* 1996), do not consider the possibility that in a low-inflation environment the wage-formation process can change. The difficulty lies in other aspects. In an expansionary period there is no doubt that both wage and employment flexibility work very well and are favourable to growth. It is not clear that they do the same job during a recessionary period. And this is particularly true in a macro-environment where aggregate demand is not a target.

We need to understand whether this leads back to a nineteenth-century kind of labour market or to something new.

8. Macro-laws, reconciliation mechanisms, and instability

After discussing the peculiarities of wage dynamics in these different historical contexts, it is worth investigating whether there are common elements characterizing the various environments.[18] In this effort, however, we do not accept the suggestion of the supporters of the Lucas critique to look at the fundamentals, and therefore to microfoundations, to arrive at stable functions. On the contrary, in our view, one must be conscious of the instability of the Phillips curve, which is a system result, compatible with different laws governing the economy in general and the labour market in particular.

---

[17] In this case, the Phillips curve must have not only unemployment as an explanatory variable, but possibly also changes in that variable. See Fazzari *et al.* (1998).

[18] There are links between these questions and those raised by econometricians by means of cointegration analysis. See, for instance, Hendry in this volume for the case of inflation.

To answer the question about common features, one has to simultaneously consider three levels of analysis: (i) the constraints deriving from macro-conditions; (ii) the so called mechanisms of reconciliation of different claims about the income share; (iii) the nature of the labour and product markets. The answer is ambiguous because it is affirmative with respect to the first level and negative as far as the others are concerned.

The macro-condition refers to the so-called Phelps Brown's law. As we already said, this law states that the share of labour in total income is roughly constant, at least in the medium–long-run period. Since the dynamics of this share can be written as

$$\hat{p} = \hat{w} - \hat{pr}, \tag{13}$$

where $^\wedge$ represents percentage rates of change, respectively, of prices (p), wages (w), and productivity (pr), it follows that wage dynamics must be compatible with this macro-relationship.

In a monetarist environment, the price dynamics would be fixed by the growth of money, while the productivity change would set the dynamics of real wages. The nominal wage dynamics would follow as a consequence. In the other paradigms, however, the conflicting claims by the workers and the entrepreneurs can be reconciled by means of different mechanisms within this macro-relationship. For instance, a high rate of growth of productivity can be compatible with increasing nominal and real wages as well as with price stability. On the other hand, the mechanisms of reconciliation can be different: inflation can be one of these. Another can be unemployment, where the 'reserve army' hypothesis of the classical authors can manifest itself.

It follows that wage dynamics can assume different patterns according to both the macro-conditions that hold and the particular mechanism of reconciliation of conflicting claims that depends on the historical period.

In the first historical period considered, it is the high rate of growth that allows a reconciliation between the various requests. It is worth stressing that the role of aggregate demand in that case is interlinked with the forces of supply. In fact, a sustained demand allows both the diffusion of economies of scale that favours productivity and the enlargement of industrial employment. Price stability is accompanied by increasing purchasing power for the workers, while the causal nexus between wages and unemployment proceeds primarily from the former to the latter, contrary to the 'reserve army' hypothesis of the classical authors.

In the conflict regime considered, the mechanisms of reconciliation are different; they are, respectively, inflation, unemployment, or both (see Sawyer 1995). In the case of reconciliation brought about by inflation, the equilibrium can be temporary because if the rate of inflation becomes particularly high a different monetary policy (i.e. a different regime) is bound to occur. As for as reconciliation through the rate of unemployment, the stability can last for a longer period because changes that can break the situation are more on the real sphere and require a longer period of time to take place.

Finally, in the last historical period considered, the weakness in the labour market and the presence of more competitive forces in the product market pass on to the consumer the gains in productivity. This does not necessarily imply that a zero-inflation era is dawning: that result depends also on world conditions, where the price of raw materials must be considered.

9. Concluding remarks

For a long time the literature has considered the Phillips curve as a dynamic version of the wage equation to be appended into the IS–LM model. In this context, the debate has been carried out in terms of money illusion to differentiate the Keynesian from the neoclassical paradigm.

In this article we have tried to stress two methodological points. First, we have shown that the Phillips curve is fundamentally a macro-relationship, and therefore it is compatible with different micro-behaviour. Its macro-shape depends on the working of the whole economy. It follows that it depends on the policy environment (as rightly stated by Lucas 1981) but not only the policy environment. It also depends on the set of rules, actors, and institutions that we call a 'regime', which disciplines the distribution of the results of the technical progress and how the full-employment problem is settled. The Phillips curve can be generated by different mechanisms and does not necessarily imply the presence of some form of money illusion. On the contrary, we have shown that it can be generated within a model of rational expectations.

In the second place, it is this system nature of the curve that justifies its change in time, according to the different regimes prevailing. In this perspective, the Keynesian period, the stagflation era, and the emergence of a new paradigm based upon a more flexible labour-market functioning have been examined for their common features as well as according to their specificities.

In this sense the argument of Tobin (1972) is still valid, according to whom wage dynamics is mainly an indeterminate topic. We have tried to show, however, how this indeterminacy can be understood as a result of institutional environments that are historically determined.

REFERENCES

Acemoglu, D. and A. Scott (1994) 'Asymmetries in the cyclical behavior of UK labour markets', *Economic Journal* 104: 1303–23.
Akerlof, G. A., W. T. Dickens, and G. L. Perry (1996) 'The macroeconomics of low inflation', *Brookings Papers on Economic Activity* 1: 1–76.
Blinder, A. S. (1997) 'Is there a core of practical macroeconomics that we should all believe?' *American Economic Review*, Papers and Proceedings 87: 240–7.
Clark, P. and D. Laxton (1997) 'Phillips curves, Phillips lines and the unemployment costs of overheating', Centre for Economic Performance, Discussion Paper 334, London School of Economics, London.

Davidson, P. (1994) *Post-Keynesian Macroeconomic Theory* (Aldershot: Edward Elgar).

Fazzari, S., P. Ferri, and E. Greenberg (1998) 'Aggregate demand and micro-behavior: a new perspective on Keynesian macroeconomics', *Journal of Post-Keynesian Economics* 20: 527–58.

Ferri, P. (1997) 'La curva di Phillips rivisitata', in AA. VV. *Mercato, Stato e Giustizia Sociale, Essays in Honour of Giancarlo Mazzocchi* (Milan: Giuffrè).

—— (1978): *I salari nell'Economia Post-Keynesiana* (Milan: EtasLibri).

—— and E. Greenberg (1992) *'Wages, Regime Switching and Cycles'* (New York: Springer-Verlag).

—— and H. P. Minsky (1992) 'Market processes and thwarting systems', *Structural Change and Economic Dynamics*, iii: 79–91.

Flaschel, P., R. Franke, and W. Semmler (1997) *Dynamic Macroeconomics* (Cambridge, Mass.: MIT Press).

Friedman, M. (1966) 'Comments', in G. P. Shultz and R. Z. Aliber (eds.), *Guidelines, Informal Controls and the Market Place* (Chicago: Chicago University Press).

—— (1968) 'The role of monetary policy', *American Economic Review* 58: 1–17.

—— (1975) 'Unemployment versus Inflation? An evaluation of the Phillips curve', Occasional Paper 44, Institute of Economic Affairs, London.

Granger, C. W. J. and T. Terasvirta (1993) *Modelling Non-linear Economic Relationships* (Oxford: Oxford University Press).

Hahn, F. and R. Solow (1995) *A Critical Essay on Modern Macroeconomic Theory* (Cambridge, Mass.: MIT Press).

Hicks, J. R. (1974) *The Crisis in Keynesian Economics* (Oxford: Blackwell).

Layard, R., S. Nickell, and R. Jackman (1991): *Unemployment* (Oxford: Oxford University Press).

Leijonhufvud, A. (1981) *Information and Coordination* (Oxford: Oxford University Press).

Lucas R. E. Jun. (1981) *Studies in Business-Cycle Theory* (Cambridge, Mass.: MIT Press).

Keynes, J. M. (1936) *The General Theory of Employment, Interest and Money* (London: Macmillan).

Maital, S. and I. Lipnowski (eds.) (1985) *Macroeconomic Conflict and Social Institutions* (Cambridge, Mass.: Ballinger Publishing Co.).

McCallum, B. T. (1989) *Monetary Economics* (New York: Macmillan).

Minsky, H. P. (1975) *John Maynard Keynes* (New York: Columbia University Press).

Nickell, S. J. (1988) 'Wages and economic activity' in W. Eltis and P. Sinclair (eds.), *Keynes and Economic Policy: The Relevance of the General Theory after Fifty Years* (London: Macmillan): 65–75.

Phelps, E. S. (1967) 'Phillips curves, expectations of inflation, and optimal unemployment over time', *Economica* 34: 254–81.

—— (1994) *Structural Slumps* (Cambridge, Mass.: Cambridge University Press).

—— et al. (eds.) (1973): *The Microeconomic Foundations of Employment and Inflation Theory* (New York: Norton).

Phillips, A. W. (1958) 'The relation between unemployment and the rate of change of money wage rates in the United Kingdom, 1861–1957', *Economica* 25: 283–300.

Ramsey, J. B. (1996) 'On the existence of macro variables and of macro relationships', *Journal of Economic Behavior and Organization* 30: 275–299.

Robinson, J. (1971) *Economic Heresies* (London: Macmillan).

Rogerson, R. (1997) 'Theory ahead of language in the economics of unemployment', *Journal of Economic Perspectives*, 11: 73–92.

Rowthorn, R. E. (1977) 'Conflict, inflation and money', *Cambridge Journal of Economics* 1: 215–39.

Samuelson, P. and R. M. Solow (1960) 'Analytical aspects of anti-inflation policy', *American Economic Review*, Papers and Proceedings, 50: 177–94.

Sargan, J. (1964): 'Wages and prices in the United Kingdom', in Hart *et al.* (eds.), *Econometric Analysis for National Economic Planning* (Butterworths: Colston Research Society): 25–54.

Sargent, T. J. (1987) *Macroeconomic Theory* (San Diego: Academic Press).

——(1993) *Bounded Rationality in Macroeconomics* (Oxford: Clarendon Press).

Sawyer, M. C. (1995) *Unemployment, Imperfect Competition and Macroeconomics* (Aldershot: Edward Elgar).

Tobin, J. (1972) 'Inflation and unemployment', *American Economic Review*, 62: 1–18.

——(1975) 'Keynesian models of recession and depression', *American Economic Review* 65: 195–202.

Tong, H. (1990) *Non-linear Time Series* (Oxford: Clarendon Press).

6 What can recent labour research teach us about macroeconomics?

ANDREW J. OSWALD AND PHILIP A. TROSTEL

1. Introduction

Perhaps more than any other sub-discipline, research in labour economics is empirical. The content of the most recent issue of the *Journal of Labor Economics* (*JOLE*) is indicative.[1] This issue has eight papers. Only one of these contains no empirical evidence. The other seven articles are primarily empirical: they employ data and report various kinds of regression equations. All seven use micro-data, that is, information on individual units like randomly sampled workers. Only one uses non-US data. Before presenting their empirical work, most of the papers construct a theoretical model that would be too technical to be understood by most graduating economics majors. This issue of *JOLE* is representative of modern labour economics.[2] It is dominated by empirical reasoning and US-based evidence, but is not devoid of theory.

Some economists, such as Krugman (1998), think that labour economics is setting a trend that the rest of the profession will follow. Krugman notes that two recent Bates Clark Medal winners (biannual award to the top young US economist) have been empirical labour economists, David Card and Kevin Murphy. This, the argument goes, signals that economics is moving away from rewarding 'home-run hitting the-oretical work' to rewarding 'careful, data-intensive research'. Krugman argues that research in the style done in labour economics will come to dominate the profession. Some support for this conjecture is borne out by, for example, the recent appointment of noted empirical economists, James Poterba and Roger Gordon, to the editorship of the *Journal of Public Economics*, the leading field journal in public economics (a field not traditionally known for its empirical nature).

Although emphasis on evidence may be increasing in the profession, that does not necessarily imply that empirical findings are having a greater influence on formal or informal thinking about the economy. Indeed, in the following selective survey, we highlight some empirical findings about labour markets that seem to be relevant for

We are grateful to Russell Cooper, Martin Eichenbaum, Jonathan Gardner, Gaelle Pierre, and Ed Prescott for helpful discussions.

[1] The *JOLE* is the leading field journal in labour economics and is influential within the profession generally. On the basis of impact-adjusted citations, it is ranked slightly above publications like the *Review of Economics and Statistics*, *Economic Journal*, and *International Economic Review*.

[2] Angrist and Krueger (1998) recently categorized articles in eight leading journals from 1994 to mid-1997 and found that 79 per cent of the articles in labour economics examined empirical evidence, compared to 50 per cent in non-labour fields; 83 per cent of the empirical articles in labour economics examined micro-data, compared to 27 per cent in other fields.

macroeconomic theory, but, as yet, do not seem to have had much influence. This, however, is not meant as a general indictment of the lack of interaction between empirical evidence and macroeconomic theory. We simply note areas where more interaction between labour evidence and macrotheory appears worthwhile.

There is always going to be some gestation lag between the production of evidence and its impact on theory, particularly when boundaries between sub-disciplines are being crossed. Indeed, as some empirical findings do not hold up over time, it is rational to wait until the amount of evidence is considerable before changing para-digms. But we suspect that there is some truth in the saying 'human beings never change their minds; they simply die, and that is how new ideas take over.'

Perhaps surprisingly, few labour economists currently give a lot of thought to testing theories at a high level. Most see their job more as measuring the sizes of parameters. Determining how much training raises wages, for instance, is viewed by most labour economists, rightly or wrongly, as a question for which one needs good data and a powerful methodological approach rather than a detailed theory. In this sense, many modern labour economists fit Keynes's vision that one day economists would be practical and useful in the way that, he thought, plumbers are practical and useful. Indeed, some labour economists are suspicious of purely theoretical work. Perhaps for this reason, labour economics is also a branch of economics where the inductive method is used more than in most of economics. It is relatively easy to publish measurement without theory. As in a great deal of science, there is labour research that assumes a theoretical framework is true and then makes empirical cal-culations based on that presumption. Some labour economists are even beginning to wonder if the swing from theory has gone too far (Hamermesh 1999). But generally, aside from the occasional anti-theory banter, in labour economics it is hard to discern any obvious methodological conflict between theorists and empiricists. The great bulk of labour research has an empirical flavour, but few labour economists would argue that the field can do without theoretical models.

Labour economists have not, however, been entirely successful in their practical and useful endeavours to measure and publicize the sizes of parameters. For example, hundreds of studies have estimated the rate of return to education, yet there is still debate about its value (see e.g. Psacharopoulus 1994 and Card 1995). Even in the case of the USA, where the quantity and quality of analyses is generally the highest, we cannot safely rule out a rate of return which is more than 10 per cent (per year of schooling) or less than 5 per cent. Moreover, there is some disagreement among labour specialists about the robustness of findings.[3] Thus, it may not be all that surprising that economic theorizing often seems to be ignorant of empirical evidence.

Despite the current limitations in trying to establish empirical regularities, we believe that recent empirical studies about labour markets can teach us about the

---

[3] e.g., the evidence on the output-constant wage elasticity of labour demand is about as robust as it gets. After surveying the evidence, Hamermesh (1993) concluded that it was about −0.3. Fuchs *et al.* (1998) surveyed sixty-five labour economists at forty leading research universities in the USA about the size of this and other parameters. The mean and median answers were very close to Hamermesh's figure, but the standard deviation of the answers was 0.39!

economy. Given that roughly three-fourths of net national income is determined in labour markets, empirical evidence about labour markets should be relevant for macroeconomic theory. This survey of recent findings about labour markets is selective. The focus is on results about two related themes—unemployment and imperfect competition in labour markets.

1.1. Six empirical regularities in labour-market data

Involuntary unemployment. Microeconometric and psychological research suggests that the unemployed have much lower levels of life satisfaction, happiness, and mental health than those in work. This result holds in cross-sections and panels, and in all countries so far studied. It is consistent with the idea that unemployment is involuntary (i.e. unemployment in the Keynesian tradition as opposed to the neoclassical view).

Rent sharing. The data show a positive microeconomic link between profitability and pay. This result, which conjures up images of bargaining, suggests that the law of one price fails and that labour markets are not perfectly competitive.

Wages and unemployment. The data indicate a robust negative link between wages and the unemployment rate in the local area. This downward-sloping 'wage-curve' appears to be inconsistent with the perfect-competition model of labour markets. Simple Phillips-curve models also fail to predict a negative relation between the rate of pay and the amount of joblessness. The curve is consistent with imperfectly competitive theories such as the efficiency-wage model. Shapiro and Stiglz (1984), for instance, predict such a curve.

Minimum wages and unemployment. Recent research by Card and Krueger (1995) and others suggests that, at existing levels in the USA, minimum wages do not raise unemployment rates. This evidence is also contrary to the prediction in the standard competitive model of labour markets. The data suggest that firms, even those hiring in seemingly competitive labour markets, may have some monopsony control over wage rates.

Education and unemployment. Numerous studies have documented a negative correlation between education attainment and unemployment. This (and other) evidence seems to suggest that labour markets may be characterized by firm-specific investments and long-term implicit contracts, as opposed to the standard spot-market model of labour markets.

Home ownership and unemployment. There is a positive correlation, across countries, between the extent of home ownership and the unemployment rate. One possible explanation is that lack of private renting in the housing market induces low labour mobility, so that large amounts of home ownership tend to ossify a labour market.

Using the terminology of Angrist and Krueger (1999), some of the empirical findings reviewed here might be classified under the category of 'descriptive analysis', whereas modern empirical research in labour economics is more typically of the 'casual inference' variety. This choice reflects our view that, at the current stage of development of data resources and econometric methods, the marginal value product of descriptive research is high. Regardless of exact theoretical interpretation, patterns and trends in the data help to shape academic and non-academic economic thought.

2. Unhappiness and unemployment

The unemployment rate in OECD countries is now more than 10 per cent. In nations like Spain, it is closer to 20 per cent. Many politicians and journalists, for theoretical rather than empirical reasons, think that this is something to do with high unemployment benefits: 'Unemployment is higher in Europe than America because Europe's labour markets are riddled with rigidities . . . and generous unemployment benefits' (*The Economist*, 11 Oct. 1997).

Blaming high unemployment rates on high unemployment benefits suggests that large numbers of individuals are, in some sense, contentedly choosing to be unemployed. If this is the case, the State might wish to reduce the attractiveness of being without work. But if this is not the case, the State may have to look elsewhere for ways to tackle unemployment, such as perhaps methods to raise the number of jobs and to get people into work directly.

As this seems a necessary starting question for the analysis of unemployment policy (as well as being a methodological difference between schools of macroeconomic thought), it might be thought that economics journals would be full of studies that attempt to evaluate the voluntariness of unemployment. Clark and Oswald (1994), however, point out that such studies are few. In principle, there are extensive survey data available to shed light on this issue. But economists have traditionally been hostile to these data—for two reasons. Economists tend to be suspicious of subjective survey data. And economists are even more suspicious of the idea that subjective well-being, i.e. utility, can be measured. A different attitude is found among psychologists (who, paradoxically, might be thought better qualified than economists to judge such things). Thousands of papers in the psychology literature are concerned with the statistical analysis of subjective well-being information.

Taking their lead from the psychologists, Clark and Oswald try to test for the voluntariness of unemployment using data on reported well-being. The test is to see if unemployed people are relatively unhappy. It is based on the underlying idea that people do not voluntarily choose misery. But unemployment appears to be associated with a great deal of unhappiness (after controlling for other personal circumstances and characteristics), and therefore does not look voluntary.

Clark and Oswald use data from the first sweep of the new British Household Panel Study, which provides information on a random sample of approximately 6,000 Britons in the labour force in 1991. Among other things, it contains mental well-being scores from a form of psychiatric evaluation known as the General Health Questionnaire (GHQ). In its simplest form this assessment asks the following set of questions.

Have you recently

1. been able to concentrate on whatever you are doing?*
2. lost much sleep over worry?

3. felt that you are playing a useful part in things?*
4. felt capable of making decisions about things?*
5. felt constantly under strain?
6. felt you couldn't overcome your difficulties?
7. been able to enjoy your normal day-to-day activities?*
8. been able to face up to your problems?*
9. been feeling unhappy and depressed?
10. been losing confidence in yourself?
11. been thinking of yourself as a worthless person?
12. been feeling reasonably happy all things considered?*

The answers to these questions are coded on a four-point scale running from 'disagree strongly' to 'agree strongly'. Starred items are coded in reverse (thus a zero then corresponds to 'agree strongly'). These twelve answers are combined into a total GHQ level of mental distress in which high numbers correspond to low feelings of well-being. The data provide a mental stress or, less accurately, 'unhappiness' level for each individual in the sample.

There are various ways to work with GHQ responses. Clark and Oswald calculate so-called 'caseness scores'. These are the number of answers in the fairly stressed or highly stressed categories. With this method, the lowest measure of well-being corresponds to a caseness level of 12 (the individual felt stressed on all twelve questions). Individuals with high caseness levels are viewed by psychologists as people who would benefit from psychiatric treatment. We interpret these caseness levels as measures of mental distress.

The data in Table 6.1 seem to reveal evidence of involuntary unemployment. The unemployed show high levels of mental distress. The mean level of distress is 2.98 for the jobless and 1.45 for the employed (both measured on a scale from 0 to 12). The 522 jobless people in the sample had approximately twice the mean mental distress score of the 4,893 individuals with jobs. This difference between the employed and unemployed is statistically significant with a t-statistic of over 10.

To understand the size of this effect, which is large, it is necessary to have some feel for the distribution of the 6,000 scores. More than half of the sample report a mental-distress score of zero. Just under 1,000 individuals have a distress level of 1, and

TABLE 6.1. *'Unhappiness' of Britons in the labour force in 1991*

Labour market status	Number	Mean mental distress
Unemployed	522	2.98
Employee	4,893	1.45
Self-employed	736	1.54

Note: Mental distress is the GHS score, a standard psychological measure. It is measured on a scale from 0 to 12. Calculating its mean imposes an implicit assumption of cardinality.

Source: Clark and Oswald (1994).

roughly 500 have a distress level of 2. The great majority of Britons, therefore, show low degrees of GHQ distress. Moving through the remaining scores from 3 to 12, the numbers of individuals become gradually smaller. Thus the mean difference of approximately $1\frac{1}{2}$ points means that the unemployed appear to be substantially more distressed than the employed. Joblessness is apparently extremely unpleasant. Its effect on mental well-being exceeds everything else in the data except major illness. As Clark and Oswald note, the effect of unemployment is larger than the effect of divorce, for example.

The raw data also show (not reported) that mental distress is found disproportionately among women, those in their thirties, and those with high levels of education. For each subgroup, unemployed individuals report much lower well-being. A cross-tabulation by education is an interesting illustration, and is given in Table 6.2. This table shows that distress from joblessness is, at 3.44, the greatest for those who are highly educated. Although we are not sure why this is, the result fits the presumption that, because of the higher forgone wage, the cost of unemployment is larger for the highly educated.

The basic patterns found in the data are confirmed when more formal multivariate techniques are employed. Clark and Oswald report ordered-probit equations. The size of the unemployment coefficient continues to be large. It is economically, and not merely statistically, significant.

Within the last few years there has been an outpouring of work looking at psychological measures of well-being. Many countries are studied. Di Tella *et al.* (1997), for example, estimate life-satisfaction equations for a dozen European countries and the USA. Table 6.3, based on US data, is indicative of one finding. They also show that, controlling for country fixed effects, unemployment movements significantly lower people's reported well-being scores. This effect holds in a country panel over and above the microeconomic correlation between simply being unemployed and low well-being. When the unemployment rate in a country rises, the life-satisfaction levels

TABLE 6.2. *Disaggregating 'unhappiness' by educational attainment*

Education	Number	Mental distress
High (HNC up to degree)		
In work	1,612	1.48
Unemployed	86	3.44
Medium (GCSE up to A level)		
In work	2,157	1.43
Unemployed	161	3.15
Low (less or no qualifications)		
In work	1,848	1.43
Unemployed	273	2.70

Note: Mental distress is the GHS score, a standard psychological measure. It is measured on a scale from 0 to 12. Calculating its mean imposes an implicit assumption of cardinality.

Source: Clark and Oswald (1994).

TABLE 6.3. *Patterns in reported happiness of 26,668 Americans, 1972–94*

	All individuals %	Unemployed individuals %
Not too happy	11.7	29.6
Pretty happy	55.6	52.7
Very happy	32.7	17.7

Source: Di Tella, MacCulloch, and Oswald 1997.

of employees fall. This suggests that the fear of unemployment affects people who are in work. Blanchflower and Freeman (1994) study well-being in a range of Western and transition nations, and also discover that unemployment is the most important economic correlate. Whelan (1992) finds in Irish data that unemployment is correlated with poor mental-health levels and high 'financial strain' scores. Gerlach and Stephan (1996) and Winkelmann and Winkelmann (1998) find in German panel data that falling into unemployment produces a large drop in life satisfaction, and that this drop is much greater than can be explained by the decline in income. This is important, because panel evidence is intrinsically preferable to cross-section results. In Sweden, new work by Korpi (1997) suggests a strong link of the sort just discussed for other countries.

A puzzle to emerge from this is why the market itself does not provide more insurance against the apparently bad event of being jobless. In the USA, what private unemployment insurance exists is sporadic (Oswald 1986). This missing market seems an avenue worth exploration.

Obviously the involuntariness of unemployment is not the only possible explanation of the above empirical findings. In cross-section analyses by social scientists, lines of causality are often open to debate. The same is true in this case. If the unemployed appear to be less happy and to have poorer mental health than those in jobs, it could be that this is because such people are inherently less desirable as employees. In other words, psychological status might be the cause, rather than the effect, of joblessness. However, there is a great deal of longitudinal evidence, collected by psychologists for smaller samples, that sheds doubt on such an interpretation. A summary of small psychological field experiments is provided by Warr, Jackson, and Banks (1988).

It is also possible that the empirical correlation between unemployment and subjective well-being is simply due to *ex post* bad luck. That is, if unemployment is often the result of adverse shocks, then that may be the real cause of unhappiness rather than the involuntariness of unemployment. In other words, bad things happen and people are going to be unhappy about it until job search eventually offsets (perhaps only partially) the bad event.[4] There is obviously something to this sort of explanation. But there are two difficulties. First, it is not clear why the wage rate does not adjust immediately to clear the market. Second, we would be surprised if it could account for the extent of the observed correlation. If people are reasonably far-sighted, it seems

---

[4] This seems to be the view expressed to us in correspondence with Martin Eichenbaum.

unlikely adverse shocks should increase mental distress so dramatically. As usual, more research is needed to explore this issue.

3. Rent-sharing

The long-standing debate between competitive and non-competitive theories of wage determination (sometimes referred to, perhaps not accurately, as the Harvard-versus-Chicago debate) has recently been revived. Sumner Slichter (1950) first pointed out that similar people appear to be paid dramatically different amounts, and that the wage premia are highest in highly profitable industries. This evidence, he suggested, is consistent with non-competitive rent-sharing theories. Dickens and Katz (1987) and Krueger and Summers (1987, 1988) found that Slichter's patterns exist in modern data. These studies have revived the old debate and have sparked a great deal of recent research.

The recent work on rent-sharing draws upon information unavailable to those in the original debate, namely microeconomic and especially longitudinal data on contracts, establishments, firms, and people. The new papers estimate versions of the simple wage equation:

$$w = \bar{w} + \phi \pi / n,$$

where, the employer's equilibrium wage, w, is shaped by a mixture of outside wage opportunities, $\bar{w}$, and profit-per-employee, π/n (where ϕ is the relative bargaining power of workers). It is straightforward to derive this equation from a bargaining model. Contrary to the prediction of the competitive wage-taking model, the new empirical studies find that profit-per-employee matters in wage determination. The studies have largely been produced in unknowing isolation from one another; they have only recently begun to appear in journals. These papers cover various countries and settings. Yet, intriguingly, the studies paint a consistent picture. Profits of the employer affect the pay of its employees. The new literature is summarized in Table 6.4.[5] Moreover, profits affect pay in non-unionized as well as unionized settings. This is also true at the macrolevel. If a picture speaks a thousand words, then Figure 6.1 may be enlightening. This figure, from Brosius (1998) using quarterly macro-data in the UK from 1970 through 1997, illustrates just how closely the detrended wages track (lagged) detrended profits per employee. While other interpretations are certainly possible, perhaps there are empirical grounds to apply bargaining models in more widespread circumstances than has been presumed.

It is sometimes claimed by European labour economists that the labour market is 'obviously' non-competitive. This is more easily said than proved. Perhaps for this reason, such claims have left comparatively little impression. What seems to make the

---

[5] Nickell and Wadhwani (1990) fail to find an effect from profits in their wage equations. They do, however, obtain a positive effect from the closely related sales-per-employee.

TABLE 6.4. *Recent microeconometric tests for profits (or quasi-rents) in a wage equation*

Study	Dep Var	Data on	No.	FE	$\hat{\beta}$ (%)
Blanchflower et al. (1990)	Weekly earnings	UK establishments	1,100	No	15
Denny and Machin (1991)	Average pay	UK firms	2,000	Yes	4
Christofides and Oswald (1992)	Contract wage	Canadian union contracts	600	Yes	6
Currie and McConell (1992)	Average pay	US union contracts	1,300	Yes	
Abowd and Lemieux (1993)	Contract wage	Canadian union contracts	1,100	Yes	90*
Hildreth and Oswald (1997)	Average pay	UK firms and establishments	3,700	Yes	16
Teal (1996)	Weekly earnings	Ghanaian establishments	700	No	100*
Van Reenen (1996)	Average pay	UK firms	2,600	Yes	120*
Blanchflower et al. (1996)	Hourly earnings	US industry profits/worker	400	Yes	24
Estevao and Tevlin (1994)	Annual earnings	US 4-digit industries	1,700	Yes	70*
Nickell and Nicolitsas (1994)	Average pay	UK firms	200	Yes	25
Smith (1996)	Basic wage	UK bargaining units	400	Yes	4

Notes: No. is the approximate sample size. FE refers to fixed effects included in the regression.

$\hat{\beta}$ is the coefficient estimate on profit or quasi-rent variables in microeconometric wage equations. These estimates are expressed here as the approximate percentage rise in wages induced by a move up the profit or quasi-rent distribution of four standard deviations. It can be thought of as the estimated spread of pay that is produced by rent-sharing. Hence 15 means a spread of 15%, and so on.

* The profit (quasi-rent) variable is instrumented by something other than lagged values of independent variables.

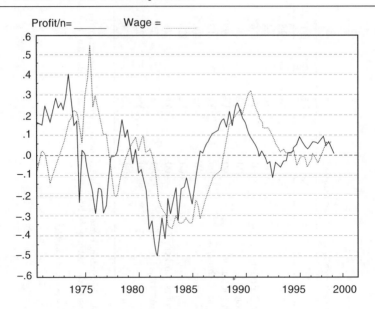

FIG. 6.1. *Time-series of real earnings and profits per employee in UK*

Note: Profit/n (log of real profits per employee) and wage (log of real earnings) are derived after regressing on a constant and a trend

Source: Brosius (1998)

new literature more persuasive is the quality of its underlying data and methods. While no single study is free of flaws, weaknesses in one appear to be covered by strengths in another. Especially dramatic findings are produced when researchers correct for endogeneity with a sensible economic variable. For example, Abowd and Lemieux (1993) use import and export prices to instrument profitability; Van Reenen (1996) uses firms' earlier technical innovations; Teal (1996) uses firms' financial and banking characteristics; and Estevao and Tevlin (1994) use output movements in up-stream sectors. On the face of it, this kind of work is a substantive methodological contribution to applied economics. However, at the time of writing, there is a difficulty with this group of papers. Their estimated rent-sharing effects are too large to be believable.

If the impact of profits on pay were statistically significant but small, the material summarized here would be of intellectual interest but not of great practical import. The competitive model would probably be close enough to the truth to be sufficient. This is not, however, what emerges from Table 6.4. Indeed, some results imply that the majority of wage dispersion is due to rent-sharing. Even if such remarkable conclusions do not survive future scrutiny (our instincts are that they will not), they hint at the importance of this research, and at likely controversy ahead. The latest step in rent-sharing work is new research on matched-panels by economists such as John Abowd at Cornell, Francis Kramarz at Paris, Andrew Hildreth at Berkeley, and Jonathan Gardner at Warwick.

4. Wages and unemployment

The new macroeconomics textbook by Blanchard (1997) draws many diagrams in which the key role is played by a negatively sloped curve linking the level of wage to the level of unemployment. He does this without appealing to any proof, but there now exists much evidence. This new microeconometric evidence has also started to raise doubts about the idea in the large time-series literature that the extent of pay flexibility is very different across nations (Layard *et al.* 1991).

If only a short run of aggregate data is available, it is extremely difficult to disentangle the true responsiveness of pay to unemployment in a world where many aggregate variables move together. An approach with more statistical power is to exploit a mixture of cross-section and longitudinal data. This makes it natural to study, say, regions through time. Microeconomic data drawn from internationally comparable random samples provide economists with a rich resource for testing hypotheses. In this spirit, Blanchflower and Oswald (1994) use random samples of individuals from twelve nations to document the existence of an empirical regularity or economic 'law' between wage rates and the local unemployment rate, which they term the wage curve.

The samples by Blanchflower and Oswald have statistical information on about three and a half million people. Pooled regressions for each of the countries are estimated using wages or earnings as the dependent variable and a local unemployment rate as one of the regressors. In most instances, this local rate is the degree of joblessness within the geographical area where the individual works. In a few cases, such as the USA and Korea, data are also available for the industry rate of unemployment. Other control variables included in the earnings equations are conventional: age, gender, education, and so forth. Unemployment is usually entered as a logarithm in the wage equations, so that, because the dependent variable is also in logs, its coefficient can be read off as an elasticity. The unemployment elasticity of pay is the obvious name to describe this number.

This elasticity is found to be negative and close to one-tenth.[6] This implies that a doubling of unemployment in a region or industry is associated with a fall of 10 percentage points in the level of pay in that region or industry. The nature of this relationship, or wage curve, is almost identical across countries. It is also present, within nations, across different periods of time. A representative table of international unemployment elasticities derived from Blanchflower and Oswald is given in Table 6.5.

Britain, Canada, and the USA produce rather similar results. The estimates of the unemployment elasticity of pay lie in a range from −0.08 to −0.11 in almost all specifications. For the US data it is important to control for regional fixed effects, that is, to include a set of region dummies or to difference the data. Once this is done, Hall's (1970, 1972) positive spatial correlation between pay and joblessness becomes strongly negative. The twelve coefficients summarized in Table 6.5 are negative and in most

---

[6] For Britain, discussion of this kind of number goes back to time-series work such as Layard and Nickell (1986).

TABLE 6.5. *International wage curves*

Country	Period	Sample size	Fixed efffects	Unemployment elasticity of pay	statistics
United States	1963–90	1,730,175	Yes	−0.10	up to 25
Britain	1973–90	175,500	Yes	−0.08	6.23
Canada	1972–87	82,739	Yes	−0.09	6.10
South Korea	1971–86	1,359,387	Yes	−0.04*	25.70
Austria	1986,89	1,587	Some	−0.09	1.59
Italy	1986–89	1,041	Yes	−0.10	0.63
Holland	1988–91	1,867	Some	−0.17	2.35
Switzerland	1987	645	No	−0.12	3.60
Norway	1989–91	2,599	Some	−0.08	2.19
Eire	1988–91	1,363	No	−0.36	1.92
Australia	1986	8,429	No	−0.19	5.80
Germany	1986–91	4,629	Yes	−0.13	1.75

Notes: The dependent variable is the logarithm of pay. The independent variable is the logarithm of the area unemployment rate (at various levels of disaggregation), except in the case denoted by *, where unemployment is measured at the industry level. In all equations, personal variables (gender, race, age, schooling, etc.) are included as controls.

Fixed effects refers to the inclusion of dummy variables for regions or industries in the regressions. A few countries' unemployment coefficients weaken when full regional dummies are added. The Eire results are unstable.

Source: Blanchflower and Oswald (1994).

cases well defined. For some nations there are few years of data across which to pool, and it is then to be expected that the inclusion of regional dummies will lead to low *t*-statistics. Eire is the analysis's only real outlier. Its coefficient is unstable and should be treated sceptically.[7] Korea, for which an industry wage curve alone can be estimated, has a low unemployment elasticity of −0.04. Future research, no doubt, will aim to chart divergences from the minus-point-one rule.

The same kind of wage curve has been shown for additional countries. Montgomery (1993) obtains an unemployment elasticity of pay for Japan of between −0.10 and −0.15. As this is close to the estimates just described for other countries, he finds little sign, contrary to the popular preconception, that Japan's labour market is unusually flexible. Although not well known, Rebick's (1990) Japanese results are similar. Edin and Holmlund (1989), Holmlund and Skedinger (1993), and Edin, Holmlund, and Ostros (1993) estimate a small but well-determined negative coefficient for regional unemployment in Sweden. Card (1990*a,b*) and Christofides and Oswald (1992) obtain an elasticity close to −0.1 in Canada. Hoddinott (1996) produces an estimate of −0.13 for Cote d'Ivoire. This case is doubly interesting. It is one of the first estimates of the local unemployment elasticity of pay for a developing country, and it is similar to those in the industrialized West. Bhalotra (1993) finds a negative effect for India. Although the coefficient is not always well determined, once regional dummies are included the

[7] In the case of Eire it proved impossible to even get a reliable-looking Mincer wage equation, so, regardless of wage curve estimation, there is something strange about the Irish data.

estimated elasticity at the mean is, somewhat remarkably, again −0.13. Kingdon and Knight (1998) find a well-defined wage curve in newly collected South African data. This country is interesting because it has an unemployment rate of approximately 30 per cent. Kingdon and Knight have micro-data on 6,500 randomly sampled workers placed in one of up to 300 different local areas within South Africa. They obtain, for a large range of sub-samples and different estimation methods, an unemployment elasticity of between −0.07 and −0.12.

This evidence suggests that the degree of wage flexibility may be more similar across countries than has been believed. If this is indeed the case, European politicians and journalists have been focusing too much on this policy area.

To economists raised on the Harris and Todaro (1970) and Hall (1970, 1972) models, the results described in this new literature are probably a surprise. Those models predict that, to satisfy the spatial-equilibrium requirement that all regions provide the same expected utility, high-unemployment areas will also be high-wage regions. In other words, the wage locus should slope up. This hypothesis is rejected by the international microeconomic data. The early empirical literature, stemming from Hall (1970), failed to control for regional fixed effects. This does not mean that the idea of compensating differentials is wrong or irrelevant. Movements in actual wages can be negatively correlated with actual unemployment while at the same time 'permanent' unemployment, put loosely, is positively related to 'permanent' wages.

Three potential criticisms of the wage-curve literature are taken up in the Blanchflower and Oswald monograph. First, a check is made on the hypothesis that, because unemployment depends upon pay (perhaps through the functioning of a downward-sloping labour-demand curve), OLS estimation of the wage curve is subject to simultaneity bias. Attractive though such thinking is theoretically, little support for it could be found empirically. In US data, instrumenting regional unemployment by weather variables, military spending, industry mix, or lagged unemployment produces estimates of the unemployment elasticity of pay that are only fractionally higher than those from OLS methods. Although, as usual in applied economics, we could always hope for better instruments, unemployment apparently has the characteristics of a predetermined variable. Second, it is shown that, for Britain and the USA, it is necessary to correct the standard errors for bias caused, in estimation where the independent variable is more highly aggregated than the dependent variable, by common group effects. The nature of the difficulty, which until recently was routinely ignored in empirical research, is explained in sources such as Moulton (1986). When a correction is done, the substantive findings remain unchanged. Third, for only one country are regional price indices available, but theory suggests that it is real wages that are depressed by local unemployment. Although undesirable, there are reasons to think that this problem is not too serious. Controlling for regional prices in the British case leaves the wage curve intact. Nominal wages are likely to be sufficient whenever year dummies and regional dummies can be, as for most countries studied, included in the regression equations. The evidence for an industry wage curve is presumably immune to the criticism. Finally, if prices depend on wages and a constant, they can be substituted out to leave a nominal reduced-form wage equation.

A simple logarithmic function of unemployment seems to do a reasonable job of capturing the patterns in the data.[8] For example, experiments using British data do not find statistically significant effects from either long-term unemployment or non-linear unemployment terms. More research will be needed, however, before definite conclusions can be drawn. Pierre (1998) finds some evidence for a long-term unemployment variable in a wage equation.

One feature of the wage–curve work has attracted particular attention and criticism. This is the Blanchflower–Oswald finding that the degree of autoregression in region panel wage equations is low. In other words, traditional estimation of the Phillips curve may be open to doubt. Blanchard and Katz (1997) have challenged this by using a slightly different data source. They replicate the Blanchflower–Oswald results on the March CPS, but not on the Outgoing Rotation Group Files. The Blanchard–Katz results have the unusual feature that they imply a huge unemployment elasticity of pay in long-run equilibrium. In other words, in the steady state implied by the authors' equations, the effect on the wage level of a rise in unemployment is much more negative than in the Blanchflower–Oswald work.

The existence of the wage curve seems to cast doubt on the relevance of the text-book competitive model of the labour market. It is difficult to see how the wage curve can be compatible within the simple standard framework. Nor can it be explained in a simple Phillips-curve framework. In contrast, the observed curve is consistent with predictions in bargainng and efficiency-wage models. Before getting swept away by this fact, however, it is as well to bear in mind that the test is not a sharp one. These models predict a downward-sloping locus in wage–unemployment space, and there appears to be one. But there may be other explanations for the pattern.

At this point in time, however, the wage curve seems to help provide the missing empirical foundation for a new class of non-competitive macroeconomic models (the missing flat quasi-supply curve discussed by Woodford 1992). Over the last few years, a small tide of new macroeconomics papers has swelled to become a movement to be taken seriously. Rowthorn (1977), David Soskice's unpublished Oxford lectures in the 1970s, Shapiro and Stiglitz (1984), Layard and Nickell (1986), Akerlof and Yellen (1990), Carlin and Soskice (1990), Layard *et al.* (1991), Lindbeck (1993), and Phelps (1990, 1992, 1993, 1994) have constructed macroeconomic models in which an aggregate wage curve not only appears but plays the principal role that marks the approach as different from convention. Hoon and Phelps (1992: 889) call it a new paradigm in the economics of booms and slumps: the 'hallmark of this theoretical approach is a labour market that exhibits involuntary unemployment.' Lindbeck (1993) lucidly chronicles a similar framework. The crucial constituent in these ana-lyses, which are longer on theoretical ideas than on empirical proof, is what Phelps (1992) describes as a quasi-labour supply curve or equilibrium wage locus. In Europe, perhaps because persistent high unemployment has seemingly become part of the wallpaper, this way of thinking is better developed than in the USA. Layard and

---

[8] Early discussions of some of these issues can be found in Nickell (1987), Carruth and Oswald (1989), and Blackaby, Bladen-Hovell, and Symons (1991).

Nickell's (1986) paper brings aggregate data, as well as new theory, to bear on the problem. But aggregate evidence is less convincing than the more modern micro-econometric findings.

The bottom line is that there is evidence consistent with the locus drawn in new texts such as Blanchard (1997), or the efficiency-wage no-shirking locus of papers such as Shapiro and Stiglitz (1984).

5. Minimum wages and unemployment

Countless textbooks have used minimum-wage laws as an example of a price floor. As Brown (1988: 134) puts it, 'an introductory textbook without a discussion of minimum wage laws might not be like a day without sunshine, but it would certainly rank with a morning without caffeine.' The standard textbook analysis is in the context of supply and demand curves. Thus, minimum wages are predicted to increase unemployment, particularly among the least skilled, such as teenagers. Relatively high-unemployment rates among teenagers is often cited as evidence of this effect, although there are obviously other contributing factors.

Such was the conventional wisdom about minimum-wage laws until the recent book by Card and Krueger (1995). In the words of Card and Krueger, their 'research provides fairly compelling evidence that minimum-wage increases have no systematic effect on employment. Indeed, some of the research . . . suggests that a rise in the minimum wage may actually increase employment. . . . This conclusion poses a stark challenge to the standard textbook model of the minimum wage (1995: 13–14)'.

Actually, Card and Krueger's evidence is not greatly different from the previous evidence on the employment effect of the minimum wage. In a well-known survey of the earlier evidence, Brown *et al.* (1982: 508) conclude that their 'survey indicates a reduction of between 1 and 3 per cent in teenage employment as a result of a 10 per cent increase in the federal minimum wage. We regard the lower part of this range as the most plausible.' Moreover, the coefficient estimates of the effect of the minimum wage on employment in many of the studies in their review are not statistically greater than zero. In addition, minimum wages were found to have an even smaller effect on young adults than on teenagers, and a smaller effect on the teenage unemployment rate than on the teenage employment rate. If Brown (1988) had concluded that the minimum wage is 'overrated', then Card and Krueger results simply show that it is really overrated.

There are two features of Card and Krueger's work, however, which make it particularly interesting. First, they exploit 'quasi-experimental' data generated by legislated increases in the minimum wage. Their primary quasi-experiment occurred when New Jersey raised its minimum wage in 1992, while its neighbour Pennsylvania did not. The neighbouring state thus served as a control for unobserved factors which could contaminate the estimated impact of the minimum wage. Second, they collected microeconomic data from firms. This, in addition to obvious advantages of dis-aggregated data, allows them to test for possible compensating changes in fringe benefits, full-time versus part-time work, etc. These two features allow Card and Krueger to estimate the impact of the minimum wage with a relatively high degree of precision and confidence. Moreover, they show that their results are consistent over a wide range of data sources. In short, the evidence that Card and Krueger provide on the impact of minimum wages on employment is both smaller (i.e. roughly nil) and apparently more believable than previous evidence.[9]

Card and Krueger's main finding is summarized in Table 6.6. Employment in fast-food restaurants in New Jersey increased slightly after the increase in the minimum wage there. At the same time employment in fast-food restaurants in neighbouring eastern Pennsylvania decreased. Thus, relative to the control group, employment increased significantly after the increase in the minimum wage. Moreover, this result is quite robust over various specifications and after controlling for various factors. Their implied minimum-wage elasticity of employment is 0.3 (as compared to the −0.1 to −0.3 range suggested by the Brown *et al.* survey).[10] They also find comparable results using broader data from the CPS; using Texas data from the 1991 increase in the federal minimum wage; using data from the 1988 increase in the minimum wage in California; and so on.[11]

TABLE 6.6. *Full-time equivalent workers per restaurant before and after the NJ minimum wage increase*

	NJ	PA	Difference
Before	20.44	23.33	−2.89
	(0.51)	(1.35)	(1.44)
After	21.03	21.17	−0.14
	(0.52)	(0.94)	(1.07)
Change	0.59	−2.16	2.75
	(0.54)	(1.25)	(1.36)

Note: Standard errors are in parentheses.

Source: Card and Krueger (1995: Table 2.2).

[9] Most of the numerous reviews of the book are quite favourable. For instance, according to Ehrenberg (1995: 827), the 'extraordinarily important book ... may well be the most important labor economics monograph of the 1990s.' Hamermesh (1995) and Welch (1995), however, are less than convinced of Card and Krueger's findings.

[10] Although the estimated impact on employment is statistically greater than zero in their primary case shown in Table 6.6, and greater than zero in all their specifications, in most of their cases the estimated effect is not statistically different from zero.

[11] Card and Krueger also provide evidence suggestive of a publication bias towards confirming the standard theoretical prediction. They show two pieces of evidence for this. First, if there is no publication bias, the *t*-statistic should increase proportionally with the square root of the degrees of freedom. Their 'meta-analysis' of the previous evidence shows that *t*-statistic actually decreases slightly with the square root of the degrees of freedom. Second, their meta-analysis shows that the coefficient estimates are positively related to their standard errors (apparently quite close to double, i.e. *t*-statistics seem to cluster around two), while they should be uncorrelated if there is no publication bias. Further examination by Neumark and Wascher (1998), however, failed to indicate publication bias.

Moreover, similar findings have recently been found in other countries. According to the Machin and Manning (1996: 670) survey, 'there seems to be a clear pattern of results suggesting that one cannot identify any evidence of a negative impact' on employment from minimum wages in Britain (operating through Wages Councils). And according to Machin and Manning (1997: 741), 'on the basis of our analysis of four countries (France, Netherlands, Spain, and Britain) we find little evidence that minimum wages have a bad impact on jobs.'

Given the controversial nature of these findings, however, there is little doubt that there will be further empirical testing of the employment effect of minimum wages. Indeed, Neumark and Wascher (1995) use an alternative data set and claim to overturn Card and Krueger's findings.[12] Using macroeconomic data, Deere *et al.* (1995) find a significant negative impact from minimum wage increases. Brown (1995) and Hamermesh (1995) stress that long-run responses are likely to be considerably larger than the short-run responses measured by Card and Krueger. Thus, the empirical issue is not yet completely settled. But it does seem safe to conclude that minimum wages have a much smaller impact on employment than can be explained within the context of the standard competitive model of labour markets.[13] As Machin and Manning (1996: 667) state, 'the emphasis seems to have shifted from "how negative are the employment effects?" to "is there an employment effect?"'

The competitive model unambiguously predicts that minimum wages discourage employment, regardless of the functional forms of preferences and technology, or the degree of competition in output markets. Thus, the empirical evidence suggests that labour markets are not adequately characterized by a simple supply-and-demand framework. A possible explanation for the empirical findings is that firms have some degree of monopsony power over the wages they pay, even in the market for low-skilled labour (i.e. where the degree of monopsony power should be the least).[14] But, as discussed in Card and Krueger, there are other possible explanations. Burdett and Mortensen (1998) show that monopsony-like behaviour can emerge in an equilibrium model of job search. Rebitzer and Taylor (1995) and Manning (1995) demonstrate monopsony-like behaviour in an efficiency-wage model. Lang and Kahn (1998) show that the empirical findings can be explained within an equilibrium model of bilateral search. And Bhaskar and To (1998) reconcile Card and Krueger's findings in a model where monopolistically competitive firms have some monopsony power arising from heterogeneous job characteristics.

---

[12] Using yet another data set, however, Card and Krueger (1998) confirm their original findings and argue that Neumark and Wascher's data is non-representative.

[13] In the competitive model, the minimum-wage elasticity of employment should be equal to the total wage elasticity of labour demand, which even in the short run is probably about -0.5 or less (according to the Fuchs *et al.* (1998) survey of labour economists).

[14] It should be noted, however, that not all of Card and Krueger's findings are completely consistent with the simple monopsony story either. They find conflicting evidence that the cost of the minimum wages is passed on to consumers in the form of higher prices (the cost is not passed on to consumers in the monopsony model).

6. Education and unemployment

Numerous studies, for example, Mincer (1974, 1993), Ashenfelter and Ham (1979), Nickell (1979), Nickell and Bell (1995, 1996), and Phelps and Zoega (1996, 1997), have documented the empirical regularity that groups with high levels of education have much lower unemployment rates than those with less education. Indeed, Mincer (1993) argues that this is one of the three major benefits of education (along with higher wages and greater upward mobility). Table 6.7, taken from Nickell and Bell (1995, 1996), is suggestive of this empirical regularity.[15] There is a strong negative relationship between unemployment and education across (developed) countries and over time.[16] The evidence in Table 6.7 indicates that the low-education group has an unemployment rate which is about three times that of the high-education group.

Table 6.8, from Mincer (1993), yields more light on the empirical relationship between education and unemployment (for American men during the period 1976– 81).[17] Along with the unemployment rate, this table shows for various education groups the yearly probability of being unemployed during the year (unemployment incidence), the yearly probability of separating from a job (job separation rate), the conditional probability of becoming unemployed given a job separation (unemployment probability of job separators), the average unemployment spell (unemployment duration), and the labour-force participation rate. This table shows that those with more education have somewhat lower durations of unemployment on average. Unemployment durations are almost three weeks (26 per cent) longer for secondary-school drop-outs compared to university graduates. But this only explains a small part of their dramatically different unemployment rates. The differences in unemployment rates are primarily due to the differences in unemployment incidence. Secondary-school drop-outs are 2.7 times more likely than university graduates to experience unemployment during a year. This accounts for roughly three-quarters of the differences in unemployment rates across education groups.

Table 6.8 also reveals that the differences in unemployment incidence are due in roughly equal parts to the differences in the frequency of job separations and in the conditional probability of unemployment for job separators. By construction, the unemployment incidence rate equals the job separation rate times the unemployment probability of job separators. Thus the fact that secondary-school drop-outs are 2.7 times more likely than university graduates to experience unemployment during a year can be decomposed into a 1.7 times higher frequency of job separations times a 1.6 times higher conditional unemployment incidence. Apparently those with more

---

[15] The education groupings in Table 6.7 vary across countries, but typically the low-education group consists of those with less than a full secondary education, and the high-education group consists of those with at least some higher education.

[16] Italy is the only exception to the rule in Table 6.7. Phelps and Zoega (1996), however, show that this case is misleading due primarily to demographic change. When they examine the unemployment rates for those over 30, they show a low/high ratio of 2.4 over the 1977–92 period.

[17] Remarkably similar patterns were found by Nickell (1979) using 1972 British data.

TABLE 6.7. *Unemployment rates and education*

Country and education group	1971–82	1983–90	1991–3
Australia			
Low	8.3[a]	11.1	13.6
High	3.5[a]	4.2	5.6
Ratio	2.4	2.7	2.4
Canada			
Low	8.2[b]	11.8[c]	16.1
High	2.6[b]	3.8[c]	5.1
Ratio	3.2	3.1	3.1
Finland			
Low		7.4[c]	14.8[d]
High		1.4[c]	4.7[d]
Ratio		5.3	3.1
France			
Low	6.5[a]	10.0[e]	12.1
High	2.1[a]	2.6[e]	4.2
Ratio	3.1	3.8	2.9
Germany			
Low	6.4[f]	13.0	10.7[d]
High	1.7[f]	3.1	2.2[d]
Ratio	3.8	4.2	4.9
Italy*			
Low	4.6[f]	7.3	7.5[d]
High	12.2[f]	13.1	12.5[d]
Ratio	0.4	0.6	0.6
Netherlands*			
Low	7.0[g]	14.0[h]	9.9
High	3.2[g]	5.7[h]	5.0
Ratio	2.2	2.5	2.0
New Zealand			
Low		8.8[i]	16.3
High		2.2[i]	6.0
Ratio		4.0	2.7
Norway			
Low	2.4[j]	4.9	8.9[d]
High	0.9[j]	1.2	2.6[d]
Ratio	2.7	4.3	3.5
Spain			
Low	10.6[f]	19.6	20.0
High	6.2[f]	9.9	9.0
Ratio	1.7	2.0	2.2
Sweden			
Low	2.9	3.3	6.9
High	1.0	1.1	2.8
Ratio	2.9	3.0	2.5

TABLE 6.7. (*cont.*)

Country and education group	1971–82	1983–90	1991–3
UK			
Low	7.5[k]	15.9	17.1[d]
High	2.4[k]	4.4	6.2[d]
Ratio	3.1	3.6	2.6
USA			
Low	7.8	11.3	11.0
High	2.0	2.4	3.0
Ratio	3.9	4.7	3.7

Notes: [*]For men and women. All other cases are for men only.
[a]1979–82; [b]1975–9; [c]1984–90; [d]1991–2; [e]1983, 86–90; [f]1975–82; [g]1975, 77, 79, 81; [h]1983, 85, 90; [i]1987–90; [j]1972–82; [k]1973–82.
Sources: Nickell and Bell (1995: Table 2a) and Nickell and Bell (1996: Table 1).

TABLE 6.8. *Unemployment components and education*

Years of education	< 12	12	13–15	16+
Unemployment rate[a]	7.0	4.1	3.3	1.9
Unemployment incidence	9.5	6.4	4.7	3.5
Job separation rate	17.9	13.4	12.8	10.5
Unemployment probability of job separators	53.2	48.6	37.8	33.2
Unemployment duration (in weeks)	13.8	12.1	11.6	11.0
Labour force participation[b]	92.1	97.0	96.4	98.2

Notes: All numbers are percentages.
[a]BLS data, white men, age 25–54, 1979;
[b]BLS data, white men, age 35–44, 1979;
All other rows: PSID data, white men, 11–25 years of work experience, 1976–81.
Source: Mincer (1993: Table 7.1).

education not only switch jobs less frequently, but when they do, they are much more likely to move straight into another job without experiencing unemployment.

It is tempting to conclude that this empirical pattern occurs because job separations are much more likely to be the workers' decisions (that is, quits rather than lay-offs) for those with more education, and thus this group generally has more chance to engage in job search during employment. But, apparently, this is not the explanation. The data indicate that the effect of education on quit and lay-off probabilities are almost proportional. Thus education increases the ratio of quits to lay-offs only slightly. Mincer concludes that this can explain no more than one-sixth of the differences in conditional unemployment probabilities across education groups.

Moreover, Mincer shows that the basic patterns revealed in Table 6.8 remain after controlling for other explanatory variables such as experience, union status, marriage status, and so forth. Controlling for job tenure and rough measures of on-the-job training, however, significantly reduces, but does not remove, the estimated impact of education on both unemployment-incidence components. The effect of education on unemployment incidence is almost halved after controlling for these factors.

As yet the empirical and theoretical relationship between education and unemployment has not been thoroughly researched. Thus, it is not entirely clear what forces drive these empirical findings. The evidence seems to point to two important types of effects at work. One of these is that job search appears to be significantly more successful for those with more education. This is the only apparent explanation for the moderate negative correlation between education and unemployment durations. It also seems to provide most of the explanation for the strong negative correlation between education and conditional unemployment incidence. Moreover, there are three theoretical reasons to expect more successful job search for those with more education. Those with more education have incentives for greater search intensity because of their higher relative opportunity costs (because unemployment benefits are generally less than proportional). Those with more education are likely to be more efficient in acquiring and processing job-search information. And firms are likely to have greater incentives to engage in job search for positions which are typically filled by more-educated workers, because these positions are likely to have relatively higher fixed costs.

But differences in job-search behaviour cannot easily explain why education is strongly negatively correlated with the frequency of job separations. The other force at work is probably that the quasi-rents from employment relationships are correlated with education. Quasi-rents arise from employment relationships because of turnover costs and because of firm-specific investments in human capital. These rents are lost when an employment relationship is broken. Thus, the presence of quasi-rents in labour markets means that there will generally be an incentive for both employees and employers parties to continue employment relationships.[18] Moreover, those with more education are likely to obtain more on-the-job training, and this type of investment in human capital will be firm-specific to some extent. Mincer provides some evidence of this. This is also likely theoretically because those with more education are likely to be relatively better learners. In addition, this provides a well-known explanation of the significantly steeper earnings profiles of those with more education. As noted earlier, however, much of the significant negative correlation between education and the frequency of job separations remains after attempting to control for job tenure and on-the-job training. Thus it appears that turnover costs are also correlated with education.

There are a number of obvious and not-so-obvious implications of the empirical evidence on education and unemployment. It suggests that unemployment outcomes

[18] For more this point see, for example, Oi (1962), Parsons (1972), Becker (1975) and the recent survey by Malcomson (1997).

are sensitive to job-search effort and technology, which in turn implies that there is scope for policies to affect long-run unemployment rates. For example, Phelps and Zoega's (1996) cross-country data indicate that the unemployment rates across education groups are not significantly affected by the relative sizes of the groups. Thus, they contend, educational upgrading of a country's labour force can significantly reduce its unemployment rate. Their simulations suggest that the unemployment rate in the USA would be two percentage points higher in 1994 if not for its educational upgrading since 1970, and the unemployment rate in Britain would be 1.5 percentage points higher in 1992 if not for its educational upgrading since 1973. Although estimates this large are hard to believe, they warrant further study.

The evidence on education and unemployment suggests that labour markets are characterized by long-term implicit contracts, as opposed to the standard spot-market model of labour markets. This in turn may have some implications for helping to understand business-cycle phenomena, such as apparent wage stickiness and labour hoarding. Less obviously, some recent research by Caballero and Hammour (1996, 1998) argues that the 'specificity' of investments is fundamental in driving business-cycle phenomena. Although these authors may not be aware of it, the empirical relationship between education and unemployment highlights the importance of specific investments in labour markets.

The evidence also suggests that investments in human capital may reduce earnings risk. Such a finding is at odds with numerous theoretical models of human capital and uncertainty that have assumed these investments are risky. The policy prescriptions for education and training in these studies will clearly vary depending on the riskiness of investments in human capital. Moreover, the apparent risk-reducing nature of investments in education will affect and be affected by precautionary motives, which recent research suggests are a crucial element of saving behaviour.

In addition, these results indicate that investment in human capital and time spent working are not independent. A number of studies have shown that, theoretically, human capital and work are jointly determined (*ex ante*).[19] To a large extent, however, the implications of this seem to have been forgotten. For instance, because human capital may be crucial in driving endogenous growth, models with human capital accumulation have become increasingly common over the past decade. Most of these models, however, have been considerably simplified by assuming that work time is independent of human capital. Moreover, in addition to being untenable empirically, this simplifying assumption has been shown to be quite limiting in some recent research. Trostel (1993) found that the interdependency between human capital investment and subsequent work is crucial in the controversy over the extent that taxation affects human capital accumulation. Similarly, Stokey and Rebelo (1995) found that this interdependency is crucial in the controversy over the extent that taxation affects economic growth. In addition, empirical research on labour supply has

---

[19] See Ghez and Becker (1975), Blinder and Weiss (1976), Heckman (1976), Ryder, Stafford, and Stephen (1976), Weiss and Gronau (1981), and Trostel and Walker (1999). Trostel and Walker also examine the empirical link between human capital and work.

ignored the interaction between education and work. Education is implicitly assumed to affect the wage rate, but not hours of work. In a full life-cycle perspective, however, education is endogenously determined along with hours of work. Therefore, previous estimates of labour supply responses may be biased. Similarly, empirical research on the rate of return to education may be also biased because the interaction between education and hours worked has been ignored. In particular, the failure to control for the correlation between schooling and employment causes a sample-selection problem.

7. Home ownership and unemployment

One way to assess the value of modern research on the labour market and macro-economics is to ask how much it has helped to answer pressing policy issues. For example, has research allowed us to understand why unemployment rates are so high? The OECD Jobs Study of June 1994 referred to unemployment as 'probably the most widely feared phenomenon of our time'. As high levels of joblessness are seen by politicians and journalists as perhaps Europe's major economic-policy issue, here there is a chance for labour and macro-research to show its mettle. Moreover, the criterion for success is sharp. Can economists suggest ideas that would lead to visibly lower rates of unemployment?

Journalists have written a great deal about the causes of Western unemployment, and seem to have firm views: 'Europe's unemployment crisis is deep-seated and self-inflicted. Over-generous social protection and labour market rigidity have resulted in a situation where continental economies have forgotten how to create jobs' (*Sunday Times*, editorial, 9 Febr. 1997); 'Unemployment rates ... are particularly high in countries with heavy labour-market restrictions ... high minimum wages, payroll taxes, ... and job protection laws' (*The Economist*, 22 August 1998). Researchers, however, usually put it more cautiously, for example: 'We do appear to be able to gain some under-standing of why unemployment varies such a great deal across different countries ... [but] why unemployment is so much higher now than in the 1960s is a much harder question ... and we do not have a really satisfactory answer' (Nickell 1998: 813).

What is the quality of the evidence supporting the journalists' statements? Not terribly strong, if one looks at the data. For example, taking statistics for a cross-section of twenty countries in the 1990s and running unemployment regressions with a single variable each time on the right-hand side gives Table 6.9. In almost all cases it is impossible to reject the null of zero on the relevant coefficient. These right-hand side numbers are R-squared values. These regressions are based on only twenty obser-vations. They are not to be thought of as serious attempts to explain unemployment, but rather to give a feel for how poor the cross-section correlations are. Yet it is such simple correlations, presumably, that motivate journalists' writings (if they use evidence).

These data were generously supplied by Steve Nickell, except that the home-ownership numbers come from Oswald (1996). It is worth bearing in mind that many of the variables above are measured in mechanical ways and are likely to be prone to severe error. For instance, benefit duration takes only values up to the integer 4. Those countries with indefinite unemployment benefits are assigned the number 4, which is

TABLE 6.9. *Correlates with countries' unemployment rates*

Variable	Explanatory power (%)
Home–ownership rate	33
Benefit duration	28
Employer coordination	26
Active labour–market policy	7
Union coverage	6
Labour standards	4
Union coordination	3
Benefit replacement ratio	1
Union density	1

Note: These numbers are R-squared values from univariate regressions on a cross-section of twenty countries in the 1990s. Benefit duration and employer coordination are probably not well measured.

not a good approximation to infinity, and may be less than ideal even for the longest observed levels of jobless duration of particular individuals.

Some of the influential work on unemployment has been done by economists at the London School of Economics. Here we take a recent example of that long-running research programme, Nickell (1998), and study its arguments.

Nickell addresses the question: why does unemployment vary so much across the OECD? He concludes by blaming the following culprits: high unemployment benefits, long-lasting unemployment benefits, trade unionism, and the tax wedge. Nickell also finds (following Oswald 1996) that high unemployment is associated with large amounts of owner-occupation in the housing market. Table 6.10, which gives the home-ownership and unemployment rates in OECD countries around 1990, shows this correlation. Nickell also concludes that some countries manage to have better unemployment performance by running 'active labour-market' policies and by having coordination between unions and employers. Apart from the new addition of a housing variable (prompted by the argument in Oswald (1996, 1997*a*,*b*) that lack of renting reduces labour mobility and worsens the efficiency of the labour market), the analysis is essentially identical to that produced by the LSE team (also including Richard Layard and Richard Jackman) since the mid-1980s. The method of analysis, however, is fractionally different from that done in the group's earlier work. Layard, Nickell, and Jackman (1991), for example, contains no country panel estimation of the sort described below.

Nickell examines data on twenty Western countries for two time-periods. The first period is an average of years from 1983 to 1988, and the second is 1989 to 1994. Nickell then has forty observations with which to work, and he estimates, by GLS random effects, the kind of equation shown in Table 6.11. The dependent variable here is the log of the unemployment rate. The regressors are measured in percentage points. According to Nickell, a 10 percentage point increase in the unemployment benefit replacement rate combined with an increase of one year in duration entitlement would

TABLE 6.10. *Unemployment and home-ownership rates by country: c.* 1990

Country	Unemployment (%)	Home ownership (%)
Austria	3.7	54
Belgium	8.1	65
Denmark	10.8	55
Finland	10.5	78
France	10.4	56
W. Germany	5.4	42
Ireland	14.8	76
Italy	8.2	68
Netherlands	7.0	45
Norway	5.5	60
Portugal	5.0	58
Spain	18.9	75
Sweden	4.4	43
Switzerland	2.3	28
UK	8.9	65
Canada	9.8	63
US	6.2	64
Japan	2.3	59
Australia	9.0	70
N. Zealand	8.9	71

Note: These countries' unemployment figures are similar today, except that unemployment in Finland is around 15 per cent and has been higher than that for most of the decade.

TABLE 6.11. *Regression to explain the log of unemployment across countries (estimated by random effects)*

Independent variable	Coefficient	t
Owner-occupation rate	0.013	2.6
Replacement rate	0.013	3.4
Benefit duration	0.10	2.2
Active labour policy	−0.02	3.3
Union density	0.01	2.3
Union coverage index	0.38	2.7
Coordination	−0.43	6.1
Total tax rate	0.03	4.0
Change in inflation	−0.21	2.2
Dummy for 1989–94	0.15	1.5

R-Squared = 0.82

Hausman test of RE model Chi-sq = 6.35

Note: The sample is two observations (averages over 1983–8 and 1989–94) from twenty countries.

Source: Nickell (1998: Table 2).

make unemployment rise by a quarter. Nickell also checks, but finds no strong statistical role for, real interest rates, hiring and firing restrictions, and pay-roll taxes.

What should one make of the regression equation given in Table 6.11? An immediate difficulty is that there are so few observations (moreover, the forty are not independent, as they are two periods from twenty nations). One reaction, and presumably the philosophy of Steve Nickell, is that this topic is of immense importance to social welfare, so that, while the scientific quality of such correlations cannot be persuasive, looking at panel regression equations is an important antidote to journalists' penchant for looking at cross-sections and simple means. There seems a certain amount to be said for this.

An alternative view is that the regression equation is probably over-fitted—in other words, that including nine regressors with a small sample is not sensible. Furthermore, it might be argued, it is not clear what causal interpretation to put on the regression. Among many potential identification issues is the important point made by Di Tella and MacCulloch (1995) that the generosity of unemployment benefits is influenced, for straightforward political reasons, by how much unemployment there is in a country. Another possibility is that country fixed-effects could make the estimation of such a regression unreliable. When one experiments with the data, the Hausman test tends to hover around the border of rejecting the null (that the random-effects restrictions are satisfied). Then there is the issue of robustness. Most of the variables have poorly determined t-statistics and do not appear terribly robust. It is when many variables are entered together that Nickell's apparently strong results are found. In passing, it is worth noting what happens if the unemployment equation is re-estimated allowing only two regressors each time: home ownership and benefit duration, home ownership and employer coordination, home ownership and ..., etc. In such regressions (available on request), the coefficient and well-determined t-statistic on home ownership hardly alters from one specification to another but the other coefficients are unstable; it is the coefficient estimate on home ownership that is much less fragile than others. The link between unemployment and home ownership also holds in panels of states for the USA, and in other settings (Oswald 1996, 1997b). But here too, there is a great deal more to be learned.

The influential work by Nickell seems to illustrate a standard dilemma faced by applied economists. The more interesting the problem, the less one can say for sure. Measuring the correlation of variable X with some variable Y using a giant micro-data set is simply a much easier task than discovering why Europe has high unemployment.

8. Conclusion

This paper has summarized six recent empirical findings about labour markets. We believe these are relevant to macroeconomics.

Psychological data indicate that unemployment substantially reduces people's well-being. There is evidence of rent-sharing in the labour market. The data suggest a wage curve, with an elasticity of about -0.1. Minimum wages do not appear to have a noticeable negative impact on low-skilled employment. The data show that, at the personal level, education is associated with lower unemployment. There is evidence, at the national level, that unemployment rates are more highly associated with home-ownership rates than with other variables. Most of these are not easy to reconcile with the textbook view of the labour market.

These disparate types of evidence suggest that labour markets do not operate in a simple competitive spot-market fashion. The emerging findings will face opposition—because the competitive-spot-market paradigm is the dominant way the profession thinks (both formally and informally). The majority of macroeconomic models of labour markets are explicitly based on this framework. Similarly, much macro-economic research rests upon the implicit assumption that unemployment is voluntary.

The profession's modelling strategies will not change quickly. There are significant obstacles. First, and probably most importantly, the appropriate alternative strategy is not clear. At this point, the empirical evidence does not point decisively to a precise form of alternative non-competitive paradigm (although rent-sharing and efficiency-wage models look promising). Second, from the orthodox economist's point of view, there are significant fixed costs associated with any such change away from convention. Third, ideology may get in the way.

REFERENCES

Abowd, John M. and Thomas Lemieux (1993) 'The effects of product market competition on collective bargaining agreements: the case of foreign competition in Canada', *Quarterly Journal of Economics* 108: 983–1014.

Akerlof, George A. and Janet L. Yellen (1990) 'The fair wage-effort hypothesis and unemployment', *Quarterly Journal of Economics* 105: 255–84.

Angrist, Joshua D. and Alan B. Krueger (1999) 'Empirical strategies in labor economics', in *Handbook of Labor Economics* (Amsterdam, North Holland).

Ashenfelter, Orley and John Ham (1979) 'Education, unemployment, and earnings', *Journal of Political Economy* 87: S99–116.

Becker, Gary S. (1975) *Human Capital*, 2nd edn. (New York: Columbia University Press).

Bhalotra, S. (1993) 'Geographical differences in unemployment and wage rates in India', Wolfson College, Oxford University, mimeo.

Bhaskar, V. and Ted To (1999) 'Minimum wages for Ronald McDonald monopsonies: a theory of monopsonistic competition', *Economic Journal* 109: 190–203.

Blackaby, D. H., R. C. Bladen-Hovell, and E. J. Symons (1991) 'Unemployment, duration and wage determination in the UK: evidence from the FES, 1980–86', *Oxford Bulletin of Economics and Statistics* 53: 377–99.

Blanchard, Olivier (1997) *Macroeconomics* (London: Prentice Hall).

—— and Lawrence F. Katz (1997) 'What we know and do not know about the natural rate of unemployment', *Journal of Economic Perspectives* 11: 51–72.

Blanchflower, David G. and Richard B. Freeman (1994) 'The legacy of communist labor relations', *Industrial and Labor Relations Review* 50: 438–59.

Blanchflower, David G. and Andrew J. Oswald (1994) *The Wage Curve* (Cambridge, Mass.: MIT Press).

——, ——, and Mario D. Garrett (1990) 'Insider power in wage determination', *Economica* 57: 363–70.

——, ——, and Peter Sanfey (1996) 'Wages, profits and rent-sharing', *Quarterly Journal of Economics* 111: 227–52.

Blinder, Alan S. and Yoram Weiss (1976) 'Human capital and labor supply: a synthesis', *Journal of Political Economy* 84: 449–72.

Brosius, Jacques (1998) 'Rent-sharing in the UK labour market: a co-integration analysis', Dissertation, University of Warwick.

Brown, Charles (1988) 'Minimum wage laws: are they overrated?', *Journal of Economic Perspectives* 2: 133–45.

—— (1995) 'Comment on *Myth and Measurement: The New Economics of the Minimum Wage*', *Industrial and Labor Relations Review* 48: 828–30.

——, Curtis Gilroy, and Andrew Kohen (1982) 'The effect of the minimum wage on employment and unemployment', *Journal of Economic Literature* 20: 487–528.

Burdett, Kenneth and Dale T. Mortensen (1998) 'Wage differentials, employer size, and unemployment', *International Economic Review* 39: 257–73.

Caballero, Ricardo J. and Mohamad L. Hammour (1996) 'The "Fundamental Transformation", in macroeconomics', *American Economic Review* 86: 181–6.

—— and —— (1998) 'The macroeconomics of specificity', *Journal of Political Economy* 106: 724–67.

Card, David (1990*a*) 'Unexpected inflation, real wages, and employment determination in union contracts', *American Economic Review* 80: 669–88.

—— (1990*b*) 'Strikes and wages: a test of an asymmetric information model', *Quarterly Journal of Economics* 105: 625–60.

—— (1995) 'Earnings, schooling, and ability revisited', *Research in Labor Economics* 14: 23–48.

—— and Alan B. Krueger (1995) *Myth and Measurement: The New Economics of the Minimum Wage* (Princeton: Princeton University Press).

—— and —— (1998) 'A reanalysis of the effect of the New Jersey minimum wage increase on the fast-food industry with *representative* payroll data', *NBER Working Paper 6386*.

Carlin, Wendy and David Soskice (1990) *Macroeconomics and the Wage Bargain* (Oxford: Oxford University Press).

Carruth, Alan A. and Andrew J. Oswald (1989) *Pay Determination and Industrial Prosperity* (Oxford: Oxford University Press).

Christofides, Louis N. and Andrew J. Oswald (1992) 'Real wage determination and rent-sharing in collective bargaining agreements', *Quarterly Journal of Economics* 107: 985–1002.

Clark, Andrew E. and Andrew J. Oswald (1994) 'Unhappiness and unemployment', *Economic Journal* 104: 648–59.

—— and —— (1996) 'Satisfaction and comparison income', *Journal of Public Economics* 61: 359–81.

—— and —— (1998) 'Unhappiness and unemployment: panel findings', University of Orleans, France, mimeo.

Currie, Janet and Sheena, McConnell (1992) 'Firm-specific determinants of the real wage', *Review of Economics and Statistics* 74: 297–304.

Deere, Donald, Kevin M. Murphy, and Finis Welch (1995) 'Employment and the 1990–1991 minimum-wage hike', *American Economic Review* 85: 232–7.

Denny, Kevin, and Stephen Machin (1991) 'The role of profitability and industrial wages in firm-level wage determination', *Fiscal Studies* 12: 34–45.

Dickens, William T. and Lawrence F. Katz (1987) 'Inter-industry wage differences and industry characteristics', in Kevin Lang and Jonathan S. Leonard (eds.), *Unemployment and the Structure of Labor Markets* (Oxford: Blackwell).

Di Tella, Rafael, and Robert MacCulloch (1995) 'The determination of unemployment benefits', Oxford University, mimeo.

——, ——, and Andrew J. Oswald (1997) 'The macroeconomics of happiness', Harvard Business School, mimeo.

Edin, P. A. and B. Holmlund (1989) 'The unemployment elasticity of pay: evidence from Swedish micro data', University of Uppsala, mimeo.

——, ——, and T. Ostros (1993) 'Wage behavior and labor market programs in Sweden: evidence from micro data', Working Paper 93-1, University of Uppsala forthcoming; in T. Tachibanaki (ed.), *Labour Markets and Economic Performance: Europe, Japan and the US* (London: Macmillan).

Ehrenberg, Ronald G. (1995) 'Editor's introduction to review symposium on *Myth and Measurement: The New Economics of the Minimum Wage*', *Industrial and Labor Relations Review* 48: 827–8.

Estevao, Marcello and Stacey Tevlin (1994) 'The role of profits in wage determination: evidence from US Manufacturing', MIT, mimeo.

Fuchs, Victor R., Alan B. Krueger, and James M. Poterba (1998) 'Why do economists disagree about policy? The roles of beliefs about parameters and values', *Journal of Economic Perspectives* (forthcoming).

Gardner, Jonathan (1998) 'Rent sharing and matched panels', University of Warwick, mimeo.

Gerlach, K. and G. Stephan (1996) 'A paper on unhappiness and unemployment in Germany', *Economics Letters* 52: 325–30.

Ghez, Gilbert R. and Gary S. Becker (1975) *The Allocation of Time and Goods Over the Life Cycle*, Columbia University Press.

Hall, R. E. (1970) 'Why is the unemployment rate so high at full employment?' *Brookings Papers on Economic Activity* 3: 369–402.

——(1972) 'Turnover in the labor force', *Brookings Papers on Economic Activity* 3: 709–56.

Hamermesh, Daniel S. (1993) *Labor Demand* (Princeton: Princeton University Press).

——(1995) 'Comment on *Myth and Measurement: The New Economics of the Minimum Wage*', *Industrial and Labor Relations Review* 48: 835–8.

——(1999) 'The Art of Labormetrics', *Handbook of Econometrics* (Amsterdam: North-Holland).

Harris, J. R. and M. P. Todaro (1970) 'Migration, unemployment and development: a two-sector analysis', *American Economic Review* 60: 126–42.

Heckman, James J. (1976) 'A life-cycle model of earnings, learning, and consumption', *Journal of Political Economy* 84: S11–44.

Hildreth, Andrew K. G. and Andrew J. Oswald (1997) 'Rent-sharing and wages: evidence from company and establishment panels', *Journal of Labor Economics*, 15: 318–37.

Hoddinott, J. (1996) 'Wages and unemployment in an urban African labour market', *Economic Journal* 106: 1610–26.

Holmlund, B. and P. Skedinger (1990) 'Wage bargaining and wage drift: evidence from the Swedish wood industry', in Lars Calmfors (ed.), *Wage Formation and Macroeconomic Policy in the Nordic Countries* (Oxford: Oxford University Press).

Hoon, Hian T. and Edmund S. Phelps (1992) 'Macroeconomic shocks in a dynamized model of the natural rate of unemployment', *American Economic Review* 82: 889–900.

Kingdon, G. and J. Knight (1998) 'Unemployment and wages in South Africa: a spatial approach', Institute of Economics and Statistics, Oxford University, mimeo.

Korpi, T. (1997) 'Is utility related to employment status? Employment, unemployment, labor market policies and subjective well-being among Swedish youth', *Labour Economics* 4: 125–48.

Krueger, Alan B. and Lawrence H. Summers (1987) 'Reflections on the inter-industry wage structure', in Kevin Lang and Jonathan S. Leonard (eds.), *Unemployment and the Structure of Labor Markets* (Oxford: Blackwell).

—— and —— (1988) 'Efficiency wages and the inter-industry wage structure', *Econometrica* 56: 259–93.

Krugman, Paul (1998) 'The $300,000 man: the strange economics of economists', *Slate*, or www.mit.edu/krugman.

Lang, Kevin and Shulamit Kahn (1998) 'The effect of minimum-wage laws on the distribution of employment: theory and evidence', *Journal of Public Economics* 69: 67–82.

Layard, P. R. G. and Stephen J. Nickell (1986) 'Unemployment in Britain', *Economica* 53: S121–70.

——, ——, and Richard Jackman (1991) *Unemployment: Macroeconomic Performance and the Labour Market* (Oxford: Oxford University Press).

Lindbeck, Assar (1993) *Unemployment and Macroeconomics* (Cambridge, Mass.: MIT Press).

Machin, Stephen and Alan Manning (1996) 'Employment and the introduction of a minimum wage in Britain', *Economic Journal* 106: 667–76.

—— and —— (1997) 'Minimum wages and economic outcomes in Europe', *European Economic Review* 41: 733–42.

Malcomson, James M. (1997) 'Contracts, hold-up, and labor markets', *Journal of Economic Literature* 35: 1916–57.

Manning, Alan (1995) 'How do we know that real wages are too high?' *Quarterly Journal of Economics* 110: 1111–25.

Mincer, Jacob (1974) *Schooling Experience, and Earnings* (New York: Columbia University Press).

—— (1993) *Studies in Human Capital* (*Collected Essays of Jacob Mincer*) (Chelknham: Edward Elgar).

Montgomery, E. B. (1993) 'Patterns in regional labor market adjustment: the US versus Japan', *NBER Working Paper* 4414.

Moulton, B. R. (1986) 'Random group effects and the precision of regression estimates', *Journal of Econometrics* 32: 385–97.

Neumark, David, and William Wascher (1995) 'The effect of New Jersey's minimum wage increase on fast-food employment: a re-evaluation using payroll records', *NBER Working Paper* 5224.

—— and —— (1998) 'Is the time-series evidence on minimum wage effects contaminated by publication bias?' *Economic Inquiry* (forthcoming).

Nickell, Stephen (1979) 'Education and lifetime patterns of unemployment', *Journal of Political Economy* 87: S117–31.

—— (1987) 'Why is wage inflation in Britain so high?' *Oxford Bulletin of Economics and Statistics* 49: 103–28.

—— (1998) 'Unemployment: questions and some answers', *Economic Journal* 108: 802–16.

—— and Brian Bell (1995) 'The collapse in demand for the unskilled and unemployment across the OECD', *Oxford Review of Economic Policy* 11: 40–62.

Nickell, Stephen and Brian Bell (1996) 'Changes in the distribution of wages and unemployment in OECD countries', *American Economic Review* 86: 302–8.

—— and Daphne Nicolitsas (1994) 'Wages, effort and productivity', Oxford University, mimeo.

—— Sushil Wadhwani (1990) 'Insider forces and wage determination', *Economic Journal* 100: 496–509.

Oi, Walter Y. (1962) 'Labor as a quasi-fixed factor', *Journal of Political Economy* 70: 538–55.

Oswald, Andrew J. (1986) 'Unemployment insurance and labor contracts under asymmetric information: theory and facts', *American Economic Review* 76: 365–77.

—— (1996) 'A conjecture on the explanation for high unemployment in the industrialized nations: Part I', Working Paper 475.

—— (1997a) 'Thoughts on NAIRU', *Journal of Economic Perspectives* 11: 227–8.

—— (1997b) 'The missing piece of the unemployment puzzle', inaugural lecture.

Parsons, Donald O. (1972) 'Specific human capital: an application to quit rates and layoff rates', *Journal of Political Economy* 80: 1120–43.

Phelps, Edmund S. (1990) 'Effects of productivity, total domestic product demand and incentive wages on unemployment in a non-monetary customer-market model of the small open economy', *Scandinavian Journal of Economics* 92: 353–68.

—— (1992) 'Consumer demand and equilibrium unemployment in a working model of the customer-market incentive-wage economy', *Quarterly Journal of Economics* 107: 1003–32.

—— (1993) 'Foreign and domestic determinants of unemployment rates through real-interest and real-exchange rate channels', seminar paper presented at LSE.

—— (1998) *Structural Slumps* (Cambridge, Mass.: Harvard University Press).

—— and Gylfi Zoega (1996) 'The incidence of increased unemployment in the Group of Seven, 1979–1994', Institute of Economic Studies, Working Paper 97: 03.

—— and —— (1997) 'The rise and downward trend of the natural rate', *American Economic Review* 87: 283–9.

Pierre, Gaelle (1998) 'Testing for long-term unemployment in a wage equation', University of Warwick, mimeo.

Psacharopoulos, George (1994) 'Returns to investment in education: a global update', *World Development* 22: 1325–43.

Rebick, M. (1990) 'Widening firm size differentials in Japan', Harvard University, mimeo.

Rebitzer, James B. and Lowell J. Taylor (1995) 'The consequences of minimum wage laws: some new theoretical ideas', *Journal of Public Economics* 56: 245–55.

Rowthorn, R. E. (1977) 'Conflict, inflation and Money', *Cambridge Journal of Economics* 1: 215–39.

Ryder, Harl E., Frank P. Stafford, and Paula E. Stephan (1976) 'Labor, leisure and training over the life cycle', *International Economic Review* 17: 651–74.

Shapiro, Carl, and Joseph E. Stiglitz (1984) 'Equilibrium unemployment as a worker discipline device', *American Economic Review* 74: 433–44.

Slichter, Sumner (1950) 'Notes on the structure of wages', *Review of Economics and Statistics* 32: 80–91.

Smith, Jennifer C. (1996) 'Wage interactions: comparisons or fall-back options?' *Economic Journal* 106: 495–506.

Stokey, Nancy L. and Sergio Rebelo (1995) 'Growth effects of flat-rate taxes', *Journal of Political Economy* 103: 519–50.

Teal, Francis (1996) 'The size and sources of economic rents in a developing country manufacturing labour market', *Economic Journal* 106: 963–76.

Trostel, Philip A. (1993) 'The effect of taxation on human capital', *Journal of Political Economy* 101: 327–50.

—— and Ian Walker (1999) 'Education and work', University of Warwick, mimeo.

Van Reenen, John (1996) 'The creation and capture of rents: wages and innovation in a panel of UK companies', *Quarterly Journal of Economics* 111: 195–226.

Warr, P. B., P. Jackson, and M. Banks (1988) 'Unemployment and mental health: some British studies', *Journal of Social Issues* 44: 47–68.

Weiss, Yoram and Reuben Gronau (1981) 'Expected interruptions in labour force participation and sex-related differences in earnings growth', *Review of Economic Studies* 48: 607–19.

Welch, Finis (1995) 'Comment on *Myth and Measurement: The New Economics of the Minimum Wage*', *Industrial and Labor Relations Review* 48: 842–9.

Whelan, C. T. (1992) 'The role of income, life-style deprivation and financial strain in mediating the impact of unemployment on psychological distress: evidence from the Republic of Ireland', *Journal of Occupational and Organizational Psychology* 65: 331–44.

Winkelmann, L. and R. Winkelmann (1998) 'Why are the unemployed so unhappy? Evidence from panel data', *Economica* 65: 1–15.

Woodford, M. (1992) 'A book review, 'Seven Schools of Macroeconomic Thought', by E. S. Phelps', *Journal of Economic Dynamics and Control* 16: 391–8.

7A   Theory, evidence, and the labour market

ROGER E. BACKHOUSE

1. Introduction

At one level these two papers (chs. 5 and 6) are very different indeed, but it is possible to discern strong similarities. They both accept (as too obvious to need documenting) that macroeconomics is generally based on the premiss that the labour market can be analysed as a perfectly competitive market in which individual agents maximize utility and wages rise or fall according to whether excess demand for labour is positive or negative. They both provide a methodological critique of what they see as the prevailing orthodoxy. Ferri's (ch. 5) critique is theoretical. He argues that the Phillips curve should be viewed as an equation describing the operation of the whole system, not as a single component of a macromodel (as a reduced form rather than a structural equation). Oswald and Trostel (ch. 6), on the other hand, argue that the competitive model is inconsistent with well-established facts about the labour market.

In discussing these two papers, I do not wish to get embroiled in the question of who is right and who is wrong. Instead, I would like to draw out some of the methodological questions raised by the two papers, and to suggest how one might start to answer them. The paper by Oswald and Trostel raises the question of why macroeconomists might ignore microeconomic evidence on the labour market. Ferri's paper raises the question of what causes transformations in macroeconomics, such as the shift from Phillips-curve models of inflation to ones based on a natural rate of unemployment and rational expectations. After discussing these two issues, I turn to wider questions concerning the relationship between theory and evidence in macroeconomics.

2. Why might macroeconomists ignore evidence on the labour market?

Oswald and Trostel point to clear psychological evidence that unemployed workers experience a lower level of psychological well-being than their employed counterparts. This is something that clearly accords with commonsense and it is hard to believe that many economists would seriously doubt the findings. Aside from economists' general scepticism about certain types of questionnaire evidence,[1] one explanation of why they ignore the implications for theories of the labour market of such evidence is that they are committed to what Hausman (1992) has called the 'separateness' of economics. Taking as a case study the literature dealing with experimental evidence on preference

---

[1] Boulier and Goldfarb (1998) point out that whilst economists profess scepticism about evidence derived from questionnaires, they are very happy to use government statistics that are derived in this way.

reversals, Hausman argued that the way economists responded to apparently anomalous evidence was one of trying to keep economics separate from other sciences, notably psychology. The theoretical strategy that underlies this response is one of seeking theories that are of maximal scope—theories that apply to the largest possible range of situations. To acknowledge the psychological evidence adduced by Oswald and Trostel would not have the same implications as would accepting the theories with which psychologists explain preference reversal, but it would be the thin end of the wedge.

Hausman (1992) has also suggested that when empirical evidence appears to conflict with theory, economists may frequently be justified in having more confidence in their theories than in the data. Such problems arise very clearly in Oswald and Trostel's paper. The obvious question concerns the robustness of the results. Whilst the clear implication of the paper is that the six empirical findings listed in Section 1 are well established, they admit that there is 'disagreement even among labour specialists about the robustness of findings'. Equally important, even where evidence is conclusive at a microeconomic level, its implications for macroeconomics may remain ambiguous. Thus Oswald and Trostel are careful to hedge the claims that they make. They write that the positive link between profits and pay at the microeconomic level 'suggests' that labour markets are imperfectly competitive, that the negative correlation between educational attainment and unemployment 'suggests' the importance of firm-specific investments and long-term contracts, and that 'one cause' of the correlation between home-ownership and unemployment may be the link between private renting and mobility. Space is left to accept their empirical findings but to remain sceptical about their macroeconomic significance.

The other side of this coin is economists' confidence in established theories. One reason for this confidence in modern economic theories is that they are based on assumptions about behaviour and the interaction between individuals that are extremely broad in their scope (cf. Hausman 1992). They apply to a wide variety of situations. Successful application of essentially the same theory to many situations can be regarded as corroborating the theory. Against this, it is arguable that, because of the inter-connectedness of contemporary economic theory, the costs of questioning any significant part of it are simply too high. As a result, economists have an enormous incentive to hold on to it, even in the face of strong contrary evidence. A second reason for confidence in established theory is that it has a strong intuitive appeal. However, though this can be read as evidence in the theory's favour, it can also be read another way. Our view of what is intuitively reasonable will be influenced by our training—prolonged exposure to the theory of general competitive equilibrium, for example, blinds us to the absence from it of features that almost any non-economist would consider 'obvious' features of competition (non-price competition, market power, innovation, etc.). Furthermore, as Blanchflower and Oswald point out, models might have considerable appeal for linguistic reasons. For example, 'the terms "insiders" and "outsiders" evocatively describe what happens in the world—they are never forgotten once heard in a seminar' (Blanchflower and Oswald 1994: 7). How much of the popularity of 'efficiency wages' is attributable to the label attached to the phenomenon? Related to this is the importance, for teaching, of being able to express theories in easily grasped language and terminology. There is thus considerable reason to be open to the possibility that economists' confidence in established economic theory might be misplaced.

The research discussed by Oswald and Trostel lies at the boundaries of two subdisciplines within economics: labour economics and macroeconomics. Clearly, macroeconomists are justified in not attending to all the details about labour markets that arise within labour economics, from some of which macroeconomic theories must, of necessity, abstract. In the same way that they work with stylized representations of product markets, they work with stylized representations of labour markets. Is it possible that macroeconomists are too concerned with the operation of their models, for which their stylized representations of labour markets are very convenient, that they ignore important evidence as lying within another discipline?

To say that academics are influenced by the need to publish and are hence forced to write types of article that are likely to be published in the right journals *in itself* explains nothing. It leaves open the question of why editors, referees, promotions committees, and so on have the criteria that they do. However, such factors may matter. I give two examples of how professional pressures on economists may distort the incentive to respond fully to evidence.

Though it cannot be the whole story, it is arguable that the US dominance of the profession might cause potential problems in labour markets if labour markets are significantly different in the USA and Europe.[2] If 'international', high-prestige journals are effectively US-dominated, career pressures will require economists to write for a US audience, which may mean playing down, or even ignoring altogether, arguments that are specific to another country. The result might thus be that arguments based on institutions specific to European labour markets, even if they became established in European journals and policy discussions, might never go beyond this to affect macroeconomic theory in general, simply because they are not relevant to the USA, the audience that, because of its size, dominates general macroeconomics. Thus, for the past decade or so, the Layard–Nickell model has dominated European analysis of unemployment and inflation, but has had little impact beyond that.

Another possible source of 'market failure' in the academic market place is that the effective refereeing of articles is sometimes prohibitively costly. It can be very time-consuming to check that all the conclusions reached in an empirical paper are justified inferences from the data set being analysed, and that they are plausible in the light of evidence available elsewhere in the literature. Furthermore, imposing standards that are too strict, or out of line with generally accepted standards, may reduce submissions or lead to economists regarding the journal as having an idiosyncratic policy.

3. Transitions in macroeconomics

Ferri's paper raises the question of why economists' views on the labour market have changed substantially several times since the 1950s. He picks out the rise in interest in

---

[2] I leave out the rest of the world, but the arguments clearly generalize.

labour-market dynamics in the 1950s; the years of stagflation following the 1970s' oil crises; and more recent developments. Consider first the Phillips curve.

Thomas Kuhn (1970) taught us that in science unsolved problems may persist for many years, without becoming a problem that scientists need to solve. It is only when an unsolved problem becomes crucial to the fate of a paradigm that it becomes an anomaly that needs to be explained. Ferri makes the interesting observation that prior to the 1950s, economists were not particularly concerned with wage dynamics. Why was this? Several possibilities suggest themselves. The first is that for most of Keynes's *General Theory*, the money wage rate was taken as a parameter rather than a variable whose dynamics were endogenous (this assumption was then relaxed near the end of the book). This is also true, to a certain extent, of Hicks's IS–LM model where wage and price changes were assumed to take place at full employment, but were not modelled formally in the same way as the static equilibrium. Patinkin's *Money, Interest and Prices* (1956, 1965), perhaps the definitive work in the neoclassical synthesis, modelled dynamics explicitly, but the emphasis was still on the analysis of static equilibria. On top of this, the Keynesian framework, with its assumption that output was demand-determined, minimized any role for real wages and aggregate supply.

Such a situation increasingly became unsatisfactory, for a variety of reasons. The use of Keynesian policies to control the level of aggregate demand meant that inflation was an issue in a way not true of the interwar period. Governments had to consider whether they might be running their economies at an inflationary level of demand. In addition, the development of econometric forecasting models made an equation for price dynamics essential. Numerous models, prior to Phillips's curve, contained equations in which inflation was negatively related to unemployment. In this sense, the Phillips curve was not new.

Having said all this, Phillips's curve had an immense impact, especially after Samuelson and Solow (1960) interpreted it as the trade-off facing policy-makers and Lipsey (1960) had shown it could be derived from wage dynamics of the type assumed by Patinkin and frictional unemployment. Though the evidence for it was perhaps shakier than many economists assumed,[3] it appeared to suggest that the relationship between inflation and unemployment was stable in the face of the many changes that had affected the labour market since the nineteenth century.[4] It was an example of a perceived empirical regularity having a profound effect on the way economists thought about a crucial macroeconomic relationship. Clearly, there was more to wages than simply unemployment but, instead of being seen to undermine the theory, the inadequacies of the Phillips curve provided a research agenda for the emerging discipline of econometrics. Numerous additional variables were introduced into the equation and new econometric techniques applied.

The Phillips curve, therefore, had such a large impact because it did three things. It simultaneously provided economists with (i) a framework within which to think about

---

[3] cf. Leeson (1998).

[4] Ferri argues that the late-1950s/early-1960s Phillips curve should be seen as reflecting the outcome of a tripartite bargaining process. Whilst some economists no doubt held this view, the textbook consensus was to see it as deriving from competitive markets in the manner suggested by Lipsey.

urgent policy issues; (ii) the concept with which to fill a theoretical gap; and (iii) a research agenda appropriate for econometrics as it existed at that time.

Ferri is right to point out that, though the Phillips curve has lived through many incarnations since 1958, but in moving straight from the early 1960s to Layard–Nickell-type bargaining models of the NAIRU, he misses three vital points. The first is the *enormous* impact of Friedman's 1967 AEA Presidential Address (Friedman 1969: ch. 1) in which he proposed the idea of a natural rate of unemployment. The second was the failure of Keynesian economics to provide a framework within which to conduct macroeconomic policy. In Britain this point is illustrated by a sometimes forgotten episode—the brief interest in 'New Cambridge Economics' in the mid-1970s.[5] In the face of stagflation, Keynesian economics did not provide policy-makers with the guidance they needed, with the result that they looked round for an alternative. After (in Britain at least) a brief flirtation with the New Cambridge approach, they turned to monetarism. The third is the impact of rational expectations and ideas about dynamic optimization on macroeconomic theory.

In establishing the reasons why macroeconomic theory changed so radically in the 1970s, the problem is that there are too many explanations, all of which seem plausible.[6] Take, for example, Friedman's natural rate hypothesis.

1. Friedman presented the natural rate hypothesis as what emerged if theory was correctly formulated. It did not involve any novel assumptions but simply the application of well-established price theory, in which supply and demand depended on relative prices, not money prices. In a sense, therefore, the question of evidence being required to justify the theory was beside the point.

2. When the Phillips curve was modified to an equation like $\pi = \alpha\pi^e - f(u)$, where $\dot{\pi} = \beta(\pi - \pi^e)$ the crucial question concerned the value of α and β. If either of these was less than unity, there would still be a Phillips curve in the long run. Numerous estimates were made. In the late 1960s, values less than unity were generally found, but estimates moved upwards, till by the early 1970s they supported the idea of a vertical long-run Phillips curve. Had economists been taking note of evidence, they would have changed their views at just this time.

3. Simultaneously with Friedman's Presidential Address, Phelps (1967) applied search models to the same problem, reaching essentially the same conclusion. Phelps (1970) sought to show that this was part of an emerging research programme. The Phelps–Friedman version of the Phillips curve, therefore, provided a theoretical research agenda.

4. It provided clear guidelines for policy in the turbulent years of the early 1970s (which arguably dated from the Vietnam War, the oil price rises being part of a much broader explosion in commodity prices).

Similar remarks could be made about the new classical macroeconomics later in the 1970s. This programme provided a research agenda, it claimed to be based on

---

[5] The central plank of the NCE was the constancy of the private-sector surplus, which implied a direct inverse link between the government and foreign-sector surpluses.

[6] It would perhaps be going too far to describe them all as sufficient conditions, but Lipsey's remark that in history we often find an excess of sufficient conditions is not too wide of the mark.

long-established economic principles (rationality was applied to the formation of expectations; account was taken of time; markets were assumed to be competitive), not on any novel assumptions or empirical regularities. The main difference is, arguably, that the empirical evidence was much less clear-cut. Lucas, Barro, and others tested what they claimed were key predictions of the new classical macroeconomics but their results remained controversial.[7]

This is the background against which the Layard–Nickell model has to be seen.[8] When European unemployment rose dramatically at the end of the 1970s and remained high throughout the 1980s, it became necessary to find a new theory. The Friedman–Phelps model was a reasonable explanation of the relationship between inflation and unemployment only if the greater part of fluctuations in unemployment were movements around the natural rate. If the main cause was changes in the natural rate itself, then the theory ceased to provide any explanation, beyond linking them to unanalysed microeconomic phenomena. The Layard–Nickell model sought to remedy the situation by breaking down changes in unemployment into changes in the natural rate and fluctuations around it, and explaining why the natural rate (in the guise of the NAIRU) itself changed. In order to do this, Layard and Nickell moved away from the perfect-competition paradigm to a bargaining model. Like the Phelps–Friedman Phillips curve in the early 1970s, it also provided a theoretical and econometric research agendas.

4. Microeconomic evidence and macroeconomic theory

The methodological perspective underlying Oswald and Trostel's paper is clearly summarized by Blanchflower and Oswald at the end of *The Wage Curve*, in a paragraph that is worth quoting in full.

Some economists may look upon this methodological approach as unconvincing. They may see it as overly ambitious or as mistaken in principle. Economics textbooks, according to a common point of view, do not write down empirical discoveries. The subject is about how to think; economics is more like history than engineering; it is not about the detection of empirical regularities; there will never be a Boyle's law or a coefficient of friction, and to believe otherwise is to deny people their humanity. These views, which may have been conveyed unconsciously in some university economics courses over the last few decades, are out of step with the philosophy underlying the book. In a sense, the work reported here is an attempt to prove them wrong. (Blanchflower and Oswald 1994: 360)

They go on to argue that it is new types of high-quality microeconomic data that make this possible, and that these new data are the result of computing and other technological advances. Three points are worth making about this paragraph.

---

[7] I refrain from speculating as to why there was this contrast. There are many possibilities including, somewhat controversially, the idea that the failure to reach a consensus on what the data showed was a consequence of economists' failure to agree on the underlying theory. Had economists been agreed that the theory underlying NCM was correct, would they have found that the data spoke to them more clearly?

[8] I focus on the Layard–Nickell model even though it was predated by Rowthorn (1977) on the grounds that it was only with the Layard–Nickell model that the theory 'took off'.

1. Though Blanchflower and Oswald suggest that their book's target is a single view of economics, it in fact calls into question two very different attitudes towards economic theory. One is the view, articulated in the recent methodological literature by Tony Lawson (1997) and Nancy Cartwright (1999), that the world is too complex for econometric modelling to be expected to work and also that formal, deductive theorizing, based on tightly specified premises, is unlikely to be feasible either.[9] They advocate instead more informal 'historical' reasoning. The other is the view that because theory cannot be based on empirical regularities, it has to be based on more 'basic' assumptions such as rationality and competition. According to this view, theorizing can be pursued largely independently of econometric evidence. As Frank Knight put it, 'The testable facts are not really economic' (1941: 753).

2. It is claimed that data analysis can establish not only qualitative generalizations (that there is a negative relationship) but the parameter values (the elasticity of the wage with respect to unemployment is −0.1). Given that critics have questioned the ability of econometric methods to establish even qualitative relationships, this is a strong claim indeed.

3. Even if the claim made by Blanchflower and Oswald, and Oswald and Trostel, are accepted, it does not establish how evidence such as they produce should be used in economic theory. There are two possibilities: (i) Estimated coefficients, once established, could be used as parameters in economic models. Comparison with Boyle's Law or coefficients of friction suggests this. (ii) Theorizing could be pursued in much the same way as at present, but consistency with estimated coefficients is used to choose between theories. This involves a less radical shift in contemporary attitudes towards economic theory.

This last point raises important questions about the nature of economic theory. How far theory should be based on empirical evidence depends on how we view economic theory. If theories are thought of as bodies of propositions about the real world, then there is no reason why we should not build a theory around, for example, the elasticity of the wage with respect to unemployment. We create a structure that can generate testable propositions and can provide explanations. Such theory would have the advantage of a strong empirical basis. The danger, however, as Bliss (1975: 125) has argued in the context of 'Cambridge' theories of distribution (based on the assumption of constant saving propensities), is that 'factors which ought to be analysed and made the subject of economic theories remain unanalysed, or are analysed only crudely'. The current fashion is to say that any factor needs further analysis if it has not been reduced to the behaviour of fully rational individuals. Against this, however, it would seem arguable that the problem ought to be seen as an empirical one: if the evidence is sufficiently strong, a case can be made for pursuing theories that do not reduce to individual rationality.

---

[9] Lawson argues that economic systems are, because of the fact of human choice, inherently open, and that closed systems will inevitably fail to represent them adequately. Cartwright argues that we can have confidence that modelled processes operate as tendencies in reality only if their effects can simply be added together. She argues that the interaction between causes is typically complex and non-linear, with the result that there is no reason to believe that modelling them individually is going to be informative.

Much of the evidence discussed by Oswald and Trostel is microeconomic, which raises further questions concerning how such evidence is used. It could be an input into a calibration exercise of the type that has become common in business–cycle theory. Microeconomic evidence that was sufficiently hard to fix more of the parameters in calibrated macroeconomic models would serve to raise the hurdles they had to jump. Alternatively, microeconomic evidence could be used to rule out, for example, certain types of behaviour or certain market structures, thereby constraining not simply certain parameters in macromodels, but the basic structure of their microfoundations. This is the way Oswald and Trostel see most of their evidence being used. If we accept it, their data on the effect of unemployment and well-being rules out models in which the marginal worker is indifferent between employment and unemployment. The connection between profitability and wages rules out perfect competition. And so on. This would seem to constitute progress when compared with a situation where the main justification for microfoundations is simply their plausibility or tractability or simply what McCloskey (1986) has dubbed 'the lore of the academy'.

There are, of course, problems with using evidence in these ways. The main ones can be summed up as replication, aggregation, and interpretation.

Economists and econometricians frequently use the term 'replication' to refer to the ability of one investigator to reproduce another's results using the same data set. It amounts to checking that the calculations have been done correctly and that the methods that an investigator claims to have used to actually produce the results that they are claimed to produce. What this type of checking does not do is to establish the existence of any real-world phenomenon that the economist needs to explain or take into account. It might be, for example, that the results are simply the result of the techniques being employed or of some accident in the way the data are constructed.[10] Such checking of results, therefore, does not perform the same function as that performed by the replication of an experimental result. If one experimenter successfully replicates the results obtained by an experimenter, he or she will establish that the phenomenon concerned is not simply the result of some peculiarity of the way the original experiment was undertaken—that there is a phenomenon there to be explained. Replication, therefore, is the process of establishing that there is a phenomenon that needs to be explained.

This way of expressing it should make it clear that replication is an economic as well as a statistical problem. Statistical criteria establish the features of the data sets that are analysed. They are, however, insufficient to establish that these features indicate the existence of real-world phenomena rather than simply quirks of those particular data sets that tell us little about the economic world. It is here that microeconomics appears to be at an advantage: more and more samples can be taken, using data collected by

---

[10] The points made in this and the following paragraph are developed in more detail in Backhouse (1997).

different investigators under different circumstances, in the same way that experimental scientists can replicate experiments. As Oswald and Trostel show, the result can be a body of evidence that is apparently very strong. In contrast, the problem with macroeconomic data is that, to replicate one's results, it is normally necessary either to use data from another country or from another time-period. In the former case there is the problem that the economy may have changed and in the latter case there is the problem that there may be significant cross-country differences. There are thus many reasons, in addition to the non-existence of the phenomenon in question, why it may be impossible to replicate a result.

The second problem is aggregation. Given that the conditions required for aggregate behaviour to mimic individual behaviour are never satisfied (for example, agents are heterogeneous) there will always be explanations of why parameters in aggregate models are not exactly the same as their microeconomic counterparts. All microeconomic evidence can do is establish that either a macroeconomic theory is wrong or that the conditions required for aggregation are not satisfied.[11] The asymmetry involved is shown in Table 7A.1. Microeconomic evidence can rule out possibility A. The one case where it can falsify a theory is where the theory includes a hypothesis about the possibility of aggregation (as with representative agent models).

A difficulty here is that, even if theorists construct theories with microfoundations, they may nonetheless be aware that the conditions required for aggregation are not satisfied. They will, therefore, draw only limited conclusions from their models. They use models to explore how certain mechanisms might work and do not regard them as complete models of what is going on in the world. The result is that they consider it justifiable to persist with them in the face of apparently contrary evidence.

This leads to the crucial question, of interpretation. If statistical evidence establishes that there is some phenomenon out there, what does it mean? This would seem to be why microeconomic evidence is so important. The current fashion in the discipline is to argue that, in order to understand a macroeconomic phenomenon, it is necessary to interpret in terms of the actions of individual agents. As long as this fashion persists, microeconomic evidence ought to be important, which brings us back to the question considered in Section 2. On the other hand, if macroeconomic theories deal with emergent phenomena, not found at the microeconomic level, then the importance of microeconomic evidence will be much less.

TABLE 7A.1

	Aggregation possible	Aggregation not possible
Theory true	A	B
Theory false	C	D

---

[11] This is, of course, an example of the Duhem–Quine problem.

5. Conclusions

It is arguable that research on the labour market has exhibited enormous progress over the past twenty or thirty years. Theories from the 1950s and 1960s now look almost naïve in that the theories are much simpler and appear to take account of a much narrower range of phenomena. There would also seem to be progress in that it appears to be the case that it now takes more evidence before an empirical result is accepted than was required forty years ago. The Phillips curve was widely accepted on the basis of what nowadays seems very flimsy evidence—so flimsy that some scholars have questioned whether the curve ever existed.[12] The Phelps–Friedman version of the Phillips curve, downward-sloping in the short run and vertical in the long run, required more evidence, but it nonetheless became widely accepted. Since then, it is harder to argue that any theory has been so widely accepted (whether real business-cycle theory or the Layard–Nickell model). Macroeconomists are entertaining more theories, and individuals are as committed to their own theories as they ever were, but general acceptance of a new theory seems to be harder to achieve. At the same time, there has been convergence on the acceptance of a standard microeconomic framework in which individual optimization is central. New phenomena have been explained in terms of this framework through introducing a variety of auxiliary assumptions, many of which have evidence in their favour.

Research on the labour market, however, reveals some fundamental tensions lying behind this picture. The main one is the use of macroeconomic data to test theories that rest on microeconomic foundations. If microeconomics really did provide the foundations of macroeconomics, one would expect microeconomic evidence, which bears directly on those foundations, to be more telling. The alternative method would be to assume that macroeconomics deals with properties of economic systems, many of which emerge only at the macroeconomic level. The possibility of such emergent properties, however, is largely eliminated by devices such as the representative agent which ensure that macroeconomic behaviour mimics that of individual agents. The reason this causes such a tension in the subject is that, at least at the macroeconomic level, these two approaches to macroeconomic phenomena imply different methods. If one takes seriously the idea that macroeconomics deals with properties that emerge only at the macroeconomic level, there is a case for exploring the consequences of stable relationships that are found in macroeconomic data, even if one is not sure what lies behind them.

REFERENCES

Backhouse, Roger E. (1997) *Truth and Progress in Economic Knowledge* (Cheltenham: Edward Elgar).

---

[12] cf. Leeson (1998).

Blanchflower, David G., and Oswald, Andrew (1994) *The Wage Curve* (Cambridge, Mass. and London: MIT Press).

Bliss, Christopher J. (1975) *Capital Theory and the Distribution of Income* (Amsterdam: North Holland).

Boulier, Bryan J. and Goldfarb, Robert S. (1998) 'On the use and nonuse of surveys in economics', *Journal of Economic Methodology* 5(1): 1–22.

Cartwright, Nancy (1999) *The Dappled World: A Study of Science* (Cambridge and New York: Cambridge University Press).

Ferri, Piero (1997) 'Wage dynamics and the Phillips curve', this volume.

Friedman, Milton (1969) *The Optimum Quantity of Money and Other Essays* (Chicago: Chicago University Press).

Hausman, Daniel M. (1992) *The Inexact and Separate Science of Economics* (Cambridge and New York: Cambridge University Press).

Knight, Frank (1941) ' "What is truth" in economics?' *Journal of Political Economy* 68(1): 1–32.

Kuhn, Thomas S. (1970) *The Structure of Scientific Revolution*, 2nd edition (Chicago: Chicago University Press).

Lawson, Tony (1997) *Economics and Reality* (London and New York: Routledge).

Leeson, Robert (1998) 'Early doubts about the Phillips curve trade-off', *Journal of the History of Economic Thought* 20(1): 83–102.

Lipsey, Richard G. (1960) 'The relation between unemployment and the rate of change of money wage rates in the United Kingdom, 1862–1957: a further analysis', *Economica*, n.s. 27(1): 1–31.

McCloskey, D. N. (1986) *The Rhetoric of Economics* (Brighton: Harvester Wheatsheaf).

Oswald, Andrew J. and Trostel, Philip A. (1998) 'What can recent labour research teach us about macroeconomics?', this volume.

Rowthorn, R. E. (1977) 'Conflict, inflation and money', *Cambridge Journal of Economics* 1: 215–39.

Samuelson, Paul A. and Solow, Robert M. (1960) 'Analytical aspects of anti-inflation policy', *American Economic Review* 50: 177–94.

Stafford, Frank (1986) 'Forestalling the demise of empirical economics: the role of microdata in labor economics research', in Orley Ashenfelter and Richard Layard (eds.), *Handbook of Labor Economics*, i (Amsterdam: North-Holland): 387–423.

Piero Ferri: I will say just two things. One is that I look at this story from a different perspective. I did not look at people who wrote about the Phillips curve but about the facts that made people theorize about the Phillips curve. To use a slogan, it is the inflation that created Friedman, not vice versa. Friedman, when he wrote his address, wrote when the rate of inflation was starting to increase, so I was looking at the inflation, not Friedman. The other point refers to the other paper. The basic question seems to be 'How can you make the micro-research agree with the macro-results?' I have been looking at this problem for twenty years and don't have the answer. It is the basic question about macroeconomics because, nowadays, macroeconomics is nothing but general equilibrium. This is not macroeconomics. This comes up in Sims's paper (2-3) but it is worth mentioning here. It is astonishing that Oswald and Trostel found a very robust coefficient. It is the first time in economics that you find a parameter that changes so little and, as far as I know, it is really new. However, in going from micro to macro, there are methodological jumps. There is the challenge that macroeconomics is not reducible to microeconomics.

David Hendry: I have been asked on numerous occasions why I don't apply the things I do to cross-sections or panels and the answer bears quite a lot on the sort of things Oswald has presented today. It all begins in the early 1970s, just after the oil price had changed, when I was at conferences where people were estimating demand for housing equations using cross-section data. I simply noted that London and a place like Aberdeen had phenomenal house-price–income ratios relative to the rest of Britain and that if you took the two extremes and ran a regression, you got a unit elasticity, whereas everyone else who had done the estimates got about 0.1. It crossed my mind that the nonsense regressions problem is just as serious in cross-section as it is in any time-series, but it is ignored. No attention is paid to it. Few people rank cross-section data from smallest to largest and look at the gigantic trends that are in there, that are hidden, dominating all the results they are getting. Let's take Oswald's result on housing. In 1900, 5 per cent of the housing stock in Britain was owner-occupied. Today it is well over 65 per cent. In 1900, 8 per cent of the population were unemployed. Today, 8 per cent of the population are unemployed. This suggests there is simply no relationship whatsoever between house-ownership and unemployment over a grand scale of time. What they are picking up is probably some sort of nonsense regressions in the data. These are very profound methodological viewpoints on which we differ. I don't think that cross-section data are any more reliable than time-series data. Once I fully understand time-series data I will move on to the even greater problems involved in trying to understand a series of snapshots in time, when there are hundreds of confounding factors on top of those that wash out, in my view, at the aggregate level.

I think the sort of work that John Muellbauer has done on the housing market, would fit in quite well with your views. He argues that owner-occupation does reduce mobility, which reduces the susceptibility of agents in the regions to falls in house prices. House prices fall when unemployment goes up, people get locked in and they can't move, and we should all adopt John Flemming's suggestion that everybody should own a house but they should rent it out. The two decisions would be separated.

Shadman-Mehta (2000) has done an enormously long study of the Phillips curve historically. Applying modern cointegration techniques to Phillips's data (the underlying data that Lipsey was the first to start analysing) you exactly replicate Phillips's result. It passes every diagnostic test. This fits in with your view of the army of the unemployed being the driving factor. It disappears pretty much totally in the interwar period when you get huge levels of unemployment and almost no change in wages. It goes the opposite direction using the same techniques in the post-war period. The causality, if you want to call it that, or the adjustment if you want to use a slightly silly pseudonym for what you really mean, goes the opposite direction. It seems to come on to unemployment from what is happening in the wage–price sectors, as if firms are maintaining the right to manage but they don't have the right to control what they pay their workers, so they sack them when it gets too expensive. I think her work would throw some light on the quantitative background to your paper.

Katarina Juselius: I would also like to comment on Ferri's paper. I think it is a nice result that you have to look at the Phillips curve in a system context. This relates to some empirical results I have found when using Danish wage data (*wages, prices, productivity, and unemployment*). When I analyse the data as a system I find very clear evidence of a Phillips curve. This is not usually the case if you look at the data taking just inflation and unemployment, but in the system context the Phillips curve is there and is quite strong. There is of course the problem that the coefficient changes with changes in regimes. In that sense it is not a regularity that is independent of institutional regimes. What I think is important, in order to understand the Phillips curve *empirically*, are the *ceteris paribus* assumptions *of the theoretical models*. As an empirical econometrician you have to condition on the *ceteris paribus* variables. But when controlling for the latter effects the Phillips curve appears again. I think it is important to see how this relationship changes with changes in regimes because it is important to look at institutional rigidities in the labour market. For instance, if labour unions are very strong they might be able to influence it. If they are not very strong, you have the opposite effect. In the USA, you see labour unions that are not very strong and you have a different relationship.

I think the relation that Oswald and Trostel find between unemployment and housing could also be explained in terms of resistance to *mobility because of* another factor that clearly influences the search process when you get unemployed. That is that if your spouse is also in the labour market, he/she will become unemployed if you move and one does not really gain anything in terms of the unemployment rate in total. Female participation may affect labour mobility and, hence, the unemployment rate.

Martin Eichenbaum: I found this an interesting session and would like to make a few comments about a tension I note in the conference. Some people want us to become more macro in the sense of more systems, and some want us to become more micro in the sense of paying more attention to micro-details. Since we also have the IS–LM session, I don't want to get into the larger debate right now about systems versus non-systems, but I do want to talk about what I think is one of the key virtues of 'optimization-based' or micro-based models. I think it was at the centre of Lucas's and Prescott's programmes to break down what I think someone referred to as separateness—this notion that there was a bunch of macro-guys who rarely talked to the micro-guys in some formal way. One really does see that in conferences in the USA—first of all when someone comes up with a model, they have been very explicit. Someone can come up to me and say, 'Marty, I hate that assumption and the reason I hate it is because I have got all this micro-evidence that it's really stupid.' I can talk about, for example, the Frisch elasticity of labour supply, which was very difficult to do twenty years ago. We did a study of this at Northwestern where we did a correlation of how students did in macro and micro and who the members of their committees were. It used to be that micro and macro were negatively correlated to prelims, but they are now positively correlated (about 0.9). Committees seem to be drawn almost at random so that a lot of the time I will be on a committee with two micro-guys. That is an extremely positive way to break down this separateness and let a macro-student use the information that has been generated in other fields. That seems, from the point of view of producing better science, to be an enormous virtue of micro-based macromodels.

There are very difficult issues about how to formally incorporate those micro-findings into aggregative models. Some of those tensions are displayed nicely in an issue of the *Journal of Economic Perspectives* (1996) where Prescott takes a very bold stand, saying 'I know what these parameters are, I stick them in and that is that.' Hansen and Heckman, to my taste, have a much more nuanced view of the difficulties of going from micro to macro. Agents don't wear their preferences on their foreheads saying what their Frisch labour supply elasticity is. These things are generated under maintained assumptions—and there is a tendency among young macro-guys to pluck out a number that was maintained under strong assumptions by a microeconomist and plunk it into a macromodel, and often it is not appropriate at all. There are deep scientific issues about how to do that and yet, when all is said and done, I would say that there is a body of things we believe that come from the micro viewed as a whole. When we see certain assumptions—that the labour-supply elasticity has to be some enormous number—we take from the micro-literature that that seems to be implausible. I don't think it is possible, if you start from a systems approach, to ask that kind of question and yell at me for making a dumb assumption.

Adrian Pagan: I don't think I can resist referring to an interview with Eichenbaum that is on his web page in which Northwestern students complain about the degree of mathematics in the courses and he says 'Only the bad ones!'.

I want to comment briefly on both papers. Ferri's paper makes a very interesting point about this question of what happened when the inflation rate started to accelerate. If you go back and look at Phillips's original paper you will see that he talked about estimating an equation in which there was on the right-hand side a cost-of-living term and that was the price of British exports. He was thinking of it in terms of real wages but because he couldn't find this in the data he threw it out. When he came to Australia and produced the second Phillips curve, the one that never got published, he faced the fact that wages were frequently being determined through a legal system in which there was essentially indexation, and so he had to think in terms of real wages. It was quite clear that he had that concept in the first place. But if you use data, and if you do estimation in a period in which that doesn't happen, then you just don't find it.

This raises the issue of whether you should stick to your theory: whether you should say 'I really believe this should be a real wage equation. Maybe I should put that regressor in there even though it isn't there in the data.' I wonder whether today we wouldn't have done that.

The second thing is that not only did the expected inflation rate change but increasingly there was the problem that even if you adjusted for that it was still unstable. In a lot of countries people said there was an increase in the NAIRU, and a large literature evolved on how we could allow the NAIRU to change. I would have liked to see something of this in the paper. Sooner or later we can add enough things into the equations to make them stable and we have to ask when we stop doing this. When does it cease to be a useful relationship.

One of the problems I have when I read Oswald and Trostel's paper is exactly what I am intended to learn from it. Do I take away from this sort of evidence the fact that labour mobility might be a problem and this affects the natural rate? I could believe that, but I don't get a handle on what the implication of all this material is. The one thing I did get a handle on was the question of the relationship between real wages and lagged profits, which you comment was important. That sort of equation appeared in Australian relationships many, many years ago. People discovered very early on that it was quite spurious because the biggest influence on the cyclical variability of profits is productivity variations, so if you build any real-wage equation you are going to have them influenced by productivity, but it is a moving average of productivity. Once you have allowed for that, the real profitability variable just disappears.

Daniel Hausman: In terms of the issue of what should we make of these empirical relationships—Backhouse asked to what extent we should be using them in theory. Obviously using them as the basis for further theorizing is a very precarious endeavour if we don't understand why those relationships obtain, even apart from doubts we might have about whether they are spurious or we have been mistaken in finding them, for a variety of well-known reasons that I don't need to repeat. I thought Oswald was, in addition, raising the question of whether we shouldn't be taking these seriously as facts that we might want to explain. Maybe this elasticity of the wage relationship is something that will break down shortly, and we wouldn't want to base any theory on it.

On the other hand, if it is indeed there and not a mistaken reading of the evidence, it seems as though it is precisely the thing we would want to explain. In trying to explain it we might learn something. So I think there is a real challenge to macroeconomists, not that they should throw these things casually into theories, but that they should regard them as needing explanation, unless you have very strong priors that these things are mistakes in using the data.

Tom Mayer: There used to be a lot of discussion in Britain about council housing inhibiting labour mobility because if you took a job in another area you ended up at the bottom of the housing list. I wonder if there are countries where this does not happen—where there is a high public housing component but you do not lose your housing preference by moving. If so, do they have a different coefficient for the housing term from countries like Britain?

Bennett McCallum: Oswald and Trostel's paper gives an interesting review of evidence that is evidently inconsistent with the view that labour markets operate in a simple competitive spot fashion. The evidence is interesting and none of it is particularly upsetting, except perhaps that about minimum wage laws. But I don't quite see what the implication is for what they call macro-type models of labour markets. I am attracted to Phillips-curve models that are of some of the most stringent neoclassical types, namely types that satisfy the strict version of the natural rate hypothesis, but I don't think that those depend on any assumption that labour markets operate in a simple competitive spot fashion. For me the issue is whether monetary policy will have any permanent effect on the characteristics of these things that you are talking about. I don't quite follow the message that macroeconomists are supposed to get from this.

Richard Lipsey: The question has been raised as to what would Phillips have done and I guess that as I was there I can say something about that. We had long discussions about real and nominal variables and indeed Milton Friedman looked me up in 1961 and said 'You should have had w/p as the independent variable.' My answer was also Phillips's, which was, 'No. What workers really bargain about is money wages. With some rare exceptions, that should be the behaviour to explain. If people care about real wages, then some price variable should be on the other side as one of the explanatory variables.' Phillips thought he had found it in his catch-up variable but when I applied standard statistical analysis (what was then accepted statistical analysis) we couldn't identify a significant relation. So we dropped it, not because we thought in principle it should not be there, but because it wasn't statistically significant. I am sure that if we had done the job ten years later the same form of price variable, actual or expected, would have come up as significant. In that case I would have said something quite different in my paper. But we held out against putting the real wage on the left-hand side of the equation because workers do not bargain about the real wage.

In so far as we can get micro-explanations of macro-relations, searching for them is a good research programme, but we don't want to turn it into a dogma. If we look at other sciences, we know that there are emerging properties such that, what you see at one level of observation cannot be deduced from behaviour at a lower level of observation. For example, you can never deduce the behaviour of water by looking at the behaviour of oxygen and hydrogen, nor could you deduce Boyle's law by looking at the behaviour of a single atom of a gas. These are emergent properties at a higher level of observation. We can't rule out in principle the existence of such emerging properties in economics, so the dogma that says everything must be rooted in a particular micro-branch is dangerous. Nonetheless, two rules matter: you shouldn't have a macro-relation that is obviously inconsistent with something we know at the micro-level, and in so far as you can deduce things at the microlevel it just provides links that are valuable and useful.

Observed empirical regularities are facts. There is no question about that. But they may or may not reflect structural relations. The facts are interesting and it is fun to ask what is behind them. Note, for example that it is much harder to sell a house in Britain than it is in America. Because neither offers to buy by a potential purchaser nor acceptances of such offers by potential sellers are binding, one gets this crazy situation that, after your offer is accepted, you may get gazumped. You also get long chains of conditional offers and acceptances that often collapse after long months of negotiations and legal expenses. In America, and I think also in Scotland, my offer to buy is binding if the seller accepts it and, if I offer the seller his asking price, he is bound to sell to me. The resulting high transactions costs of selling and buying real estate in England is a force you might be able to pick up if it is affecting labour mobility. Finally, I think there is some independent evidence about rent-sharing that can be derived from the experience of American deregulation. It turns out that the rents created by regulations were partly shared by the staff, and once deregulated competition hit, employees such as airline pilots, found themselves facing large drops in their incomes.

Ron Smith: It happens to be the case that macroeconometrics is time-series and microeconometrics is cross-section but the two issues are quite separate and raise quite different sorts of point. The other problem is that panel data are not the solution, because the cross-section dimension will be telling you a completely different story from the time-series dimension. In many cases what you are doing by doing panel data is, by chance, imposing one or the other depending on which happens to have the largest variance. I think that cross-section/time-series and the micro/macro both have distinct roles.

Grayham Mizon: I would like to comment on two issues. One is the theme of the conference—the role of evidence and theory—and the other, which was underlined in both these papers today, is the micro–macro distinction. I think they are related. I think that in considering the distinction between micro and macro it is important, or at least valuable, to separate the phenomenon in which we are interested from the methods and tools that we would use to analyse that phenomenon. Once it is clear what the phenomenon of interest is, often that will determine what is the appropriate empirical evidence to use. For macro-phenomena we will use macro-data. Equally for a micro one we use micro-data. When it comes to developing models as a framework for analysing the phenomena of interest though, the methods of analysis should be good but the choice between micro- or macro-based tools is less clear-cut. However, whilst I personally would be happiest with a macrotheory for analysing a macro-problem, I would be equally happy for people to develop micro-based theories if they could demonstrate that they have relevant implications for the macro-phenomenon under study.

Turning to Andrew Oswald's presentation and the unemployment–ownership relationship, which has attracted attention from many people, I too felt that this may well be a nonsense regression. Also, looking at the graph presented today, the cluster of points seems to be very much like a circular cloud with a few errant observations giving -0.1 as the estimated slope. So this appears to be a case of outliers determining the relationship. But then if we have this empirical relationship, and maybe it is coming about because of outliers, we need an interpretation. Maybe what you have in own-ership is a proxy for mobility. I was impressed by your reference to Spain. Spain has the highest unemployment and ownership in Europe. But then I thought of where I am living at the moment in Italy. There is high unemployment, particularly in the South. My observation is that home-ownership is not high, so that wouldn't work. However, from what I have observed in Italy there are other social reasons why people are less mobile than they would be otherwise. To look for a relationship between unemployment and mobility may be valuable.

Ferri:[1] I found the discussion particularly encouraging. In my paper, I raised three methodological points that have been touched in the discussion by different people: a nice division of labour.

The first methodological point concerns the status of the Phillips curve as a system result. This aspect has been underlined by Juselius who also stresses the importance of studying the Phillips curve in a system context. This approach opens the way to understanding the nature of the various regimes that had a big impact on the shape and the nature of the Phillips curve.

The second aspect of my paper refers to the nature of the dependent variable, i.e. the debate on nominal versus real wage determination. Even though it is true that people consider real targets, it is also true that in a monetary economy you can only get nominal wages. This does not mean that prices are not important, but that they play different roles according to different institutional regimes prevailing. This has been underlined by both Lipsey and Pagan.

The third methodological aspect concerns the possibility of explaining within a unified framework the different kinds of the Phillips curve that appeared in time. According to Hendry, applying modern cointegration techniques to Phillips's data, one can replicate the different patterns. This is very encouraging. However, from an economic point of view, this is not enough because one has to put forward reasonable explanations.

---

[1] Because of a failure of the tape recording, the responses by Ferri and Oswald to the discussion were added after the conference.

More generally, one can realise that most of the discussants have touched upon the two papers. This is evidence for the strong methodological link between them. I underlined the relationship between the labour market and the system (i.e. the other markets), while Oswald and Trostel stressed the micro-relationships underlying macro-results. I worked on widening and they opted for deepening. Both these aspects receive relatively simple answers within a neoclassical framework, while all the other attempts look more problematic. However, one must remember that simple does not mean correct.

Andrew Oswald: [Because of recording problems at the conference, I have been asked to write this comment after the conference, so can do so from the calm of my study.] Let me stick to two things. First, is the positive correlation between unemployment and home-ownership simply spurious? This is suggested by David Hendry and Graham Mizon—admittedly after only a brief look at one type of evidence. There are many worse snap reactions to have in economics.

It does, though, remind me of what the tobacco companies said in the 1950s—my current non-economics reading so it is in my mind—when they discovered the scientific work fairly early in the twentieth century on a cross-section correlation between cancer and smoking. Those companies also were fond of finding examples of ninety-year-olds who had smoked a pack a day—like Mizon's Italian example (though Southern Italy has a high home-ownership rate, in fact). And they were fond of pointing out that the growth of traffic pollution was a better time-series correlate with the growth of lung cancer in Western society.

Hendry and Mizon are absolutely right. It is entirely possible, and even likely at first glance, that the correlation is spurious. For that reason I kept quiet about this evidence for a couple of years, while I did checks and gathered other data, and found out whether the correlation survived tests for fixed effects. Philip and I also discussed this issue in constructing the paper.

But I have come to believe that they are substantively wrong. There are two reasons to believe in a causal link. (i) Standard neoclassical theory tells us both that mobility rates will affect the natural rate of unemployment (indeed Milton Friedman said this in his famous AEA address), and that the nature of the housing market will affect people's mobility, so there is nothing unusual about the underlying theoretical idea. (ii) The statistical link between unemployment rates and low levels of private renting has now shown up in the data too many times and in too many settings to be in any simple sense spurious: for example in cross-sections for countries (as shown at the conference), panels of countries in which year dummies and many other variables are included to mop up some of the omitted things Hendry is rightly worried about, panels of European regions, and panels of US states. The correlation certainly could be spurious, in some deep sense that we do not currently understand (as is true of every published piece of applied economics, incidentally), but it is not spurious in an elementary sense. No variable known to me in the history of unemployment research is as well correlated. Since the conference, I have discovered that the new Layard–Nickell chapter in the North-Holland *Labour Economics Handbook* will include a statistically significant role for one of my home-ownership variables. Moreover, as this writing goes to press, I have been looking at the latest 1999 OECD *Employment Outlook*. In Table 2.8, its unemployment equations find only one statistically significant variable in a panel of European nations—and it is not benefits, unions, labour taxes, and all those other things we routinely hear about in newspaper leaders. You can guess.

In short, it is perfectly sensible, and necessary, to ask whether economists' correlations are believable. I do it all the time. Indeed applied economics is about little else. But we need to have criteria by which we come to believe, or at least not to disbelieve; there is no point in immediately being against a pattern in data because we are not used to it.

Second, David Hendry gets at interesting methodological issues. I cannot do justice to them in a paragraph. My own view is that it pays to use a range of types of complementary evidence. That is always my main piece of advice to a young economist. In this sense, I am against what I take to be the implicit opinion put forward by Hendry that 'you will have to show it to me in aggregate time-series data to get my attention.' If that is his view, and perhaps it is not, then I think he is dead wrong.

It is an excellent and important point that the UK had high levels of private renting early in the century. It may even be that unemployment then was the same as now (the jobless data, imputed from limited union records, are open to more dispute than Hendry implies). But in any case this is a problem for every existing theory of high unemployment—not just mine. Most of the variables commonly blamed for Europe's high joblessness were low at the beginning of the century. So we all have a lot to learn and must be missing some part of the picture.

On spurious correlations in time-series versus in cross-sections, well, I do not see a strong distinction. The issue continues to be: is there a believable theoretical reason for a relationship, and are we seeing a correlation in so many different ways and with so many robustness and causality checks that we start to believe in it? Economics is as simple, and difficult, as that.

REFERENCES

Kydland, F. E. and Prescott, E. C. (1996) 'The computational experiment: an econometric tool', *Journal of Economic Perspectives* 10(1): 69–85.

Shadman-Mehta, F. (2000) 'An empirical study of the determinants of real wages and employment: the Phillips curve revisited', in R. Leeson (ed.), *A. W. H. Phillips: Collected Works in Contemporary Perspective* (Cambridge: Cambridge University Press).

Part III

NEW KEYNESIAN ECONOMICS

8 Imperfect capital markets: a new macroeconomic paradigm?

DOMENICO DELLI GATTI AND ROBERTO TAMBORINI

Introduction

Today's macroeconomic theoretical, empirical and normative analysis is essentially split between the scholars who base their work on the first principles of the Walrasian paradigm of perfectly competitive markets—and do not attach any scientific value to Keynesian economics at large—and those who believe that Keynes's view of possible misfunctioning of market economies was fundamentally correct though Keynesian economics needs accurate restructuring at the (micro)foundations level.

The latter approach, that following Greenwald and Stiglitz (1987), is known as New Keynesian (NK) economics, is usually identified with a large body of literature concerned with imperfect competition and the microfoundations of real or nominal rigidities as if it were the only 'typical' NK brand (e.g. Gordon 1990). With this paper we wish to draw attention to a different NK line of research claiming that the core of the Keynesian view of the world need not rely upon rigidities but on the macroeconomic consequences of capital market failures due to imperfect information (see e.g. Greenwald and Stiglitz 1987, 1993*b*; Stiglitz 1992*a*). Indeed, this distinction between wage and price rigidities, on the one hand, and capital market failures on the other is reminiscent of the two basic interpretations of Keynes's original message throughout its history. Hence our aim is not only to survey the results of the NK economics of imperfect capital markets, but also to assess whether this body of literature has the characteristics of a macroeconomic paradigm alternative to the Walrasian one.

We devote Section 1 to an overview of the main theories of capital markets, emphasizing, in particular, the new approaches based on the pervasive role of asymmetric information. This phenomenon has far-reaching implications, not only for the analysis of the working mechanism of capital markets, but also for the theory of financial intermediation and of the capital structure of firms. We shall emphasize, in particular, the fact that asymmetric information can explain the presence of a *financing hierarchy* in firms' capital structure. This is the root of the macroeconomic models surveyed in Sections 2 and 3. In Section 2 we present and discuss macromodels of income, employment, and price determination. In particular, we will review models of income determination in a *fix-price* framework in which equilibrium output is basically *demand-led* and the terms at which credit is extended by banks to finance investment

The authors wish to thank Mark Blaug and Axel Leijonhufvud for their comments. R. Tamborini gratefully acknowledges financial support by MURST, grant no. 9813624037.

expenditure play a crucial role in shaping aggregate demand (Bernanke and Blinder 1988) and models of income determination in a *flex-price* framework in which equilibrium output is *supply-driven* and the risk of bankruptcy affects employment and production decisions on the part of firms (Greenwald and Stiglitz 1988*b*, 1990, 1993*a*). Section 3 deals with macrodynamic models, i.e. models in which financial factors are important in the determination of the business cycle. First of all, we discuss the dynamic extension of the Greenwald and Stiglitz framework. Then, we analyse the framework put forward by Bernanke and Gertler (1989, 1990) in which the supply of the capital stock entirely depends upon the flow of entrepreneurial saving (internal finance). Finally we will briefly discuss the most recent work by Kiyotaki and Moore (1997) on 'credit cycles'. Section 4 is devoted to conclusions.

1. Theories of capital markets

1.1. Capital market failures, Keynes, and the Keynesians

The paradigm of perfect capital markets is essentially a set of conditions such that any investor considering an investment with a given rate of return faces a unique cost of capital *r*. Consequently, *the decision as to whether the investment under consideration is feasible or not is independent of the form of capital supply*. Indeed, as long as the market rate of return to any investment (real or financial) is *r*, no rational agent in no form would supply capital to obtain less than *r*. This fundamental property of perfect capital markets is nothing but an application of the 'law of one price' (which financial economists prefer to call 'no arbitrage condition'). This argument is also the core of the well-known Modigliani–Miller 'indifference theorem' (1958) which applies to the financial structure of a whole firm as well as to the financing of any new investment. The efficient amount of investment in the economy is uniquely determined by available projects whose real returns exceed the market interest rate.

Capital markets are 'perfect' under a number of conditions underlying the law of one price of capitals. A list of conditions is the following:

- *perfect competition*: all agents are price-takers, have no market power, and enjoy free entry and exit
- *no transaction costs*: there are zero non-price costs whatsoever as agents perform spot exchanges or stipulate contracts
- *perfect information*: all agents have free access to the same information set which may be complete (certainty) or incomplete (risk)

Accordingly, capital market failures may, theoretically, emerge when one or more of these conditions is not met. The whole history of monetary and financial economics witnesses an ongoing debate between scholars who argue that almost all relevant aspects of capital markets and financial institutions can only be explained as a response to the absence of one or the other condition of perfection, so that availability of financial resources, if not strict money, cannot be neutral on the level of economic activity, and scholars who think that the perfect capital markets paradigm remains the best guideline for positive as well as normative research. The NK literature that we shall examine in this paper has decidedly swung the pendulum back towards the first type of view. However, before probing into this new wave of the debate, it is worth throwing a glance to the peculiar path of Keynesian thought.

Throughout the first half of its parable, the 'Keynesian revolution' was understood, explained, and taught precisely as a departure from the neoclassical macroeconomic general equilibrium theory on the grounds of perfect capital markets (Leijonhufvud 1992). We do not wish to engage in the exegetics of Keynes here, but there is no doubt that a large part—someone would say the core—of the *General Theory* was devoted to explain unemployment equilibrium as a result of a mismatch between investment and saving due to a capital market failure—essentially related to the 'monetary nature of the rate of interest' as opposed to the 'real' nature of it.[1] From this point of view, Keynes's discussion in the *General Theory* of the role of the labour market in the adjustment process in the event of excess saving, and in particular of the possibility that the real wage may not fall *enough*, should be understood as a warning that there is no reason to expect that the misallocational effects of a 'wrong' price of capital will necessarily be corrected through changes in the price of labour by market forces. Wage stickiness, though possibly a fact of real life, is a side issue in this theoretical picture. As a matter of fact, the theoretical debate in the aftermath of the *General Theory* concentrated on the theory of the interest rate (see Moggridge 1987: 201–367) with little or no reference at all to wage stickiness. In this perspective, one of the most challenging theoretical legacies of the *General Theory* was that a 'flex-price economy' *with imperfect capital markets* is not reducible to the usual properties of the neoclassical macroeconomic model.

After sixty years of macroeconomic research we have a clear understanding of the functioning of a Walrasian 'flex-price economy' and of a Keynesian 'fix-price economy', whereas our knowledge of a flex-price economy with imperfect capital market is still very limited. This backwardness in macroeconomic theory finds one main reason in the fact that early Keynesian research was soon trapped in the fix-price–flex-price alternative as if any 'flex-price economy' were *ipso facto* a Walrasian economy. After the early debates between Keynes and his critics mentioned above and their continuation in the loanable-funds versus liquidity-preference controversy, and after the textbook tradition of the 1950s and 1960s, where saving–investment equality rather than aggregate demand–supply equality was at the centre of analysis, by the mid-1970s the idea that capital market failures had an integral part in Keynes's theory was buried under the mountain of the fix-price–flex-price debate. The brand of Keynesian economics that had kept closer to that idea, the Hicks–Tobin extension of portfolio theory to macroeconomics, proved unable to overcome the attacks of the various 'irrelevance theorems'—in the specific case new editions of

---

[1] 'Real' here refers not simply to the interest rate net of inflation but to its role in the allocation of resources between present and future consumption (i.e. saving and investment) in intertemporal equilibrium.

the Modigliani–Miller theorem—that were launched by the New Classicals from the grounds of the Walrasian paradigm of rational behaviour and perfectly competitive markets.[2]

Apart from the sparse works of few applied financial economists or heretics (such as Minsky 1975, 1982), the theoretical research on the role of capital markets was carried on by few scholars who drew on the developments of the Walrasian paradigm as a key to understanding the origin and extent of the 'Keynesian revolution' (e.g. Brechling and Hahn 1965; Leijonhufvud 1968, 1969, 1981; Hahn 1977; Weintraub 1979). They contributed to the idea that the recovery and development of a programme centred on Keynes's view would require an alternative paradigm whose (minimal) key points of (successful) distinction from the Walrasian one would be one, or a combination, of the following: (a) bounded rationality, (b) imperfect information, (c) incomplete markets.[3] The line of NK research based on imperfect capital markets is grafted onto these previous results, and hence it tends to some extent to present itself as alternative to the other NK family (e.g. Greenwald and Stiglitz 1988a, 1993b; Stiglitz 1992a)[4]

For more than a decade now, I and several of my coauthors (. . .) have been exploring the thesis that it is imperfections in the capital market—imperfections that themselves can be explained by imperfect information—which account for many of the peculiar aspects of the behaviour of the economy which macroeconomics attempts to explain. (Stiglitz 1992a: 269)

[This] second strand of New Keynesian literature explores another path suggested by Keynes: that increased flexibility of prices and wages might exacerbate the economy's downturn. This insight implies that wage and price rigidity are not the only problem, and perhaps not even the central problem. (Greenwald and Stiglitz 1993b: 25)

1.2. New Keynesian foundations

Although Stiglitz and his co-authors stress their interest in pursuing Keynes's legacy, it is fair to notice that, as is typical in the NK approach in general, research is mostly oriented by 'macroeconomic stylized facts and puzzles' rather than by pure doctrinal issues. As Stiglitz (1992a) argues, the perfect capital market paradigm underlying the

---

[2] Nor can we overlook the fact that Tobin himself was fully within the fix-price–flex-price divide arguing time and again that complete wage–price flexibility and continuous market clearing are theoretical abstractions, whereas 'all Keynesian macroeconomics really requires is that product prices and money wages are not perfectly flexible' but are adjusted slowly through time (1993: 56).

[3] See also Colander (1998). With a totally different theoretical and methodological background, and a plea for a more radical divorce from all aspects of orthodoxy, the so-called Post-Keynesians reached basically the same conclusions, and contributed for their part to the breakdown of the Keynesian–Neoclassical synthesis and to the search for an autonomous Keynesian paradigm. Though the Post-Keynesians are fiercely adverse to any orthodox treatment of rational decision-making under uncertainty, imperfect information, and incomplete markets, of which they blame the NKs, the role of capital markets and financial institutions in the macroeconomic processes is certainly the area of less distance, if not of dialogue, between the two families of Keynes's heirs (see esp. Davidson (1972) and Minsky (1975, 1982). For a detailed discussion see Rotheim (1998: pt. III).).

[4] The reader interested in more extended methodological aspects of the NK economics of imperfect capital markets can especially see Stiglitz (1992a,b) and Greenwald and Stiglitz (1983, 1993).

neoclassical tradition as well as modern New Classical and real business-cycle theories is first of all under attack as being sharply in contrast with basic facts of economic cycles. Three of them are of particular significance in this context:

- investment is almost everywhere the most unstable (large variance) component of GDP by such an extent that it seems hard to justify by changes in social inter-temporal preferences,
- changes in real interest rates do not display the amplitude that would be necessary to stabilize aggregate demand in the event of the observed investment shocks, and
- consequently, we observe the ubiquitous co-movements between investment, consumption, and GDP over the cycle.

As everyone sees, these are indeed the key predictions of the Keynesian real business-cycle theory, and what the NKs wish is to discover better explanations than those provided by the 'Keynesian–Neoclassical synthesis'. Moreover, the NKs concerned with imperfect capital markets argue that old and new business-cycle explanations merely based on the stickiness of wages and prices are unsatisfactory.

The foundations of the NK macroeconomics of imperfect capital markets essentially rest on the above paradigmatic points (b) and (c), i.e. imperfect information and incomplete markets.[5] Although some leading NKs are on the forefront of current research on these issues, it would be misleading to label *all* this vast and multifaceted foundational work as NK. Rather, what qualifies the NK programme is the use of these foundations for macroeconomic purposes. The NKs embed imperfect information and incomplete markets in a methodological choice concerning the treatment of time and a methodological consequence concerning the 'special nature' of financial 'goods'. Thus we may identify four foundational points whose content we shall recall very briefly

1. *Agents heterogeneity.* Markets exist and trades take place because agents differ. Traditional microeconomics concentrates on differences in preferences and/or endowments as inducements to trade; the NK economics concentrates on differences in information endowments.
2. *Imperfect information.* Agents have free access to a *public information set* on relevant current and future state variables, which may be incomplete for the future variables (probabilistic risk), but do not have free access to each other's *private information set* on individual pay-off-relevant variables or actions (asymmetric information).
3. *Incomplete markets.* Agents are constrained not to trade for goods to which they attach positive value. Note that the definition of asymmetric information implies at least one missing market, the market for private information.[6]

---

[5] As to bounded rationality, Stiglitz's methodological writings recognize the importance of the issue and its relevance to the NK programme, but NK models have so far dispensed with this assumption.

[6] On the impossibility of a market for private information when it is costly and valuable to the owner see Grossman and Stiglitz (1980).

4. *Sequential time and transactions.* Markets operate and trades take place in discrete 'calendar' time-periods. In each period, only spot transactions take place.[7] Hence, the definition of sequential time and transactions implies in addition the absence of future contingent markets.

5. *The 'special nature' of financial 'goods'.* Capital markets treat 'special goods', namely financial contracts. They are special for a number of reasons: (a) they are immaterial entitlements to *future* delivery of *money* payments, (b) the transaction involved is opened spot (the purchase of the entitlement), but is closed in the future (the delivery of the money payment), and (c) the open end of the transaction is dependent upon both general market states and specific individual states or actions of the party due to deliver the money payment.

It is the combination of the first four points with the fifth that places capital markets outside the Walrasian paradigm. In a financial relationiship three informational activities are involved as it unfolds over time:

- *screening* (before entering the contractual relationship) to ascertain the distribution of the characteristics of the demanders,
- *monitoring* (during a specific contractual relationship) to ascertain that the use of resources made by the demander is consistent with the contractual commitment, and
- *auditing* (at the end of a specific relationship) to ascertain the final value of the resources employed.

Imperfect information is not removed when any of the above-mentioned informational activities is lacking. Table 8.1 summarizes the relevant taxonomy.

In turn each of these activites may have an *opportunity cost* to the supplier, and/or some of the bits of information involved *may not be attainable* at all. In the first case, when paying the cost is sufficient for the supplier to obtain all the relevant information, the market operates with *transaction costs*. In the second case, when some information remains hidden to the supplier, the market operates under *asymmetric information* as defined previously.[8]

---

[7] On the method of sequential time or 'sequence economies' see also Hahn (1988).

[8] Transaction costs are a well-known fact in capital markets activities and have long been considered a source of imperfections—they have been the first and more traditional approach to the problem (e.g. Gurley and Shaw 1960; Brainard and Tobin 1967). These early studies led to explanations of *financial intermediation* as a means to minimize transaction costs. They moved from a relatively simple type of transaction costs—basically fixed cost per unit of transaction—and hence viewed the efficiency gain of intermediation in the exploitation of *operation economies of scale*. In retrospect, these explanations reveal two main limits: the first is their inability to distinguish between different types of financial intermediaries—namely non-bank and bank intermediaries; the second is that they leave the perfect capital market paradigm unaffected (if not stronger) showing that if there are 'frictions' these are minimized through intermediation. By contrast, the modern theory of intermediation focuses on the information-related transaction costs recalled above and points to explain different types of intermediation as solutions for different types of informational cost. On the other hand, the presumption that the emergence of intermediaries ensures the absence of capital market failures can no longer be taken for granted. We shall present some of these results in due time.

TABLE 8.1. *Summary of relevant taxonomy*

	Type of asymmetry	Consequence
Screening	*Ex ante*	*Adverse selection*: probability of transacting with low-quality subjects
Monitoring Auditing	*Ex post*	*Moral hazard*: opportunity of non-observable actions by the counter-party

Analyses of financial relationships under costly or asymmetric information produce results that as a rule imply some form of capital market failure. Market failures emerge as a consequence of two possible responses of rational agents to imperfect information: one, in a context of predefined contracts, *ex ante* asymmetry and adverse selection, is the uninformed party's use of the price of the financial transaction as an indicator of the hidden information about the other party (e.g. Stiglitz 1987), the other, in a context of *ex post* asymmetry and moral hazard, is the design of financial contracts apt to regulate the conflict of interests between the better-informed and the worse-informed party once the relationship is established (e.g. Hart 1995: pt. II). In both contexts, the optimal solution for individuals may entail a loss of allocative efficiency at the market level. We shall see some relevant cases in the following parts of the paper.

1.3. Financial hierarchy, financial constraints, and capital rationing

Capital market failures in the NK approach are generally related to violations of the Modigliani–Miller theorem in any of the following forms:

- *financial hierarchy* (or *pecking order*): first comes a violation of the law of one price, i.e. different forms of capital supply have different costs to the investing firm; consequently, the firm finances investment starting from the cheapest form of capital supply and resorts to other forms only as the scale and the expected return of investment increase sufficiently.
- *financial constraints*: some classes of firms may have no access at all to some forms of capital supply; hence their ability to invest is constrained by the amount of external resources available in the forms which they have access to or by the amount of internal resources.

As to the first type of violation, it has long been noticed in the business and applied finance literature that the cost of capital is far from being uniform in capital markets, and that investing firms typically display a diversified structure of investment finance. The evidence on financial hierarchy collected in the past and in the present is extremely vast: Fazzari *et al.* (1988), Mayer (1988, 1990, 1994), Hubbard (1990, 1998), and Bond and Jenkinson (1996), to mention only few among the most recent works.

Mayer (1994: 4) summarizes the evidence thus:

Two stylized facts about corporate financing are, first, that internally generated funds are the most significant source of finance for firms in most developed countries and, second, that bank finance is the most importante source of external finance.

Therefore, the increasing order of magnitude of the cost of capital seems to go from internal funds to bank debt up to market debt and equity. Accordingly, the decreasing order of magnitude of investment finance goes from equity to internal funds. Given the key role that the equity market plays in all models of perfect capital markets and even in the popular idea of what is a good and well-functioning capitalism, this evidence is certainly astonishing. One of the most important achievements of the new theories of capital markets with imperfect information has been to give rigorous and fruitful explanations of these well-known facts.

1.3.1. Equity cost and equity rationing. As a prototype of equity-market failures, let us consider the case of *ex ante* asymmetric information between managers and the equity market, where managers are better informed than the market. This class of situations derives from Akerlof's (1970) 'lemon problem' of adverse selection, and was extended to the equity market by Leland and Pyle (1977), Myers and Majluf (1984), and Greenwald *et al.* (1984). The key problem is that if two companies are identical except that one has higher expected return to investment than the other, but the market treats their investment as equally valuable, it quotes them at the same price. Pooling companies of different quality together underprices those of good quality and overprices those of bad quality. As long as the market is unable to discriminate investments perfectly, equities represent a source of high-cost capital for good companies. Hence these companies may refrain from financing investments in the equity market or may even be unable to finance all valuable investments on this market—what is usually known as 'equity rationing'.

Stiglitz (1985) discusses in detail the reasons why small shareholders in a competitive equity market may not have incentives to bear the costs to reduce *ex ante* asymmetric information (the 'small voter' paradox), while managers may not have incentives to bear the costs necessary to disseminate insider information. Thus *ex ante* asymmetric information and adverse selection seem endemic in a competitive equity market.

Stiglitz's argument extends to *ex post* asymmetric information too, in particular to the lack of management monitoring which is typical of small shareholders. Yet a competitive equity market (many small public companies and many small shareholders) is a good case for pure theory, but in reality in developed equity markets we find large controlled corporations and huge institutional investors like investment funds, pension funds, etc. The small voter paradox certainly applies with less force to these financial intermediaries; indeed, their incentive and skills in reducing asymmetric information may be invoked to explain their existence and efficiency. The marginal role of the equity market in investment finance has thus to be sought for in other directions too. One is the design of the firm's financial structure in order to regulate the agency problems that arise in connection with *ex post* asymmetric information between shareholders and managers as suggested by Jensen and Meckling (1976). Another is the problem of control: as Leland and Pyle (1977) point out, removing asymmetric information is a double-edged knife, for private information may also be valuable to the owner, and all means that reduce asymmetric information entail an erosion of value of private information and of control of insiders in favour of outsiders.[9]

1.3.2. Bank debt and credit rationing. We have seen that the evidence on investment finance across industrialized countries shows that bank debt is the second substantial source of capital supply for investing firms after internal funds. This fact prompts an important theoretical question: why is it that investing firms prefer a debt relationship with a bank to equity capital? A second related question is then: does the bank solve the capital markets informational problems in such a way that we may safely ignore capital markets imperfections (for pure theoretical purposes)? Here we are not concerned with the theory of banking for its own sake,[10] but with how information-based theories of banking are embodied by NK macroeconomic models of capital markets.

The specificity of the bank as it emerges from the research on imperfect capital markets hinges on the fact that the bank offers a peculiar *personal, non-marketable, non-contingent* contract.[11] Townsend (1979), Diamond (1984), and Gale and Hellwig (1985) are the seminal works that have examined this question, and they have found that the bank 'standard debt contract' (see below) can be explained as the optimal financial contract whenever removing the lender's asymmetric information is costly.[12]

Let us approach this idea with a simple introductory model. Consider a population of firms j each having an investment project of money value I_j with quality defined by its probability of success α_j. First, there may be an *ex ante* screening problem: the quality of each project is not freely observable to outsiders, but it can be ascertained at a cost θI_j. Second, there may be an *ex post* monitoring and auditing problem: the true amount of the firm's resources can only be established by incurring a cost M_j. The optimal financial relationship has two stages:

(i) individual lenders confer funds to an intermediary at the fixed rate i,
(ii) the intermediary offers the borrower a debt contract that specifies: the money value of the loan L_j; the amount due in case of success $L_j(1 + r_j)$; and the sum G_j that the borrower is commited to pay in case of default.[13]

[9] See futher development in Hart (1995).
[10] See e.g. Battacharya and Thakor (1993), Marotta and Pittaluga (1993), Mayer (1994), and Van Damme (1994), for thorough reviews of the literature.
[11] This view is reminiscent of Keynes's complaint that equity market relationships have exactly the opposite characteristics (1936: ch.12).
[12] The contract is optimal in the sense that it maximizes the borrower's expected profit from being truthful under the constraint of minimizing the informational costs of the lender.
[13] Generally the optimal amount of G_j is the firm's revenue.

Given that the intermediary pays the market risk-free rate i its expected profit is:

$$z^e = (G_j - M_j)(1 - \alpha_j) + (1 + r_j)L_j\alpha_j - (1 + i + \theta)L_j. \tag{1.1}$$

The competitive condition of zero expected profit implies that the interest rate charged to firm j must be:

$$1 + r_j = \frac{1 + i + \theta - (1 - \alpha_j)\gamma_j}{\alpha_j} \tag{1.2}$$

with $\gamma_j = (G_j - M_j)/L_j$.

Therefore, this financial relationship implies: (a) perfect price discrimination of borrowers, and (b) a premium of the interest rate over the risk-free rate increasing in the unit screening cost and decreasing in the quality of the borrower and in the value of the borrower's commitments net of monitoring costs.

The efficiency of the debt contract arises to the extent that the bank may have a *comparative advantage in the informational activities* (see also Stiglitz and Weiss 1988).[14] It is clear that the key variables in this approach are the costs of removing asymmetric information (θ and M_j) which are supposed to be lower for the bank than for any other agent. Such advantage may in turn arise from two features of bank activity. The first is specialization, that is the possession of knowledge and skills such that these costs are minimized. The second relates to the bank's nature of intermediary and to the old wisdom of economies of scale with respect to small independent savers. Moreover, as Mayer (1988, 1990, 1994) and Hellwig (1991) have stressed forcefully, whereas economies of scale in screening or auditing may be common to all financial intermediaries, what is typical and most important in the bank is just that bank loans are *long-term relationships* such that all information remains between the firm and the bank. Analyses of these features of banking are less developed (see Van Damme 1994: Section 6; Marotta and Pittaluga 1993: ch. 3), but focus on the idea that the solution to financial informational problems has to be seen not simply in the optimal design of the standard debt contract, or in static advantages in information technology, but in the *set of services and instruments* that the bank can activate *throughout the whole life of the investment*.

But also banks may face imperfect information, as shown by one of the best-known NK models of capital market failure: credit rationing (Stiglitz and Weiss 1981). Suppose that: (a) firms differ in their probability of success α_j as before, but all firms' investments have the same expected value (as a consequence, the return to investment in case of success must be inversely related to α_j); (b) the bank cannot achieve perfect screening of the exact quality of each investment, but only the correct probability distribution of the quality of investments in the population of firms.

Therefore, with respect to the previous case, the bank operates on the basis of a single (average) probability of success α, and a single interest rate r for all firms (for

---

[14] The idea goes back to Schumpeter (1934) who put credit availability at the centre stage in the capitalistic development.

simplicity let $\theta = 0$, $G_j = 0$, $M_j = 0$). However, in a heterogeneous market α is no longer independent of r, for an increase in r increases the weight of more risky—low α—firms in the population; hence the bank faces a problem of adverse selection.[15] Hence, let simply posit a function $\alpha(r) \in [0, 1]$, $\alpha_r < 0$, $\alpha_{rr} < 0$. Now the bank's expected profit is

$$z^e = (1 + r)L\alpha(r) - (1 + i)L, \tag{1.3}$$

which is no longer monotocally increasing in r because of the adverse selection effect captured by the function $\alpha(r)$. In fact, the expected profit function, under the above assumptions, is concave, and reaches a maximum at a particular value r^*, where the increase in the expected revenue from each loan is exactly offset by the decrease of the probability of success. Therefore, each bank is willing to lend to any firm only within a limited range of interest rates $r \in [\underline{r}, r^*]$, where $\underline{r}$ is the zero expected-profit interest rate. A major consequence *may be* credit rationing: i.e. *if* capital demand at r^* exceeds credit supply, $I(r^*) > L(r^*)$, then the level of investment is constrained by credit supply, $I = \min(I(r^*), L(r^*))$, and some firms are (randomly) rationed by the amount $I(r^*) - L^*(r^*)$.

Credit rationing is a controversial result that seems quite sensitive to the initial assumptions concerning information and the means, other than the interest rate, the bank can use to screen the quality of firms.[16] Also, credit rationing has received less empirical support than equity rationing. Italy, for instance, is a country were equity finance is much less developed than in other industrial economies and credit is a pervasive form of business finance; nonetheless, the evidence in favour of credit rationing is rather weak, perhaps with the exception of less developed, more risky Southern regions (e.g. Pittaluga 1988; Angeloni *et al.* 1997). King (1986) has found only mixed support for credit rationing in the US data, while Berger and Udell (1992) openly criticize the Stiglitz–Weiss approach in the light of direct analysis of banking practices.

In the whole, it seems plausible to argue that bank debt *is* a substitute for equity capital just because banks provide a whole set of instruments and activities that in some circumstances deal with asymmetric information *more efficiently* than the equity market, and hence firms perceive *lower or no* rationing probability in the credit market. However, even in the absence of credit rationing, the shift from equity capital to bank debt changes dramatically the macroeconomic picture with respect to the neoclassical theory of perfect capital markets (possibly with 'neutral' intermediaries) for three main reasons that will emerge in the remaining parts of the paper. The first is that credit supply may still be traced back to Keynes's principle of liquidity preference and of 'the monetary nature of the rate of interest'. The second is that credit supply is related to

---

[15] This problem can arise either because the firms have a predetermined quality, but a higher interest rates discriminates against those with low return and high α_j (see assumption (a)), or because the firms can choose among different projects and, for the same reason, are forced to choose those with high return and low α_j. See also Jaffee and Russell (1976) and Keeton (1979).

[16] For reviews of the debate see also Jaffee and Stiglitz (1990) and Ardeni and Messori (1996).

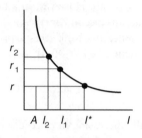

FIG. 8.1.

monetary policy both because of the previous reason and because of the special ties between banks and the central bank. The third is that bank debt changes managers' behaviour in a way that modifies profoundly the theory of production underlying aggregate supply.[17]

1.3.3. Aggregate investment when capital markets are imperfect. The thrust of the NK view is that asymmetric information can produce capital market failures both in the equity market (equity rationing) and in the credit market (credit rationing). Hence the economy has a tendency to underinvest with consequences on the activity level as well as the growth rate. However, even milder violations of the Modigliani–Miller law of one price of capital—i.e. an increasing cost of external versus internal capital—may account for significant departures from Walrasian macroeconomics, notably in the form of underinvestment. Figure 8.1 (see also Fazzari *et al.* 1988), portrays a distribution function of investment projects in the economy according to their expected return, hence the horizontal axis measures total investment *I*. The vertical axis measures the cost of capital to firms. The base rate *r* is representative of the opportunity cost for those firms who own the money value of investment; r_1 and r_2 measure the cost of capital for those firms that resort to external finance, say bank debt and equity capital respectively. The three rates differ for the reasons discussed above.

The level of investment in the economy now depends on the access of firms to the different sources of finance:

(1) *unconstrained firms*: I^* is the level of investment if all firms have internal funds no less than the money value of their respective investment, say $A_j \geq I_j$, all *j*;
(2) *constrained firms*: suppose that only the amount *A* of internal funds is available to firms. The resulting level of investment in the economy depends on the access of constrained firms to (a) bank debt at the rate $r_1(I_1)$, (b) equity capital at the rate $r_2(I_2)$.

Consequently, aggregate investment can be found somewhere between *A* and I^* depending on the characteristics and financial structure of firms. *Heterogeneity of firms,*

[17] For a wider discussion of these points see Messori and Tamborini (1995).

as already stressed, is a key feature of the determination of aggregate investment, but in any case the extent of investment loss below the potential level I^* can be related to the amount of internal funds of firms. This general conclusion has been exploited in the proliferation of empirical works aimed at testing the incidence of capital market imperfections on investment.

Generally, these tests are based on an investment equation that blends the neo-classical determinants of investment (usually captured by an average Tobin's Q with adjustment costs) with a measure of firms' internal resources (net worth or cash flow) (e.g. Schiantarelli 1996; Hubbard 1998):

$$I(Q, \beta, \gamma, A, \varepsilon), \tag{1.4}$$

where β is a parameter of the adjustment cost function, γ is a technology shock, and ε represents optimization errors. As suggested by the path-breaking test run by Fazzari *et al.* (1988), if the problem with the neoclassical investment equation lies in the perfect capital market hypothesis, the inclusion of A in the equation should improve the quality of the estimation in the sense that A's coefficient should be significantly positive, and the residuals should pass the white-noise test whereas in the pure neo-classical version they do not. Notwithstanding the severe technical difficulties in collecting appropriate data (e.g. Hubbard 1998) which should induce everyone to handle the results with care, it seems possible to say that there is now general agreement among researchers about the importance of firms' financial constraints in determining aggregate investment. As is important to note, in addition to the US data examined by Fazzari *et al.* (1988), Fazzari and Petersen (1993), Hu and Schiantarelli (1994), and others, evidence has been found in nearly all major industrial countries as testified by the works of Deveraux and Schiantarelli (1990) and Bond and Meghir (1994) for the UK, Hoshi *et al.* (1991) for Japan, Elston (1993) for Germany, Calcagnini (1993), and Faini *et al.* (1993) for Italy. In Hubbard's words (1998: 193):

The principal findings of these studies are that: (1) all else being equal, investment is significantly correlated with proxies for changes in net worth or internal funds; and (2) that correlation is most important for firms likely to face information related capital-market imperfections.

2. Economic activity, employment, and prices

2.1. Models of fixed investment and aggregate demand

Given the pivotal role attributed by Keynes and Keynesian economics to fixed investment among the determinants of aggregate demand and of the level of economic acitivity, it was only natural that the first wave of macroeconomic models based on imperfect capital markets focused on the way in which such imperfections may affect the ability of firms to invest.

As already explained, these models hinge on violations of the Modigliani–Miller indifference principle either in the form of increasing cost of external finance or in the form of equity or credit rationing. Consequently, analysis centres on the way in which availability of internal funds or credit affects the level of aggregate investment. These models can be grouped into two main types of explanations of investment and aggregate demand determination.

(1) *Net-worth (or balance-sheet) channel.* The main source of investment finance is seen in firms' internal funds, broadly identified with the firm's net worth or 'equity base' (the reference model is Greenwald *et al.* 1984). Given the amount of profitable investment opportunities, the actual level of investment in the economy changes according to changes in the value of internal resources available to firms, which in turn mainly depend on: (a) previous cash flow and retained profits, and (b) the market value of firms' assets (Gertler and Hubbard 1988; Bernanke and Gertler 1989, 1990). This 'channel' of investment determination has two important consequences. The first is that investment takes a marked procyclical pattern—the so-called 'financial accelerator'; for in a depression both factors (a) and (b) worsen and hence investment is reduced, and vice versa in a boom. The second is that monetary policy, say open-market operations that alter asset prices, affects investment not only via the cost of equity capital but also, indeed mostly, through wealth effects on firms' internal means of investment.

(2) *Credit channel.* Here the view is that one of the prominent sources of external investment finance is bank credit, not equity capital. Therefore, the level of investment in the economy is essentially related to the price and amount of credit available, and, indirectly, to the determinants of credit supply (reference papers are Blinder (1987); Bernanke and Blinder (1988); Greenwald and Stiglitz (1990: Section 1.3); and Stiglitz and Weiss (1992). These in turn are basically: (a) the portfolio policy of banks in relation to information on firms and to commitments with depositors, and (b) monetary policy interventions capable of altering the portfolio policy or the loanable funds of banks.

Neither approach to investment determination is entirely new, though it is worth stressing that none of them can be explicitly traced back to the *General Theory* and to the subsequent Keynesian literature.[18] As usual, the NK models have provided an up-to-date framework that has made these ideas competitive with the mainstream one, and that, more importantly, has improved our knowledge of the causes and consequences of these phenomena. Of course, there are important linkages between the

---

[18] Stiglitz (1992*a*: 299) argues that this absence was due the Keynes's 'error' of having too neoclassical theory of investment which led him to ignore investment finance diversification and credit. Effects of net worth and retained profits on investment were present to Kalecki (1935, 1937), Kaldor (1940, 1956), Fisher (1933), and more recently to Minsky (e.g. 1982) to whom the terms 'financial accelerator' and 'financial fragility' largely used in this literature are owed. The credit channel—or else 'availability doctrine'—is a long-lived approach to monetary analysis and policy that was obscured in the last fifty years by the dominant view of the monetary transmission among Keynesians and monetarists based on real money balances. Early fundamental contributions to the 'credit view' date back to Wicksell (1898), Hawtrey (1927), and Keynes (1930), to name only a few. The 'credit view' was never fully dismissed. In the 1960s it was revived by the Radcliffe Report (1959) and later by Kaldor's works on 'endogenous money' (1982).

two 'channels' of investment determination and it is only for expository purposes that one may try to draw a distinction between them. In fact, a firm's net worth is generally part of the bank's assessment of creditworthiness, so that when net worth say falls a firm has less internal funds for investment and, at the same time, will also face tighter credit conditions. On the other hand, a bank is itself a firm, and negative shocks to asset values may also impair banks' ability to invest, i.e. to make loans. These joint effects strenghten the financial accelerator phenomenon (Mishkin 1991; Bernanke 1983). Net worth models have especially been developed towards business-cycle analysis, which is examined in the next section. In this section we shall consider the contribution of credit-channel models.[19]

One of the most successful macroeconomic models is the one proposed by Bernanke and Blinder (1988). They start from a traditional IS–LM model of aggregate demand and examine the consequences of diversification of investment finance. This feature is introduced by assuming imperfect substitution between market loans (bonds) and bank loans for firms' investment. Symmetrically, banks are assumed to diversify their portfolios between bonds and loans, but do not ration credit. This allows the author to show that credit rationing is not essential to the credit channel of investment determination. Extensions with credit rationing have been studied by Blinder (1987), Greenwald and Stiglitz (1990: Section 1.3), and Stiglitz and Weiss (1992).

In the Bernanke–Blinder model aggregate demand in any given period of time consists of real consumption and investment as usual, but investment is financed by issuing bonds B or by demanding bank loans L^d, both measured in real terms. The two components of investment finance differ in their real cost, r and i, respectively, and each component is assumed to be gross substitute with the other, so that firms' demand for bank credit is

$$L^d = L(\rho, r, i) \quad L_\rho > 0, \ L_r > 0, \ L_i < 0, \tag{2.1}$$

where ρ is a measure of the marginal efficiency of capital.

Output market equilibrium obtains when aggregate supply equates aggregate demand or, equivalently, when real saving equates investment at the level of real incomes that exhaust output. Therefore, the locus of aggregate demand equilibrium is

$$y = d(\underset{+}{\rho}, \underset{-}{r}, \underset{-}{i}) \tag{2.2}$$

Note that, in comparison with the IS locus, this also embodies the interest rate on bank loans i; hence Bernanke and Blinder call it the CC (commodity and credit) curve, which plays a crucial role in their analysis.

The model now requires an explicit treatment of banks' behaviour. The authors assume a simplified bank activity such that banks accept deposits from households, hold a fraction τ of deposits as reserves H^b with the central bank,[20] and the remainder

---

[19] Further suggested readings are Gertler and Hubbard (1988) and Bernanke and Gertler (1995).
[20] The addition of free reserves would not change essentially the results of the model.

is lent to firms by granting loans L^s or by buying bonds B^b. The diversification of the banks' portfolio of assets is again derived from the gross substitution hypothesis. The credit market must equate real supply of bank loans with real demand which is related to investment; therefore:

$$\lambda(r,i)D(1-\tau) = L^d(\rho,r,i), \tag{2.3}$$

where λ is the portfolio share of loans to firms.

Since in equilibrium $D = H^b/\tau$, the credit market determines i for any given value of ρ, r, τ, and H^b:

$$i = i(\rho,r,H^b,\tau). \tag{2.4}$$
$${+\ +\ -\ +}$$

The sign of the partial derivative with respect to r is noteworthy: it is positive because an increase in r shifts the demand for investment finance from bonds to bank loans, and hence, *ceteris paribus*, i should rise.

Taking into account the equations for y and i and the LM equation the reduced form of y results:

$$y = y(\rho,H^b,\tau). \tag{2.5}$$
$${+\ +\ -}$$

This result resembles the usual one in the IS–LM model. There is, however, an important difference that has drawn a lot of attention from monetary scholars: the so-called 'transmission mechanism' from the monetary variables, H^b and τ, to output is *qualitatively* and *quantitatively* different than in traditional models:

(i) changes in monetary variables affect both the money market (and hence the interest rate on bonds as usual) and the credit market (and hence the interest rate on bank loans),

(ii) such changes have magnified effects to the extent that investment is financed on the credit market, and

(iii) the credit channel operates in such a way that monetary policy interventions can produce large effects on output with small changes in open-market interest rates.

The peculiar features of the Bernanke–Blinder model can easily be seen graphically in Figure 8.2. Consider a monetary contraction in the form of a cut in H^b. The effect is twofold: (a) there is the traditional shift of the LM curve and (b), there is also a shift of the CC curve due to a fall in credit supply and a rise in i. Thus investment finance is cut both in the form of bonds and of bank loans, and the reduction of aggregate demand is amplified *vis-à-vis* a dampened change in the market rate of interest. As we know, these are among the empirical challenges that the NKs wish to explain, and the Bernanke–Blinder model offers an explanation alternative to credit rationing or other forms of interest-rate rigidity. As the authors warn, the credit-channel effects hinge on

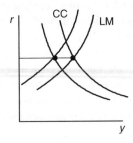

Fɪɢ. 8.2.

two preconditions:

- the diversification hypothesis—the fact that firms and banks do not consider bonds and loans as perfect substitutes,[21]
- the central bank's ability to alter banks' portfolio choices.

These conditions have prompted extensive empirical research. First of all, the propagation of monetary impulses to real activity through the bank sector was examined by Romer and Romer (1990). They used the minutes of the Open Market Committee of the Federal Reserve to identify expansionary and contractionary interventions and then sought to track the effects of these interventions on the bank and non-bank financial sectors in the subsequent months. They deny the existence of a specific credit channel in the USA. Another group of studies has focused directly on the diversification hypothesis underlying the credit channel: Bernanke and Blinder (1992), Friedman and Kuttner (1992), Kashyap *et al.* (1993), Kashyap and Stein (1994*b*) all have found sizeable substitution effects in US banks' and firms' balance sheets following changes in monetary policy according to the credit view. A number of studies made at the Bank of Italy has confirmed the financial exposure to monetary shocks for a large part of Italian firms in relation to their dependence on bank credit (Angeloni *et al.* 1997). Tests of the macroeconomic model of the credit channel have also been run with more formal statistical instruments such as VAR models with impulse–response analysis. Results supportive of the credit channel with US data are provided by Bernanke and Mihov (1995), Bernanke and Gertler (1995), and Christiano *et al.* (1996), and with UK data by Dale and Haldane (1993). Bagliano and Favero (1995, 1996) have run a VAR based on the Bernanke–Blinder model on Italian data and have found broad confirmation of the expected results. However, a serious problem in this kind of empirical analysis of the credit channel is the 'identification problem': observing that credit and output are correlated after a monetary shock is not sufficient evidence in favour of the credit channel, for credit may follow output instead of the other way round (e.g. Kashyap and Stein 1994*a*; Bernanke and Gertler 1995).

---

[21] It can be proved formally that the monetary effect on output dy/dH^b becomes equal to the usual one obtained in the IS–LM model if $L_i^d \to \infty$ and/or $\lambda_i \to \infty$.

An important remark is in order. Having clarified the conditions whereby capital markets fail to dampen the effects of investment fluctuations on aggregate demand, or they indeed amplify them, the CC–LM class of models have covered only halfway. It remains to explain why saving–investment imbalances, if they leave excess aggregate supply on the output market, are not corrected by changes in prices.[22] After the *General Theory*, the solution to the problem was the real balance effect. Yet, according to Greenwald and Stiglitz (1993*b*: 36): 'The enormous attention that the real balance effect has received over the years hardly speaks well for the profession. Quantitatively, it is surely an *n*th order effect.'

Theoretically, the real balance effect is a complex dynamic process whose convergence to equilibrium cannot be taken for granted. Most important difficulties may arise from expectations formation (e.g. Neary and Stiglitz 1982; Grandmont 1983, 1985),[23] and from Fisherian redistributional effects (e.g. Tobin 1980: ch. 1; Stiglitz 1992*a*). If anything, the real balance effect is an example that *supports* Keynes's intuition that price flexibility may be disruptive of, rather than conducive to, general equilibrium. 'This intuition is now at the heart of another development in the NK research on imperfect capital markets (e.g. Stiglitz 1992*b*; Greenwald and Stiglitz 1993*b*; Rosser 1998): This view holds that even if wages and prices were perfectly flexible, output and employment would be highly volatile. It sees the economy as amplifying the shocks that it experiences, and making its effects persist' (Greenwald and Stiglitz 1993*b*: 25).

2.2. Models of working capital and aggregate supply

We now turn our attention to another important NK approach to economic activity determination in imperfect capital markets, one which focuses on working capital and aggregate supply, instead of fixed investment and aggregate demand, and one where flexible prices and wages do find a place. The general framework is the same as the one we have presented above, though now analysis concerns how firms can finance purchases of inputs for current production (working capital) in situations where typically money payments for inputs anticipate the money proceeds from sales of output due to the production time lag. The reference model is Greenwald *et al.* 1984, with its subsequent refinements (Greenwald and Stiglitz 1988*a,b*, 1990, 1993*a*). The connection of this approach with the theory of money demand as a means to bridge time gaps between payments and proceeds—what Keynes named the 'finance motive' (1937)—and with Keynes's idea of a 'monetary theory of production' (1933) is apparent. However, the task of these models in the NK view is more specifically to complete the macroeconomic set-up with an aggregate supply function consistent with

---

[22] For instance, Bernanke and Gertler (1995) and Kashyap and Stein (1994*a*) still maintain that nominal rigidities are an integral part of the real effects of aggregate demand and monetary policy impulses through the credit channel.

[23] The problem the real balance effect is supposed to relieve is that the real cost of capital is too high. If the general price level falls today, and is expected to fall in the future, the real cost of capital *rises further* unless the nominal interest rates fall faster than prices.

the general premises of imperfect capital markets and, at the same time, comparable with the orthodox aggregate supply function.

The key ingredients of the Greenwald–Stiglitz aggregate supply model (GS–AS) are: (a) a sequential economy such that firms have to pay for inputs (labour) before they are able to sell output, (b) firms' output price uncertainty in the form of a probability distribution of each firm's individual sale price around the average 'market price' of output, (c) full 'equity rationing' of firms, so that firms' demand for working capital (the wage bill) is met either by internal funds ('equity base') or by bank credit in a competitive credit market (each firm may borrow from many banks and each bank can lend to many firms), and (d) standard debt contracts between banks and firms.

Formally, it is assumed that all firms j produce a homogeneous output by means of a common labour technology with decreasing marginal returns, and one-period production time, so that $y_{jt+1} = y(n_{jt})$, $y_n > 0$, $y_{nn} < 0$. The selling price of each firm in $t+1$ is the outcome of a random market process around the 'average market price' of output P_{t+1}, given by the law $p_{jt+1} = P_{t+1}u_{jt+1}$, where u_{jt+1} is a i.i.d. random variable with cumulative function F and expected value $E(u_{jt+1}) = 1$. To pay for labour, firms can spend out of their existing equity base A_{jt} or can borrow from banks. Given the money-wage rate W_t, the amount of borrowing of a firm is therefore $B_{jt} = W_t n_{jt} - A_{jt}$.

Banks offer standard debt contracts in a competitive market. Since firms are homogeneous, banks face no screening problems. Hence interest rate determination, $R_t \equiv (1 + r_t)$, is essentially the same as in equation (1.2) for all firms, where the screening cost is $\theta = 0$, the repayment in case of bankruptcy is $G_j = p_{jt+1}y_{jt+1}$, and the risk-free return on deposits is set exogenously in real terms $(1 + i_t) = x_t P_{t+1}/P_t$. If the firm declares its inability to repay $B_{jt}R_t$, it is forced into a bankruptcy procedure such that it pays its whole revenue $p_{jt+1}y_{jt+1}$ to the bank and bears (non-pecuniary) fixed bankruptcy costs valued in monetary terms Φ_{jt+1}.[24]

Bankruptcy occurs in all states such that $B_{jt}R_t > p_{jt+1}y_{jt+1}$ or, after little manipulation, $u_{jt+1} < B_{jt}R_t/P_{t+1}y_{jt+1} \equiv u^*_{jt+1}$. That is to say, whenever the individual price relative to the market u_{jt+1} falls below a critical value u^*_{jt+1} equal to the firm's debt/revenue ratio. Knowing the probability distribution $F(u_{jt+1})$, the bankruptcy probability of the firm is:

$$\text{Prob}(u_{jt+1} \leq u^*_{jt+1}) = F(u^*_{jt+1}). \tag{2.6}$$

Under these conditions, a *levered* firm's expected profit in $t+1$ is ((^{e}) denotes the firm's expectation):

$$\pi^e_{jt+1} = p^e_{jt+1}y_{jt+1} - B_{jt}R_t - \Phi_{jt+1}F(u^*_{jt+1}). \tag{2.7}$$

Hence the key variables in the levered firm's problem are its outstanding debt $B_{jt}R_t$ and the related expected bankruptcy costs $\Phi_{jt+1}F(u^*_{jt+1})$. Therefore, assuming rational expectations, i.e. $p^e_{jt+1} = P_{t+1}$, the firm will choose n_{jt} to maximize the following

---

[24] G–S assume that bankruptcy costs are increasing in the borrowed amount but this is not strictly necessary.

expression:

$$\max \pi_{jt+1}^{e} = P_{t+1} y_{jt+1}(n_{jt}) - (W_t n_{jt} - A_{jt}) Rt - \Phi_{jt+1} F(u_{jt+1}^*). \tag{2.8}$$

The peculiar role of financial variables in the firm's employment decision is immediately grasped observing the first-order condition for maximization (where all variables are now in real terms):[25]

$$y_n = w_t r_t + \phi_{t+1} F_u u_n^*. \tag{2.9}$$

Since $F_u > 0$ and $u_n^* > 0$, the gross real marginal cost (the right-hand side of the expression) is necessarily greater than the pure real wage rate; hence the firm should obtain a higher marginal product of labour by employing less labour. The labour-demand schedule of a levered firm systematically lies below the one of the standard firm theory. This fundamental fact of the G–S model hinges on two factors: (a) the real interest rate paid on the wage bill and (b) the bankruptcy marginal cost.[26] Consequently, the aggregate supply function results to be as follows:

$$Y_{t+1} = Y(N(w_t, r_t, \phi_{t+1}, F_u, a_t)). \tag{2.10}$$
$$\phantom{Y_{t+1} = Y(N(} - \quad - \quad - \quad - \quad +$$

Now let us plot this function on a (Y, P) space, and assume a standard downward-sloping AD function as in Figure 8.3. The result looks like the standard New Classical one. However there are substantial differences.

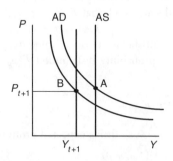

FIG. 8.3.

<hr />

[25] We are using the following definitions: $w_t = W_t/P_t$ is the real wage rate, $a_t = A_t/P_t$ is the real equity base, $\Pi_t = P_{t+1}/P_t$ is inflation factor, $r_t = R_t/\Pi_{t+1}$ is the real capitalization factor, $\phi_{t+1} = \Phi_{t+1}/P_{t+1}$ is the real bankruptcy cost.

[26] Obviously, a non-zero marginal cost of bankruptcy requires that $u_n^* > 0$, i.e. the bankruptcy threshold must be increasing in employment. This in turn depends on the underlying production function which should generate an increasing average cost function.

First, the rational-expectations equilibrium level of output (the vertical AS curve) depends not only on technology and the real wage, but also on real financial variables $(r_t, \phi_{t+1}, F_u, a_t)$.[27] A negative shock is transmitted to labour demand and aggregate supply (the AS curve shifts leftward) whenever the real interest rate, the real bankruptcy costs, the bankruptcy risk rise, or when the real equity base falls.

Second, some of the financial variables, say r_t, can also affect the AD function. Co-movements of the AD and AS functions in the same direction, such as the example in Figure 8.3, may account for large output adjustments with seemingly sticky prices while they are not (see also Stiglitz 1992*a,b*).

The G–S AS model lends itself to being developed in various directions. At present, it has mainly been applied in business-cycle analysis thanks to the fact that the dependence of supply on the equity base, which in turn depends on past cash flow, generates endogenous cycles (e.g. Greenwald and Stiglitz 1993*a*)—this research field is matter of Section 3. The other field of application of the G–S model concerns the debate on employment, output, and price determination. So far, this important aspect has received less attention than it deserves.

The first point to be clarified at the outset is that the G–S model does not generate Keynesian unemployment by itself. It is a model that can explain low levels of *equilibrium* employment and activity in relation to the financial variables identified above. At first sight one might conclude that the G–S model is at most an explanation of a 'high' natural rate of unemployment. The obvious question that arises is whether monetary policy can affect the financial factors in the G–S AS function. How this can be possible has been explored by Delli Gatti and Gallegati (1997), Tamborini (1997), and Fiorentini and Tamborini (1998). Though in different specifications of the G–S set-up, these authors have found that monetary policy shocks transmitted through bank credit supply may induce competitive adjustments in the wage rate, the bank interest rate, and the price level that *may not leave firms' real marginal costs unaffected.* For instance, in a deflation there is no guarantee that the real wage rate falls as much as necessary to compensate for the rise in the real expected interest rate paid by firms. Thus the (expected) real marginal costs of levered firms grow and output and employment are cut.

In conclusion, this shift in theoretical focus towards the supply-side credit channel is important, yet whether the credit transmission mechanism has stronger effect than the money transmission mechanism largely remains an empirical matter depending on a number of 'fine' factors such as the time structure of transactions, the contractual arrangements in the labour and credit markets, and the formation and effect of price expectations. These are all critical elements on the way of viable macroeconomic models of credit economies that at present need much more intensive research.

---

[27] The G–S AS function, too, can accommodate a 'price suprise' *à la* Lucas if firms misperceive the future price level in the computation of their real interest rate (see Delli Gatti and Gallegati 1997). The reasons of this factor, however, are different. In Lucas' framework, in fact, a positive price surprise affects production stimulating labour supply. In the case of G–S, on the contrary, a positive price surprise affects production reducing debt commitments *as perceived* by firms (a sort of Fisher effect).

3. Financial fragility and the business cycle

The study of the macroeconomic implications of imperfect capital markets has been extended to economic fluctuations. In this literature one can find both approaches that characterize modern business-cycle theory: the *impulse-propagation* approach, which is the core of the so-called *exogenous* theories of the cycle, and the *endogenous* approach.[28]

In the following we review three models of business fluctuations. First of all, we dig deeper into the model by Greenwald and Stiglitz (1993)—presented and discussed in Section 2.2 in a static framework. Second, we briefly review the approach pioneered by Bernanke and Gertler (1989, 1990). Third we focus on the model recently put forward by Kiyotaki and Moore (1997).

3.1. Bankruptcy costs, aggregate supply, and business fluctuations

The framework developed by Greenwald and Stiglitz can be used to analyse the emergence of financially driven fluctuations and cycles. In order to do so, following up our previous treatment, we start from the definition of the real equity base of the jth firm in period $t + 1$:

$$a_{jt+1} = u_{jt+1}y_{jt+1} - r_t(w_t n_{jt} - a_{jt}) - d_{jt+1}, \tag{3.1}$$

where d_{jt+1} are real dividends distributed in $t + 1$.

We can now recall that, according to equation (2.9), individual optimal supply is $y_{jt+1} = y(n(w_t, r_t, F_u, a_{jt}))$. In order to simplify the exposition, in the following we will drop the cost of bankruptcy and the parameters of the distribution function. Moreover, Greenwald and Stiglitz assume that dividends paid in $t + 1$ are an increasing function of the equity base in t, $d_{jt+1} = d(a_{jt})$. Substituting these expressions into (3.1), averaging over firms and assuming that the law of large numbers applies, we obtain:

$$a_{t+1} = y(n(w_t, r_t, a_t)) - r_t(w_t(n(w_t, r_t, a_t)) - a_t) - d(a_t). \tag{3.2}$$

This is the *law of motion* of the *average* equity base. It describes the relation between the average equity base in period t and in period $t + 1$ given the real wage, the gross real interest rate, and the price surprise. It is a first-order non-linear difference equation. The steady states of (3.2) will be denoted by: $a^* = a(w_t, r_t)$ so that average output will be: $y^* = y(w_t, r_t, a^*) = g(w_t, r_t)$. The steady-state output is a function of the real wage and the real interest rate. This completes the result already presented and discussed in Section 2.2.

---

[28] According to the approach pioneered by Slutsky and Frisch the business cycle is the result of an exogenous shock (the impulse) which trickles down (by means of a propagation mechanism) producing bursts of economic activity which eventually peter out. The cycle persists inasmuch as the economy is continuously hit by exogenous shocks. According to the alternative approach, the business cycle is the working mechanism of a market economy. In other words, economic activity 'naturally' and 'spontaneously' follows an oscillatory pattern (a self-sustained business cycle) which need not be rooted in the continuous occurrence of exogenous shocks.

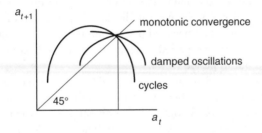

FIG. 8.4.

Let us now examine more closely the dynamics of the equity base. The phase diagram of equation (3.2) on the positive orthant of the (a_t, a_{t+1}) plane can assume many different shapes (see Figure 8.4). If $\partial a_{t+1}/\partial a_t$ is smaller than 1 in absolute value, the steady state is unique and stable. In this case fluctuations can be generated only by the recurrence of exogenous shocks.

The dynamics is more interesting if we assume that the phase diagram is non-monotonic, which may generate financially driven, endogenous, irregular business cycle. This is the case of the hump-shaped phase diagram in Figure 8.4. Suppose the phase diagram is a quadratic map: this can produce a wide range of different types of dynamics: convergence—monotonic or by means of dampening oscillations—to the steady state; limit cycles (invariant attracting orbits); 'chaos'; divergence—monotonic or by means of exploding oscillations—from the steady state (Delli Gatti and Gallegati 1998).

3.2. Monitoring costs, capital accumulation, and business fluctuations

Bernanke and Gertler (1989, 1990) (B–G hereafter) have put forward a different theoretical framework which yields basically the same results as those of Greenwald and Stiglitz. B–G assume that in a principal–agent relationship between borrowers and lenders, the latter can assess the return on investment only incurring monitoring costs. As a consequence, also in their framework the scale of production depends upon net worth. In fact, the higher is borrowers' 'net worth'—or, more precisely, the volume of internal finance—the lower is the cost of monitoring on the part of lenders and the higher the volume of credit extended, investment, and production.

B–G assume that there are overlapping generations of agents who live for two periods. In each generation there is a constant proportion η of entrepreneurs, i.e. agents endowed with an investment project. Non-entrepreneurs, on the contrary, cannot access the investment technology. There are two types of goods, output and capital. Output can be consumed, invested—i.e. used up as an input of the investment project—or 'stored'. If stored, each unit of output yields a constant return r. In a sense, stored output is the volume of saving which is lent at the exogenous interest rate r. Output is produced by means of a constant returns to scale technology which uses capital and labour. The production function in per-capita terms is: $y = \theta f(k)$ where y is per-capita output, θ is a technological shock, k is per-capita capital (the capital/labour ratio), and $f(\cdot)$ is a well-behaved production function.[29] Assuming that capital depreciates completely in one period, capital in period $t + 1$ is equal to the flow of investment carried out in period t.

Each entrepreneur is characterized by a different degree ω of inefficiency. Therefore ω is a random variable distributed uniformly with support $[0, 1]$. The volume of output needed to carry out each investment project is an increasing function of the degree of inefficiency: $x = x(\omega)$, $x' > 0$. The return on investment—i.e. the quantity of capital generated by each investment project—is a discrete random variable with expected value $E(\tilde{k})$.

Each agent is endowed with one unit of labour which is supplied inelastically. The real wage will be represented by w. In equilibrium the real wage will be equal to the marginal productivity of labour, i.e. $w = \theta[f(k) - kf'(k)]$. Preferences are such that entrepreneurs save all their labour income when young.

An entrepreneur would carry out his investment project if the return on investment, i.e. the product of the price of capital times the expected real return of the investment project, $qE(\tilde{k})$, were greater than or equal to the opportunity cost of investing, i.e. the return on storage times the output needed to carry out the investment project $rx(\omega)$. Therefore, we can detect a critical degree of inefficiency:

$$\bar{\omega} = x^{-1}\left[\frac{qE(\tilde{k})}{r}\right] \tag{3.3}$$

such that all the entrepreneurs with inefficiency lower (higher) than $\bar{\omega}$ will invest (not invest). The critical degree of inefficiency represents also the proportion of entrepreneurs who invest.

The return to investment is known to the entrepreneur. Non-entrepreneurs can observe the return on investment only incurring monitoring costs. If information were perfect, there would not be monitoring costs. In the presence of asymmetric information between borrower and lender, the former has an incentive to lie to the latter, declaring the bad outcome of the investment project and avoiding the payment of debt commitments when the good one has occurred. The lender can ascertain the true return on investment only incurring monitoring costs. B–G derive the optimal financial contract and show that auditing/monitoring occurs only if the bad state of the world is declared. The probability of auditing is decreasing with internal finance.

Entrepreneurs with inefficiency higher than $\bar{\omega}$ will not invest in the perfect information case. Therefore, they will not invest even in the imperfect information case, whatever their level of internal finance. They will be labelled *poor entrepreneurs* for short. Poor entrepreneurs are lenders.

---

[29] From now on, in this section we will refer to per-capita variables.

If the probability of auditing were $p_a = 1$, we could derive a second critical degree of inefficiency:

$$\underline{\omega} = x^{-1} \left[\frac{q(1 - \pi\gamma)}{r} \right], \tag{3.4}$$

where π is the probability of the bad outcome and γ represents monitoring costs. Entrepreneurs with inefficiency lower than $\underline{\omega}$ (*good entrepreneurs* for short) will invest even if the probability of auditing is 1, whatever their level of internal finance. Entrepreneurs with inefficiency $\underline{\omega} < \omega < \bar{\omega}$ will be labelled *fair entrepreneurs*. By assumption a fair entrepreneur will invest only if he is fully collateralized, that is if his internal finance is 'sufficiently high'.

Good entrepreneurs and fully collateralized fair entrepreneurs will always invest. Only incompletely collateralized good entrepreneurs, however, will demand loanable funds and run the risk of being audited. Incompletely collateralized fair entrepreneurs, poor entrepreneurs, and non-entrepreneurs will not invest: they will employ their savings supplying loanable funds. Therefore, the supply of capital will be increasing with the volume of entrepreneurial savings (internal finances). An increase of internal finance, in fact, reduces the probability of auditing for incompletely collateralized good entrepreneurs—thus reducing the loss of capital associated with monitoring costs—and increases the number of fully collateralized fair entrepreneurs.

From the usual condition according to which the marginal productivity of capital must be equal to the real remuneration of capital follows the demand for capital: $q_{t+1} = \theta f'(k_{t+1})$. Equilibrium in the market for capital implies:

$$k_{t+1}^* = k(r, \eta, \theta, S). \tag{3.5}$$

Recall now that: $w = \theta[f(k) - kf'(k_t)]$ and w is internal finance for the investing entrepreneur. Substituting this expression in the equation for the equilibrium stock of capital we get:

$$k_{t+1} = k(r, \eta, \theta, \theta[f(k_t) - k_t f'(k_t)]) = h(r, \eta, \theta, k_t). \tag{3.6}$$

This is the law of motion of the (equilibrium) stock of capital. It describes the relation between the stock of capital in period t and in period $t + 1$ given the gross real interest rate, the proportion of entrepreneurs in total population, and the technological shock. (3.6) is a first-order non-linear difference equation. Its phase diagram on the positive orthant of the (k_t, k_{t+1}) plane is upward-sloping. The steady state of (3.6) is: $k^* = k(r, \eta, \theta)$. The associated average output will be: $y^* = \theta f(k(r, \eta, \theta))$. If $0 < \partial k_{t+1}/\partial k_t < 1$ the steady state is unique and stable. In this case oscillations of the stock of capital and output can be generated only by an exogenous shock (an impulse) which propagates through the system. The core of the mechanism is the financial accelerator (Bernanke *et al.* 1996).

3.3. The inalienability of human capital, financial constraints, and business fluctuations

Kiyotaki and Moore (1997) (K–M hereafter) assume that in a principal–agent relationship between a borrower and a lender, characterized by asymmetric information and moral hazard, the former faces a financing constraint: the loan he obtains is smaller or equal to the value of his collateralizable assets, which plays in this framework a role analogous to that of net worth or the equity base in G–S and entrepreneurs' savings (internal finance) in B–G. As a consequence, also in their framework, the scale of production depends on 'net worth' (collateralizable wealth). In fact, the higher is net worth, the higher is the volume of credit extended, investment, and production.

K–M assume that there are infinitely lived agents. Population consists of financially constrained and of unconstrained agents ('farmers' and 'gatherers' respectively) in constant proportions. A farmer is an agent endowed with inalienable human capital. Therefore, he can get from lenders no more than the value of his collateralizable assets. This is the reason of the financing constraint. Notice that the financing constraint here is binding. In a sense farmers are credit rationed.

Non-farmers ('gatherers'), on the contrary, are not endowed with inalienable human capital. Therefore they do not face financing constraints. It will turn out that all the farmers (gatherers) will be borrowers (lenders).

There are two types of goods, output ('fruit') and a collateralizable, durable, non-reproducible asset ('land') whose total supply is fixed. Output can be consumed or lent. If lent, each unit of output yields a constant return of r. Output is produced by means of a technology which uses land and labour.

By assumption farmers and gatherers have access to different technologies. The production function of each *farmer* is: $y = (\alpha + \beta)k_{t-1}$, where y is output, k is land, α and β are parameters. βk_{t-1} is the output which deteriorates ('bruised fruit') and is therefore non-tradable. K–M model the farmer's preferences in such a way as to obtain that farmers consume only non-tradable output.

Each farmer's technology is idiosyncratic in the sense that once production has started only he has the skills necessary to successfully complete the production process, i.e. to make land bear fruit. If the farmer were to withdraw his labour, production would not be carried out, i.e. land would bear no fruit. In the words of Hart and Moore, the farmer's human capital is inalienable. As a consequence, if the farmer is indebted, he may have an incentive to threaten his creditors by withdrawing his labour and repudiating his debt. Creditors protect themselves against this threat by collateralizing the farmer's land. This is the reason why farmers face a financing constraint. For the sake of simplicity we will assume in the following that there is only one farmer and one borrower. The financing constraint that the farmer faces is $b = (q_{t+1}k)/r$. Accordingly, the maximum amount of debt the farmer succeeds to obtain 'today' is such that the sum of principal and interest rb is equal to the value of the farmer's land when the debt is due, i.e. $q_{t+1}k$, where q_{t+1} is the price of land at time $t + 1$.

As far as the gatherer is concerned, K–M assume that he adopts a well-behaved production function $G(\overline{K} - k_{t-1})$ where $\overline{K}$ is the total supply of land. The gatherer's human capital is not inalienable. Therefore, he faces no financing constraint. In order to maximize utility, the gatherer has to equate the marginal productivity of his land to the opportunity cost of cultivating it.

With a few manipualtions K–M end up with the following:

$$k = \frac{r}{G'(\overline{K} - k_{t-1})} \alpha k_{t-1}. \tag{3.7}$$

This is the law of motion of the farmer's land. It describes the relation between land in period t and in period $t+1$ given the real interest rate, the technological parameter α, and the total supply of land. (3.7) is a first-order non-linear difference equation. Its phase diagram on the positive orthant of the (k_t, k_{t+1}) plane is upward-sloping. The steady state of (3.7) will be denoted by: $k^* = \overline{K} - G'^{-1}(r\alpha)$. The associated average output supplied will be: $Y^* = (\alpha + \beta)(\overline{K} - G'^{-1}(r\alpha)) + G(G'^{-1}(r\alpha))$. If $0 < \partial k_{t+1}/\partial k_t < 1$, oscillations of the farmer's land and output can be generated only by an exogenous shock (an impulse) which propagates through the system.

In this setting K–M show that small shocks—for instance to technology—can produce large and persistent fluctuations in output and asset prices. In their model, in fact, the durable, non-reproducible asset (land) plays the dual role of a factor of production for both constrained and unconstrained agents and of collateralizable wealth for financially constrained agents. Therefore the price of assets affects the borrowers' financing constraint. At the same time, the size of the borrowers' credit limits feed-back on asset prices. 'The dynamic interaction between credit limits and asset prices turns out to be a powerful transmission mechanism by which the effects of shocks persist, amplify, and spread out', (Kiyotaki and Moore 1997: 212).

Two comments are in order at this point. First of all, in a sense, all the models surveyed so far implicitly or explicitly adopt a notion of financial fragility. The degree of financial fragility is decreasing with the volume of the equity base in the case of G–S, with the capital stock in the case of B–G, with the value of land in the case of K–M.

Second, they all generate fluctuations of the impulse-propagation type. In a sense, these New Keynesian models share with the New Classical ones the same view of a market economy, i.e. an inherently 'stable' system continuously hit by random disturbances. The most important difference between New Keynesian and New Classical models of fluctuations seems to lie in the nature of the *propagation mechanism*. While the New Keynesian propagation mechanism and the source of persistence is essentially the degree of financial fragility—even though the meaning of this expression is different from one author to the other in this literature as we have already pointed out above—the New Classical propagation mechanism operates without financial factors, which are irrelevant, and the transmission of the shock rests essentially on the labour/leisure choices of agents. As far as the impulse is concerned, some of the New Keynesian models start from a technological shock (B–G, K–M) as in the real business-cycle school, others assume that a 'price shock' occurs, as in the misperception models *à la* Lucas–Sargent.

As we have seen, however, the G–S approach can be adapted to study the emergence of endogenous fluctuations due to a non-linear deterministic setting. This model can generate chaotic dynamics in a straightforward way. This a promising line of research which could and should be exploited more thoroughly.

4. Conclusions

In our opinion, the literature we have reviewed has five major results.

First of all, these works have strengthened with analytical rigour the view that capital market failures have a role in explaining fluctuations in employment and the non-neutrality of money even in competitive markets. Moreover, these financial factors are important not only for aggregate demand but also for supply decisions. This is not without consequences for the assessment of the impact of monetary shocks. If demand (supply) shocks have transitory (permanent) effects on the growth path of the economy—as it is commonly understood—a monetary shock can have some persistence. In other words, its influence on real variables is not bound to vanish 'in the long run'.

Second, we now have a more sophisticated view of the transmission mechanism of monetary policy. For instance, the real-balance and liquidity effects, which are the core of the traditional analysis of the transmission mechanism, have been complemented by the credit and net-worth channels.

Third, this literature has provided a set of new explanations of the business cycle. Even though the wording is different from one author to the other, changes in financial fragility are the main determinants of self-sustained oscillations and/or of the propagation of exogenous nominal (monetary) and real (technological) shocks.

Fourth, we have reached a better understanding of the importance of heterogeneity in economic models. Heterogeneity is important at least for two reasons. One is its role in the borrower–lender relationship. The other concerns the transmission of monetary impulses, with the distinction between large and small borrowers.

Last but not least, this literature has dignified, in academic circles, a view of the economy which is conventional wisdom for the business community. In this view, differential costs of capital, the importance of firms' financial structure, and financial constraints are basic 'facts of life' corroborated by a huge body of empirical evidence since the early days of capitalism.

Of course, there are also weaknesses. The microfoundations of capital market imperfections makes it hard to build a simple and powerful macroeconomic model. For instance a fully specified model of aggregate demand and supply is still in its infancy. At the level of the microfoundations themselves, one may argue that deeper implications of imperfect information such as bounded rationality, learning processes, and deviations from rational expectation equilibria are not adequately addressed yet. Also, the proliferation of different models in this framework leaves us with a sense of *embarass de richesse*. Those who look for a unified and tightly connected paradigm or even for the unique 'grand model' of the economy will be disappointed. The list of the causes of capital market failures is long and varied, and for each cause one may find a specific set of consequences. Not surprisingly, one can hardly find a shared view of policy prescriptions.

Finally, we think it is worth stressing that NK capital rationing *per se* is hardly the kind of capital market failure that lies at the core of Keynes's macroeconomic theory. Capital rationing certainly implies a loss of aggregate investment, as Keynes's theory does, but for a completely different reason and with a striking difference as regards the role of interest rates in the adjustment process. The problem with NK capital rationing is asymmetric information between borrowers and lenders, and the consequence is the *upward* rigidity of the interest rate in the event of *excess capital demand*, whereas Keynes's problem is savers' liquidity preference that prevents the interest rate from *falling* as much as necessary in the event of *excess capital* supply. In other words, Keynes had a 'monetary theory' of capital market failures whereas the NKs have a 'non-monetary' one. We are not arguing that the NK contribution should exclusively be assessed according to its faithful adherence to Keynes's ideas, but we think that liquidity preference as a cause of capital market failure remains a key issue in macro-economic theory which is not addressed in NK models.

REFERENCES

Akerlof, G. (1970) 'The market for "lemons": qualitative uncertainty and the market mechanism', *Quarterly Journal of Economics* 84: 488–500.

Angeloni I., Conti, V., and Passacantando, F. (1997) *Le banche e il finanziamento delle imprese* (Bologna: Il Mulino).

Ardeni, P. and Messori, M. (1996) *Il razionamento del credito* (Bari: Laterza).

Bagliano, F. C. and Favero, C. A. (1995) 'The credit channel of monetary transmission. The case of Italy', Paper presented at the conference: 'I meccanismi di trasmissione della politica monetaria', Catholic University, Milan.

——(1996) 'Measuring monetary policy with VAR models: an evaluation', mimeo.

Battacharya, S. and Thakor, A. (1993) 'Contemporary banking theory', *Journal of Financial Intermediation* 2–50.

Berger, A. N. and Udell, G. F. (1992) 'Some evidence on the empirical significance of credit rationing', *Journal of Political Economy* 100: 1047–77.

Bernanke, B. (1983) 'Non-monetary effects of the financial crises in the propagation of the Great Depression', *American Economic Review* 73: 257–76.

——and Blinder, A. (1988) 'Credit, money, and aggregate demand', Papers and Proceedings of the American Economic Association, *American Economic Review* 78: 435–9.

—— and ——(1992) 'The federal funds rate and the channels of monetary transmission', *American Economic Review* 82: 901–21.

——and Gertler, M. (1989) 'Agency costs, net worth and business fluctuations', *American Economic Review* 79: 14–31.

—— and ——(1990) 'Financial fragility and economic performance', *Quarterly Journal of Economics* 105: 87–114.

—— and ——(1995) 'Inside the black box: the credit channel of monetary policy transmission', *Journal of Economic Perspectives* 9: 27–48.

——, ——, and Gilchrist, S. (1996) 'The financial accelerator and the flight to quality', *Review of Economics and Statistics* 78: 1–15.

——and Mihov, I. (1995) 'Measuring Monetary Policy', *NBER Working Paper* 5145.

Blinder, A. (1987) 'Credit rationing and effective supply failures', *Economic Journal* 97(3): 327–52.

Bond, S. and Meghir, C. (1994) 'Dynamic investment models and the firm's financial policy', *Review of Economic Studies* 61: 197–222.

—— and Jenkinson, T. (1996) 'The assessment: investment performance and policy', *Oxford Review of Economic Policy* 12: 1–33.

Brainard, W. C. and Tobin, J. (1967) 'Financial intermediaries and the effectiveness of monetary controls', in D. Hester and J. Tobin (eds.), *Financial Markets and Economic Activity* (New Haven, Conn.: Yale University).

Brechling, F. P. R. and Hahn, F. H. (eds.) (1965) *The Theory of Interest Rates* (London: Macmillan).

Buttiglione, L. and Ferri, G. (1994) 'Monetary policy transmission via lending rates in Italy: any lessons from recent experience?', Temi di Discussione, 224 (Rome: Bank of Italy).

Calcagnini, G. (1993) 'Market valuations and investment decisions: An empirical analysis of the Italian case', *Economic Notes* 22: 464–77.

Christiano, L. J., Eichenbaum, M., and Evans, C. L. (1996) 'The effects of monetary policy shocks: evidence from the flow of funds', *Review of Economics and Statistics* 78: 16–34.

Colander, D. (1998) 'Beyond New Keynesian economics: towards a post-Walrasian economics', in R. J. Rotheim (ed.), *New Keynesian Economics / Post Keynesian Alternatives* (London: Routledge).

Dale, S. and Haldane, S. (1993) 'Bank behaviour and the monetary transmission mechanism', *Bank of England Quarterly Bulletin*: 478–90.

Davidson, P. (1972) *Money and the Real World* (London: Macmillan).

Delli Gatti, D. and Gallegati, M. (1997) 'Financial constraints, aggregate supply and the monetary transmission mechanism', *Manchester School* 65: 101–26.

Devereux, M. and Schiantarelli, F. (1990) 'Investment, financial factors and cash flow: evidence from UK panel data', in R. G. Hubbard (ed.), *Asymmetric Information, Corporate Finance and Investment* (Chicago: Chicago University Press).

Diamond, D. W. (1984) 'Financial intermediation and delegated monitoring', *Review of Economic Studies* 51: 393–414.

—— (1989) 'Reputation acquisition in debt markets', *Journal of Political Economy* 97: 828–62.

—— and Dybvig, P. (1983) 'Bank runs, deposit insurance and liquidity', *Journal of Political Economy* 91: 401–19.

Elston, J. E. (1993) 'Firm ownership structure and investment: evidence from German manufacturing 1968–84', Wissenschaftzentrum Berlin.

Faini, R., Galli, G., and Giannini, C. (1993) 'Finance and development: the case of Southern Italy', in A. Giovannini (ed.), *Finance and Development: Issues and Experiences* (Cambridge: Cambridge University Press).

Fazzari, S., Hubbard, R. G., and Petersen, B. (1988) 'Financing constraints and corporate investment', *Brookings Papers on Economic Activity* 1: 141–206.

—— and Petersen, B. (1993) 'Working capital and fixed investment: new evidence on financing constraints', *RAND Journal of Economics* 24: 328–42.

Fiorentini, R. and Tamborini, R. (1998) 'Monetary policy, credit and aggregate supply: the evidence from Italy', Discussion Paper, Dipartimento di Economia dell' Università di Trento, Trento.

Fisher, I. (1933) 'The debt deflation theory of Great Depressions', *Econometrica* 1: 337–57.

Friedman, B. M. and Kuttner, K. N. (1992) 'Money, income, prices, and interest rates', *American Economic Review* 82: 472–92.

Gale, D. and Hellwig, M. (1985) 'Incentive-compatible debt contracts: the one period problem', *Review of Economic Studies* 52: 647–63.

Gertler, M. (1988) 'Financial structure and aggregate activity: an overview', *Journal of Money, Credit and Banking* 20: 559–88.

—— and Gilchrist, S. (1993) 'The role of credit market imperfections in the monetary transmission mechanism: arguments and evidence', *Scandinavian Journal of Economics* 93: 43–64.

—— and —— (1994) 'Monetary policy, business cycles and the behaviour of small manufacturing firms', *Quarterly Journal of Economics* 109: 309–40.

—— and Hubbard, R. G. (1988) 'Financial factors in business fluctuations', in Federal Reserve Bank of Kansas City, *Financial Market Volatility*, Kansas City.

Gordon, R. (1990) 'What is New Keynesian economics?', *Journal of Economic Literature* 28: 1115–71.

Grandmont, J. (1983) *Money and Value. A Reconsideration of Classical and Neoclassical Monetary Theory* (Cambrdige: Cambridge University Press).

—— (1985) 'On endogenous competitive business cycles', *Econometrica* 53: 995–1045.

Greenwald, B. and Stiglitz, J. E. (1987) 'Keynesian, New Keynesian and New Classical economics', *Oxford Economic Papers* 31(1): 119–33.

—— and —— (1988a) 'Examining alternative macroeconomic theories', *Brookings Papers on Economic Activity* 1: 207–60.

—— and —— (1988b) 'Imperfect information, finance constraints and business fluctuations', in M. Kohn and S. C. Tsiang (eds.), *Finance Constraints, Expectations and Macroeconomics* (Oxford: Clarendon Press).

—— and —— (1988c) 'Money, imperfect information and economic fluctuations', in M. Kohn and S. C. Tsiang (eds.), *Finance Constraints, Expectations and Macroeconomics* (Oxford: Clarendon Press).

—— and —— (1990) 'Macroeconomic models with equity and credit rationing', in R. G. Hubbard (ed.), *Information, Capital Markets and Investment* (Chicago: Chicago University Press).

—— and —— (1991) *Towards a Reformulation of Monetary Theory*, Caffe' Lectures, Universita' Bocconi, Milan.

—— and —— (1993a) 'Financial market imperfections and business cycles', *Quarterly Journal of Economics* 108: 77–113.

—— and —— (1993b) 'New and Old Keynesians', *Journal of Economic Perspectives* 7: 23–44.

——, ——, and Weiss, A. (1984) 'Imperfect information, credit markets and unemployment', *European Economic Review* 31: 444–56.

Grossman, S. J. and Stiglitz, J. E. (1980) 'On the impossibility of informationally efficient markets', *American Economic Review* 72: 884–907.

Gurley, J. G. and Shaw, E. S. (1960) *Money in a Theory of Finance* (Washington, DC: Brookings Institution).

Hahn, F. H. (1977) 'Keynesian economics and general equilibrium theory: reflections on some current debates', in G. C. Harcourt (ed.), *The Microeconomic Foundations of Macroeconomics* (London: Macmillan).

—— (1988) 'On Monetary Theory', *Economic Journal* 98: 932–50.

—— and Solow, R. (1995) *A Critical Essay on Modern Macroeconomic Theory* (Cambridge, Mass.: MIT Press).

Hargreaves Heap, S. P. (1992) *The New Keynesian Macroeconomics. Time, Belief and Social Interdependence* (London: Elgar).

Hart, O. (1995) *Firms, Contracts and Financial Structure* (Oxford: Clarendon Press).

Hawtrey, R. G. (1927) *Currency and Credit*, 3rd edn. (London: Macmillan).

Hellwig, M. (1991) 'Banking, financial intermediation and corporate finance', in A. Giovannini and C. Mayer (eds.), *European Financial Integration* (Cambridge: Cambridge University Press).

Hicks, J. R. (1980) 'IS–LM: an explanation', *Journal of Post Keynesian Economics* 3: 230–51.

Hoshi, T., Kashyap, S., and Scharfstein, D. (1991) 'Corporate structure, liquidity and investment: evidence from Japan's industrial groups', *Quarterly Journal of Economics* 106: 33–60.

Hu, X. and Schiantarelli, F. (1994) 'Investment and financing constraints: a switching regression approach using US firms panel data', Boston College, Working Paper 284.

Hubbard, R. G. (ed.) (1990) *Asymmetric Information, Corporate Finance and Investment* (Chicago: Chicago University Press).

——(1998) 'Capital market imperfections and investment', *Journal of Economic Literature* 36: 193–225.

Jaffee, D. and Russell, T. (1976) 'Imperfect information, uncertainty and credit rationing', *Quarterly Journal of Economics* 91: 651–66.

——and Stiglitz, J. E. (1990) 'Credit rationing', in B. M. Friedman and F. H. Hahn (eds.), *Handbook of Monetary Economics* (Amsterdam: North-Holland).

Jensen, M. C. and Meckling, W. H. (1976) 'Theory of the firm: managerial behaviour, agency cost, and ownership structure', *Journal of Financial Economics* 3: 306–60.

Kaldor, N. (1940) 'A model of the trade cycle', *Economic Journal* 50: 78–92.

——(1956) 'Alternative theories of distribution', *Review of Economic Studies* 23: 94–100.

——(1982) *The Scourge of Monetarism* (Oxford: Blackwell).

Kalecki, M. (1935) 'A macrodynamic theory of business cycles', *Econometrica* 3: 327–44.

——(1937) 'The principle of increasing risk', *Economica* 4: 440–7.

Kashyap, A. K. *et al.* (1993) 'Monetary policy and credit conditions: evidence from the composition of external finance', *American Economic Review* 83: 78–9.

——and Stein, J. C. (1994*a*) 'Monetary policy and bank lending', in N. G. Mankiw (ed.), *Monetary Policy* (Chicago: Chicago University Press).

——(1994*b*) 'The Impact of monetary policy on bank balance sheet', *NBER Working Paper* 4821.

Keeton, W. R. (1979) *Equilibrium Credit Rationing* (New York: Garland).

Keynes, J. M. (1933) 'A monetary theory of production', in *The Collected Writings of John Maynard Keynes*, xiv, ed. by E. Moggridge, 2nd edn., 1987 (London: Macmillan).

——(1930) *A Treatise on Money*, in *The Collected Writings of John Maynard Keynes*, ix, ed. by E. Moggridge, 1973 (London: Macmillan).

——(1936) *The General Theory of Employment, Interest and Money*, in *The Collected Writings of John Maynard Keynes*, vii, ed. by E. Moggridge, 1973 (London: Macmillan).

——(1937) 'Alternative theories of the rate of interest', in *The Collected Writings of John Maynard Keynes*, xiv, ed. by E. Moggridge, 2nd edn., 1987 (London: Macmillan).

King, S. (1986) 'Monetary transmission: through bank loans or bank liabilities?, *Journal of Money Credit and Banking* 18: 290–303.

Kiyotaki, N. and Moore, J. (1997) 'Credit cycles', *Journal of Political Economy* 105: 211–48.

Leijonhufvud, A. (1968) *On Keynesian Economics and the Economics of Keynes* (London: Oxford University Press).

——(1969) 'Keynes and the classics' (London: Institute of Economic Affairs).

——(1981) *Information and Coordination: Essays in Macroeconomic Theory* (New York: Oxford University Press).

—— (1992) 'Keynesian economics: past confusions and future prospects', in N. Dimitri and A. Vercelli (eds.), *Macroeconomics. A Survey of Research Strategies* (Oxford: Oxford University Press).

Leland, H. and Pyle, D. (1977) 'Informational asymmetries, financial structure and financial intermediation', *Journal of Finance* 32: 371–87.

Marotta, P. and Pittaluga, G. B. (1993) *La teoria degli intermediari bancari* (Bologna: Il Mulino).

Mayer, C. P. (1988) 'New issues in corporate finance', *European Economic Review* 32: 1167–88.

—— (1990) 'Financial systems, corporate finance and economic development', in R. G. Hubbard (ed.), *Asymmetric Information, Corporate Finance and Investment* (Chicago: Chicago University Press).

—— (1994) 'The assessment: money and banking, theory and evidence', *Oxford Review of Economic Policy* 10: 1–13.

Messori, M. and Tamborini, R. (1995) 'Fallibility, precautionary behaviour and the New Keynesian monetary theory', *Scottish Journal of Political Economy* 42: 443–64.

Minsky, H. P. (1972) 'An exposition of a Keynesian theory of investment', in *Can It Happen Again? Essays on Instability and Finance* (New York: Sharpe).

—— (1975) *John Maynard Keynes* (London: Macmillan).

—— (1982) *Can It Happen Again? Essays on Instability and Finance* (New York: Sharpe).

Miron, J. A., Romer, C., and Weil, D. N. (1994) 'Historical perspectives on the monetary transmission mechanism', in G. Mankiw (ed.), *Monetary Policy* (Chicago: Chicago University Press).

Mishkin, F. S. (1991) 'Anatomy of a Financial Crisis', *NBER Working Paper* 3934.

Modigliani, F. and Miller, M. (1958) 'The cost of capital, corporation finance and the theory of investment', *American Economic Review* 48: 261–77.

Moggridge, D. (ed.) (1987) *The Collected Writings of John Maynard Keynes*, xiv, pt. 2, 2nd edn. (London: Macmillan).

Moore, B. (1988) *Horizontalists and Verticalists* (Cambridge: Cambridge University Press).

Myers, M. and Majluf, N. (1984) 'Corporate financial decisions when firms have information that investors do not have', *Journal of Financial Economics* 13: 187–220.

Neary, P. and Stiglitz, J. E. (1983) 'Toward a Reconstruction of Keynesian Economics', *Quarterly Journal of Economics* 98(Suppl): 119–228.

Pittaluga, G. B. (1998) *Il razionamento del credito* (Milan: F. Angeli).

Radcliffe Committee (1959) *Report on the Working of the Monetary System* (London: HMSO).

Romer, C. and Romer, D. (1990) 'New evidence on the monetary transmission mechanism', *Brookings Papers on Economic Activity* 1: 149–214.

Rosser, J. B. (1998) 'Complex dynamics in New Keynesian and Post-Keynesian models', in R. J. Rotheim (ed.), *New Keynesian Economics/Post Keynesian Alternatives* (London: Routledge).

Rotheim, R. J. (ed.) (1998) *New Keynesian Economics/Post Keynesian Alternatives* (London: Routledge).

Schiantarelli, F. (1996) 'Financial constraints and investment: methodological issues and international evidence', *Oxford Review of Economic Policy* 12: 73–95.

Schumpeter, J. A. (1934) *A Theory of Economic Development* (Cambridge, Mass.: Harvard University Press).

Stiglitz, J. E. (1985) 'Credit markets and the control of capital', *Journal of Money Credit and Banking* 17: 234–56.

—— (1987) 'The causes and consequences of the dependence of quality on price', *Journal of Economic Literature* 25.

Stiglitz, J. E. (1992*a*) 'Capital markets and economic fluctuations in capitalist economies', Paper and Proceedings of the European Economic Association, *European Economic Review* 36: 269–306.

——(1992*b*) 'Methodological issues and the New Keynesian economics', in N. Dimitri and A. Vercelli (eds.), *Macroeconomics. A Survey of Research Strategies* (Oxford: Oxford University Press).

——and Weiss, A. (1981) 'Credit rationing in markets with imperfect information', *American Economic Review* 71: 393–410.

—— and ——(1988) 'Banks as social accountants and screening devices for the allocation of credit', *NBER Working Paper* 2710.

—— and ——(1992) 'Asymmetric information in credit markets and its implications for macroeconomics', *Oxford Economic Papers* 44: 694–724.

Tamborini, R. (1997) 'An investigation into the New Keynesian macroeconomics of imperfect capital markets', Discussion Paper, Dipartimento di Economia dell' Università di Trento, Trento, 11; in M. Messori (ed.) 1999 *Financial Constraints and Market Failures. The Microeconomic Foundations of New Keynesian Economics* (London: Elgar).

Tobin, J. (1969) 'A general equilibrium approach to monetary theory', *Journal of Money Credit and Banking* 1(1).

——(1980) *Asset Accumulation and Economic Activity* (Oxford: Blackwell).

——(1993) 'Price flexibility and output stability: an Old Keynesian view', *Journal of Economic Perspectives* 7: 46–66.

Townsend, R. (1979) 'Optimal contracts and competitive markets with costly state verification', *Journal of Economic Theory* 20: 265–93.

Van Damme, E. (1994) 'Banking: a survey of recent microeconomic theory', *Oxford Review of Economic Policy* 10: 14–33.

Weintraub, E. R. (1979) *Microfoundations. The Compatibility of Microeconomics and Macroeconomics* (Cambridge: Cambridge University Press).

Wicksell, K. (1898) *Interest and Prices*, 1936 edn. (London: Macmillan).

9 New Keynesian macroeconomics: the role of theory and evidence

HUW D. DIXON

One can say that the new classical challenge has been met: Keynesian economics
has been reincarnated with a firm microeconomic muscle

Mankiw (1992: 560)

In this paper I wish to focus on some of the main developments associated with new
Keynesian macrotheory (NKM) in the 1980s and early 1990s. Let me preface the
paper with two observations about my own perspective. I will argue that empirical
evidence in itself has little to do with the choice of the macroeconomic framework
adopted. *This is because the theory itself determines the way the evidence is interpreted and
indeed what evidence is considered at all.* At the base of macroeconomists' worldviews are
basic preconceptions about what is really going on, what needs explaining, and what is
worth taking seriously (and hence what can be ignored). Within a given theoretical
framework evidence can matter, because there is then an agreed framework both for
what is admissible evidence and for its interpretation. I would argue this as a general
statement which applies to most of economics. In this paper, however, I try to explore
its validity primarily in the context of NKM and related developments.

The paper proceeds in the following manner. In Section 1 I try to define the basic
tenets of NKM. These tenets constitute the 'attitude' and gut feelings (core beliefs) of
the NKM macroeconomist. The next sections go on to explore the concrete issues of
nominal rigidities and involuntary unemployment, attempting to differentiate the
theoretical and empirical motivation behind them. Section 2 looks at Menu-cost
theory, surely one of the major reincarnations of the traditional Keynesian concerns
with nominal rigidity. Section 3 explores the 'new synthesis', in which nominal
rigidities have become a central focus for most macroeconomists. Section 4 looks at the
idea of involuntary unemployment (IU). Whilst IU is perhaps not a central NKM idea,
it plays an important role in differentiating NKM (and traditional Keynesians) from
new classical and RBC counterparts.

The basic story of the paper is the following. The prime motivation behind new
Keynesian theory was a theoretical one: to provide microfoundations for nominal
rigidities and involuntary unemployment (amongst other phenomena). These phenomena were seen as being almost self-evidently important features that needed
explaining (the agenda). This does not mean that empirical evidence did not play a
role: rather the evidence was not decisive and there was certainly no important 'new'
evidence driving the theory or determining the agenda. Indeed, in the mid-1990s there
has been 'new synthesis': a desire to combine the key features of nominal rigidities
within the general equilibrium dynamic model built up by new classical and RBC
economists in the 1980s and early 1990s. Again, there is a shift of sentiment amongst

macroeconomists: this cannot be explained by some decisive new evidence. Involuntary unempoyment is a phenomenon that some people see as self-evident and others as an irrelevant theoretical construct. Again, whilst this underlying belief determines the theoretical framework, there is no generally accepted empirical test. I do, however, argue that there is strong evidence for the existence of involuntary unemployment, but in a data source that is usually ignored by economists (surveys of well-being).

1. The New Keynesian agenda

I have written elsewhere in some detail about the origins and precursors of NKM (Dixon and Rankin 1995: introduction; Dixon 1998). However, for the purposes of this paper, I will take the discussion in the introducton to Mankiw and Romer's collection '*New Keynesian Economics*' (Mankiw and Romer 1991: 2–3). Here the authors argue that New Keynesians *do* believe that:

- nominal variables can affect real variables (the classical dichotomy is violated), and
- market imperfections are crucial for understanding the economy.

Indeed, putting together these two points Mankiw and Romer state that 'the interaction of nominal and real imperfections is a distinguishing feature of new Keynesian economics' (ibid.). It should be noted that when this statement was written, this clearly differentiated New Keynesians from new classical and real business cycle (RBC) economists. The authors also stress the break with the 'old Keynesian' beliefs, in that New Keynesians *do not* necessarily believe that

- fiscal policy is more effective than monetary policy, and
- government intervention is desirable.

The real questions that I wish to ask are to what extent these core beliefs are driven by theoretical as opposed to empirical considerations. This discussion will inevitably lead to a consideration of the role of theory and evidence in applied economics and economics in general.

David Romer's article 'The New Keynesian synthesis' (1993) puts the matter quite explicitly, so I quote (selectively) at some length:

The *famous* 'neoclassical synthesis' . . . postulated that prices in money units adjusted only slowly to imbalances in supply and demand . . . . the remainder of the neoclassical synthesis was Walrasian. The neoclassical synthesis foundered on an obvious question: in an environment so . . . competitive, how can one glaring departure from Walrasian behaviour persist? . . . This question lead to the collapse of the neoclassical school and split mainstream macroeconomics into two schools. . . . RBC theory abandoned Keynesian macroeconomics [and] deny the existence of involuntary unemployment NKM: *members of this school believe that the appropriate response was to determine whether a correct description of the microeconomy would give rise to the phenomena that they believed characterized the economy*'. (Romer (1993: 5–6, italics my own)

From his quote it is quite clear that the main aim is to 'provide adequate foundations for Keynesian macroeconomics', a concern is also apparent from the opening quote by

Mankiw about 'microeconomic muscle'. One of the key phenomena that Romer sees as essential to Keynesian macroeconomics is the importance of unemployment and in particular involuntary unemployment: 'after all, accepting the belief that the labour market was continuously in Walrasian equilibrium would require denying that unemployment was an important phenomenon.' I think that it is fair to say that he views the existence of IU as almost self-evident: the very fact that unemployment matters means that there must be IU. It is part of the basic agenda that must be explained. RBC and new classical economists are in a state of denial: they 'deny the existence of involuntary unemployment'.

In the rest of the paper, we will explore the theoretical and empirical motivations for two of the basic NKM agenda items: nominal rigidities and IU.

2. Menu costs

The ideas that there exist nominal rigidities of some kind have always been central to Keynesian economics, from Keynes *General Theory* onwards. To some extent, however, the existence of such nominal rigidities was seen as *ad hoc* or unexplained in some fundamental sense. Perhaps the most influential research in this tradition was the Fischer–Taylor model of overlapping labour contracts (Fischer 1977 and Taylor 1979). This took as a given that labour contracts were overlapping and staggered and then analysed the macroeconomic implications of this. There was still possibly a question that the theoretical foundations of the staggering of contracts was not fully explained.

The theory of menu costs is a very good example which illustrates the two essential features of NKM highlighted by Mankiw and Romer: (a) a real imperfection leads to a nominal rigidity and (b) imperfect competition is central. In addition, as Gordon (1990) has pointed out, there is a shift of emphasis from rigidities in the labour market to the product market.

2.1. Menu costs: theoretical motivation

The theoretical motivation for menu costs is very clear. I have explored this in some detail in Dixon (1998): in this paper I will restrict myself to the overview. The key relationships are the following. If the following hold true, then an increase in nominal demand can increase output and welfare simultaneously:

- price exceeds marginal cost,
- nominal prices are rigid.

To see how these two features interact, let us consider a simple partial equilibrium consumer surplus argument, as in Figure 9.1. Consider an increase in demand (due to an increase in nominal demand for example) at some fixed nominal price P_a in excess of MC. This will lead to an increase in output from X_a to X'_a. This will cause an

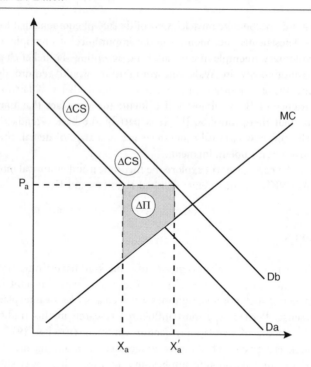

FIG. 9.1. *Increase in welfare as demand increases with a fixed price*

increase in producer surplus represented by the area $\Delta\Pi$[1] and also an increase in consumer surplus ΔCS. If price were equal to marginal cost (as in the Walrasian case), nominal rigidity would affect output in the same way (excepting that there is a question as to whether suppliers would wish to supply consumers at outputs where price is less than MC). However, since welfare (the sum of producer and consumer surplus) is maximized at the Walrasian outcome, any deviation in welfare is merely second order. If price were below MC, then increases in output would cause reductions in welfare and decreases in output increases (there is a clear problem as to why firms would voluntarily satisfy demand when price is below marginal cost). Hence, nominal rigidity is needed to have output affected by nominal demand: price needs to exceed MC in order to have a first-order positive welfare effect.

The theories of menu costs and imperfect competition together provide exactly these two preconditions. Firstly, the condition that price exceeds marginal cost is implied by almost any theory of oligopoly/monopolistic competition[2] except when (industry) demand is perfectly elastic (a limiting exception). Secondly, the theory of menu costs provides a direct explanation of price-rigidity in itself. When added

---

[1] Which is in effect integrating the excess of price over MC as output increases.

[2] The only exception are theories based on Bertrand price competition with a homogeneous product and perfect consumer market (see for a discussion Dixon 1988). Even here, a price greater than MC is possible though not inevitable).

together, the monopolistic theory also implies that the menu costs need only be small, since the initial price will satisfy some optimality condition.

Clearly, whilst some authors have concentrated on imperfect competition in the output market, others have focused on the labour market: (Akerlof-Yellen 1985*a*,*b*; Ball and Romer 1990). In this case, the condition which is equivalent to the excess of price over marginal cost is that the real wage exceeds the marginal disutility of labour (or the marginal rate of substitution between leisure and consumption).

2.2. Menu costs: the empirical motivation

What about the empirical evidence? I think that it is fair to say that there is almost no discussion of the evidence for menu costs in the NKM literature itself. The only contemporary paper that tests for the menu-cost theory in a rather indirect manner is Ball–Mankiw–Romer (1988).[3] In this paper the authors consider the cross-country evidence for the inflation-output trade-off. Since the trade-off depends on nominal rigidity of prices, one would expect economies where prices change frequently (i.e. high-inflation economies) to have less of a trade-off, which is indeed what they find. However, the evidence is at best indirect, since other factors could cause the inflation effect, not the specific mechanism postulated.

However, there is a long history of analysing price-rigidities in oligopolistic markets: this is known in the IO literature as the *administered pricing controversy* (see Mills 1927; Means 1935, 1972; Humphrey 1937; Tucker 1938; Hall and Hitch 1951; Stigler and Kindahl 1970; and Weiss 1977, *inter alia*). The administered price hypothesis (APH) arose out of the observation that in some oligopolistic industries nominal prices seemed unresponsive to demand and supply pressures, being 'administered' by oligopolists. The empirical debate here has tended to centre on two features. First, the question of whether there is a relationship between concentration and the flexibility of prices. Here there has not been any decisive empirical evidence either way. Second, there is the issue of *list* prices (the prices on the 'menu') and the actual *transaction* prices: Stigler and Kindahl argued that the evidence of rigidity in list prices was consistent with the flexibility of actual transaction prices, due to discounting.

The more recent debate about price flexibility was instigated by Carlton (1986). He re-examined the Stigler–Kindahl data on transactions prices: amongst several other findings he concluded that.

- 'The degree of price rigidity in many industries is significant.'
- 'The level of industry concentration is strongly correlated with rigid prices. The more concentrated the industry, the longer is the average spell of price rigidity.'
- 'The more rigid are prices, the greater is the price change when they do change.'

There have been many studies in the IO literature exploring these and other relationships (see e.g. Slade 1991; Caucutt *et al.* 1994; Roberts *et al.* 1994; Geroski 1992). Most of these (though not all, it must be said) tend to support the main findings of Carlton. For example, using UK data from the 1980s Geroski (1992) finds 'prices

---

[3] See also Kandil (1991) and Defina (1991).

responded sluggishly to costs but virtually not at all to demand' and, 'pricing dynamics were more sluggish in less competitive industries.'

There have also been studies looking directly at menu costs (Levy *et al.* 1997) and also comparing the partial-adjustment cost model[4] with the lump-sum approach (Carlson 1992). Levy *et al.* (1997) conclude from a detailed study of supermarket chains that 'menu costs may be forming a barrier to price changes'; 'that those chains with higher menu costs change price less frequently' and 'find that menu-costs are significant element of profits and revenue.' Carlson compares the partial adjustment and lump-sum cost models at the firm level and finds that whilst the evidence is mixed, 'the high percentage of firms which fix prices for a quarter or more casts doubt on the plausibility of the partial-adjustment hypothesis' (Carlson 1992).

One criticism of the menu-cost model has been that although it might explain price rigidity at the *individual firm* level, this is quite consistent with *aggregate* price flexibility (Caplin and Spulber 1987). As Sutherland (1995) has shown, the Caplin–Spulber result is something of a special case. In general, individual price rigidity will carry over to the aggregate price-level if there is any *clustering* of price changer. Whilst there has not been any empirical work specifically on this point that I am aware of, casual empiricism seems to point to strong clustering in particular markets along with more general seasonal effects. Roberts *et al.* (1994) examine the relationship between individual and aggregate price rigidity and conclude that 'The results suggest that to the extent that aggregate price rigidity exists, it can be explained by sluggishness of individual price adjustment.'

I would conclude that the NKM literature on menu costs was almost entirely motivated by a combination of theoretical considerations. There has been a long-standing debate over the relationship between price rigidity and industrial concentration in the IO literature. However, the primary NKM literature did not develop this (perhaps largely because the IO debate was at the microeconomic level). The specific idea of menu costs has however received more recent attention, which has been largely supportive of the original notion, although the macroeconomists seem to have moved on more to other issues.

3. Nominal rigidities and the 'new synthesis'

The main reason to be interested in sticky prices is that they provide one of the few means of generating large monetary non-neutralities. The basic evidence for the existence of large non-neutralities is the evidence assembled by Friedman and Schwarz (1963), together with events after the end of their sample.

I will try to hint at a joint research programme for New Keynesians and real business cycle theorists. Kimball (1995: 1242–3)

Moving on to the present, most macroeconomists now accept that nominal rigidities are an important, not to say essential part of any viable macromodel. Kimball (1995) argues forcefully for this viewpoint: very few RBC economists now use exclusively real models. It is worth looking at Kimball's statement in more detail. First, note that the

---

[4] The partial-adjustment model is based on convex costs of price adjustment (e.g. Rotemberg 1982).

evidence he cites for the non-neutrality of money is not at all new: indeed, Friedman and Schwarz's study has been very well known since its publication (not least for the controversy it has generated). Secondly, the evidence is not *direct*. He argues that we need to have nominal rigidity not because of any direct evidence for price or wage rigidity: rather, he argues that such rigidity *provides* 'one of the few means of generating large monetary non-neutralities'. This statement is very significant, since Miles Kimball himself was previously very much a self-confessed RBC man. Whilst Kimball does not make the point, it is implicit in his statement that RBC theorists were wrong to ignore nominal rigidities and focus on 'real' models that implicitly assumed perfect price flexibility. From the methodological perspective, it indicates again that it is not the evidence that is decisive: evidence was there all of the time, but was ignored because of theoretical priors.[5]

Again, whilst Kimball does not state it as such, he is arguing that one of the core new Keynesian propositions *à la* Mankiw–Romer be adopted. In this sense the New Keynesian perspective has been victorious in forcing one of its key beliefs back on to the centre-stage of the macroeconomic debate. Kimball calls this *neo-monetarist*: however, this is a neologism that has not caught on (not as yet).

Since Kimball's paper, there has been a growing tide of research on the topic of nominal rigidities in dynamic macromodels. There have been writers who have been associated with the standard RBC approach who have been moving towards the integration of nominal variables into the dynamic general equilibrium model (e.g Cooley and Hansen 1995; Chari *et al*. 1996). However, more recently the driving force behind this has not so much been a desire to explain the importance of monetary non-neutrality *per se*, but the fact that nominal rigidities can generate a persistence mechanism for real or monetary shocks. This is now a rapidly growing literature which puts an overlapping contract framework into a dynamic general equilibrium model— see for example (Guido Ascari 1997, 1998; Ascari and Rankin 1997). In these models employment is determined by labour demand—there is involuntary unemployment. This enables the authors to explore the effects of policy in some detail: in particular Ascari and Rankin (1998) shows the mechanics of how disinflation (both anticipated and unanticipated) causes a slump. In fact, the literature integrating nominal rigidities into dynamic general equilibrium is growing so rapidly that it is not really appropriate to attempt to summarize it here.[6]

However, there is a more general move towards integrating nominal rigidities apparent in the monetary policy literature. There has been a move towards modelling central banks as using the interest rate to try to control inflation. The usual way this is modelled is using a Phillips curve relationship which puts the rate of inflation as a (lagged) function of output (see for example Ball 1997; Bean 1998; and

---

[5] I should point out that we should not think of the RBC exercise as primarily empirical despite that: it was based on the presumption of a particular theory and made no rigorous attempt to test between alternatives (this is what was meant by 'calibration'). This has changed in recent years as the theoretical models have become richer.

[6] Some of the papers of particular interest are Ellison and Scott (1998), Erceg (1997), Hansen (1998), Jeanne (1997), and Kiley (1997), all as yet unpublished.

Svensson 1997). This marks an interesting change in perspective. The original policy credibility literature was based on the surprise supply function in which a surprise in inflation caused a change in output. The whole argument for central bank independence was that by delegating monetary policy to conservative central bankers the temptation to have a bout of inflation to reap the reward of some extra output and employment could be avoided. This model is perfectly compatible with the notion that prices and wages are perfectly flexible, with output variations caused by expectational errors (as in the Friedmatn–Lucas story). When authors are now modelling actual policy rules, they reverse the relationship and have changes in output (caused by interest rate policy directly or via the exchange rate) causing changes in inflation. This marks an interesting historical cycle.

4. Involuntary unemployment

The possibility of involuntary unemployment (IU) and its analysis has always been a central feature of Keynesian economics. Clearly, from Keynes's own definition of involuntary unemployment,[7] the essence of IU is that an individual is willing to supply more labour than is demanded at the prevailing wage (or one slightly lower). It is thus defined in terms of the individual on the assumption that there is a unique wage rate facing him. Clearly, Romer sees the concept of unemployment (and by implication IU) as central to his view of how the macroeconomy works.

Its role in NKM is less clear. In particular, many authors have been happy to model the labour market as a competitive market (Mankiw 1985, 1988; Dixon 1987). However, many papers have looked in some detail at the issue, often using the efficiency wage model in order to generate a wage that exceeds the competitive (Ball and Romer 1990; Hairault and Portier 1993).

New classical economists have largely ignored the phenomenon of involuntary unemployment. Lucas puts the case against IU admirably in an article on 'Unemployment policy' (Lucas 1978). Collecting together some of his statements from this article:

> The worker who loses a job does not *volunteer* to be in this situation. Nevertheless the unemployed worker can always find *some* job at once ... there is an involuntary element in *all* unemployment, in the sense that no one chooses bad luck over good.
>
> Involuntary unemployment is not a fact or a phenomenon to which it is the task of theorists to explain. It is, on the contrary, a theoretical construct which Keynes introduced (in order to explain) large scale fluctuations in measured, total unemployment.[8]
>
> [I]t does not appear possible, even in principle, to classify individual unemployed people as either voluntarily or involuntarily employed.

---

[7] By looking at Keynes I do not mean to support Mankiw's 'dubious Keynesian Proposition No. 1', Mankiw (1992: 560). It is simply a useful reference point.

[8] In a similar vein from about the same time Fisher remarked 'I would maintain that involuntary unemployment as a phenomenon still lacks ... empirical support' (Fisher 1976).

Without going into a detailed textual analysis of an article written over two decades ago, the essence of the point Lucas makes is that the concept of IU is only useful insofar as it helps us to explain aggregate fluctuations. He was obviously of the opinion that the assumption that all unemployment is voluntary (Walrasian) was the most promising way to proceed.

Clearly, one must agree that any exact decomposition between voluntary and involuntary is not possible. There is a literature that tried to decompose unemployment into components (cyclical, structural, etc.). However, few would argue with Lucas's assertion that it is difficult to categorize individuals. The key point is that involuntary unemployment is useful in that it enables us to understand fluctuations in employment and unemployment that occur even when (real) wages do not vary much. It is this feature that makes it useful in a practical sense. For a standard classical view, this raises the problem of the fact that individual labour-supply elasticities are small. RBC models have adopted the view that the aggregate labour-supply elasticity can nevertheless be high since variations in employment take the form of number of people employed rather than hours per worker (this is consistent with US data). The story is (following Hansen 1985) that labour is indivisible and the labour-supply function is roughly the cumulative density of the reservation wages. For other countries, such as the UK, changes in total hours break up more evenly between employment and hours per worker (see for example Holland and Scott 1998), so this explanation will not work so easily.[9]

I would argue that there is no *decisive* empirical test as to whether employment is usefully viewed as having a high IU content or not. However, I would certainly argue that there is evidence that unemployment has a high IU content, at least at certain times and places. This evidence comes from a source not usually given a high prominence by economists: survey evidence on welfare or happiness.[10] As Oswald has found, the evidence here is very strong that becoming unemployed makes people very unhappy (Oswald 1997). As I argue in Dixon (1999), this basic fact is very hard if not impossible to explain in a competitive labour market. The basic reason is that a competitive labour market will allocate changes in employment efficiently: those becoming unemployed will be those who (at the margin) value work the least. In fact competitive models will generally predict that those remaining employed will have a larger reduction in welfare than those becoming unemployed. Of course, whilst I may find this evidence convincing, many do not at present. Unless the profession as a whole decides that this is evidence worth taking seriously, there remains no real test of whether unemployment is involuntary or not.

It is worth noting that part of the new synthesis in macroeconomics has involved some researchers taking IU seriously. In particular, Ascari (1997, 1998) Ascari and Rankin (1997), and Andersen and Holden (1998) adopt an imperfectly competitive labour market with IU. It remains to be seen whether this becomes as generally accepted as an agenda item along with nominal rigidity. As I argue in Dixon (1999),

---

[9] Holland and Scott remain within the Walrasian paradigm by assuming preference shocks.

[10] Whilst economists have rejected the notion of measurable cardinal utility for the last fifty years or so, there is a groundswell of opinion that this should be reconsidered: see for example the Controversy on Economics and Happiness in the *Economic Journal* 107 (November 1997).

I believe that it is not possible to have a coherent account of wage or price rigidity without modelling the process of wage or price determination, which implies that there must be a non-competitive approach which abandons the assumption of price-taking.

5. Conclusion

We all have priors of varying strengths, which influence how we interpret the world. The choice of prior is important, since it determines where we start from when we interpret the world. Indeed, a prior is important because in many cases we do not update our prior unless we have to. Many economists have a 'classical' prior: they believe that fundamentally the world is best explained as being one where markets are more or less perfect. Clearly, there is some question as to how far the assumption of perfect markets is completely accurate. However, in practice, it is merely a question as to how far we can go in explaining phenomena. In recent years, one chosen battle-ground (data to be explained) has been the business cycle and growth. Many of the earlier RBC models completely ignored data and issues that were seen as important by others (e.g. the nominal and monetary side of the economy).

NKM starts from a different view of the world: one where market imperfections of one sort or another are seen as essential to understand the way the economy works. For me the reasons here are partly aesthetic. No one understands very well the microfoundations of perfect competition: supply equals demand is familiar yet in many ways mysterious. Looking at imperfect markets at least gives us a way of understanding how almost perfect economies might operate: the competitive economy is usually the limiting and special case of some model with market imperfections. Clearly, however, I write as a theorist. Much of NKM is concerned with more empirical issues. Most importantly, this comes down to the importance of nominal variables in affecting real variables and the explanation of labour-market institutions and unemployment. Thus, for example, NKM economists might be interested in the role of unions in wage-setting and in particular whether the degree of centralization matters (the so-called Calmfors–Driffill hump-hypothesis). This is a question which is of no interest to the classical view and which uses data which is at worst not relevant, at best simply ignored.

REFERENCES

Akerlof, G. and Yellen, J. (1985*a*) 'A near-rational model of the business cycle with wage and price inertia', *Quarterly Journal of Economics* 100 (suppl): 823–38.
—— and —— (1985*b*) 'Can small deviations from rationality make significant differences to economic equilibria?', *American Economic Review* 75: 708–21.
Andersen, T. M. and Holden, S. (1998) 'Stabilization policy in an open economy', Dept. of Economics, mimeo, University of Oslo, Sept., mimeo.
Ascari, G. (1997) 'Optimising agents, staggered wages and persistence in the real effects of money shocks', Warwick Economic Research Paper 486, Sept.

—— and Rankin, N. (1997) 'Staggered wages and disinflation dynamics: what can more microfoundations tell us?', *LEPR DP* No. 1763.

——(1998) 'Superneutrality of money in staggered wage-setting models', *Macroeconomic Dynamics* 2: 383–400.

—— and Rankin, N. (1997) 'Staggered wages and disinflation dynamics: what can more microfoundations tell us?', CEPR DP 1763.

Ball, L. (1997) 'Efficient rules for monetary policy', Johns Hopkins University, mimeo.

—— and Romer, D. (1990) 'Real rigidities and the non-neutrality of money', *Review of Economic Studies* 57: 179–98.

——, Mankiw, N. G. and Romer, D. (1998) 'The New Keynesian economics and the output inflation trade-off', *Brookings Papers on Economic Activity* 1: 1–82.

Bean, C. (1998) 'The New UK monetary arrangements', *Economic Journal* 108: 1795–809.

Caplin, A. and Spulber, D. (1987) 'Menu costs and the neutrality of money', *Quarterly Journal of Economics* 102: 703–26.

Carlson, J. (1992) 'Some evidence on lump-sum versus convex costs of changing prices', *Economic Inquiry* 30: 322–31.

Carlton, D. (1986) 'The rigidity of prices', *American Economic Review* 76: 637–58.

Caucutt, E. M., Ghosh, M., and Kelton, C. (1994) 'Pricing behaviour in United States manufacturing industries—a statistical analysis using dissagregated data, *Review of Industrial Organisation* 9: 745–72.

Chari, V. V., Kehoe, P. J. and McGratten, E. R. (1996) 'Sticky price models of the business cycle: can the contract multiplier solve the persistence problem?', *NBER WP* No. 5809.

Danthine, J. P. and Donaldson, J. B. (1990) 'Efficiency wages and the business cycle puzzle', *European Economic Review* 34: 1275–301.

——(1993) 'Methodological and empirical issues in real business cycle theory', *European Economic Review* 37: 1–35.

Defina, R. (1991) 'International evidence on a new Keyensain theory of the output-inflation trade-off', *Journal of Money, Credit and Banking* 23: 410–42.

Dixon, H. (1987) 'A simple model of imperfect competition with Walrasian features', *Oxford Economic Papers*, 39: 134–60.

——(1998) 'Reflections on New Keynesian economics; the role of imperfect competition', in Vane and Snowden (eds.), *Reflections on Modern Macroeconomics* (London: Edward Elgar): 158–203.

——(1999) 'New Keynesian economics, nominal rigidities and involuntary unemployment', *Journal of Economic Methodology* 6: 221–38.

—— and Rankin, N. (1995) *The New Macroeconomics* (Cambridge: Cambridge University Press).

Ellison, M. and Scott, A. (1998) 'Sticky prices and volatile output: or when is a Phillips curve not a Phillips curve', *CEPR Discussion Paper* 1849.

Erceg, C. (1997) 'Nominal wage rigidities and the propagation of monetary disturbances', Board of Governors of the Federal Reserve System, mimeo.

Fisher, M. (1976) 'The new microeconomics of unemployment', in G. Worswick (ed.), *The Concept and Measurement of Involuntary Unemployment*: 35–58.

Geroski, P. (1992). 'Price dynamics in UK manufacturing—a microeconomic view', *Economica* 59 (236): 403–19.

Hairault, J. O. and Portier, F. (1993) 'Money, new-Keynesian macroeconomics and the business cycle, *European Economic Review* 37: 1533–68.

Hansen, Claus Thustrup (1998) 'Monetary stabilization policy in a dynamic, stochastic menu cost model', Discussion Paper 1998-18, Institute of Economics, University of Copenhagen.

Hansen, G. (1985) 'Indivisible labour and the business cycle', *Journal of Monetary Economics* 16: 309–27.

Holland, A. and Scott, A. (1998) 'The determinants of UK business cycles', *Economic Journal* 108: 1067–92.

Jeanne, O. (1997) 'Generating real persistent effects of monetary shocks: how much nominal rigidity do we really need?', *European Economic Review* 42: 1009–32.

Kandil, M. (1991) 'Variations in the response of real output to aggregate demand shocks—a cross industry analysis', *Review of Economics and Statistics* 73(3): 480–8.

Kiley, M. T. (1997) 'Staggered price setting, partial adjustment, real rigidities, and sunspots', Board of Governors of the Federal Reserve System, mimeo.

Kimball, M. (1995) 'The quantitative analytics of the basic neomonetarist model', *Journal of Money, Credit and Banking* 27(4): 1241–77.

Levy, D., Bergen, M., Dutta, S., and Venable, R. (1997) 'The magnitude of menu costs: Direct evidence from large US supermarket chains', *Quarterly Journal of Economics* 112: 791–825.

Mankiw, N. G. (1985) 'Small menu costs and large business cycles: a macroeconomic model of monopoly', *Quarterly Journal of Economics* 100: 529–39.

——(1986) 'Issues in Keynesian macroeconomics: a review essay', *Journal of Monetary Economics* 18: 217–23.

——(1988) 'Imperfect competition and the Keynesian Cross', *Economics Letters* 26: 7–13.

——(1992) 'The reincarnation of Keynesian economics', *European Economic Review* 36: 559–65.

Oswald, A. (1997) 'Happiness and economic performance', *Economic Journal* 107: 1815–31.

Prescott, E. (1986) 'Theory ahead of business cycle measurement', *Federal Reserve Bank of Minneapolis Quarterly Review* 10: 9–22.

Roberts, J. (1992) 'Evidence on price-adjustment costs in the United States manufacturing industry', *Economic Inquiry* 30: 399–417.

—— Stockson, D. and Struckmeyer, C. (1994) 'Evidence of flexibility of prices', *Review of Economics and Statistics* 76: 142–50.

Romer, D. (1993) 'The new Keyensian synthesis', *Journal of Economic Perspectives* 7: 5–22.

Rotemberg, J. J. and Woodford, M. (1995) 'Dynamic general models with imperfectly competitive product markets', *Annales d'économie et de statistique* 37–38: 357–410.

—— Woodford, M. (1996) 'Imperfect competition and the effects of energy price increases on economic activity', *Journal of Money, Credit and Banking* 28(4): 549–77.

Slade, M. (1991) 'Market-structure marketing method, and price instability', *Quarterly Journal of Economics* 106: 1311–40.

Sutherland, A. (1995) 'Menu costs and aggregate price dynamics'. In Dixon, H. and Rankin, N. (eds.) *The New Macroeconomics: Imperfect Markets and Policy Effectiveness* (Cambridge University Press).

Svensson, L. (1997) 'Inflation targeting: implementing and monitoring inflation targets', *European Economic Review* 41: 1111–46.

10A Equity finance, internal funds, and involuntary unemployment

MARK BLAUG

There is one and only one thing wrong with the paper by Delli Gatti and Tamborini: there is too much in it, being in fact two or even three papers in one. It has a grand theme, namely that asymmetric information between lenders and borrowers in loan markets and between issuing companies and shareholders in equity markets gives rise to both equilibrium credit-rationing and equilibrium equity-rationing; in short, capital markets are inherently imperfect. Following Bernard Greenwald and Joseph Stiglitz, who invented this type of New Keynesian Economics (NKE) in the 1970s, Delli Gatti and Tamborini systematically explore the macroeconomic impact of these capital-market imperfections on aggregate income determination, on the possibilities of demand management, on economic growth, and finally on the business cycle.

They begin by noting that a popular account of 'what Keynes really meant, associated with the names of Axel Leijonhufvud and Paul Davidson, traces unemployment equilibrium in capitalist economies to the essentially monetary determination of the rate of interest, irrespective of whether wages and prices are flexible or not. Post-Keynesians hold that this capital-market failure is in turn the result of radical uncertainty, bounded rationality, imperfect information, and incomplete markets. New Keynesians, however, add to these the special nature of the financial contracts that are traded in capital markets, which inevitably give rise to asymmetric information as between demanders and suppliers: they involve *ex ante* screening and *ex post* monitoring and auditing, which leads to adverse selection in the former and moral hazard in the latter case. In short, the perfect market paradigm is totally inappropriate to a study of capital markets.

In one sense, all this amounts to reinventing the wheel. More than fifty years ago, Friedrich Hayek (1942: 235–6) pointed out that perfect competition in product markets is not like perfect competition in capital markets:

It would of course be absurd to assume [he said] that even in the most perfectly competitive money market every borrower (or, for that matter, any borrower) can at the given rate of interest borrow any amount he likes. This is precluded by the fact that in any given circumstances the security a borrower has to offer is not so good for a large amount as for a small one. In consequence, every prospective borrower will have to face an upward-sloping supply curve of credit—or, rather, not a continuous supply curve, but an upward stepped 'curve'.

Of course, he should have said that the supply curve of credit is kinked at the rationing level, after which it becomes perfectly inelastic. He might also have added that a perfectly elastic credit-supply curve to each firm in a perfectly competitive capital market is, strictly speaking, a contradiction in terms: if a firm is able to borrow funds without some absolute ceiling or expectation of a ceiling to the amount it can borrow at a finite rate of interest, it will borrow enough to push the marginal yield of the invested loan down to zero, knowing it can always borrow to repay interest and principal, and so on *ad infinitum*. This is tantamount, however, to command of funds in perpetuity; since the funds are now also commanded with perfect certainty, this is equivalent to ownership of the funds. Thus, the indefinite opportunity to borrow at any finite rate of interest turns out paradoxically to be equivalent to a zero rate of interest. Some kind of credit rationing, therefore, is an indispensable logical element in the theory of business finance. To be sure, Hayek did not say all that in 1942 but George Stigler (1967) did say it in 1967.

Apart from credit rationing, imperfect capital markets are also characterized by what Delli Gatti and Tamborini call 'financial hierarchy (or pecking order)': the marginal cost of borrowing to firms depends on the source of capital supply, in consequence of which the Modigliani–Miller theorem is invariably violated. Indeed, a considerable body of empirical research on financial hierarchy testifies to two well-established stylized facts about corporate finance: first, internally generated funds are the most significant source of finance for firms in developed countries and, second, external finance is more often provided by banks than by stock markets; the cost of capital to firms rises as we go from internal funds to bank debt to market debt and equity. As they say: 'Given the key role that the equity market plays in all models of perfect capital markets and even in the popular idea of what is a good and well-functioning capitalism, this evidence is certainly astonishing'. That the bulk of investment in capitalist countries is financed by business and not by personal saving and that business saving consists of internally retained profits and unused depreciation accruals is a fact that was well known to macroeconomists of Keynes's generation (Baran 1952: 359–60) but that bank credit dwarfs stock-market finance, not just in France and Germany but in the USA, the UK, and Japan, is by no means a widely known fact.[1]

To me, the tendency of NK economists to begin with so-called 'stylized facts' and then to model the behaviour of markets in order to provide explanations of these facts is one of the most attractive features of this style of economics. Unfortunately, this is not how we usually proceed in modern economics. We typically begin with laying down a core of microfoundational concepts, such as autonomous rational agents trading in perfect markets with perfect information to maximize utility or profits, and then we endorse only those macroeconomic explanations that are consistent with this microfoundational core; in the eagerness to display technical ingenuity in the elaboration of models that remain true to the core, we virtually lose sight of the empirical phenomena that we are supposed to be illuminating, which indeed we often fail to specify precisely. It is as if economics as a discipline amounts to a particular approach to explanation and not to the investigation of an empirical domain of economic phenomena. What is at issue is how we allocate our intellectual resources: NK economists rightly spend more time establishing the facts to be explained than perfecting the

---

[1] A search of the leading current elementary texts (Samuelson and Nordhaus, Lipsey and Chrystal, Fischer and Dornbusch, Parkin, Phelps, Sloman, and Mankiw) shows that only Stiglitz (1993: 555) recognizes it.

models that do the explaining. Delli Gatti and Tamborini point out that 'financial hierarchy' is a better-established stylized fact than credit rationing, but that may be because credit rationing can take a variety of forms with consequent differential effects on the credit channel to investment. These credit channels take up Section 2 of the paper on the transmission mechanism of monetary policy. Time does not permit comment on the many interesting points in these pages, not to mention the provocative asides in Section 3 on the role of 'financial fragility' in the business cycle.

Dixon's paper begins with an extreme statement of the facts-are-theory-ladened thesis: 'the theory itself determines the way the evidence is interpreted and indeed what evidence is considered at all but, of course, qualifies it immediately: 'Within a given theoretical framework evidence can matter.' I say 'Of course because if it were really true that all evidence is determined by theory, between and not merely within theories, then we would be left with purely logical and aesthetic criteria for choosing between theories'. This is about as radical an anti-realist position as it is possible to adopt.

I agree, however, that 'there is no generally accepted empirical test among macro-economists for distinguishing between voluntary and involuntary unemployment'. I also agree that the distinction is at best one of degree and, resting as it does on the subjective feelings of workers, there can be no such thing as an absolutely decisive, totally compelling definition of involuntary unemployment. Nevertheless, the continued denial of RBC and new classical macroeconomists of the very existence of involuntary unemployment must be ascribed to the extraordinary obeisance that virtually all mainstream economists display to purely theoretical constructs, in this case, Walrasian general equilibrium theory and its central implication that all resources, including labour, are optimally employed. Apart from survey evidence *à la* Oswald and Trostel (Chapter 6), there is the curious fact that rising unemployment in a recession is associated with sharp rises in lay-offs, not quits, at least in countries like the USA which collect evidence on quits and lay-offs in special labour-force surveys. If lay-offs are not involuntarily unemployed workers, it is difficult to see what they are. Even when unemployment data are not categorized as quits or lay-offs, it is difficult to believe that the intertemporal substitution of leisure for work should suddenly seize tens and indeed hundreds of thousands of workers simultaneously. To call such sharp increases in unemployment merely voluntary unemployment is to fall prey to the reification of theoretical concepts.

Dixon argues vehemently, as he has done in all his published works, in favour of the notion of imperfect competition as an essential element in a coherent account of wage or price rigidity and hence cyclical fluctuations in output and incomes. I agree with his conclusion but can only marvel that it is necessary to fight so hard for the notion of imperfect competition when all economists before Arrow and Debreu, right back to Adam Smith, have known that Cournot's perfect competition is a cloud-cuckoo-land, a case of 'black-board economics' that could never exist outside the classroom (see Blaug 1997). 'Clearly', he says, 'there is some question as to how far the assumption of perfect markets is completely accurate.' Completely accurate in a descriptive sense? To write such a sentence is not simply to display one's 'priors' but rather to display extreme intellectual malformation. Alas, that is what we are all prone to after years of studying modern economics!

REFERENCES

Baran, P. A. (1952) 'National economic planning', in B. F. Haley (ed.), *A Survey of Contemporary Economics* (Homewood, Ill.: Richard D. Irwin): 355–407.

Blaug, M. (1997) 'Competition as an end-state and competition as a process', in B. C. Eaton (ed.), Trade, Technology and Economics: Essays in Honour of Richard G. Lipsey (Aldershot: Edward Elgar).

Hayek, F. A. (1942) 'The Ricardo Effect', *Economica* 34 (May); repr. in *Individualism and Economic Order* (London: Routledge & Kegan Paul 1949): 220–54.

Stigler, G. J. (1967) 'Imperfections in the capital market', *Journal of Political Economy* 75 (June): 287–92.

Stiglitz, J. E. (1993) *Economics* (New York: W. W. Norton).

10B   New Keynesian macroeconomics: general discussion

Huw Dixon: The view I am trying to put forward here is not that empirical evidence has nothing to do with it. In fact, what Blaug finally articulated at the end of his talk was very much my view—it drops into the background. But I still think that there is a problem. If there was agreement on a set of stylized facts, that would be great, but people can just ignore things. They can say, 'OK, there may be these imperfections, but they are very small. They don't really matter.' How do you know whether a particular imperfection is important or not? I agree with you entirely. I think imperfect competition does matter but others say it doesn't and they write down models which don't have any imperfections at all—no involuntary unemployment and so on—and they think that these are quite adequate to explain things. They are interested in other evidence.

Delli Gatti: I just want to point out the following. It is true that, methodologically, this kind of model starts from stylized facts. We can discuss whether these stylized facts are the right ones or not. From this point of view you can find a distinction, methodologically, from the mainstream way of modelling macroeconomic models. But I want to stress that there is a point that is methodologically shared with mainstream models, which is microfoundations. From the point of view of the way in which you model the macroeconomy, these New Keynesian models at least try to start from first principles. You can of course discuss whether these microfoundations are good or bad but this is what they try to do. I am not particularly fond of microfoundations but from the point of view of communication within the profession, they are an asset compared with other Keynesian schools that explicitly reject microfoundations as being too neoclassical.

Richard Lipsey: There is an interesting question in the fine paper by Delli Gatti and Tamborini about being embarrassed by too many imperfections. Now that, I think is a fairly general point that, since we are interested in methodology, we should reflect on. When we build models we are trained to go for the minimum set of assumptions to produce the result. If we have an extra assumption, Occam's razor comes in and we strip it away. That is fair enough for building models but the problem is that it makes us think the world is like that. When you start to study history, as I have been doing in the last eight years when I have been studying the last 10,000 years of technological change, you realize that many, many times in history you have an excess of sufficient conditions. The sign of it is that the historians are all arguing about which was the sufficient condition that really did the job. That, of course, is really a non-question, because if there are eight sufficient conditions and any one of them would do the job, that is all you need to know. It seems to me that it is a very common situation. It is not an embarrassment because that is the way the world is but it is not the kind of world we expect because of the way we are trained in modelling. So I am pleased to see yet another historical illustration of my principle that, almost any time you get a really interesting event in the world, there are more than enough sufficient conditions to explain it.

One of the problems with the stylized facts is that, as you know, Kaldor invented them to constrain theorists and they constrain too much. So we often ignore them because it is hard to deal with them. In the paper that Curt Eaton and I wrote on product differentiation in the North-Holland series on the new IO (1989) we listed eight stylized facts that a model of product differentiation taking off from Chamberlin should explain. In fact, when you build a model to explain that, you are driven (as Kaldor long ago pointed out) into a model of overlapping oligopolies. It is a very difficult model and it is intractable in the sense that you can't aggregate it up to a macro-phenomenon. But those are the stylized facts about the world. What happened, of course, is that we all use the Dixit–Stiglitz model of monopolistic competition, which is directly contradictory to five of those stylized facts, because we can aggregate it up to the whole economy, derive welfare predictions (see Helpman and Grossman 1991), and so on. What on earth do you make of welfare predictions, firmly stated, on the basis of a model that violates five well-known, established stylized facts? But it is a tractable model, so we use it. So though I support what you say, I think very often the problem for the theorists is that because it is far too constraining and it leads you in the direction of fairly intractable models, we throw away some of those stylized facts in order to get a tractable model. Maybe we have to do this, but we ought to have great big warning signs up that say, 'This model that I am going to confidently use is in contradiction to several stylized facts.' I have discussed this matter of the inappropratieness of the accepted GE version of monopolistic competition in Eaton and Lipsey (1997) and Lipsey (2000).

Kevin Hoover: I think Dixon is wrong to think that evidence doesn't matter in a fairly important way. It isn't just background—it actually matters, sometimes crucially, in the development of a theory—but I think the reason why he and a lot of people go down that path can be laid at the door of methodologists. Falsificationism and other versions of positivism that have led to a view that has become really embedded in our thinking: that we deduce consequences and we come up with a crucial test by which we can dispose of a theory or, perhaps, support it. But that is not the way that evidence actually works in this case, or in most cases in economics.

There is some evidence in Dixon's paper for this claim—namely the reason he restricted himself to the 1980s. He said that in the 1990s, the New Keynesian and the new classical macroeconomics look a lot more alike than they did in the 1980s. We see that in the Burnside, Eichenbaum, and Fisher paper (1-3), where they have embedded an efficiency-wage hypothesis in their model. There is a coming together of what before we might have thought were oil and water, that couldn't mix. And they are mixing them. Why are they doing that? It is because the cumulative evidence, the cumulative experience of working with the model, has forced them and the rest of the group working in this area into the position of saying, 'It is no longer worthwhile to maintain a separation between the new classical and the new Keynesian. It is worthwhile to explore this other avenue and to bring these disparate schools of thought together.' We have seen other examples of that. I cite just one more—the abandonment by the new classical macro types of the Lucas surprise-only aggregate supply function in favour of real business-cycle models and other explanations. You can't point to a single crucial experiment that drives that result, but what you can point to is a lot of empirical evidence, a lot of different kinds of tests, gradually making the position seem less tenable. As a result, there is no point where you can say 'It was abandoned.' What you see is a drift away into another direction but that drift is driven by evidence.

David Hendry: I certainly want to disagree with all those who have spoken in favour of stylized facts because in general they are not stylized and they are almost never facts. For the most part, they are extremely time-dependent—it very much depends on which particular bit of history you have looked at, and it is usually very measure-dependent (there are some measures in which this thing exists and others in which it doesn't). I also think it is extremely dangerous to hang things around stylized facts rather than what I would consider evidential summaries which are much more widespread to take account of the uncertainty attached to the alternative measures that might exist and the fact that they might be changing over time. A typical example came up in this morning's session, where someone referred to consumption smoothing as being a well-established fact in empirical economics. It is simply not true. Quarterly data on consumption have vastly more variation than quarterly data on income— something like four to five times the size of quarterly variation in income. You say, 'That's all due to seasonality. We don't count that when we look at it.' OK, then let's look at the seasonally adjusted data. From 1986 to 1992, the variance of consumers' expenditure on non-durables and services in the UK greatly exceeded the variance of income. That caused enormous policy problems—they got the Lawson boom wrong and then they got the crash wrong in 1989. On the one hand, consumption growth exceeded income growth for nearly four years in the late 1980s and then consumption growth went negative when income growth did not, which is the most strong violation of all the conventional theories that we have of consumers' expenditure smoothing. Why did this happen? It happened because of credit rationing or, the case that is missing from the paper, because of legal changes in what credit rationing is allowed in the economy. In 1986 the government passed the Building Societies Act that allowed building societies to borrow on wholesale markets, it removed restrictions on their lending, and you got an explosion in credit, from this legal change, to people who had previously been rationed. The net result was that most of them, who had never had the chance to get credit before, over-borrowed enormously and when the crunch came in 1989, incomes fell and interest rates went up, they had either to lose their house or to cut back massively on expenditure. So credit rationing of a kind that isn't discussed, but which I think is quite fundamental in the economy, was the driver of that set of episodes—legal changes.

The final point is slightly different. I am a bit puzzled by one of the remarks about the cost of equity being so high. It has puzzled me for many years and my colleagues in Oxford haven't solved it, but maybe someone knows the solution. Lots of British companies offer scrip shares as dividends. Some British companies are clever enough to offer a premium to encourage you to take the scrip dividend rather than the cash dividend. The premium that P&O and BP, the two biggest companies that, to my knowledge, do this, is 20 per cent of the dividend. The average dividend is 5 per cent. I do not think that is a very high cost of getting equity. Half the people who take dividends do so in scrip form, which means the companies are raising $2\frac{1}{2}$ per cent per annum of their total equity base for about 1 per cent. So it is hard to believe that the cost of equity is all that high. What puzzles me is why other companies have not adopted this obvious mechanism for raising new equity when they want to.

Grayham Mizon: I would like to respond to Dixon's provocative talk. Evidence is usually taken as part of the background, usually prior to the theory. I won't say any more about that, but one of the things that I think has been puzzling Dixon, or perhaps annoying him, is that evidence has never yet been decisive in his mind. Evidence has been used, definitely, but whenever we come up with more than one apparently acceptable explanation for a phenomenon and the empirical evidence is there, it has not, Dixon believes, been decisive. Were that the case, it would be very disappointing but I would argue that often this arises because of the way that the evidence, in this narrow econometric sense, is used. We have a theory, we develop it well theoretically, we implement it, we don't use econometric evidence to evaluate and reveal weaknesses but we use it to confirm the theory. We can get many theories that are confirmed in this way. I can then refer back to the point Hendry made this morning; the Ericsson–Hendry paper says that when you have more than one confirmed that establishes the inadequacy of all. This is one aspect of the phenomenon you are seeing.

Often when evidence is used, it is used in a framework where all the evidence hasn't been exploited. So the particular models developed conform to a theory and may be conform to some stylized facts, if they exist, and if the overall quality of the model, judged from a theoretical perspective, is thought to be good, that is said to be sufficient. But we can look at the statistical qualities of the model. Does it exploit all the information? Are the residuals of the model serially correlated? Is there evidence of functional form misspecification, and so on? I think that is often missing when evidence is used, and if you miss that then there will be problems.

Bennett McCallum: From listening to the discussion it seemed to me that the imperfections in the financial markets that Delli Gatti and Tamborini build upon are all real imperfections. They have nothing to do with monetary phenomena at all. Financial market participants are interested in real things just like everyone else. So at the end of the analysis there is really no explanation of why monetary policy actions should have any effect on any real variables. Maybe that is OK, but it is inconsistent with what a lot of people think of as New Keynesian work, such as Dixon's. So I would like to know whether that is true and whether we are still left with the puzzle of trying to figure out why, it seems, although not everyone agrees that it is true, that the monetary authorities do have a substantial effect on real aggregates when they take strong action.

Dixon gets monetary effects by assuming that menu costs pertain to nominal magnitudes but in the literature the rationalization for menu costs is all in real terms. It is unexplained why these menu costs do not relate to indexed prices rather than nominal prices. So that literature also doesn't succeed in explaining why actions by the monetary authority have real effects.

Delli Gatti: We did not have time to discuss the monetary factors in these models in detail but there is something in the paper. In models in which there is an explicit credit channel, a monetary shock has a real impact both through the liquidity effect, which is traditionally in IS–LM-type models, and through the credit availability effect. However, in a sense, these results on the real impact of a monetary shock, depend indirectly on an implicit price-rigidity assumption. Basically the Bernanke–Blinder (1988) model is a modified IS–LM fixed-price model. In that case, of course, the trick is the usual one. In the paper the focus was on the channels of transmission of the monetary impulse. As far as the Greenwald–Stiglitz (1993), Bernanke–Gertler (1989), or Kiyotaki–Moore (1997) models are concerned, you are perfectly right—these are real models, so there is no explicit room for monetary variables in those models. As far as the Greenwald–Stiglitz model is concerned, however, and this is an example of a way of reasoning upon monetary impulses, the impact of a monetary shock should go through a price shock. Greenwald and Stiglitz explicitly talk of a price shock as a way in which a monetary impulse can have real effects. Of course, there is an immediate similarity between a price shock and a price surprise in a Lucas/Sargent-and-Wallace type of framework, so you could say that this is only a variant of a standard monetary misperceptions model. That is true, but only in part. The reason is that the way in which a price shock impacts on real variables in the Greenwald–Stiglitz framework is not through any misunderstanding of real and nominal price effects. It is through a sort of Fisher effect in the sense that the real burden of firms' debt goes down if there is a positive price surprise. In any case, these are only details. It is perfectly true that it is difficult, in a sense, to deal satisfactorily with the effects of a monetary shock in this type of 'real' model. We think there is room for modifying the model in order to deal with the aggregate demand side. In a sense, the curious aspect of this type of model is that although they are New Keynesian, income determination is basically supply driven. So there is a very unsatisfactory treatment of aggregate demand effects.

The paper by Kiyotaki and Moore, which is probably the most successful in the profession right now, deals explicitly with one type of price effect—the asset price effect. There is no explicit treatment of monetary policy there but if you think of monetary policy as being, in a sense, responsible for asset price inflation or deflation, that type of model can in a sense be a theoretical explanation of this type of effect.

Adrian Pagan: Whenever I read this literature, I always find myself nodding agreement—yes, there are imperfections in capital markets—and then I get to the end and try to understand what it says to me about the economy I am sitting in. I am sometimes reminded of Ragnar Frisch's comment—that it is a little like playometrics. In a way, unlike the real business cycle or stochastic general equilibrium model approach, where I can get a pretty good handle on the implications of the model for the data, I almost never see any applications of this framework to actual data and actual economies. The closest we ever get is the Bernanke stuff but largely this is all to do with one little sector of the economy. You want to explain investment decisions by small firms and large firms, etc. I am very interested in whether we are ever going to see a full-fledged neo-Keynesian view of the economy that I can get a handle on. There was a comment that Kiyotaki and Moore represents the state of the art. When I look at Kiyotaki and Moore, one of the things I take away from it is the amazingly complicated dynamics you get for output, none of which I actually see in the data. I am left to wonder whether we aren't playing games here rather than trying to describe something in a realistic way.

Martin Eichenbaum: I have two comments related to Pagan's and McCallum's. There is a strand in the literature that tries to grapple with the point that McCallum raises about how this real rigidity or market imperfection gets translated when there is a monetary policy shock. One is, of course, explicitly having sticky prices in there. There is a lovely piece in the *Handbook* by Bernanke, Gilchrist, and Gertler (forthcoming) where they actually solve a GE model with these sorts of imperfections and they try to answer the questions that McCallum asks now. The other, of course, has to do with imperfections in which the essence of a central bank open-market operation is to flood the banking sector with reserves. How does that happen in GE? They take seriously the notion that agents do not find it optimal to undo the injection of reserves into the banking sector. Fuerst (1992) worked on this stuff and Lucas (1990) of course did, and there is some work that Jonas Fisher, in general equilibrium, did putting these two things together. Both those avenues, whether you like them or not, do help cross this barrier and translate an open-market operation into real effects.

Greg Mankiw often kids me about being New Keynesian and I kid him about being a New Friedmanian. I think he actually agrees with me. The essence of the New Keynesian programme, as it was outlined on that blackboard, is filling out the details of Friedman's 1968 paper. That's it. You could have just read this in Friedman and then asked what it would take to get those effects. It is very much a Friedman vision. Tobin took the same view and said explicitly that what you guys do is interesting but it is not what he thinks of as Keynes. He was much more interested in multiple equilibrium and coordination failures, which is a more distinct sort of thing than what Mankiw and his colleagues have worked on.

Andrew Oswald: I thought I would say a word about unhappiness data. Dixon conjectured that unemployed people would look very unhappy and that is certainly true if you take large random samples. It is true if you control for fixed effects. That is, if people fall into unemployment, they experience a dramatic drop in well-being and when they find a job they experience a huge surge in well-being, however you measure it. Second, though the models McCallum appeals to seem rather sensible in that nominal things won't have real effects, it is interesting to note the latest thing we have found with really big samples of happiness data (say on hundreds of thousands of people across countries). This is that when inflation rises in your country (controlling for everything about you) you give systematically lower scores for happiness, life satisfaction, psychiatric mental health, or whatever. So although we do not understand the mechanism, people certainly feel very much less happy when inflation rises. This is indicative of some kind of real effect that we don't yet understand.

Mark Blaug: These are just stylized facts!

Oswald: No, I am rather on the side of Hendry. I am hoping that he will think of these giant econometric facts as more than what is traditionally called 'stylized'.

Christopher Sims: To contribute to the trashing of stylized facts, I like to think of there being two kinds of facts: ugly facts and stylized facts. Ugly facts refer to the famous quote by, was it Niels Bohr?, there is nothing sadder than a beautiful theory killed by an ugly fact. I think of stylized facts as facts that have been polished by theorists to the point where they won't kill any of their beautiful theories. On the question of whether evidence, and in particular econometric evidence, has any effect, I think if you look at the history of the last forty or fifty years or so of macroeconomics, it is really hard to take that position. In the early post-war Keynesianism, some of which I was exposed to in graduate school (I think people stopped being exposed to it at all shortly after that) people were quite sure that monetary policy had very little effect and that interest rates were, at least to the extent that interest rates could influence them, not important. Friedman and Schwartz, not just in their history book, did a lot of econometric work. There was a lot of critical response to this and this process conditioned the theorist's thought, for good or ill (I think a lot for ill). I remember a seminar that James Duisenberry taught in which he discussed some of the regression results that were coming out relating money and income and attempting to compare them, and with relationships of government expenditure to income. He was surprised by what people were finding econometrically—puzzled by it—and I think those kind of facts were influencing people then. Since then, the breakdown of relationships between monetary aggregates and income, which has been documented econometrically, and the process of criticism and debate have influenced people's attitudes towards monetarist theories. I like to think that the VAR evidence on the relationships between interest rates and real quantities in the business cycle has had an influence on the way theorists think. The Phillips curve and the huge empirical literature, exploring and documenting the different ways that unemployment and price rises and wages are not related—it is hard for me to imagine that has not had any impact on theory.

Blaug: It is very interesting how, whenever you mention the idea of stylized facts it makes econometricians in the room bristle because a lot of them were not collected econometrically. A lot of them were collected by non-econometric quantitative data.

They were simply historical series. They have an in-built resistance to any facts about the economic world that were not established using econometrics. Examples include one referred to in the 1930s (that we now realize is not a stylized fact) called Bowley's Law on the constancy of labour's relative share in national income in developed economies over the centuries. Another is the constancy of the capital/output ratio, which Kaldor cited incorrectly as a well-established stylized fact. In presenting the data, nothing was done except to average it.

Sims: You are citing two old stylized facts, developed at a time when there were hardly any econometricians, and which are now discredited. These do not seem strong examples to me. The issue is to what extent it was constant, so one needs to characterize how much variation there was.

Lipsey: Having started out defending Blaug, I am on Sims's side. Stylized facts is a terrible term and I wish we had never had it. What I was saying, and I still think it is important, is that there are many reasons for building theories. One of them is that you just build a nice-looking theory and see what comes from it. Another is that you think there is some phenomenon in the world and you are going to try to build a theory that will account for that phenomenon, hoping it will have other implications. In that case, it is worth stating, 'Here are the facts that I think exist in the world and that I am going to build a theory to try to explain.' If we said that, then people would look at those facts and discover that some of them were and weren't right. I think it is just a plea that if I am trying to explain something I should tell you clearly what it is that I am trying to explain.

Let me then defend Blaug by giving him a class of stylized facts that I think are not established using econometrics. They are ones that are so obvious that a thought experiment will convince you and you don't need to do the econometrics. Take something from the article of mine that I cited on product differentiation. One of the stylized facts is that there are far fewer variations of any generic product in existence than you can imagine. You can imagine a continuum of variations of automobiles (a little more acceleration, a little stronger frame, and so on). We realize a very small proportion of the total number. That is a very interesting stylized fact. Incidentally, you have to invoke scale economies to explain it. I am very willing to have an econometric experiment for that but every time I tell someone they say, 'Yes, it's true. We don't need to do the econometrics.' It is potentially econometric. The other one is that people, faced with the same incomes, choose different bundles of the realizations of differentiated products. That is another interesting thing. These are stylized facts that you say you are going to explain in your theory of product differentiation.

Hendry: I think Blaug is mixing up data and summaries of data. The capital/output ratio that Kuznets *et al.* calculate are data calculations that do not necessarily, though they could, involve econometrics, particularly the notions of capital, what comes into capital stock, what rates of depreciation are used, and so on that could have been estimated econometrically. The key thing is that the moment you start to summarize it, a summary requires a statistic. That statistic has properties. Sims alluded to some of these properties: what is its variability? Is it actually a constant statistic? How does it change over time? Is it the appropriate statistic as a summary statistic? All of these things are indeed econometric issues. One of the reasons econometricians bristle when so-called stylized facts come up is that they are often based on statistics that we think have got wholly unreasonable properties. Claims that the average propensity to consume is constant over time were based on misunderstandings of what variability was conceptually possible in the statistics that had been calculated. That is the reason why, I think, we bristle. I think we have to be very clear in the distinction between the actual facts—the data on which a thing is based, and which are open to all sorts of corrections (the measurements could be wrong, it could be added up wrongly—there are lots of issues that could come in there) and these starry things reported like second moments of certain statistics or certain correlations between things which have econometric properties that are often absolutely appalling because they are based on things that are non-stationary, have got enormous auto-correlated errors, and the variability that is recorded has got nothing to do with the actual variability it will have, etc. That is why I don't think they are facts.

McCallum: I am sort of a defender of the practice of using stylized facts, in a way very similar to that in which Lipsey described it. What I thought people were doing when they used stylized facts, and I guess the popularity of the term, though it was invented by Kaldor, really sprang from the fact that Lucas used it several times in the early 1970s. What he was doing was saying, 'Here are some empirical regularities that other people have laid out. I am writing a theory paper so I am not going to take twenty-five pages to go over all of these myself but I believe these are things that most people would regard as correct. If they don't, then fine.' In his hands, what they were was an attempt to carefully select some empirical regularities that were of fundamental importance and to have those as background information while writing a theoretical paper. I can see nothing whatsoever wrong in that. It is just a division of labour.

Hoover: I also don't like the term stylized facts because I think it has become cast-iron idiom. Economists can't say the word 'facts' without putting 'stylized' in front of it any more. If stylized is to mean anything, it has to mean something like, 'The actual behaviour of whatever is being characterized doesn't agree completely with the stylization.' So if we look at capital/output ratio and say that the stylized fact is that it is constant, we know that it isn't literally constant, but that a constant is a good enough approximation for many purposes. I would like to point out, however, that I don't think Lipsey's examples of non-econometric stylized facts really work. What he has cited are not cases in which there is deviation of the actual facts from the stylization. They are facts, not stylized facts.

Ron Smith: One of the other reasons why it is useful to use the term 'stylized' is because theorists very often mean comprehensible. Very often we get information that is useful, like the spectral density function, which came up this morning. Theorists have great difficulty in handling that, so in a sense it is getting a relatively simple thing which can fit into that sort of structure in that way so that it is able to be communicated in a particular way. Then we go back to the question, which Hendry raises, 'How stylized are you in those circumstances?' It then gets very complicated. One starts saying, 'Conditioning on this, removing these dummy variables, doing this seasonal adjustment....' It is at this time that the theorist's eyes glaze over and wish it was just stylized.

Eichenbaum: Does anyone think it was not useful when Friedman pointed out that consumption, on average, unconditionally, was a little less volatile than income? He had a very nice insight into how one might begin to think about that. And then it is also very interesting to think about conditional moments when various factors, such as Hendry pointed out, are taken into account. Does anyone think that permanent income was a bad thing to do?

Burnside: Basically the entire research agenda in Deaton (1992), mostly by new Keynesians, is driven by what they see as the stylized facts about consumption: the stuff about excess volatility.

Hendry: And it is the fact that is undermined as soon as you look at seasonally unadjusted data. The basic proposition is false. In order to make it a stylized fact you have to use econometric manipulations of the data.

Eichenbaum: There is this shrewd conjecture that we don't have to worry about Christmas and the fact that we like to give gifts at Christmas to explain the business cycle.

Hendry: I am not disputing that. People are trying to avoid the difficulty that the world is much more complicated than these facts.

Pagan: I suppose we should sort out what we mean by stylized. My use of the word has always been as a selection of facts. I am not sure what the other use is. We often take averages over long periods. You prefer to take averages over shorter periods.

James Hartley: Surely the term has costs and benefits. The benefits are you don't have to reprove the facts all the time. The cost is that your fact is just wrong, and you are using it. If your facts are wrong, that is a problem; but if they are roughly true, that is very useful.

Lipsey: It has become a term for those facts that you are going to take for granted in your theory. Just an anecdote: we called them facts in our article and the editor pencilled in stylized, so I shook my head and said 'That is the standard term for describing what you take as true when you build your theories.' If that is all we mean by it, the term is harmless.

Roberto Tamborini: As I said in my presentation, many people dislike the trend towards piecemeal macroeconomics. I think it is not necessarily a bad thing. In any case, I think it is probably the new way in which our discipline is evolving and there is little to do against it. Why? Because we come from an age in which the world was divided into two big camps: those who thought that capitalism was always wrong and those who thought the other way round. Among those who thought that capitalism was basically good were those who thought that this was the case provided that the government made sufficient interventions, and those who thought that this was unnecessary if not negative. Now things have changed and this world is over. Probably we are all aware that we want to explain the world in which we live in terms of economic institutions and situations that may work well under some circumstances and not work well under others. This is inherently a piecemeal approach. Macroeconomics, being so close to policy concerns, is probably the first front on this change of attitude towards the world. I don't think this is bad. It is changing the mission of the discipline. It is becoming a conditional science, not an apodictic science. This change is happening right now and there is resistance to it.

The discussion of stylized facts is, in a sense, related to this change. I think that stylized facts are a very loose and unfortunate substitute for a nobler and more appropriate term that is used in other sciences, namely regularities. Regularities are the bread and butter of research in all sciences but we all know that regularities are not facts. Regularities are the act of an active intervention on crude data, even if the latter exist. They are just the first step of theorizing. This is very well known in the philosophy of science. What should change is our attitude to this new style of work and our understanding of it. We should be more prepared to show what are our precommitments and not to hide behind objective facts.

My second point concerns the relations between Keynes, New Keynesians, and money. If I were to use the ordering principle that I used in my presentation, New Keynesians and Keynes share many informal priors including the facts which are worth explaining. Also, there are some formal priors. In my view, incomplete futures markets and imperfect information are part of Keynes's view of the malfunctioning of capitalist economies. Of course he did not use these terms because they were not available then. It is true that standard New Keynesian imperfect-capital-markets models do not deal with liquidity preference. This is an interesting point and some colleagues and I have been trying to see whether we can include money in a strong way in such models. But this is not the same thing as saying that money is totally absent from these models. Greenwald and Stiglitz (1987) wrote that there is a shift from the stress on money as a store of value back to the old concern with money as a medium of payment. This is the way in which monetary policy can alter activity.

REFERENCES

Bernanke, B. and Blinder, A. (1988) 'Credit, money and aggregate demand', *American Economic Review* 78 (Papers and Proceedings): 435–9.

Bernanke, B. and Gertler, M. (1989) 'Agency costs, net worth and business fluctuations', *American Economic Review* 79: 14–31.

—— and Simon Gilchrist (forthcoming) 'The financial accelerator in a quantitative business cycle framework', NBER Working Paper W6455, in John Taylor and Michael Woodford (eds.), *Handbook of Macroeconomics.*

Deaton, A. (1992) *Understanding Consumption* (Oxford: Oxford University Press).

Eaton, B. C. and Lipsey, R. G. (1989) 'Product differentiation', in R. Schmalensee and R. D. Willig (eds.), *Handbook of Industrial Organization*, i (Amsterdam: North-Holland): 723–68.

Fuerst, T. S. (1992) 'Liquidity, loanable funds, and real activity', *Journal of Monetary Economics* 29(1): 3–24.

Greenwald, B. and Stiglitz, J. E. (1987) 'Keynesian, New Keynesian and new classical', *Oxford Economic Papers* 39(1): 119–33.

—— and —— (1993) 'Financial market imperfections and business cycles', *Quarterly Journal of Economics* 108: 77–113.

Helpman, E. and Grossman, G. (1991) *Innovation and Growth in the Global Economy* (Cambridge, Mass.: MIT Press).

Kiyotaki, N. and Moore, J. (1997) 'Credit cycles', *Journal of Political Economy* 105: 211–48.

Lipsey, Richard G. (1997) *The Collected Essays of Richard Lipsey*, i: *Microeconomics Growth and Political Economy*, ii: *Macroeconomic Theory and Policy* (Cheltenham: Edward Elgar).

—— (2000) 'New growth theories and economic policy for the knowledge society', in K. Rubenson and H. G. Schuetze (eds.), *Transition to the Knowledge Society: Public Policies and Private Strategies* (Vancouver, BC: University of British Columbia Press).

Lucas, Robert E. Jun. (1990) 'Liquidity and interest rates', *Journal of Economic Theory* 50(2): 237–64.

Part IV

MACROECONOMICS IN OFFICIAL DOCUMENTS

11 Using government documents to assess the influence of academic research on macroeconomic policy

THOMAS MAYER

Since many factors determine the choice of economic policies it is hard to pin down the role that economic analysis plays. One possibility is to see to what extent the work of academic economists is referred to in government documents. Do academic economists provide the reasons—or at least a least a rationale—for the policies that are adopted, or are they just disregarded kibitzers? More specifically, the organizers of this conference have asked me to address the following questions: do academic ideas enter official documents, and if so, how? What happens to them when they are used in official documents? Are they simplified? Is there any pattern to those that are accepted and those that are not? How long does it take for ideas to travel from the journals to official documents?

1. Coverage and procedure

I deal only with macroeconomic policies in developed economies. My coverage is also limited by the impossibility of reading more than a miniscule sample of the relevant material. This sample is not a representative one because of my limited knowledge of foreign languages, and lack of knowledge about what foreign documents are available, as well as the difficulty of obtaining them. Much of my material therefore comes from US documents, and it is only for the USA that I trace developments over time; for other countries I primarily use recent documents. This limitation is not quite as serious as may appear at first because the relative openness of the US government means that US documents provide a much richer source than do the documents of most other countries. Moreover, I am primarily trying to explain rather than enumerate the uses of academic economic research, and for that concentration on one particular country is not as serious as it would be for a more descriptive endeavour.

Within macroeconomics I look mainly at monetary policy. This is in part due to the greater availability of monetary-policy documents and my familiarity with them, but is motivated also by the widespread realization that fiscal policy is not an effective tool of macropolicy. As Gregory Mankiw (reprinted in Snowden and Vane 1997: 448) pointed out, because persistent large deficits make it impossible to obtain the consensus that would be needed for timely fiscal policy 'all attempts at stabilization are left to monetary policy.' Although since Mankiw wrote this the USA has achieved a

I am indebted for helpful comments to participants in the Conference.

balanced budget, large deficits are scheduled to reappear. Other countries face a similar problem. Since the monetary authorities tend to pay more attention to economists and to be more academically oriented than the fiscal authorities this means that my discussion is, if anything, more likely to overstate than to understate the influence of academic economists. I pay little attention to international macropolicy, because this is an area in which it is often impossible for authors of government documents to speak frankly for fear of generating speculative movements.

One way one might proceed is to select specific academic contributions and see whether, and if so when, they enter official documents. The other way is to start with government documents and record the academic contributions they contain. The latter approach is more likely than the former to show that academic contributions matter, because it counts every instance where they do appear as a success, while ignoring all those that do not make it into any of these documents. Starting with academic ideas would run into the problem that one would have to decide which contributions to select. But there is so much disagreement among economists that it would be hard to find a sufficient set of ideas that are at the same time generally accepted by academic economists and sufficiently distinct from ideas held by others, or held by others only due to the work of academic economists.[1] I therefore started with the documents.

As a participant in the conference suggested, it would be desirable to quantify the influence of academic research. However, this cannot be done in a meaningful way. The appropriate quantification is the ratio of the number of times academic research is cited to the number of times it could have been cited, with both numbers weighted in some way. But to calculate the numerator would require a complete knowledge of the relevant academic literature. As another participant suggested it would also be desirable to investigate differences among countries in the role of academic research. However, that involves a much larger question, the differences in the status of economists, and that would require a separate paper.

2. Defining academic economics and government documents

One possible definition of 'academic ideas' is the ideas that originated in universities. A broader definition includes work done by economists employed in government agencies and in the private sector who are members of the same speech community as academic economists; that is they deal with similar problems, use similar techniques and language, sometimes publish in the same places, and read each others' work. It does seem arbitrary to count as academic work a paper published in *Econometrica* if it is written by a university teacher, but not if it is written by an economist in the central bank.

The term 'government documents' is also ambiguous. One could include anything a government agency *publishes* as 'publishing' is usually defined, that is as something printed and made publicly available. But letting the definition of government

---

[1] For surveys of economists' opinions see Kearl *et al.* (1979); Alston *et al.* (1982); Frey *et al.* (1984); Ricketts and Shoesmith (1990). Not all the economists in these surveys were academics, but the overall results probably apply to academics.

documents depend on whether an item is printed or duplicated is not helpful in assessing the influence of academic research. For example, in the USA the 'Transcripts of the Federal Open Market Committee' (FOMC) are not printed and advertised for sale, but can be obtained in certain libraries or purchased as microfilms and duplicates, and future issues will be on the internet. The corresponding minutes from the Bank of England are already on the internet. Such minutes are very close to the policy-making process, so excluding them would mean ignoring a valuable source.

But if the criterion of being printed is therefore eliminated how about working-papers from research departments? I have excluded them in part because they often have little influence on policy, and also because it is obvious that they show the imprint of academic research.

That still leaves two problems. One is that official agencies sometimes publish essentially academic material, such as the proceedings of academic conferences that they sponsor. Though I mention them occasionally in passing, I do not treat these as official documents, in part out of a belief that the main purpose of many conferences is at least as much to be a pay-off to one of the central banks' constituencies, academic economists and to keep them interested in the problems that concern the central bank, as it is to help the central bank make policy decisions. Hence, such proceedings give little indication of what academic ideas the central bank takes seriously. The second problem is the treatment of international agencies, such as the IMF or OECD. Since they are not governments I exclude their documents.

3. Some other problems

Much of economics can get by with only the thinnest of psychological foundations because it deals with aggregations of individuals, so that individual idiosyncrasies usually wash out. But here this is problematic, because a particular person who happens to be in charge can sometimes make a difference. For example, the Federal Reserve Banks now publish reviews that carry many articles closely tied to academic papers. This was not so until Homer Jones became director of research at the St Louis Federal Reserve Bank. To be sure, one can argue that if he had not been there to show what the Banks' research departments could do, someone else would have done so by now. But that is not necessarily the case, and even if it is, it might have taken much longer. Similarly, when a former academic, Robert Weintraub, was appointed staff economist of the congressional Subcommittee on Domestic Monetary Policy, he induced this Committee to interact much more closely with academic economists and to publish contributions by them in several compendia. After his untimely death that ceased. Likewise, in the 1960s and 1970s Senator Proxmire successfully insisted on the appointment of economists, many of them former academics, to the Federal Reserve Board, which surely stimulated interest in academic research at the Fed.

Another problem is that many academic ideas may not appear in any government document because they deal with an issue that is not currently alive in the political arena—academic and policy-oriented researchers have different agendas (see Frey *et al.* 1997). For example, if the Fed's independence were threatened, it would probably refer in its documents to academic publications advocating central bank independence or at least use their arguments. But absent such a threat it has nothing to gain by doing so. Hence, if an academic idea appears in an official documents only, say ten years after its publication, one should not claim that it has taken ten years for government officials to absorb it.

An additional problem is that if a government document mentions an idea that is prominent in academic research this need not indicate causation. In 1968 Friedman (1968) persuaded many economists that raising the growth rate of money soon raises interest rates. The Federal Reserve had been saying that for many years before. Similarly, it anticipated the current literature arguing that price stability enhances economic growth.

Still another problem is that academic research can influence government documents in an invisible way. Surely, all of us have had the experience of our research being influenced by a paper we do not cite, because what it does is to induce us not to write something that we would otherwise have written.

A related and more important problem is that many government documents use academic research not explicitly but implicitly. One reason is that most official documents are factual and avoid explicit theory. But facts are 'theory-drenched', and which facts seem to deserve mention depends upon one's theoretical framework. For example, a 'purely factual' survey of the current state of the economy written by a post-Keynesian would spend less time on the growth rate of money than would one written by a monetarist. But such indirect influences are hard to detect. Academic work also enters government documents in another hard-to-detect way; the document's forecast is likely to be based at least in part on an econometric model developed by academics.

4. A public choice perspective on government documents

Public choice theory suggests that the relation between official documents and policy may be tenuous. The government may adopt a policy without issuing a document setting out its reasons. In other cases it may cite research that played only a minor part in its decision because it provides a convenient cover. Governments are not compelled to provide a full record of their thoughts and actions. For example, the 1982 *Report of the Council of Economic Advisers* discusses the weakness of fiscal policy as a stabilization tool. It seems likely that had the Democrats and not the Republicans won the previous election, the *Report* would not have used its limited space to make this point, though the Council might well have told the same thing to the President in private.

From a public choice viewpoint an official document is to a substantial extent a public relations tool.[2] It will therefore avoid whenever possible citing unfavourable academic research even if there is strong evidence supporting it, while citing even

---

[2] This does not necessarily mean that the reasons cited in government documents are unimportant. By influencing public opinion they can expand (or contract) the area of admissible policy discussions, and they can legitimize the positions that officials in various government agencies can safely take.

weakly supported favourable academic research. Hence, the sequence of events may often run—not from government documents to policy decisions—but from policy decisions to government documents. (Such a 'cite what fits' procedure is also not unknown in academia.) For example, the Federal Reserve's so-called 'monetarist experiment' in 1979 was in large part motivated by the failure of its prior policy. But it may well be that the Fed would not have undertaken this 'monetarist experiment' at that time had it not been for the writings of monetarist economists, and the changing perception of monetary policy among academic economists in general. Yet the statement that the Fed issued to justify its policy change attributed its policy shift to changed circumstances in financial markets, and not to a recognition of errors in its previous thinking, or changing academic beliefs. All in all, it is not surprising that Edward Kane (1974: 835–6) referred to the Annual of the Report of the Federal Reserve as: 'roseate and self-serving analysis imbedded in the typical Fed pronouncements. ... The *Report's* goal is to put the best face possible on Fed actions of the past year. ... There are, of course, no sections ... summarizing academic or business criticism of Federal Reserve policies.

Several factors ameliorate this discouraging picture. First, some government documents do not pose a potential threat to the reputation or preferred policies of a government agency. They may deal with new problems, or problems that have little political resonance, or they may be written for a narrow audience of experts. Second, doing good *is* one of the important motives of the government, and that gives it an incentive to take academic advice seriously. Third, citing the support of academic economists for one's policy may be good public relations. This will differ among countries. Thus in discussing the role of the Dutch Central Planning Bureau (CPS), which is staffed by economists, Harry van Dalen and Arjo Klamer (1997: 60) wrote that: 'whatever economic policy emerges will not pass without the stamp of approval of the CPS', so that the CPS has an influence that is greater than that of comparable institutes elsewhere in Europe, 'and is inconceivable in the US.'

Fourth, government economists themselves are a significant constituency. They care about the opinions of other economists, particularly if there is significant migration between government service and academia. So, when asked to endorse obviously bad reasoning they will tend to drag their feet. They will also try to enhance their status with academics by using the academic literature. Fifth, the authors of government documents need to care about whether academic economists respect their work because journalists sometimes talk to academic economists when they write their stories. And a good way to achieve such respectability is to refer either explicitly or implicitly to academic work. Finally the rationalizations that one gives affect one's thinking and hence one's actions.

5. Other determinants of the role of academic economics

Suppose that, as I have argued, the major function of many government documents is to persuade the public. Then, except in the rare situation in which the public is willing to accept academic analyses on faith, the role played by the work of academic economists depends in part on its plausibility to an audience not trained in economics. Since the general public is not likely to read government documents their main audience consists of journalists. Much therefore depends upon their training in economics and their willingness to take the time and effort to understand serious economic reasoning, as well as on its difficulty. Academic research is likely to play a much larger role in government documents if they can present it in a simple, intuitive way. For example, research that shows that raising the minimum wage will cause unemployment is more likely to find its way to the general public than is, say a demonstration of the uniqueness of a general equilibrium solution. Authors of government documents know this, and hence are more likely to make more use of the former type of research. And they are likely to avoid anything that seems implausible to the average person.

A related determinant is the willingness of academic economists to do the type of work that government officials find useful. That is the sophisticated use of simple tools that are mostly taught in introductory economics (see Allen 1977; Frey *et al.* 1997; Harberger 1998). It is only in academia that the term 'technical' is considered high praise. In other words, the supply as well as the demand for usable economic analysis determines the amount bought.

6. Some American documents

I will look mainly at the *Report of the Council of Economic Advisers* (CEA), at the *Transcripts of the Federal Open Market Committee* (*Transcripts*),[3] and more briefly at congressional Hearings. In the US Treasury and Commerce Department documents are generally uninformative about macropolicy.

6.1. The CEA reports

The CEA *Report* is written in non-technical language and is addressed in the first instance mainly to the media and the informed public. It contains a convenient and useful summary of economic events during the previous year, a justification for the President's proposals to Congress, and a set of chapters on specific topics reflecting the interest of the Administration or of the CEA chairperson. It is obviously a political document. Unless it chooses to preserve a discreet silence on some issues—and it may not be allowed to do even that—it must defend the Administration and its proposals.[4]

---

[3] Up to March 1976 they are called *Minutes*, but do not differ much from the later *Transcripts*, so I will call both *Transcripts*. They report what each member said, unlike the Minutes in the *Federal Reserve Bulletin*. They are voluminous and I have not read them all. I did read—rather cursorily—the January 1965–March 1976 *Transcripts* in connection with another study (Mayer 1999), but only sampled those for 1985–92. They are issued with a five-year lag, and the latest set available to me was 1992.

[4] An indication of the limits to the Council's independence is an incident during the Nixon Administration, when one of Nixon's political aides persuaded CEA Chairperson McCracken to change the estimates of GNP and unemployment he presented in congressional testimony (Matusow 1998: 179).

At the same time the Council members and senior staff, most of whom are academics on leave from their universities, need to look to their professional reputations and to the reputation of the Council in general, and hence must avoid seeming too partisan. The CEA is therefore much more open to the influence of academic economics than other US government agencies and its *Reports* come closest to fulfilling an educational mission.

An examination of the *Reports* over the last thirty years shows a strong shift in the evaluation of counter-cyclical policy. Although the 1968 *Report* conceded that stabilization policy cannot offset very minor fluctuations, the (then Democratic) CEA believed in counter-cyclical policy in other situations. It stated that fiscal policy has 'contributed to the improved record of economic stability' (63), while monetary policy 'made a major contribution to the advance of the economy' (71). In its 1969 *Report* it advocated annual changes in tax rates to make stabilization policy even more effective.

Subsequent *Reports* took a different line. The 1970 *Report* (66–7) recognized that monetary and fiscal policy may be destabilizing 'if moves are not made in the right amounts and at the right time. ... There is now abundant experience with the obstacles to the effective and flexible use of tax changes' for stabilization. Given the long and variable lags of monetary policy, it is prudent not to let monetary policy 'stray widely from the steady posture' called for by longer-run policy (68).

In 1982 another *Report* (now by a Republican CEA) advocated a stable growth rate of money instead of counter-cyclical monetary policy. It argued that fluctuations induced by productivity changes and price shocks cannot be avoided, but what is avoidable are 'the procyclical changes in the growth of the money supply that have occurred in the past' (77).[5] And with respect to fiscal policy the 1985 *Report* stated that, quite apart from the problem of lags and forecast errors 'there is increasing doubt about the effectiveness of discretionary fiscal policy' (57). Subsequently the 1889 *Report* declared that: 'Discretionary fiscal policies ... have as often been destabilizing as stabilizing' (77). The 1990 *Report* (68) added that counter-cyclical fiscal policy is 'fraught with so many difficulties that ... [it] becomes inconsistent with ambitious goals for long-run growth.'

All of the citations in the previous paragraph come from Republican CEA's. After the Democrats regained the White House in 1992 their CEAs have kept a judicious silence on the efficacy of counter-cyclical policy. Perhaps they shared the Republicans' view; that is hard to say.

Because so little information is available on academic economists' evaluation of stabilization policy only a crude comparison of their evaluation with the CEAs is possible. It seems likely that the optimistic 1968 *Report* mirrored the predominant view of academic economists. The CEA's shift to a more sceptical view of fiscal policy was probably shared by the majority of academic economists, though I suspect that the CEA shifted faster. On monetary policy academic economists also shifted in the same

---

[5] The reference to technology shocks is a rare, perhaps unique, bow to real business-cycle theory. It appeared several months prior to the Kydland–Prescott (1982) paper, and thus shows that even radical ideas can get into government documents rapidly.

direction as the CEA, but only a minority would go all the way with the monetarist CEAs of the 1980s. Yet the CEA's positions certainly did not lack support from some eminent academics, and seem based on their work. It would be hard to argue that the Republican CEA in the 1980s ignored what was going on in the academic journals. And the subsequent Democratic CEAs should not be blamed for keeping silent; they are not required to cover all aspects of a particular subject.

The CEA's treatment of the specifics of monetary policy, too, shows the influence of academia. Thus the 1968 *Report* argued that uncertainty reduces the optimal size of the response of monetary policy to fluctuations, a finding that Brainard (1967) had published only the previous year. The (Democratic) 1969 *Report* warned against an accommodative monetary policy and stated that at turning points the interest rate can be a misleading indicator of the stance of monetary policy—points that monetarists had been making for many years, but which the Fed would not absorb for many more years. Several *Reports* showed concern with the choice of a monetary target versus an interest rate target, a hotly debated issue in academia, and one of them seems to refer implicitly to the seminal Poole model. By 1983 the *Report* already dealt with GDP targeting. Money-demand functions and velocity were also discussed in informed ways in various *Reports*.

The *Reports* also show the influence of academic work in their discussions of interest rates as well as saving. Thus, while the 1968 *Report*, like the academic literature at the time, ignored the Fisher effect, the 1970 *Report*, written about two year after Friedman's (1968) presidential address, discussed it. The 1993 *Report* discussed Ricardian equivalence.

The academic literature has also influenced discussions of inflation. Thus while the 1968 *Report* still employed the loose formulation of the wage–price spiral that was then standard in the academic literature, the 1971 *Report* advanced to the expectations-augmented Phillips curve. The 1975 *Report* talked in terms of the natural rate of unemployment and a long-run vertical supply curve. This was in the year when Lipsey and Steiner (1975), as had Samuelson (1973) two years earlier, told beginning students about a long-run trade-off.[6] The 1982 *Report* rejected the policy of not lowering the inflation rate but holding it stable and letting expectations adjust, because as monetarist academics had argued: 'Once a positive rate of inflation is accepted it becomes difficult to argue against a slightly higher rate' (56). It also pointed to the positive correlation between the level and the variance of the inflation rate, a much discussed topic in academic journals.

The shift from the old macroeconomics to the new also showed up in a discussion of the importance of reputational effects for monetary policy, with the 1972 *Report* pointing to the possibility that easing monetary policy might have restrictive effects because it could raise the expected inflation rate, and hence long interest rates. Time inconsistency was discussed in the 1990 *Report*, while the 1996 *Report* took up the effects of deficit reduction in a model with forward-looking agents.

---

[6] Even in the next edition Samuelson (1976), while conceding that the short-run Phillips curve will change in the long run, did not warn about it becoming vertical.

The contributions of academic economists also appears in discussions of international macroeconomics, for example in the explanation exchange-rate overshooting in the 1977 *Report*. The 1979 *Report* presented a good discussion of exchange rate flexibility, while the 1987 *Report* took up the absorption approach. Other discussions that academic readers will find familiar deal with implicit contract theory (1978 and 1981), the coordination problem stressed by the New Keynesians (1981), Lucas's island model (1982), the effect of the Smoot–Hawley tariff on the Great Depression (1989), the role of fiscal discipline in terminating hyperinflations (1993), and hysteresis (1997).

With respect to methods, the 1968 and 1969 *Reports* mentioned econometric models as being used in the Administration's forecasts and in calculating the effects of a tax cut. But shortly after that the CEA may have become disillusioned with these models. The 1973 *Report* (61) complained about their 'poor record' in predicting the inflation rate.

The 1982 *Report* is of particular interest. Its discussion of monetary policy ranged from the choice of regimes (the gold standard, and a monetary growth rate rule) to some specifics, such as tying the discount rate to open-market rates. It has an unusual number of references to the academic literature ranging from 1930 (Cassel) to 1981 (Bordo). A plausible explanation is that this was the first *Report* issued by the Reagan Administration, which tried to institute substantial changes in economic policy. To justify such changes it helps to discuss economics in a more fundamental way than is usual in *Reports* that recommend minor adjustments to current policies. It is for such fundamental rethinking that the work of academics is most relevant.

All in all, academic research has found its way into the *Reports*. It is obvious that their authors have read the academic literature, and their arguments are professionally respectable. But the *Reports* are intended to be political documents, not scholarly endeavours. This shows up in the choice of problems discussed. The extent to which a *Report* uses the academic literature therefore depends in part on the availability of academic work on the particular problems that concern the Administration. And it depends also on whether this work supports the case that the *Report* wants to make.

6.2. The FOMC *Transcripts*

The FOMC *Transcripts* are much more closely related to actual policy decisions than are the CEA *Reports* since they record the arguments that various FOMC participants advance during the decision-making process. Both the five-year delay in their publication and the excruciating amount of technical detail they contain ensure that they have only a small scholarly audience and no influence on public opinion.

They show that the FOMC's thinking was slow to reflect the great improvement in the quality and volume of both academic research and the Federal Reserve's own research that began in the 1960s. Even now the *Transcripts* do not show much direct influence of academic research. In the 1960s they indicated that the FOMC did not value highly the analytic work of its own economic departments, not to speak of the work of academic economists. Chairman William McChesney Martin, who is quoted as saying: 'no more economists' (cited in Matusow 1998: 25), preferred to rely on his own intuition. As Robert Hetzel (1995: 2) explained: 'Martin valued [the] Research

... [department] for an ability to organize information rather than an ability to think analytically about policy. He valued individuals who could offer anecdotal information about economic activity more highly than economists.' Thus in the early 1960s the staff was actually forbidden to make any forecasts. Then, when the Board of Governors acquired its own econometric model it did not, at first, take the forecasts based in part on this model seriously. Only very gradually did it learn to trust them.

An example of how the FOMC ignored academic research is its treatment in the lag in the effect of monetary policy. Though this is clearly critical in deciding when and how to change policy, for a long time the FOMC paid it little attention. In the late 1960s the median estimate of FOMC members was probably around six to nine months. While this was in line with some of the academic estimates, it was much shorter than the lag shown by the Board's own econometric model, as well as by most other econometric models. Although subsequently, FOMC members seem on the whole to have lengthened their estimates of the lag, for a long time they did not seem to catch up with the long lags that appeared in more and more of the academic literature.

This discrepancy is probably due to several factors. One may be that Chairman Martin focused his attention predominantly on the immediate money-market effect of monetary policy rather than on its effect on GDP. Another is the FOMC's distrust of forecasts, particularly forecasts extending for a year or more. If it had conceded that the lag is long, it might then have had to admit that it could not operate an effective counter-cyclical policy. It was less disturbing to ignore the long lags shown by its own and other econometric models (see Mayer 1990).

One might expect that in the 1960s and 1970s as more and more academic economists (including several eminent ones) were appointed to the Board of Governors and to Reserve Bank presidencies (and thus became FOMC members) its discussions would have become more hospitable to the work of academics. But this did not happen, even when one of the world's leading economists, Arthur Burns, became chairman. Burns, according to some reports, did make extensive use of the expertise of the academically oriented National Bureau of Economic Research. But he made little use of other types of academic research. For example, by 1974 many money-demand functions had been successfully fitted (see Laidler 1974), but Burns did not refer to any of them when discussing velocity. Instead, he commented that velocity: 'depended on confidence in economic prospects. When confidence was weak, a large addition to the money stock might lie idle, but when confidence strengthened the existing stock of money could finance an enormous expansion' (FOMC 1974: 103–4).

The neglect of the academic literature is probably related to the FOMC's reluctance to the discuss the basic issues on which the academic literature focuses, such as the existence of a long-run unemployment–inflation trade-off.[7] With so many good economists on the FOMC that seems surprising. One likely explanation is that the FOMC is afraid that confronting such issues might generate ideological or paradigmatic splits

---

[7] This statement is subject to the caveat that for the years 1985–92 I read only one *Transcript* per year, and had neither the April 1976–84 nor the 1993–8 *Transcripts* available. Moreover, there were probably some discussions of fundamental issues among many FOMC members outside of FOMC meetings.

that would not only make it hard to agree on a specific policy at each meeting, but would also politicize the Fed. Another possibility is that if FOMC members were to make the basic ideas underlying their decisions explicit, then they would suffer feelings of regret and guilt if any of these ideas were later disconfirmed (see Mayer 1990). Furthermore, by being silent on basic issues the Fed presents less of a target to its critics. Another possibility is that not explicating even to themselves the theoretical framework that underlies their policy decisions gives FOMC members great flexibility in deciding what policy to adopt at each meeting. This flexibility permits them to make the necessary compromises between sound policy and the policy dictated by political pressures without feeling embarrassed (see Hetzel 1990).

FOMC discussions therefore focus on the current state of the economy and on how that is likely to change, as well as on the effect that a small change in the federal funds rate at this particular time would have. The academic literature has almost nothing to say directly about the former, and little to say about the latter.

Implicitly, however, academic research does make an important contribution to FOMC discussions by influencing staff research at the Board and at each of the Banks. How much of this FOMC members read is hard to say, but research by academics underlies some remarks at FOMC meetings. Thus when Greenspan (FOMC 1987: 34) stated that we 'ought to take M1 seriously in a sense', one can see the quantity theory at work at least indirectly. Such influences may well be greater now than before, because FOMC discussions now seem much more sophisticated than they were in the early 1970s. Not only do technical terms occasionally appear, but the whole tone of the discussion *seems* different. Before, even though they might have thought like economists, on the whole FOMC members did not sound like economists. Now they do. When reading the discussions during the 1970s I frequently felt that FOMC members were making arguments that someone familiar with the literature would not have made. The more recent discussions do not give this impression. Academic research now also plays an important role through the econometric models that the staff uses along with other information in preparing its forecasts, and in presenting policy simulations. And as Edison and Marquez (forthcoming) have shown, these forecasts and simulations do play an important role in FOMC deliberations.

Does the failure of academic research to play an *explicit* role in FOMC discussions signal a serious shortcoming of academic research or in the FOMC's procedures? One might well argue that it is an appropriate division of labour, that research on what policy should be followed on a month-to-month basis should be left to central-bank technicians. But one can also make a case that although academics can hardly be as knowledgeable as central bankers about the details of central banking, they should work on actual policy-making, as for example Karl Brunner and Allan Meltzer have done (see Brunner and Meltzer 1989).

6.3. *Some other federal reserve documents*

Some of the Federal Reserve Banks and occasionally the Board publish papers by their staffs (see, for instance, Board of Governors 1981) or papers given at conferences they sponsor. Many of these papers are essentially academic papers. All the Banks also issues a *Review* that contains papers interacting with the academic literature, some through literature surveys and others through original research. However, their articles are not official documents, since they do not necessarily represent the views of the Federal Reserve.

6.4. Congressional documents

Congress plays an important role in determining US macropolicy because of its power over fiscal policy, and also to a much lesser extent because of its influence over the Fed. Its documents consist primarily of transcripts of the *Hearings* and *Reports* of its committees. Some of these committees have also commissioned and published compendia of studies and other material by academics.

The Joint Committee on the Economic Report, on which sit the chairpersons of all committees with primary responsibility for macropolicy, is unusually receptive to academic work. Thus at its *Hearing* on 'Monetarism in the United States and the United Kingdom' (US Congress, Joint Economic Committee 1981) two eminent academics, David Laidler and Allen Meltzer, were the only witnesses. At a subsequent *Hearing* on 'The Future of Monetary Policy', four of the fifteen witnesses were academics (US Congr., Joint Economic Committee 1982), and so were five of twenty-one witnesses at a 1988 *Hearings* (US Congr., Joint Economic Committee 1988). At its *Hearings* on the 1992 *Report* the Committee heard from Paul Krugman, Robert Gordon, Paul Samuelson, James Tobin, and George Perry (US Congr., Joint Economic Committee 1992). How much influence such *Hearings* have is hard to say. Usually only a few committee members, sometimes only a single one, attend, but one can hope that at least some of the other members have their staff read the testimony and summarize it for them.

7. Europe and Japan

In Britain the Bank of England publishes the Minutes of its *Monetary Policy Committee* (MPC). These focus on the current and future states of the economy. Though its members may discuss more general and fundamental issues of macroeconomic theory elsewhere, in its official minutes it, too, avoids fundamental discussions.[8] Even so, academic research has an indirect effect by setting the framework for the discussion, and sometimes it also shows up in the details. For example, the MPC has used the life-cycle hypothesis to estimate the effect of windfall gains on consumption, and it has discussed a buffer-stock money-demand function (1997, June, December). It also referred to its own simulations showing that its credibility affects the Phillips curve (1997, December). While such a conclusion is impressionistic and cannot be properly documented, it seems that the MPC makes efficient use of the relevant academic research.

---

[8] I looked only at the *Minutes* from June 1997 to January 1998. It is possible, but unlikely, that much more academic discussions occurred at other meetings.

Since the Bank of England has been given an inflation target and since it aims for transparency, it also issues a quarterly *Inflation Report*. This is a factual document that uses the available economic and econometric work where it is relevant. For example, its discussion of the monetary aggregates includes a section on Divisia money (a measure which weighs various monetary components by the relative opportunity cost of holding them), and in discussing unemployment it takes up the hysteresis hypothesis (Bank of England 1994: 34).

The Bank's *Quarterly Bulletin* carries some articles that are more technical. For example, one calculates implicit forward rates from the Black–Scholes model (Bank of England: 1997, February), while others deal with the optimal rate of disinflation (1996, November), the debate about monetary policy rules (1996, August), and the concept of broad money (1996, May). These articles, which supplement less technical discussions of current policy, often cite the academic literature. Some are written by academics. The important Hendry–Ericsson critique of Friedman and Schwartz's book on monetary trends that appeared in the *American Economic Review* (Hendry and Ericsson 1991) is a condensation of a version first published by the Bank in a set of papers by its academic consultants (Bank of England 1983).

The Deputy Governor described to an academic audience the use the Bank makes of academic research: 'A considerable amount of research . . . [on how monetary policy operates] has been undertaken within the Bank for many years. And in doing so, we have drawn heavily on the ideas and techniques developed by academics outside the Bank' (Harold Davies 1996: 464). He also mentioned that the Bank includes 'within a wide range of information variables' policy rules developed by two academics, Bennett McCallum and John Taylor. They 'provide useful reference points', though they are not used as an automatic pilot (464–5). The Bank has come a long way from the time of Governor Norman, who when asked for the reason for a certain decision responded: 'Reasons, Mr Chairman? I don't have reasons, I have instincts' (cited in Boyle 1967: 327).

In France the central bank issues a *Bulletin* (Banque de France). Although it is mainly concerned with elucidating current developments it has also published some articles on issues on which academic research has something to contribute directly.[9] And these articles do make use of academic research, some carrying explicit citations to the academic literature. In addition, the Banque de France has run joint conferences with universities.

In Germany relevant documents are published by the Sachverständigenrat (Council of Economic Experts) and the Bundesbank. The Sachverständigenrat has only advisory responsibilities, and individual members can dissent from the majority's recommendations. It is essentially a government think-tank, and does not speak for the Administration. That raises the question of how much influence it has on policy, and hence whether its reports give much of a clue about the influence of academic research on policy. They are technically well informed, provide a ready home for academic

---

[9] Because of the difficulty of getting access in time to more recent issues my discussion is based on 1992 and 1993 issues.

ideas, and are not reluctant to discuss basic issues, such as the choice of targets for monetary policy (see Sachverständigenrat 1988: 171–3).

The Bundesbank's *Annual Reports* contain little economic analysis, and focus more on surveying recent events and trends, topics on which the academic literature makes more of an indirect than a direct contribution. But there are points where academic influence is direct. Two examples are a sophisticated and up-to-date discussion of the costs of inflation, and concern that, by raising the expected inflation rate, an easing of monetary policy might raise rather than lower long-term interest rates (Bundesbank 1993: 61–2). There are references to a paper by Akerlof and Perry in the *Brookings Papers on Economic Activity* and to an NBER working-paper by Feldstein (Bundesbank 1996: 81, 85). Overall, the *Annual Reports* give the impression that any lack of reference to the academic literature reflects neither ignorance of, nor disdain for the current macroeconomic literature, but primarily that this literature does not relate directly to the issues under discussion.

The situation is similar at the Bank of Italy. Again, the *Annual Report* is largely a factual survey. A section called 'The Governor's Concluding Remarks', does go beyond that and evaluates various policy options, but at least in the ones I have been able to obtain (1981–3), it is written in such general terms, that there is usually little opportunity for a discernible academic influence to show up. However, the 1981 *Report* (16) does have a sophisticated discussion of the marginal propensity to consume and the wealth effect.

The Bank of Japan publishes a *Quarterly Bulletin* that very occasionally has articles employing academic research. Summaries of speeches by the Bank's officials posted on the internet also use academic research in the few cases where it that is relevant, and give the impression of familiarity with academic research. The Bank of Japan also publishes a scholarly journal, *Monetary and Economic Studies*, that carries papers given by outstanding academic economists at a conference sponsored by the Bank.

The Swedish central bank has an official inflation target and issues a quarterly *Inflation Report*. Only occasionally does this *Report* make explicit contact with academic economics, though indirectly its forecasts are based on the work of academic modellers. The Bank also publishes a *Quarterly Review* that contains articles on topics such as monetary policy and unemployment, the management of short-term interest rates, and electronic money. In one article the Governor explained the vertical Phillips curve, and also cited publications by Krugman, Lindbeck, and Snower that had appeared only a few years earlier (Bäckström 1997).

The Swiss National Bank issues an annual volume of essays. These contain what are essentially academic papers. Thus the 1989 volume (Swiss National Bank 1989) contains essays testing the rational expectations hypothesis, a popularly written, but technically sound discussion of the role of monetary policy in a small economy, and a paper that uses an error-correction model to measure the effect of the real exchange rate on exports.

Finally, a report by the deputies to the Group of Ten (1995) provides an interesting contrast. It draws on the academic literature much more than any of the above-discussed documents. Even the most demanding academic could not ask for more.

One likely reason for this is that the deputies were asked to address technical questions, i.e. the future levels of saving, investment, and interest rates. Another reason is that it is not a political document either in the sense of being a programme for action, or an attempt to influence public opinion. Instead, it seems intended for an audience of economists, both in the national bureaucracies and in academia.

8. The specific questions

What do these documents tell us about the three questions I was asked to address? The answer to the first—how academic research enters official documents—is that presumably even though few policy-makers themselves read academic journals, their staff does, and also those policy-makers who were trained as economists may remember what they were taught.

To the second question—whether academic ideas enter in simplified form—the answer is normally, yes. That is not surprising because important policy ideas can generally be presented in simple, intuitive language. I found no evidence that such translations distort the ideas.

The third question asks whether there is a pattern in the ideas that are accepted. Yes, those that fit into policy-makers' beliefs and wishes are accepted. For example, a number of central bank documents have picked up the fashionable idea that central banks should have substantial independence. If papers were to appear that provide strong econometric evidence that central bank independence is undesirable, I doubt that they would get nearly as much attention in these documents. Similarly, it is hardly surprising that the case against counter-cyclical policy appeared in *Reports* of Republican rather than Democratic CEAs.

The final question deals with the lag in the transmission of ideas. That can be very short, even working papers can be cited—or if the idea is unwelcome—very long. One cannot be more specific because the date at which an idea is accepted by the profession is unclear, and the date of first publication is irrelevant. For example, would it be fair to say that it took the Fed more than 200 years to accept the idea that the quantity of money is the main determinant of the price level because David Hume stated this in the 1750s?

9. A summing-up

The glass is half-full and half-empty. On the one hand one can safely say that there are no major dominant views among macroeconomists that fail to find a resonance in government documents—but on the other hand there are few such (non-trivial) views. The authors of government documents are familiar with academic research and tend to employ it—but mainly when it supports, or at least does not conflict, with what they would like to say. The sequence 'academic research > government documents > policy decisions' is a seriously incomplete way to describe the situation—but the alternative sequence: 'policy decisions > government documents' does not deny any influence to academic research, because academic research can influence policy without first going through government documents. The contrasts between the publications of the Sachverständigenrat, the CEA *Reports*, and the FOMC *Transcripts* suggests that the further removed a document is from policy-making the more likely is it to explicitly use academic research. But by inspiring both the underlying analytic framework and the econometric models used in forecasting and in policy simulations, academic research has a strong implicit influence even on documents close to policy-making.

If the present role of academic research in government documents indicates that we academics do not have as much influence on policy as we think appropriate, we should remember that our record is hardly unblemished. In the USA in the 1960s and early 1970s leading economists advocated a policy that generated stagflation. Then, shortly after monetarism achieved substantial influence in academia, velocity became unstable, and monetarist advice was no longer so useful. Would the world have been better off if subsequently policy-makers had paid much attention to the rise of new classical theory? In the 1950s, Fed chairman Martin sounded naïve to economists when he stressed the dangers of inflation, and when he said that interest rates were determined by the grass roots of the country, not by the central bank. Now it no longer sounds so naïve.

But *perhaps* we finally do have it right and policy-makers should pay more attention to us. What can we do to further this? One answer might be to reduce the extent of our disagreement, but that is hard to do.[10] Also, paying more attention to the day-to-day, hands-on problems that policy-makers face would help. More contact with them and their staffs would facilitate that. Its all too easy now for central bankers to feel that academic economists do not grasp the vital details of the problems that central banks face. Estrella and Miskin (1998) provide a persuasive example of how from the viewpoint of central bankers academic discussions of the NAIRU miss the mark. There is much to be said for delineating speech communities by common problems, rather than by the source of employment or methods used.

REFERENCES

Allen, William (1977) 'Economics, economists and public policy', *History of Political Economy* 9: 48–88.

Alston, Richard, Kearl, J. R., and Vaughan, Michael (1982) 'Is there a global economic consensus?' *American Economic Association, Papers and Proceedings* 72: 203–20.

Bäckström, Urban (1997) 'Monetary policy and unemployment', Bank of Sweden, *Quarterly Review* 1: 4–16.

---

[10] Paradoxically, lack of disagreement among academic economists might reduce the frequency with which they are cited in official documents, since those on the other side of the argument would no longer be able to cite some academic economists in support.

Bank de France, *Bulletin Trimestrier*, various issues.

Bank of England, Panel of Economic Consultants (1983) *Monetary Trends in the United Kingdom*. (London: Bank of England).

——(1994) *Inflation Report* (London: Bank of England).

——(1997) *Quarterly Bulletin* (London: Bank of England).

——(1997, 1998) *Minutes of the Monetary Policy Committee* (London: Bank of England).

——(1997) *Minutes of the Monetary Policy Committee* (London: Bank of England).

Bank of Italy (1981–3) *Annual Report* (Rome: Bank of Italy).

Bank of Sweden (1966) *Inflation Report* (Stockholm: Bank of Sweden).

Board of Governors, Federal Reserve System (1971) *Open Market Policies and Policy Procedures* (Washington, DC: Board of Governors).

——(1981) *New Monetary Control Procedures* (Washington, DC: Board of Governors, duplicated).

Boyle, Andrew (1967) *Montegue Norman* (London Cassel).

Brainard, William (1967) 'Uncertainty and the effectiveness of monetary policy', *American Economic Review* 57: 411–25.

Brunner, Karl and Meltzer, Allan (1989) *Monetary Economics* (Oxford: Blackwell).

Bundesbank (1993, 1996) *Annual Report* (Frankfurt: Germany).

Davies, Howard (1996) 'Research and policy at the Bank of England: the things we would like to know, but dare not ask', *Quarterly Bulletin* 36: 463–9.

Edison, Hali and Marquez, Jaime (forthcoming) 'US monetary policy and econometric modeling: tales from the FOMC transcripts 1984–91', *Economic Modelling*.

Estralle, Arturo and Mishkin, Frederic (1998) 'Rethinking the role of NAURU in monetary policy: implications of model formulations and uncertainty', Research Paper 9806 (New York: Federal Reserve Bank of New York).

Federal Open Market Committee (FOMC) (1974) *Minutes of the Federal Open Market Committee* (Washington DC: Board of Governors).

——(1987) *Transcripts of the Federal Open Market Committee* (Washington, DC: Board of Governors).

Frey, Bruno, *et al.* (1984) 'Consensus and dissension among American economists', *American Economic Association, Papers and Proceedings* 73: 986–94.

——and Eichenberger, Reiner (1997) 'Economics, first semester, high fliers and UFO's', in Peter van Bergeijk, Lans Bovenberg, Eric van Damme, and Jarig Sinderen, *Economic Science and Practice* (Cheltenham: Edward Elgar): 15–48.

Friedman, Milton (1968) 'The role of monetary policy', *American Economic Review* 58: 1–17.

Group of Ten (1995) 'Saving, investment and real interest rates' (Rome: Instituto Poligrafico e Zecca dello Stato).

Harberger, Arnold (1998) 'A vision of the growth process', *American Economic Review* 88: 1–32.

Hendry, David and Ericsson, Neil (1991) 'The econometric analysis of UK money demand', in Milton Friedman and Anna J. Schwartz, *Monetary Trends in the United States and the United Kingdom, American Economic Review* 81: 8–38.

Hetzel, Robert (1990) 'The political economy of monetary policy', in Thomas Mayer, *The Political Economy of American Monetary Policy* (New York, Cambridge University Press): 99–115.

Hetzel, Robert (1995) 'William McChesney Martin and monetary policy in the 1960s' (unpublished MS).

Kane, Edward (1974) 'All for the best: the Federal Reserve Board's 60th Annual Report', *American Economic Review* 64: 835–50.

Kearl, J. R., *et al.* (1997) 'A confusion of economists', *American Economic Association, Papers and Proceedings* 69: 28–37.

Kydland, Finn and Prescott, Edward (1982) 'Time to build and aggregate fluctuations', *Econometrica* 50: 1345–70.

Laidler, David (1974) *The Demand for Money* (New York: Harper & Row).

Lipsey, Richard and Steiner, Peter (1975) *Economics* (New York: Harper & Row).

Mankiw, Gregory (1997) 'The reincarnation of Keynesian economics', repr. in Brian Snowden and Howard Vane, *A Macroeconomic Reader* (London: Routledge): 445–51.

Matusow, Allen (1998) *Nixon's Economy* (Lawrence, Kon.: University of Kansas Press).

Mayer, Thomas (1990) *The Political Economy of American Monetary Policy* (New York: Cambridge University Press).

——(1999) *Monetary Policy and the Great Inflation in the United States* (Cheltenham: Edward Elgar).

Ricketts, Martin and Shoesmith, Edward (1990) *British Economic Opinion: A Survey of a Thousand Economists* (London: Institute of Economic Affairs).

Sachverständigenrat (1987, 1988) *Vorrang für die Wachstumpolitik* (Stuttgart: Kohlhammer).

Samuelson, Paul (1973) *Economics* (New York: McGraw-Hill).

Swiss National Bank (1989) *Geld Wärung und Konjunktur* (Basle: Swiss National Bank).

US Congr., Joint Economic Committee (1981) *Monetarism in the United States and the United Kingdom, Hearings* (Washington, DC: GPO).

——(1982) *The future of monetary policy, hearings* (Washington, DC: GPO).

——(1988) *The 1988 Economic Report of the President, Hearings* (Washington, DC: GPO).

——(1992) *The 1992 Economic Report of the President, Hearings* (Washington, DC: GPO).

US, Executive Office of the President (various dates, 1968–97) *Economic Report of the President* (Washington, DC: GPO).

Van Dalen, Harry and Klamer, Arjo (1997) 'Blood is thicker than water: economists and the Tinbergen legacy', in Peter van Bergeijk, Lans Bovenberg, Eric van Damme, and Jarig Sinderen, *Economic Science and Practice* (Cheltenham: Edward Elgar): 60–91.

12 Macroeconomic thought at the European Commission in the first half of the 1980s

IVO MAES

1. Introduction

In this paper an analysis is presented of macroeconomic thought at the European Commission, an institution which has become increasingly influential at shaping policy formulation at the European level.

A study of economic thought at a policy-making institution encounters certain specific problems, compared to the study of traditional academic economic texts. A crucial difference is that the economic theories and paradigms are less explicit, more hidden. Moreover, official documents involve many persons and, consequently, are more heterogeneous. So, any analysis of economic thought at a policy institution will involve a greater degree of 'rational reconstruction' than more traditional analyses of economic thought.

This study concentrates on macroeconomic thought at the European Commission in the early 1980s, when unemployment became more and more the dominating economic issue in Europe. The paper starts with background sketches of the European Community in the early 1980s and policy-making instances at the European Commission. This is followed by an overview of the monitoring and forecasting of economic developments at the Commission, a crucial feature of life at a policy-making institution. Thereafter, the focus is on economic thought at the Commission, focusing on the Annual Economic Reports, the main macroeconomic policy document of the Commission. Particular attention will also be given to the debate on macroeconomic policy with the 'Dornbusch Group', an academic advisory group of the Commission. A final section compares academic economics with economics at policy-making institutions, drawing on the experiences at the European Commission in the early 1980s.

I would like to thank F. Abraham, R. Backhouse, A. P. Barten, A. W. Coats, S. Deroose, D. Dinan, M. Emerson, H. Famerée, M. M. G. Fase, M. Fratianni, H. Hagemann, D. Hausman, F. Ilzkovitz, J. Michielsen, T. Padoa-Schioppa, L. Pench, A. Salanti, and A. Sapir, as well as the participants at the Bergamo Conference on 'Theory and Evidence in Macroeconomics', and at seminars at the University of Maastricht, the European Society for the History of Economic Thought (Valencia), the European Community Studies Association (Pittsburgh), and the Federal Reserve Bank of New York for useful comments and suggestions. The usual restrictions apply.

2. The European Community in the early 1980s

The early 1980s were a period of morosity at the European Commission: the European economy was in the doldrums and the integration progress was stalling.

Europe's economic performance in the early 1980s was rather disappointing: economic growth was low and unemployment was increasing strongly, while inflation was high and declined only stubbornly. Part of the reason for it was certainly the second oil shock of the autumn of 1979, which gave a stagflationary shock to Europe's economy. Moreover, the European performance contrasted markedly with the situation in the USA, where the recovery, from 1983 onwards, was very strong and unemployment started declining, something which several observers associated with Reagan's supply-side economics. 'Eurosclerosis' was the term used to characterize the economic situation in the Community (cf. Giersch 1987).

The European integration process was also in the doldrums. The issue which dominated the European debate in the first half of the 1980s was the British contribution to the European budget, famous with Mrs Thatcher's phrase 'I want my money back.' A solution would only be reached at the Fontainebleau summit of June 1984, clearing the way for the European Community to concentrate on integration furthering projects.

The main impetus to the integration process came from the European Monetary System (EMS), which was founded in March 1979 (cf. Ludlow 1982). However, the first years of the EMS were very difficult: there was a lack of convergence of economic policies and performances, especially inflation, and there were several realignments. The development of the EMS was one of the main preoccupations of economic policy-makers at the European Commission. Tensions in the EMS were exacerbated from May 1981 onwards, when Mitterrand was elected as French President and followed an

TABLE 12.1. *Main events*

1979	March	Creation of the EMS
	Autumn	Second oil shock
1981	January	Beginning of Thorn Commission
		Reagan inaugurated as US president
	May	Mitterrand elected in France
	October	General realignment in the EMS
1982	June	General realignment in the EMS
	October	Kohl becomes Chancellor in Germany
1983	March	General realignment in the EMS
1984	June	Fontainebleau Summit, agreement on the European budget
1985	January	Beginning of Delors Commission
	March	European Council agrees on single-market project
	July	General realignment in the EMS
	November	Cooperative Growth Strategy presented in the Annual Economic Report

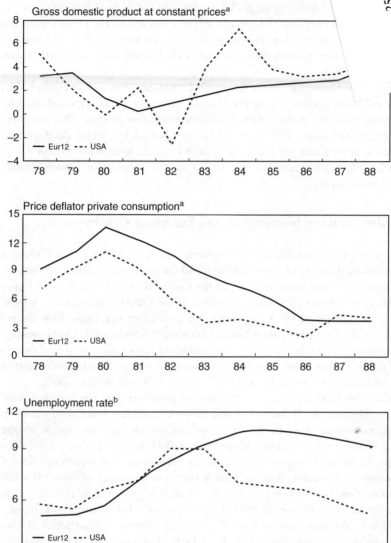

FIG. 12.1. *Main economic indicators for the European Community and the United States*

[a] Annual percentage change
[b] Percentage of civilian labour force

Source: European Commission

ısolated Keynesian policy strategy. This led to a loss of competitiveness of the French economy, capital outflows, and speculative pressures against the French franc, leading to several realignments. With the change of policy orientation in France, towards more orthodox economic policies after the March 1983 realignment, the EMS became in more stable waters.

The sphere of morosity in the European Community was further reinforced by the rather lacklustre performance of the Thorn Commission (1981–4), which did not take noticeable initiatives to further the European integration process. This would change dramatically in January 1985, with the Delors Commission, which developed several projects to reinvigorate the European economy and the integration process. Of special importance were the internal market project and the Cooperative Growth Strategy for more Employment.

3. Policy-making instances at the European Commission

It can be useful to note that the term 'commission' is used both for the College of the Commission, the body of commissioners, and for the services of the commission, the administration. Also, every member of the Commission disposes of a small group of collaborators, his so-called 'cabinet', typical of the French administrative system.

It is the College of the Commission which is ultimately responsible for policy-making at the European Commission. However, macroeconomic policy-making was mainly at the level of the Member States and so the responsibilities of the Commission were rather limited. They concerned mainly the orientation and coordination of the national macroeconomic policies (cf. Mortensen 1990 and Wegner 1989).[1]

Inside the Commission, it is mainly the president and the member with the responsibility for DG II (Economic and Financial Affairs, which can be considered as the macroeconomic research department of the Commission) who are most involved in macroeconomic policy-making. From 1981 to 1984, Gaston Thorn, a Luxemburger, was president and François-Xavier Ortoli, a Frenchman, was responsible for DG II. According to witnesses, they were both relatively easygoing persons, who left the administration a lot of freedom. Ortoli was mostly interested in monetary matters. With the new Commission in 1985, Jacques Delors, a Frenchman, took, besides the presidency, also the responsibility for monetary matters. Alois Pfeiffer, a German trade unionist, became responsible for DG II. The economic man in his cabinet, Ludwig Schubert, would play an important role in macroeconomic policy-making.[2]

The director-generals of DG II have typically been Italians. From June 1979 to March 1983, Tommaso Padoa-Schioppa was Director-General of DG II. He was succeeded by Massimo Russo.

---

[1] Over time, this coordination function of the Commission has increased in importance. So, with EMU, which started in January 1999, sovereignty in the field of monetary policy was transferred to the European Central Bank and the Commission's role in the coordination of macroeconomic policies was reinforced, especially with the Broad Economic Guidelines.
[2] Schubert had been a student of Karl Schiller, the father of the 'Konzertierte Aktion' (concerted action) in Germany, and had kept in contact with him.

TABLE 12.2 *Main macroeconomic policy-makers at the European Commission (in January 1983)*

President: G. Thorn (L)[a]

Commissioner responsible for DG II: F.-X. Ortoli (F)[b]

DG II   Director-General: T. Padoa-Schioppa (I)[c]

Deputy Director-General: M. Wegner (D)

Directorate A (National Economies): P. Van den Bempt (B)

Directorate B (Economic Structures and Community policies): . . .

Directorate C (Macroeconomic Research and Policy): M. Emerson (UK)

1. Concerted action
2. Short-term forecasts
3. Business-cycle surveys
4. Medium-term forecasts
5. Econometric models

Directorate D (Monetary Matters): J.-P. Mingassson (F)

[a]From January 1985: J. Delors (F)
[b]From January 1985: A. Pfeiffer (D)
[c]From March 1983: M. Russo (I)

Padoa-Schioppa had a profound impact on DG II: according to witnesses, he was not only a skilful administrator, but also a brilliant economist and very well connected. People describe him as combining a German rigour with Italian imagination and a profound economic culture, including mainstream Ango-Saxon economics. He was then quite young (around 40), dynamic, and rather ambitious.[3]

His main focus of attention was the reinforcement of the European Monetary System, which he considered as the 'priority of the priorities'. Another of his main preoccupations was the strengthening of the analytical level of DG II. An important element hereby was a reorganization of DG II, in March 1980.

After this reorganization, DG II consisted of four directorates:

• The A Directorate: National Economies, with P. Van Den Bempt (B) as director. The A Directorate was responsible for monitoring and analysing the economic situation on a 'vertical' basis, country by country. It consisted of four divisions, three of them followed the different countries of the Community, the fourth the rest of the world.

---

[3] Padoa-Schioppa had been for many years at the research department of the Banca d'Italia, one of the top-policy oriented research institutes in Europe, with strong connections with leading American and British universities (cf. Porta 1996: 180). Padoa-Schioppa had been a student and, later, a visiting scholar at the Massachussets Institute of Technology. He was close to Franco Modigliani: they published together (e.g. Modigliani and Padoa-Schioppa 1978) and he contributed to Modigliani's Festschrift (Padoa-Schioppa 1987).

- The B Directorate: Economic Structures and Community Policies, can be considered as a kind of 'economic service', where the various policies of the Community (sectoral, industrial, competition, etc.) were followed and analysed.
- The C Directorate: Macroeconomic Research and Policy, with M. Emerson (UK) as director. This was a newly founded directorate, which reflected a double aim. The 'methodological' purpose was to pursue more academic-oriented research, as clearly indicated in the word 'Research' in the name of the new directorate. The other purpose was to focus on macroeconomic policy for the European economy as a whole. This also reflected the idea that the Commission could have more influence on economic policies in the Member States if it could highlight the Community dimension of a certain national policy stance. The director of the C was usually the main author of the Annual Economic Report, the most important macroeconomic policy document of the Commission (cf. above).

    The directorate consisted of five units: concerted action (a newly created division, responsible for a 'horizontal' analysis of the Community economy and for policy actions at the Community level); short-term forecasts (responsible for the coordination and consistency of the twice yearly forecasting exercises); business-cycle surveys (responsible for the coordination and aggregation of business and consumer surveys, which were executed by different institutes in the Member States); medium-term forecasts; econometric models (a newly created division, the purpose was to give DG II more autonomy in econometric modelling; this group would later be merged with the unit for medium-term forecasts).
- The D directorate: Monetary Matters, with J.-P. Mingasson (F) as director. It consisted of four divisions, focusing on the EMS, the balance of payments situations, monetary policy in the different countries, and capital markets.

Also other reforms contributed to the strengthening of the intellectual and analytical capacities of DG II, like the organization of seminars (both by DG II economists and outsiders) and the reinvigoration of the group of advisers (economists, both academics and national policy-makers, who were on a temporary basis at the Commission). Padoa-Schioppa also launched a new series of publications, the *Economic Papers* (which were the sole responsibility of the author). This caused quite a stir in the Commission, as officials publishing in their own name in an official publication of the European Commission was a completely new phenomenon.

Of particular importance was certainly the collaboration with the Centre for European Policy Studies (CEPS), located in Brussels, especially with the foundation (and funding by DG II, cf. Ludlow 1983: 2) of the CEPS Macroeconomic Policy Group. This Group was also known as the Dornbusch Group, after its first Chairman.

DG II economists would have meetings with the members of the CEPS group, in which the macroeconomic situation and the policy challenges for the European Community would be discussed. The CEPS economists would offer their comments on policy documents of the Commission, especially the Annual Economic Report, and they would also, every year, write their own paper. Initially, the Dornbusch Group was set up as an internal advice group. Later, under the pushing of the academics, it was decided to publish the papers of the Dornbusch Group, both as a CEPS paper and as an *Economic Paper* of the Commission.

This triangular collaboration (Dornbusch Group, Commission, CEPS) offered DG II several advantages: it strengthened the analytical and intellectual level of the economic policy debate, it allowed the Commission to penetrate in the world of the 'economic intelligentsia', and it exposed the services of DG II to emulation and contradiction. Moreover, it was also a way to let top American academics get to know the European Community and to analyse Europe's economic problems.

The *Economic Papers* of the Dornbusch Group would cause quite some turmoil, especially in the cabinets but also among the Commissioners. Several people asked the question why the Commission should pay people 'who make our life difficult'. Senior DG II officials, like Padoa-Schioppa and Emerson, defended the principle of publishing the work of the Dornbusch Group. They argued that the cooperation with the Dornbusch Group was very important for DG II, both for improving its analytical capacity and for increasing its influence in the academic world. Consequently, one had to 'accept the rules of the game' and let the Dornbusch Group publish the results of its research. They were herein supported by Ortoli, the Member of the Commission responsible for DG II.

4. The monitoring and forecasting of economic activity at the Commission

Policy decisions need to be based on a solid understanding, not only of how the economy works and its present state, but also of its future course. In practice, policy-makers are confronted with many time lags: good data about the economic situation become only available with delay, the decision-making process itself can take time, just like the implementation of policy, and it also takes time before policy measures have an effect on the economy. Thus policy-makers have no choice but to take decisions on the basis of estimates and forecasts of economic activity (cf. Llewellyn *et al.* 1985: 73).

At the European Commission then, as at other policy-making institutions, a lot of time was and is spent with monitoring and forecasting the economic situation. This was undoubtedly, as regards time and resources, a core activity of the A and C directorates, which were the main directorates involved in macroeconomic policy-making at the Commission.

At the core of this monitoring and forecasting activity were the forecasting rounds. These forecasting rounds were organized twice a year, in the spring (April–May) and the autumn (September–October) (CEC 1984*c*: 191). They concerned the main macroeconomic data: growth, inflation, unemployment, the government deficit, etc., with the national accounts at the centre of the forecasts. They covered the current and the following year.

These forecasts performed a basic role in macroeconomic policy-making at the Commission, as they delivered the data material on which the analysis of the economic situation and the policy recommendations of the Commission would be based.[4] For instance, the data in the Annual Economic Report, which was published in November, would be the estimates and forecasts of the autumn round.

Given this crucial importance of the forecasting activities, it seems appropriate to elaborate somewhat on its organization, which was coordinated by the short-term forecast unit in the C Directorate:

- The forecasting round would start with a 'position paper'. This described the main events since the last forecasting round and the evolution of the economic situation. It also contained the basic assumptions regarding interest rates and exchange rates, oil and commodity prices, world trade, and the evolution of economic activity in the rest of the world. This position paper would be discussed in a general meeting by all the persons who were involved in the forecasts.
- Typical for the Commission, as an international institution, was a trade consistency exercise, involving both trade volume consistency (changes in countries' export volumes must have their counterpart in changes in partner countries' import volumes) and trade price consistency (each country's import price has to have its counterpart in the export prices of the countries from whom it imports).
- The country desks of the A Directorate would, on the basis of the assumptions in the position paper and all possible information about their economy, elaborate their forecasts. The national desks had a quite large degree of freedom about their methods of forecasting. In many cases a 'judgemental' approach was followed.
- There were also consultations with national experts (ministries, central banks, and national research institutes). In a first round this would happen on a bilateral basis, with the desk officers visiting their nation's capitals. Towards the end of the round, there would be a general meeting, where DG II would present its forecasts to officials from the Member States.

This would all take place in several rounds, a long iterative process, wherein forecasts were continually revised and revised, until a final storage. One should also mention the general assumption of no changes in economic policy, which is typical for forecasting at the Commission, and for policy institutions in general.

These short-term forecasts would form a kind of benchmark against which the economic situation would be monitored in the periods between two forecasting rounds. In the monitoring (and forecasting) process, the Commission relied also on surveys, for which a special unit in the C Directorate was responsible. In fact, since 1961, the Commission coordinated business surveys in industry in the Community. Later, in 1970, consumer surveys were integrated in this programme (CEC 1997: 203).

DG II would also make medium-term forecasts. Here, more use would be made of econometric models. In the early 1980s DG II invested heavily in an econometric model unit so as to be less dependent on outside experts and to acquire a greater degree of autonomy.

---

[4] One can contrast this with 'academic' analysis, which is mostly based on existing data, and is a kind of 'historical' analysis, even if often of the recent past.

DG II had already some experience with econometric modelling. In the early 1980s DG II used two models: Eurolink and Comet. Eurolink was a system of econometric models, based on four existing national models: Sysifo for Germany, Metric for France, Prometeia for Italy, and the Oxford model for the United Kingdom. There were quite some differences between these models. Sysifo was disaggregated into fifteen branches, Metric into eight, and Prometeia and the Oxford model into three. They were linked together by DG II officials, with the assistance of external advisers. Simulations with the Eurolink model were presented in the 1984 Annual Economic Review (CEC 1984*b*: ch. 9).

The Comet model was primarily a medium-term model. It was set up to improve the quality of the medium-term forecasts of the Commission. The project was started in 1969 and assigned to a team at the Centre for Operations Research and Econometrics at the Catholic University of Leuven under the responsibility of professor A. P. Barten. At times, there were tensions between the model team and DG II, partly due to the fact that the model team was at the University of Leuven and not at the Commission.

Comet consisted basically of a set of country models, one for each Member State, of similar structure. The models were then connected by a model describing the bilateral trade flows between the countries (Barten and d'Alcantara 1984). Senior DG II officials reproached the model as being too Keynesian, and not paying sufficient attention to the monetary sector and the supply side.[5] It was probably an element which induced DG II officials to set up their own model unit.

The new model unit of DG II set out to build two econometric models: the Compact model, an aggregated macromodel for the Community as a whole, and Quest, a multicountry model.[6] Simulations with the Compact model were presented in the 1985 Annual Economic review (CEC 1985*b*: ch. 6).

5. Main lines of macroeconomic thought at the Commission

The following analysis of the economic thought at the European Commission is to a large extent based on the Annual Economic Reports of the Commission, the main macroeconomic policy document of the Commission.

The drafting of the Annual Economic Report at the European Commission went through several phases. The first draft was essentially prepared in Directorate-General II, Economic and Financial Affairs, and more specifically in the C Directorate 'Macroeconomic Research and Policy'.

An important role in the conception of the Reports was also played by the cabinets, especially the cabinet of the members of the Commission responsible for DG II.

---

[5] Something which was contested by the model builders.

[6] Also the European Central Bank has constructed two models: an aggregate model for the European economy as a whole and a multicountry model, composed of similar models for the economies of the Euro area.

They determined to a large extent the general orientation of the Reports. Sometimes, they requested quite substantial revisions of a Report.

Before its acceptance by the Commission, the Report was also submitted to the Economic Policy Committee (EPC), composed of senior officials of the Member States (ministries and central banks) and the Commission. In general, the discussions in the EPC did not lead to important changes in the Report.

Macroeconomic thought at the Commission was, to a large extent, a synthesis and compromise of the main schools of macroeconomic thought in the European countries, especially the three big ones: Germany, France, and the United Kingdom.[7]

German economic thought was centred round the social market economy. Two tendencies can be distinguished. The more free-market-oriented German economists would emphasize that economic policy was, in essence, 'Ordnungspolitik', i.e. a policy to create a sound and secure framework within which markets can operate. The main tasks of economic policy are then: (a) monetary policy: assure price stability; (b) fiscal policy: rather limited task for the government; and (c) structural policy: a more passive role, competition policy is emphasized. The other tendency, more Keynesian, with Karl Schiller as an important representative, emphasized the social dimension of the 'social market economy'. It was linked to the social democrats and the trade unions and considered a dialogue between the social partners (trade unions and employers) as a crucial element of its strategy to stimulate growth and employment.

In general, German economists, mostly emphasized that economic policy consisted in the application of certain basic economic principles (especially the respect of market mechanisms and wage moderation) to the actual economic situation. It has many similarities with Roy Harrod's characterization of Keynes's view:

Following Marshall, he [Keynes] believed ... that progress in economics would be in the application of theory to practical problems. His recipe for the young economist was to know his Marshall thoroughly and read his *Times* every day carefully, without bothering too much about the large mass of contemporary publication in book form. (Harrod 1951: 381)

Initially, French economic ideas were very influential at the Commission. Robert Marjolin, the first commissioner for DG II, had been the principal assistant to Monnet at the French Planning Office, famous for its five year plans (cf. Marjolin 1986). The French Planning Office, while being part of the French 'Colbertiste' tradition, was also a spearhead of Keynesianism in France, with the national accounts at its heart (cf. Rosanvallon 1987: 40). Later, Malinvaud was influential, especially with his distinction between 'Keynesian' and 'classical' unemployment (cf. Malinvaud 1977).

Anglo-Saxon ideas in the post-war period followed different fads: Keynesianism, monetarism, and supply-side economics. This was also so at the Commission, even if monetarism was never very popular. From a methodological point of view, the Anglo-Saxons favoured generally a more analytical approach, whereby economic policy

---

[7] For an overview of post-1945 economic thought in Europe, see the contributions in Coats (1999). An interesting overview of the German ideas can also be found in Schefold (1998), who focuses on the debates in the 'Verein für Socialpolitik'.

recommendations would be based on more refined economic research. They especially favoured the developing of DG II's model-building capacity.

Initially, an important transmission channel for Anglo–Saxon ideas was the OECD. Many Commission officials, including Marjolin, had worked at the OECD and there were many interactions between the OECD and the Commission.

Anglo–Saxon ideas would receive a big boost with the nomination of Padoa-Schioppa as director-general of DG II (cf. below). Also, younger economists would have a more Anglo–Saxon education, more of them having studied in the USA and having a Ph.D.

At the beginning of the 1980s, the Commission's analytical framework was medium-term oriented, with an important role for supply-side and structural elements (Maes 1998: 14). The general view was probably best presented in the 1980 Annual Economic Report:

> The concerted response to the present general economic situation should be based on the right strategic mix of demand and supply policies and notably the right balance in their application to short and medium-term problems. Short-term adjustments should be more moderate than at times in the last decade, and a heavier weight has to be given to reducing medium-term inflationary expectations and improving supply conditions in the economy. (CEC 1980: 13)

In the early 1980s, the European economy was coping with a serious stagflation, after the second oil shock of 1979 and high US interest rates. In its analysis, the Commission strongly emphasized the structural aspects of the crisis: 'the accumulated back-log of adjustments and on our growing incapacity to respond quickly to the recent changes in the economic environment. The increased structural rigidities in our economies and social behaviour have changed profoundly the long-term dynamics of the business cycle' (CEC 1982: 11).

6. The employment debate with the CEPS group

In the 1980s, unemployment more and more dominated the economic scene.[8] This was reflected in the 1984 Annual Economic Report of the Commission, where the title of the introduction was: 'The dominant problem of unemployment' (CEC 1984a: 9). This rise of unemployment happened against a background of a hesitant recovery, but important progress in stabilization policies and monetary convergence.

Unemployment would become the main theme of the debate between the Commission and the CEPS Macroeconomic Policy Group. The CEPS Group, consisting mostly of 'sophisticated Keynesians', many with an American background, argued for a more reflationary fiscal policy. Their position was elaborated in two reports:

- *Macroeconomic Prospects and Policies for the European Community*, in April 1983, by G. Basevi, O. Blanchard, W. Buiter, R. Dornbusch, and R. Layard.

---

[8] For an analysis of Europe's unemployment and competitiveness problems, cf. Bean (1994), Nickell (1997), and Jacquemin and Pench (1997).

The Group argued that there was no evidence that 'unemployment is all and without exception, or even predominantly, a real wage problem' (Basevi *et al.* 1983: 3). They favoured a coordinated expansionary policy, accompanied by incomes policy.

- *Report of the CEPS Macroeconomic Policy Group. Europe: the Case for Unsustainable Growth*, in April 1984, by R. Layard, G. Basevi, O. Blanchard, W. Buiter, and R. Dornbusch. They argued that the European economy should, for some years, grow faster than its sustainable long-term growth rate, in order to reduce the margin of unused resources. A temporary fiscal expansion and an accommodating monetary policy was necessary.

The major disagreement between the Commission and the CEPS Group, in 1983 and 1984, was about the nature of the European unemployment problem, whether it was 'Keynesian' or classical. The CEPS Group estimated that the NAIRU was maximum $7\frac{1}{2}$ per cent, while actual unemployment was more than 10 per cent (cf. Layard *et al.* 1984: 4). The Commission, in its analysis, put more emphasis on the importance of 'classical' unemployment:

Estimates of the present level of NAIRU (non-accelerating-inflation rate of unemployment) vary widely, with the most extreme views holding that the present unemployment rate is very close to the NAIRU. Although the debate about the relative extent of Keynesian, classical and structural unemployment is still far from closed, it may at all events be concluded from the above remarks that classical and structural unemployment has increased over the past 10 years. (CEC 1984*b*: 100)

In its analysis of the unemployment problem, the Commission strongly emphasized that economic growth had become less labour-intensive. According to Commission estimates the stock of capital per employed person had risen at an average annual rate of $2\frac{1}{2}$ per cent in the preceding decade (CEC 1984*a*: 24). The rise in relative labour costs, which was at the origin of this capital deepening, was not only the consequence of increases in nominal wages but also of the rise of non-wage labour costs. Substitution was further stimulated as the cost of capital was kept low, partly due to fiscal advantages. For the Commission, the increase of public expenditure, as well as the structure of expenditures and taxes, was one of the causes of the increase in unemployment.

Another reason for the increase in classical unemployment, according to the Commission, were the growing rigidities in the labour markets in Europe. They were the result both of legislation and of collective agreements. These were generally introduced in the golden 1960s, in order to protect weaker groups. However, the Commission noted that: 'Some of these regulations have proved to be ill-adapted to new circumstances and may ... have hindered employment creation' (CEC 1984*a*: 33).[9]

---

[9] Michael Emerson, in a study published in his own name, argued that: 'in Western Europe today there is a need for some correction of excesses of labour market regulation and social security programs' (Emerson 1988: 3).

The employment strategies, proposed in the Annual Economic Reports of 1982, 1983, and 1984, were very broadly based and comprised: (i) a stable macroeconomic framework; (ii) an improvement of the competitiveness of the enterprise sector, especially the strengthening of the internal market; and (iii) measures concerning the labour market, including wage moderation, more differentiated wage settlements, and a 'systematic reappraisal of labour market regulations and conventions' (CEC 1984: 34).

In a certain sense this debate can seem somewhat paradoxical: it was the policy-makers at the European Commission who were defending the 'new' paradigm of supply-side economics, while the academics were in favour of the 'old' Keynesian paradigm. It certainly shows that policy-makers can be open to new economic theories. It is also a clear indication that DG II in the early 1980s was very alert to what was happening in the academic world and integrating this in its analysis of the economic situation in Europe. Moreover, the Commission just had a very bad, if not traumatic, experience with a coordinated Keynesian demand expansion. The 'concerted action', after the European Summit in Bremen and the G7 Summit in Bonn in 1979, led to an increase in inflation and balance of payments deficits in the early 1980s (Maes 1998: 404). It led European Commission officials to focus on the supply side, especially the increased rigidities in Europe's labour markets. These rigidities made Europe certainly different from the USA, with its flexible markets, where many of the members of CEPS Group lived.

In 1985, both the Commission and the CEPS Group refocused their analysis and policy prescriptions. The CEPS Report *Employment and Growth in Europe: A Two-Handed Approach* of June 1985 was written by O. Blanchard, R. Dornbusch, J. Drèze, H. Giersch, R. Layard, and M. Monti. It argued that the European unemployment problem did not have a single cause. Consequently, a 'two-handed' approach was necessary, combining structural measures on the supply side and a 'boost' to start the process. This boost had to come from timely supply measures, sustained and validated by demand (Blanchard *et al.* 1985: 30). One can note here that the new accents of the CEPS Report go together with certain changes in the composition of the Group, like the inclusion of Herbert Giersch, who had been emphasizing the structural aspects of Europe's economic problems.

The 1985 Annual Economic Report of the Commission proposed a more focused economic strategy: the Cooperative Growth Strategy for more Employment. This cooperative strategy called for 'balanced contributions' of different parties: the Community, the governments of the Member States, and the social partners. The aim was to strengthen growth in Europe and to make it more employment-creating. The strategy was based on a combination of moderate real wage increases, in order to improve profitability, and support for demand:

Only if wage moderation is accompanied by a sufficient level of aggregate demand can one have confidence that the process of improving profitability and restructuring demand (relatively more investment and relatively less consumption) will be rapid enough and not involve drastic deflation that would place social consensus under considerable strain. Only in this way can wage moderation fulfil its employment function. (CEC 1985a: 10)

The change in emphasis in 1985, with the Cooperative Growth Strategy, is linked to the arrival of a new European Commission, under the presidency of Jacques Delors, which revitalized the European integration process, especially with the internal market project.

The Cooperative Growth Strategy for more Employment was elaborated under A. Pfeiffer, a German trade unionist, who was the Commissioner responsible for DG II, and L. Schubert, the economic man in his cabinet. Compared to earlier Reports, the Cooperative Growth Strategy was more macroeconomic in nature, with less emphasis on differentiated patterns of wage-cost levels and labour-market flexibility. The strategy was also more based on a social dialogue between the employers and the trade unions.[10]

7. Academic economics and economics at policy-making institutions

It is interesting to make an analysis of the differences between academic economics and economics at a policy-making institution, like the European Commission. In practice the border between academic economics and economics at policy-making institutions is non-existent. Many economists have been part of both worlds, not only in the course of their life, but also simultaneously, combining jobs. The European Commission, in the early half of the 1980s, has very strongly favoured this interaction. Part of the reason for this was certainly that senior policy-makers, like Padoa-Schioppa and Emerson, had strong academic contacts and were well at home in the academic world.

However, there are some interesting and important differences. The inspiration for analysis and research at policy-making institutions is mostly very different from academic research. At policy-making institutions, concrete and actual issues, with which senior policy-makers are confronted, will mostly be at the basis of research projects. Policy-relevant research is at a premium. This contrasts with basic academic research, 'blue sky research', which is driven by theoretical problems or by possibilities of new econometric techniques (Portes 1997: 56). At policy-making institutions, theory and technique have a more ancillary function. Moreover, economists at policy-making institutions mostly need a quick judgement, as there is less time for in-depth analysis of problems.

So, for policy institutions, it is important that economic theory can select and highlight the relevant features for policy-making. One can think here of Schumpeter's characterization of the economics of J. M. Keynes:

What I admire most in these and other conceptual arrangements of his is their *adequacy*: they fit his purpose as a well-tailored coat fits the customer's body. Of course, precisely because of this, they possess but limited usefulness irrespective of Keynes's particular aims. A fruit knife is an

---

[10] It is also remarkable that, in 1984, the Annual Economic Report comprised 50 pages, compared to 136 pages for the Annual Economic Review (the analytical economic studies of the Commission services). In 1985 the Report counted 76 pages but the Review only 68 pages.

excellent instrument for peeling a pear. He who uses it in order to attack a steak has only himself to blame for unsatisfactory results. (Schumpeter 1946: 287, original italics)

There are also differences in the empirical material between economics at policy-making institutions and academic institutions. Policy-makers are strongly concerned about the actual economic situation and the future perspectives. Economists at policy-making institutions, like the European Commission, put a lot of time and effort at the monitoring and forecasting of the economic situation. This also implies that a lot of attention is given to the methodology of statistics, as a good comprehension of the coverage and quality of statistics is necessary. This rather contrasts with academic economists, who mostly work on the basis of existing economic data, leading to a more 'historical' kind of analysis, even if of the recent past. Academic economists, in general, will pay relatively less attention to the methodology of the data, as they are more concerned with theoretical refinements and econometric techniques.

Moreover, economics at policy-making institutions, like the Commission, is a compromise, a search for consensus between different tendencies and persons. This contributes naturally to the eclectic and synthetical nature of economics at policy-making institutions. This can sometimes lead to rather paradoxical situations. So was the 1983 Report of the Commission very positive on nominal income targeting, which was advocated by the CEPS Group, but praised also the strategy of monetary targeting in several Members States. This searching for a consensus implies also that economists at policy-making institutions should be good team members, also with non-economists. There are limits to 'independent originality' in policy-making institutions. As remarked by one observer, 'Economists working in government service have a vested interest in promoting consensus on basic issues of economic analysis. Academics, on the other hand, while they must ride with the tide, have a vested interest in differentiating their product' (Marris 1986: 109).

Work at international policy institutions, like the European Commission, is even more about consensus building, as the aim is to get the preferred economic policies accepted and implemented by the Member States. Hereby, one can remark that 'skills in communication and the art of persuasion are generally at a premium in international agencies, given their limited powers' (Coats 1986: 167). However, also to have an impact inside a multinational (and multilingual) organization, communication and negotiation skills are more important than in national organizations. Writing clear and accessible papers and achieving consensus in meetings can be more important than 'academic brilliance'. Marris's remarks about the OECD apply equally well to the European Commission: ' "good economics" merges almost imperceptibly into the art of persuasion' (1986: 113).

One also has to distinguish, at policy institutions, between background studies and direct policy work. The more academic background studies have certainly become more important during the last decades. Policy-makers need to know how the economy functions, so thorough analysis is needed.

For analytical studies policy-making institutions will often cooperate with academics. This interaction with the academic world was strengthened in the Commission in the early 1980s, especially under the influence of Padoa-Schioppa. Main elements were the cooperation with the CEPS Macroeconomic Policy Group and the launching of a new series of publications, the *Economic Papers*. Naturally, as there are 'cultural' differences between the worlds of academics and policy-makers, there can be clashes, often about the publication of research work, which also happened at the Commission. However, the tendency at policy-making institutions is for more analytical, academic research, even if the attitude towards the academic world of senior policy-makers play a very important role herein. This also implies that policy-making institutions will themselves do certain types of research, which earlier were done by outside academic experts. A clear example is the setting up of a modelling division at DG II in the early 1980s.

8. Conclusion

During the early 1980s the European economy was in the doldrums, with unemployment more and more dominating the scene, and the European integration process was languishing. In its Annual Economic Reports the European Commission presented its analysis of the situation and proposed its macroeconomic policy strategy.

In its analysis of the economic situation and discussion of policy proposals, the services of the Commission were clearly influenced by developments in the academic world. During the 1980s, these interactions between the academic world increased strongly, especially under the impulse of Tommaso Padoa-Schioppa, the director general of DG II (Economic and Financial Affairs). His main aim was to improve the analytical capacity of the Commission services. Strengthening contacts with the academic world was a crucial element of his strategy to reform DG II. The interaction with the academic world was even institutionalized with the foundation of the CEPS Macroeconomic Policy Group, which comprised several distinguished academics, and which held joint seminars with the economists of the Commission.

However, economics at a policy-making institution like the European Commission has several characteristics which distinguish it from academic economics. So the inspiration for analysis and research at policy-making institutions is mostly very different from academic research. At policy-making institutions, concrete and actual issues, with which senior policy-makers are confronted, will mostly be at the basis of research projects. This contrasts with basic academic research which is more driven by theoretical problems or possibilities of new techniques. There are also differences in the empirical material between economics at policy-making institutions and the academic world. Policy-makers are strongly concerned about the actual economic situation and the future perspectives. Consequently, economists at policy-making institutions, like the European Commission, put a lot of time and effort at the monitoring and forecasting of the economic situation. This rather contrasts with academic economists, who mostly work on the basis of existing economic data, leading to a more 'historical' kind of analysis, even if of the recent past. Moreover, at policy institutions, consensus building is very important. There are limits to 'independent originality', so valued in the academic world. Economics at policy institutions, like the Commission, is a compromise between different tendencies and persons, whereby an economic strategy has to be shaped which is also politically feasible. It all contributes to the eclectic and synthetical nature of economics at the Commission.

REFERENCES

Barten, A. P. and G. d'Alcantara (1984) 'COMET III: Econometric model building for the European Community' (Leuven: Katholieke Unversiteit Leuven), mimeo.
Basevi, G., Blanchard, O., Buiter, W., Dornbusch, R. and Layard, R. (1983) *Macroeconomic Prospects and Policies for the European Community* (Brussels: CEC, Economic Papers, 12).
Bean, C. (1994) 'European unemployment: A survey'. *Journal of Economic Literature*, 32: 573–619.
Blanchard, O., Dornbusch, R., Drèze, J., Giersch, H., Layard, R. and Monti, M. *et al.* (1985) *Report of the CEPS Macroeconomic Policy Group. Employment and Growth in Europe: A Two-handed Approach* (Brussels: CEC, Economic Papers, 36).
CEC (1980) Annual Economic Report. *European Economy*, 7 (Nov.): 5–29.
——(1982) Annual Economic Report. *European Economy*, 14 (Nov.): 5–32.
——(1983) Annual Economic Report. *European Economy*, 18 (Nov.): 5–44.
——(1984a) Annual Economic Report. *European Economy*, 22 (Nov.): 5–54.
——(1984b) Annual Economic Review. *European Economy*, 22 (Nov.): 55–190.
——(1984c) Technical Annex. *European Economy*, 22 (Nov.): 191–200.
——(1985a) Annual Economic Report. *European Economy*, 26 (Nov.): 5–80.
——(1985b) Annual Economic Review. *European Economy*, 26 (Nov.): 81–156.
——(1997) The joint harmonised EU programme of business and consumer surveys, *European Economy* 6: 1–231.
Coats, A. W. (ed.) (1986) *Economists in International Agencies* (New York: Praeger).
——(ed.) (1999) *The Post-1945 Development of Economics in Europe* (London: Routledge).
Emerson, M. (1988) *What Model for Europe?* (Cambridge, Mass.: MIT Press).
Giersch, H. (1987) 'Eurosclerosis. What is the cure?' *European Affairs*, 4 (Winter): 33–43.
Harrod, R. F. (1951) *The Life of John Maynard Keynes* (Harmondsworth: Penguin).
Layard, R., Basevi, G., Blanchard, O., Buiter, W., and Dornbusch, R. (1984) *Report of the CEPS Macroeconomic Policy Group. Europe: The Case for Unsustainable Growth* (Brussels: CEC, Economic Papers, 31).
Jacquemin, A. and L. Pench (1997) 'What competitiveness for Europe? in A. Jacquemin and L. Pench (eds.) *Europe Competing in the Global Economy* (Cheltenham: Edward Elgar): 1–43.
Llewellyn, J., Potter, S., and Samuelson, L. (1985) *Economic Forecasting and Policy – The International Dimension* (London: Routledge).
Ludlow, P. (1982) *The Making of the European Monetary System* (London: Butterworth).
——(1983) Introduction, in R. Dornbusch, G. Basevi, O. Blanchard, W. Buiter, and R. Layard, *Macroeconomic Prospects and Policies for the European Community* (Brussels: CEPS Paper, 1).
Maes, I. (1996) 'The development of economic thought at the European Community institutions', in A. W. Coats (ed.), 'The post-1945 internationalisation of economics', *History of Political Economy*, Annual Suppl.: 245–76.

——(1998) 'Macroeconomic thought at the European Commission in the 1970s: the first decade of Annual Economic Reports of the EEC', *Banca Nazionale del Lavoro Quarterly Review*, 207: 387–412.

Malinvaud, E. (1977) *The Theory of Unemployment Reconsidered* (Oxford: Blackwell).

Marjolin, R. (1986) *Le Travail d'une Vie. Mémoires 1911–1986* (Paris: Robert Laffont).

Marris, S. (1986) 'The role of economists in the OECD', in A. W. Coats (ed.), *Economists in International Agencies* (New York: Praeger): 98–114.

Modigliani, F. and Padoa-Schioppa, T. (1978) *The Management of an Economy with '100% Plus' Wage Indexation* (Princeton: Essays in International Finance): 130.

Mortensen, J. (1990) *Federalism vs. Co-ordination* (Brussels: CEPS Paper).

Nickell, S. (1997) 'Unemployment and labor market rigidities: Europe versus North America', *Journal of Economic Perspectives*, 11(3): 55–77.

Padoa-Schioppa, T. (1987) 'Reshaping monetary policy', in R. Dornbusch, S. Fischer, and J. Bossons (eds.), *Macroeconomics and Finance. Essays in Honor of Franco Modigliani* (Cambridge, Mass.: MIT Press): 265–85.

Porta, P. L. (1996) 'Italian economic thought in the postwar years', in A. W. Coats (ed.), 'The Post-1945 internationalisation of economics', *History of Political Economy*, Annual Suppl.: 165–83.

Portes, R. (1997) 'Users and abusers of economic research', in P. Van Bergeijk, L. Bovenberg, E. Van Damme, and J. Van Sinderen (eds.), *Economic Science and Practice* (Cheltenham: Edward Elgar): 49–59.

Rosanvallon, P. (1987) 'Histoire des idées Keynésiennes en France', *Revue Française de l'Economie* 4(2): 22–56.

Schefold, B. (1998) 'Die Wirtschafts—and Sozialordnung der Bundesrepublik Deutschland im Spiegel der Jahrestagungen des Vereins für Socialpolitik 1948 bis 1989', mimeo.

Schumpeter, J. (1946) 'John Maynard Keynes', in *Ten Great Economists* (London: Allen & Unwin): 260–91.

Wegner, M. (1989) 'The European Economic Community', in J. Pechman (ed.), *The Role of the Economist in Government* (New York: N.Y.U. Press): 279–99.

13A   In defence of two policy platitudes

D A N I E L   M .   H A U S M A N

Economists typically take for granted two propositions concerning the bearing of economic theory on policy-making. One can see these presuppositions clearly in the essays in this volume by Thomas Mayer and Ivo Maes, but there is nothing idio-syncratic about their work in this regard. My reason for pointing out these pre-suppositions is not to challenge them—on the contrary, I shall argue that they are correct. I wish to call attention to them instead because they are so important, because methodologists as well as economists have occasionally and mistakenly challenged them, and because significant currents in contemporary cultural studies purport to reject them.

The two platitudes are:

(i) To decide rationally among competing policies requires information concerning their outcomes.
(ii) Science (and even economics) can sometimes provide this information.

A number of clarifications are called for concerning the first platitude and the meaning of 'information' in this context. (Platitudes are rarely as simple as they look.) First, information concerning the outcomes of alternatives obviously does not suffice for policy-making. In addition one needs some way to *evaluate* outcomes. Although economists typically take for granted a particular method of evaluation—in terms of the satisfaction of given preferences—economics is generally supposed to play a much smaller role in formulating evaluative criteria than in determining outcomes. In any event, in insisting that rational evaluation of policies requires information concerning their outcomes, I am not asserting that nothing else is needed.

Second, appraisal may depend on more than the causal consequences of a policy. Policies may be subject to evaluation both in terms of their consequences and intrinsically. For example, a proposal to institute a system of slavery would be con-demned without regard to its effects, because slavery itself is impermissible. So sometimes information concerning consequences might be trumped by more immediate evaluations. The best way to acknowledge this point is to contrast 'out-comes'—which include the policy itself—from 'consequences' narrowly conceived as effects of the policy.

Third, some clarification is needed concerning exactly what information concerning outcomes is needed. Although point predictions of exactly the outcomes of policies P and Q would be nice to have, such predictions are rarely available. The world is a risky and uncertain place, and the most one can reasonably hope for are conditional probability distributions over possible outcomes if P is chosen or if Q is chosen. In fact, even this is too much to hope for. It is rarely possible to specify completely even what the possible outcomes might be (perhaps the Martians do not like policy P and will destroy the earth if it is instituted), let alone specify what the distribution of these outcomes would be if P or Q were chosen.

Yet rational choice is still possible when one does not know all the outcomes or their conditional probabilities. The principles to use in circumstances of genuine uncertainty are controversial. Some (subjective) Bayesians would argue that uncertainty raises no new difficulties at all. In their view one has only subjective probabilities, and no matter what one knows or does not know, one should choose the policy that maximizes expected utility. Policies chosen this way can go badly astray, but that is life. Others, such as Isaac Levi (1986), would insist that uncertainty calls for different principles of choice than does risk. One should recognize the indeterminacies in one's probability assignments and employ secondary principles of choice when the indeterminacies in probability assignments lead to indeterminacies in ranking alternatives. I am not capable of resolving these controversies, and in any event this essay is not the occasion for such an effort. The important point in this context is that all parties to these controversies agree that better information concerning outcomes is always welcome. Though it is possible that a better estimate of the likely outcome of competing alternatives will lead to a choice that will in fact have a worse outcome than the alternative one would have chosen with less information, choices are more rational and their outcomes are likely to be better when one has better information.

There is one technical issue about what sort of information is needed that deserves mention. In saying that rational choice among policies requires information concerning their outcomes, it seems that I am favouring so-called 'causal decision theory'. Suppose that an agent A is deciding whether to do P or Q and that there is only one outcome W that A is concerned about. Should A base her choice between P and Q on a comparison between $Pr(W/P)$ and $Pr(W/Q)$ or on a comparison between the specifically *causal* consequences of doing P or Q. For example, suppose that P is smoking, Q is not smoking, and that W is (avoiding) getting lung cancer. If smoking and lung cancer are related as cause and effect, the comparison of the conditional probabilities and the causal consequences will be just the same. But if smoking and lung cancer are related as effects of some common cause (for example, some genetic predisposition both to smoke and to contract lung cancer), then the conditional probability of contracting lung cancer given that one smokes might be much higher than the conditional probability of lung cancer if one does not smoke, even though smoking does nothing to *cause* lung cancer. I personally think that this contrast between so-called 'causal' and 'evidential' decision theory is mistakenly drawn (see Meek and Glymour 1994), but these issues need not be resolved here. Evidential decision theorists should simply read the first platitude as maintaining that rational choice requires information concerning conditional probabilities rather than specifically causal information.

Fourth, something should be said about how precise, accurate, and secure the required information must be. What one needs are rational *grounds* for belief concerning how the world will be if policy P is instituted compared to how it will be if policy Q is instituted. What is needed is thus *evidence* rather than *truth*. Truth is the aspiration that drives research; it provides no epistemic warrant. The object of inquiry plays a *causal* role in the process of gathering evidence rather than an evidential role;

and the correspondence between the findings of inquiries and their objects enters into an explanation of those findings, rather than into the evidence for them. What determines whether one should rely on a particular proposition in assessing policies P and Q is what sort of evidence there is for the proposition, not whether the proposition is true. So let us continue to hope that the claims that science (and economics in particular) provide are true, and let us continue to aim at the truth, but in making policy choices what matters is what sort of evidence there is for these claims.

Ideally, one would like to have decisive evidence in support of every proposition concerning the outcomes of instituting P or Q, but rational decision-making does not require decisive evidence or certainty. The better the evidence and the more certain one can be about the outcomes, the better the decision-making is likely to be (though of course in an uncertain world even the most rational decision-making can lead to fiasco). The view that one appraises alternative policies by considering their expected value is a useful idealization, but only if one recognizes how great an idealization it is. Even assuming that there were no problems concerning evaluation of outcomes, the outcomes are typically not all known, and the probabilities one assigns to them are often mere guesses.

With those clarifications in mind, the two platitudes are, I believe, correct and indeed obviously so. Yet they have nevertheless been challenged. The second platitude, the claim that science can sometimes provide the information that rational policy choice needs, has been challenged in three ways. First, there are radical sceptical challenges to the possibility of acquiring any knowledge or justified belief. It is unclear whether the radical sceptical challenge can be met, because it is unclear what would count as meeting it. Part of the problem posed by the radical sceptic is the sceptic's view of what counts as a justification. In any event, I shall not address the sceptic's challenge here; and my defence of the platitudes will be in this way incomplete.

Second, one finds a variety of 'post-structuralist', 'post-modernist', 'deconstructionist', or 'social constructivist' critiques of science as merely one language game among other. According to these critiques, truth and justification are internal to particular language games, and without relativization to a particular language game, there is no such thing as justification or rational choice. For example, Deirdre McCloskey (1985) argues that the goal of economists is persuasion. Successful economics is economics that manages to persuade. Either there is no role for rationality, or rationality is defined by the group that determines what is persuasive, and is thus an empty honour awarded automatically to the victor in the struggle to persuade.[1] This view is implausible. If economists cared only about persuading others, then they ought to use focus groups to find out what sells and, regardless of what they themselves believe, they ought to avoid any principles that have been found to be unpersuasive. There may be some economists like this, but a discipline explicitly organized around such goals would be very different from the actual discipline.

---

[1] McCloskey's formulations are ambiguous, and a case can be made that she regards the goal as *rational* persuasion, where *rationality* is not defined in such a way that the view that persuades automatically counts as persuading rationally. I would quarrel with even this more moderate view, but there is no need to do so in this paper, since it concedes the point at issue.

The sceptical conclusions many draw from current work in cultural studies cannot be accepted by those who seek to design policies to further their values and who believe that rational policy design is possible (Rosenberg 1992: ch. 7). This difficulty does not refute all of those concerned with cultural studies. Some of them may be radical sceptics, and if they are, then the following remarks do not touch their position. Others may deny that rational policy design is possible or have no interest in designing policies that will change anything in a way that they take to be for the better. But those who aspire to choose rationally among policies must believe that there are rational grounds supporting claims about how things would be if one policy rather than another were instituted. This is consistent with the view that some other activity than science provides these grounds, but I don't know of anyone who holds that view. In effect, I am using platitude one to argue for platitude two. One cannot hope to make rational choices among competing policies if one denies that there is any way to know how things would be with one policy rather than another.

Let me give one concrete illustration from the writings of one who has been highly sceptical of science. Commenting on Alan Sokal's hoax (1996*a*,*b*), Bruce Robbins, one of the editors of *Social Text*, which published Sokal's hoax, writes:

Is it in the interests of women, African Americans, and other super-exploited people to insist that truth and identity are social constructions? Yes and no. No, you can't talk about exploitation without respect for empirical evidence and a universal standard of justice. But yes, truth can be another source of oppression. It was not so long ago that scientists gave their full authority to explanations of why women and African Americans (not to speak of gays and lesbians) were inherently inferior or pathological or both. Explanations like these continue to appear in newer and subtler forms. Hence, there is a real need for a social constructionist critique of knowledge. (1996: 59)

Though it is worth pointing out Robbins's egregious conflation of 'truth' and 'truth claims', the important point here is that even in the context of supposedly challenging the objectivity of science, Robbins concedes that evidence is needed to identify exploitation and, presumably, to assess proposals about how to eliminate it. Nobody has any remotely sensible model about how rationally to decide how to act that does not require evidence concerning outcomes. Those who would deny that evidence can ever be had have to give up on the possibility of acting rationally.

A third argument against the view that science provides information about the outcomes of alternative policies is implicit in Karl Popper's falsificationism. Popper maintains that there is no such thing as supporting evidence (for example, 1974: 1043). The most one can learn is that some claims have been falsified, and even learning this requires unjustified *decisions* not to blame the apparent falsification on experimental error, disturbing causes, and so forth. Claims that have not been falsified are just as conjectural as if they had never been tested at all. Although Popper denies that he is a sceptic, and calls claims that have not been falsified 'knowledge', he accepts Hume's view that empirical generalizations cannot ever be supported or justified. But rational decision-making among competing policies requires information concerning their outcomes, not guesses honorifically dubbed 'knowledge'. Unlike a sceptic, Popper agrees that rational actions should rely on well-tested scientific theories. He insists that there is no more rational course. But he cannot explain why it is more rational to rely on a well-tested theory than on a conjecture that has never been tested at all. Without admitting some notion of confirmation or support, he cannot explain how the fact that a claim has passed (harsh) tests could be relevant to decision-making. Most Popperian economists do not take Popper's philosophy literally. They attribute to him the watered down view that theories should be harshly tested, rejected when they fail tests, and regarded as confirmed or more likely to be correct or reliable when they pass. But this is the view of inductivists (or, in Lakatos's (1970) terminology, 'justificationists') not Popper's view.

Let me then turn to challenges to the first platitude, that rational policy choice requires information concerning the outcomes of the alternatives. This view has been challenged not only by maverick methodologists, but also by major economists and philosophers of economics. A recent maverick challenge is Tony Lawson's (1997). Following Roy Bhaskar (1978), Lawson maintains that science permits predictions concerning outcomes of policies only in closed systems—that is, in systems in which the only relevant causal factors are those that our theories explicitly take account of. Since economies are open systems, no predictions are possible. Rather than conclude that rational policy-making is impossible, Lawson (again following Bhaskar) maintains that knowledge of *tendencies* suffices. A tendency for Lawson is not some sort of statistical prediction about what will happen most of the time. It is rather a 'trans-factual'. It is something 'going on' beneath the layer of observation regardless of what actually happens (1997: 23). Lawson's view is that if some feature of the world X has a *tendency* to produce something bad, then we have reason to favour a policy that tends to deactivate or counteract X, even if we have no knowledge about what the consequences of X or of our policy will be (1997: 288; see also Bhaskar 1978: 125).

Lawson's view is implausible, and it is inconsistent with economic practice. For example, by one mechanism minimum wage laws have a tendency to diminish poverty (because they raise wages of low-wage workers), and so by the reasoning above, those who seek to diminish poverty have a reason to institute or raise minimum wages—without any need for information about whether minimum-wage laws actually diminish poverty. Unfortunately, it is also the case that by another mechanism (substitution for labour of other factors of production), minimum-wage laws also have a tendency to increase unemployment and thereby to increase poverty among unskilled workers. So it appears that those who seek to diminish poverty have reason not to institute minimum-wage laws as well as reason to institute them. The way one would try to resolve the conflict would be by attempting to judge how much unemployment minimum-wage laws *in fact* lead to. But Lawson denies that this knowledge is to be had, and maintains that policy should be based merely on knowledge of tendencies. It seems to me on the contrary that knowledge of the tendencies by itself provides *no* reason to do anything. To act rationally one needs information concerning what the outcome of the policies will actually be.

Geoffrey Brennan, James Buchanan, and Alexander Rosenberg have all argued that some policy choices should be based on what the outcomes of alternative policies would be if everyone were rational and self-interested rather than on what the outcomes of alternative policies would in fact be. Brennan, Buchanan, and Rosenberg all quote the following famous remarks of David Hume's.

Political writers have established it as a maxim, that, in contriving any system of government, and fixing the several checks and controls of the constitution, every man ought to be supposed a *knave*, and to have no other end, in all his actions, than private interest. By this interest we must govern him, and, by means of it, make him, notwithstanding his insatiable avarice and action, cooperate to public good . . . .

It is, therefore, a just *political* maxim, *that every man must be supposed a knave*; though, at the same time, it appears somewhat strange, that a maxim should be true in *politics* which is false in *fact*. (Hume 1741: 40–2)

When Hume speaks of knaves, he has in mind rational and self-interested individuals who pursue their own interests without concern for the public good. Similar remarks can be found in James Madison's contributions to the *Federalist Papers*, where he argued at length for the need to establish institutions that will be robust in the face of unscrupulous and opportunistic individual behaviour. Brennan and Buchanan do not maintain that all policy-making should be made on the basis of the contrary-to-fact assumption that all men are knaves. Their view is instead that 'constitutional' decisions—that is decisions that determine the basic constraints within which individuals choose what to do—should be decided on this basis (1985: 44–5). The important point in this context is that Brennan and Buchanan are maintaining that sometimes rational policy-making should not be influenced by information concerning what the actual outcomes of alternative policies would be.

I have criticized Brennan's, Buchanan's, and Rosenberg's views at length elsewhere (1998), and shall only touch on the main difficulties here. It is best to start by asking why one should believe that some policy-making should start from the contrary-to-fact assumption that all men are knaves. (If the assumption is not contrary to fact, then there is, of course, no challenge to the claim that rational policy-making should depend on information concerning the actual outcomes of alternative policies.) There are, I think, two main answers. First, many economists would argue that, given actual motives and institutions, things may work out much as they would if everyone were a knave. Suppose for example that all penalties for tax evasion were eliminated. That would save a great deal of money on enforcement, and since a great many people are public spirited, initially a large proportion of people would still pay their taxes. But since some people would cheat and others would resent their cheating and feel exploited, commitment to paying taxes would unravel and one would reach a state of affairs very much like the one that would result if everyone were a knave.

However sensible this argument may be—and with respect to certain policies it is very sensible indeed—it is an argument for the claim that supposing everyone to be a knave is a useful short cut to determining what the actual outcomes would be, not an argument that the actual outcome doesn't matter.

Suppose then that the actual outcomes and the outcomes if everyone were a knave diverge. The reason for focusing on the latter seems to be a 'play-it-safe' attitude.

Maybe we could economize on some tax collectors, police officers, or accountants, but it is more important that our institutions be robust than that they be optimal; and given the uncertainties attached to institutional design, we had better design our institutions to work in the worst case in which everyone is a knave.

Although apparently sensible, this view has no justification. First, if one's concern is with the worst case, then one ought to assume something much worse than universal knavery. If everyone were a knave, there wouldn't be anything like the genocide witnessed this century in Germany, the former Yugoslavia, or Rwanda. Widespread irrational malevolence is a much worse case, and it is unfortunately a perfectly possible one. Second, and more generally, it is irresponsible to attend to worse-case scenarios without thinking about the costs of doing so and the probabilities of facing such scenarios. And once one does this, one returns (of course) to thinking about the actual outcomes of alternative policies. If everyone were a knave, voluntary recycling programmes would fail completely. Policy-makers who assume that everyone is a knave would never do anything as foolish as to propose such programmes. It is controversial how well these programmes work, but it is not controversial that they do work and that refusing to consider them on the grounds that policy should be based on the assumption that everyone should be assumed a knave would be foolish.

So let us have some respect for these two platitudes, and let us keep looking for information about the outcomes of policies that can help solve some of the problems we face.

REFERENCES

Bhaskar, Roy (1978) *A Realist Theory of Science* (Hemel Hempstead: Harvester Press).

Brennan, Geoffrey and James Buchanan (1985) *The Reason of Rules* (Cambridge: Cambridge University Press).

Hausman, Daniel (1998) 'Rationality and knavery', in Werner Leinfellner and Eckehart Köhler (eds.), *Game Theory, Experience, Rationality; Foundations of Social Sciences; Economics and Ethics: In Honor of John C. Harsanyi* (Dordrecht: Kluwer): 67–79.

Hume, David (1741) 'Of the independency of Parliament', *Essays Moral, Political, and Literary* (repr. Oxford: Oxford University Press 1963): 40–7.

Lakatos, I. (1970) 'Falsification and the methodology of scientific research programmes', in I. Lakatos and A. Musgrave (eds.), *Criticism and the Growth of Knowledge* (Cambridge: Cambridge University Press): 91–196.

Lawson, Tony (1997) *Economics and Reality* (London: Routledge).

Levi, Isaac (1986) 'The paradoxes of Allais and Ellsberg', *Economics and Philosophy* 2: 23–53.

McCloskey, Deirdre (1985) *The Rhetoric of Economics* (Madison: University of Wisconsin Press).

Meek, Christopher and Clark Glymour (1994) 'Conditioning and intervening', *British Journal for Philosophy of Science* 45: 1001–21.

Popper, Karl (1974) 'Replies to my critics', in P. Schilpp (ed.), *The Philosophy of Karl Popper* (La Salle, Ill.: Open Court): 961–1200.

Robbins, Bruce (1996) 'Anatomy of a hoax' *Tikkun* (Sept./Oct.): 58–9 also available at http://www.physics.nyu.edu/faculty/sokal/robbins_tikkun.html.

Rosenberg, Alexander (1992) *Economics—Mathematical Politics or Science of Diminishing Returns* (Chicago: University of Chicago Press).

Sokal, Alan (1996*a*) 'Transgressing the boundaries: toward a transformative hermeneutics of quantum gravity', *Social Text* 46/47 (Spring/Summer): 217–52.

—— (1996*b*) 'A physicist experiments with cultural studies', *Lingua Franca* 6(4): 62–4.

13B   Official documents: general discussion

Andrew Oswald: Have economists' ideas been very expensive, for good or ill, in the European Commission? Have new theories of unemployment, for example, led to large quantities of taxpayers' money being spent, whether for benefit or cost?

Adrian Pagan: I have a quotation relating to central banks that Mayer might like to use. One of our ex-research directors once said, regarding changes in opinion within the bank, that the bank was often wrong but never in doubt.

I have been working on this topic myself in relation to monetary policy in Australia, trying to work out the influence of academic work on monetary policy decisions over the last thirty years. One of the things I discovered was that it was far more important to look at the speeches of bank officials than any discussion that took place at the meetings themselves and to look at the documents that went to the monetary policy committee. The documents are where the milieu gets established. Generally there is some sort of policy proposal within these that reflect some sort of academic opinion. I think the academic opinion turns out to be very important, and can be seen in these documents.

David Hendry: I was delighted to see in Maes's paper that empirical work did have an impact in the European Commission, but having done some teaching there, in different DGs over the last few years, I have been rather frightened by the lack of quantitative skills among large numbers of the people and I didn't see anything about the method of recruitment in the discussion. It worries me the way the EU recruits people. It seems to put rather a big emphasis on what I would call European legal-type degrees rather than quantitative ones. In response to Oswald and Hausman, I was editor of the *Review of Economic Studies* along with Geoff Heal when we perpetrated such a fraud (Grandmont *et al.* 1974; we put 'Manuscript received 1st April' at the bottom of it to make this quite clear). It was on all this stuff that was going on in the Hildenbrand GE-type literature about the density of sets in each other, and whether or not it proved anything. It got quite an angry reaction from those who were spoofed, but you can certainly do it with modern economics without much difficulty. We could see it was a spoof, but most people in the profession could not see it was a spoof, even when 1st April appeared at the bottom. One might amuse oneself by doing that at a later stage for several of the methodologies that are being used in this conference.

It would be very interesting if Hausman could amplify why he thought platitude 2 posed great difficulties for Blaug's view of how we should proceed.

It obviously interests me how much impact econometricians have had within, for example, the UK. If anything, it rather falls into Hausman's first category, namely that the Treasury has been extremely rational in that as good econometric evidence, as they viewed it, came along, they built it into their econometric system with the net result that they made some extremely bad decisions. The Treasury has published a lot of documents on the econometric modelling strategy since the mid-1970s, and one can trace the evolution of the model very directly in response to econometric developments in the literature. Of course, the problem is that all these tools need to be used by people who have got the intuition to understand when they are appropriate and when they are not. It harks back to Smith's complaint that the vast majority of stuff that is done is mechanistic. It is mechanistic whether it is economic theory, whether it is econometrics, whether it is applying models or whatever. The skills needed to do these things seem, in practice, to be rather rare. One just hopes that a lot of intuition and commonsense impinge on the way these decisions are made.

Mary Morgan: I have been involved in a project looking at the way models are used in the policy process. What we found when having people from different countries come to talk about the way models were used, was an extraordinary variety. One of the things that was interesting was that discussions of the use of models tended to be a focus for discussion of both economic theory and evidence. However, you can't really tell from the official documents how influential those model discussions, and therefore those discussions of academic work, were because in the official documents all sorts of consensus had to be built in, or the academic content hidden, so that the outputs did not reveal very accurately to what extent the academic work which had been instantiated in the models had been influential. Mayer referenced Edison and Marquez's paper which is one of those from the conference (the whole set is being published in Den Butter and Morgan, forthcoming) and you can see tremendous variation in how this works in a practical context.

James Hartley: I was just wondering, when policy-makers should start using academic information. Take the new minimum-wage literature such as Card and Krueger (1995). Is this now advanced enough that policy-makers should start using it? Do we need longer streams of evidence for it? Should it have been adopted two years ago? How do we incorporate it optimally into policy?

Bennett McCallum: I thought I would put in a 15 second advertisement for the last issue of the *Carnegie-Rochester Conference Series on Public Policy* (vol. 47, December 1997). This has two papers written by people from the Board of Governors, one describing the philosophy and construction of their new econometric model, and the other one a detailed discussion of the ways in which that and other econometric models are used in the policy process at the Federal Reserve.

Christopher Sims: Even though I basically agree with Hausman, his comments go so against the grain of this conference that they haven't really drawn any fierce response. So I thought I would take the other side here. My son is a sociologist of science, so I get more exposure to this kind of discussion than most economists do. One of the things that interests me is the extent to which the two sides in this dispute between the sociologists and philosophers, science and scientists, tend to focus on the most extreme members of each group, and the most extreme formulations of the views involved. They comfort each other by chuckling over how naïve the other side is. I agree that if you want to do anything you have to act as if there is a truth and you are looking for it. However, I also think it is true that we play language games and that there is quite a bit to be learned from stepping back to ask what kind of a language game we are playing. Part of the reason is to help us do a better job in rooting out what is truth and what's the social structure of our discipline. I have occasionally been sharply reminded of this. I remember once visiting a mid-Western university and sitting around a discussion with a group of young macroeconomists and talking about open research agendas and important new ideas. I don't remember exactly what idea we were discussing and one of them said, 'But that idea seems not to be grounded in optimizing behaviour of individuals.' The whole point of the discussion was that I had thought that here was a way in which we had evidence that we did not have dynamic optimization, but this was an economist who felt he wasn't interested in theories that weren't based on dynamic optimization by individuals. We ought to be aware of the extent to which this kind of thing is going on and McCloskey (e.g. 1986) has been very useful to us in reminding us that this kind of thing does go on. I think you could even accept the extreme view of a deconstructionist that there is no truth and that we are all playing language games, and still end up being an active and socially responsible economist. Or you could just take a kind of existential view—that there isn't anything we can do except play some kind of language game and we just have to pick the one that looks best to us and play it as best we can.

Huw Dixon: I just have an observation about the sampling procedure of looking in America. There are several countries where the policy-makers and politicians are economists—Portugal, Italy—and others like Denmark where many politicians have economics degrees. It may be useful to extend your knowledge of languages to ones like Portugese and Danish because it would be interesting to compare how ideas move around in these countries with countries like Britain, where politicians and even civil servants generally do not have economics degrees, and are even antagonistic to economics.

Ron Smith: Economists have much more impact on policy than almost anyone else. I have talked a lot about this to military people. The links between academics and the military in decision-making are very remote. The common language issue is very important. It is not merely that academics are talking about problems that central bankers and the government do have to face but there is a media out there that is also talking about those issues. As Mayer made clear, you have to persuade the academics, otherwise they will write nasty things about you. That is not true in many scientific subjects and certainly not true in defence decision-making.

Giorgio Ragazzi: Just a brief, cynical comment. If one shares the view that politicians and governments have an intrinsic interest in not being transparent—in hiding the real meaning of policies—this is relevant to the problem. In my view, Italy in recent years is a good example, especially if you consider fiscal policy. Here we are able to do things in a hidden manner. Official documents approved by the Parliament—budgets, etc.— are practically meaningless with respect to what really happens to government expenditure and so on. Expenditures are controlled in administrative ways and through a number of rules which are written in laws called *Collegati Finanziaria* which tend to be extremely unreadable. I am ready to bet that practically no economist in Italy has ever read these documents or understood what their meaning is. Just one small example, there is a short line that changes certain lines in other laws. The financial impact of this kind of measure can be very large but to understand what it means and how it will be implemented is practically impossible. So economists are not in a position to know what is really happening in the rooms where decisions are made. As a consequence, perhaps, economists tend to line up with one political party or another. Most economists are labelled as belonging to one of the main parties, which means their prestige is negligible in this country. For any policy, you find a number of famous economists lined up on either side on ideological grounds. The profession lacks real prestige in terms of being autonomous, of knowing what is going on, and of publicly taking certain positions. I don't know whether I am too cynical and whether this is a problem for other countries.

Ivo Maes: In reply to Hendry, it is not just the French economic system. The philosophy of the Commission is much more legal. Another element is that it is also a hierarchical organization. This means that most people at the top are quite old and they didn't have much econometrics when they were young. They determine very much what happens. Why, for instance, was there change with Padoa-Schioppa? Padoa-Schioppa, when he became Director-General, was aged forty. The person high up in the hierarchy makes a lot of difference. What is going on now in policy institutions in Europe is that more attention is being paid, in central banks and the Commission, to reinforcing the analytical dimension. For example, at the moment there is a restructuring of DGII, and one of its elements is reinforcing the analytical dimension.

Tom Mayer: There is always a problem knowing what policy-makers read, even if they receive documents. I wouldn't be surprised, for example, if all the governors received all the staff working papers but did not read very much of them. As far as speeches are concerned, I hate to read that stuff, because it is so overblown, so full of clichés, and meaningless phrases that it is hard to find real content.

I couldn't agree more with the point that economists are using techniques mechanically. It certainly leads to bad policy. Once upon a time I would ask economists, both in academia and in government, how they got their degrees and yet not know economics. That doesn't happen any more. They know economics. They can talk examination–economics talk but they haven't got the intuition. In other words you can take somebody who lacks the ability to be an economist and tank him or her up with a lot of phrases and equations and so on. It reminds me of a phrase of Alexander Pope's: 'The learned blockhead, ignorantly read/With loads of useless numbers in his head.' I don't know what you can do about that except possibly to change the way we recruit government economists. Turning to the question of how soon economic ideas should be adopted, it is a little bit like when you are writing a textbook: you read a paper in a journal and have to decide whether to include it. It is risky because if you include it, the next issue of the journal may have an article blowing it up. Formally, of course, you ought to consult a loss function, but you don't usually have one.

Daniel Hausman: Brennan and Buchanan (1985) actually make this argument explicitly in several places. It is not a complicated interpretation on my part. It is obviously not their main concern but it is worth pointing out that I am not just arguing with straw men.

There was nothing in what I said that should be taken, explicitly or implicitly, as a criticism of the sociology of knowledge. Sociologists who study science are for the most part trying to get at what they take to be the truth about the way scientific communities are established. I don't really think this view that there are lots of different language games is a tenable one for anyone to hold. It supposes that somehow one hovers above language games, just playing them. One always participates in a language game and it is not optional whether one accepts its presuppositions or not. The language game of science and economics is not one that is peripheral to everyday life. It is heavily integrated into everyday life and although someone could, I suppose, opt out and become some sort of fairly radical sceptic, it is extremely difficult to do and I don't think such a position is available to most people. I think a lot of that literature is written, as it were, in bad faith, from a position that isn't really held by the author. It is one they pragmatically contradict the minute they put their pen down.

REFERENCES

Brennan, Geoffrey and Buchanan, James (1985) *The Reason of Rules* (Cambridge: Cambridge University Press).
Den Butter, Frank and Mary S. Morgan (forthcoming) *Empirical Models and Policy Making: Interaction and Institutions* (London: Routledge).
Card, D. E. and Krueger, A. B. (1995) *Myth and Measurement: The New Economics of the Minimum Wage* (Princeton: Princeton University Press).
Grandmont, J. M., Kirman, A. P. and Neuefeind, W. (1974) 'A new approach to the uniqueness of equilibrium', *Review of Economic Studies* 41: 289–91.

Index